Alfred Thayer Mahan

The Influence of Sea Power Upon the French Revolution and

Empire, 1793-1812

Vol.1

Alfred Thayer Mahan

The Influence of Sea Power Upon the French Revolution and Empire, 1793-1812
Vol. 1

ISBN/EAN: 9783337244507

Printed in Europe, USA, Canada, Australia, Japan

Cover: Foto ©ninafisch / pixelio.de

More available books at **www.hansebooks.com**

THE

INFLUENCE OF SEA POWER

UPON THE

FRENCH REVOLUTION AND EMPIRE

1793–1812

BY

CAPTAIN A. T. MAHAN, D.C.L., LL.D.

UNITED STATES NAVY

AUTHOR OF "THE INFLUENCE OF SEA POWER UPON
HISTORY, 1660–1783," ETC.

IN TWO VOLUMES

VOL. I.

London
SAMPSON LOW, MARSTON & COMPANY, Limited,
St. Dunstan's House, Fetter Lane, Fleet Street, E.C.

UNIVERSITY PRESS:
JOHN WILSON AND SON, CAMBRIDGE, U.S.A.

PREFACE.

THE present work, like its predecessor, "The Influence of Sea Power upon History, 1660-1783," is wholly a result of the author's connection with the United States Naval War College as lecturer upon Naval History and Naval Tactics.

When first asked to undertake that duty, the question naturally arose how to impart to the subject of Naval History an aspect which, in this very utilitarian age, should not be open to the ready reproach of having merely archaeological interest, and possessing no practical value for men called upon to use the changed materials of modern naval war. "You won't have much to say about history," was then the somewhat discouraging comment of a senior officer of his own service.

In pondering this matter, it occurred to the author — whose acquaintance with naval history was at that time wholly superficial — that the part played by navies, and by maritime power generally, as a factor in the results of history, and as shaping the destinies of nations and of the world, had received little or no particular attention. If this were so, an analysis of the course of events through a series of years, directed to show the influence of Sea Power upon History, would at least serve to imbue his hearers with an exalted sense of the mission of their calling; and might also, by throwing light upon the political bearings of naval force, contribute to give the service and the country a more definite impression of the necessity to provide a fleet adequate to great undertakings, lest, if an occasion should arise for what he has ventured to call "statesmanship directing arms," we should be found unprepared, through having no sufficient armed force to direct.

In avowing this as the original, and, for a time at least, almost the sole motive of his work, the author practically confesses that he at the beginning had no scientific appreciation or reasoned knowledge of the naval history of the past. Upon giving this the attention required by his new duties, and collating the various incidents with the teachings of recognized authorities upon land warfare, he soon came to recognize that the principles which they claimed to be of general application in their own specialty received also ample and convincing illustration in naval annals; although the development of the Art of War at sea has been slower, and is now less advanced, than on shore. This backward result has been due, partly, to uncertainties peculiar to the sea, and partly to a contempt for the study of the past, and of its experience, as "not practical," from which the naval profession has not yet wholly rid itself.

Thus, in its course, the author's former work. without abandoning its first simple motive, expanded into an attempt to analyze the strategic conduct of the naval campaigns, as well as the tactical features of the various battles — all too few — in which any clear tactical purpose was shown by the commanders engaged. The cordial reception given to the work by his professional brethren, in Great Britain as well as at home, has been to him not only most gratifying, but wholly unexpected. Its chief significance is, however, not personal. The somewhat surprised satisfaction testified is virtually an admission that, in the race for material and mechanical development, sea-officers as a class have allowed their attention to be unduly diverted from the systematic study of the Conduct of War, which is their peculiar and main concern. For, if the commendation bestowed be at all deserved, it is to be ascribed simply to the fact that the author has been led to give to the most important part of the profession an attention which it is in the power of any other officer to bestow, but which too few actually do.

That the author has done so is due, wholly and exclusively, to the Naval War College, which was instituted to promote such studies. If further success attend his present venture, it is his hope that this avowal may help to assure the long uncertain fortunes of the College, to which, — and to its founder, Rear-Admiral Stephen B. Luce, — he gratefully acknowledges his indebtedness for guiding him into a path he would not himself have found.

The term of this work is fixed at the year 1812; a date signalized by Napoleon's invasion of Russia, which wrecked his empire, — or at least gave the outward and visible token of the wreck, — and also by the outbreak of war between Great Britain and the United States. To the latter, as a subject of particular national interest, the author hopes in the near future to devote a special study.

A. T. MAHAN.

October, 1892.

CONTENTS OF VOL. I.

CHAPTER I.

INTRODUCTORY

OUTLINE OF EVENTS IN EUROPE, 1783-1793.

	PAGE
Prominence of the year 1793	1
Leading features and results of the war of 1778	2
Condition of the different belligerents at its termination	3
Success of the second Pitt as a peace minister	5
Advantage to Great Britain arising from his secure tenure of power	6
Desire of Western Europe for peace	7
Causes of disturbance	7
Accession of Joseph II. to crown of Austria	7
Commercial expansion of Austrian Netherlands during war of 1778	8
Question of the navigation of the Scheldt	9
Wide-spread interests therein involved	10
The Eastern Question, 1780-1790	11
Change of relations between Great Britain and Russia from 1770 to 1785	12
Interests of France and of Great Britain in the Levant and Baltic	14
Importance of Antwerp as a naval station	15
Interests of European States in Holland and the Netherlands	16
Relations between Russia and France, 1780-1790	17
Preponderance of French influence in Dutch politics	17
Joseph II. drops the question of the Scheldt	18
Treaty of alliance between France and Holland, 1785	18
Armed interference of Prussia in Holland, 1787	19
British party regains ascendency in Holland, 1787	19

CONTENTS.

	PAGE
Meeting of the Notables in France, February, 1787	19
Turkey declares war against Russia, August, 1787	19
Austria declares war against Turkey, February, 1788	19
Great Britain and Holland proclaim a strict neutrality	20
Consequent effect upon Russia's maritime projects	20
Sweden attacks Russian Finland, June, 1788	21
Defensive alliance between Great Britain, Prussia, and Holland, 1788	21
Denmark attacks Sweden	21
Interposition of Great Britain and Prussia in the Baltic	21
Significance of this action	22
Dawn of the modern Eastern Question	22
Conflicting views of British statesmen about Russia, 1791	23
External influence of France paralyzed by home troubles	24
Progress of the war in southeastern Europe	24
Renewed interference of Great Britain and Prussia in the Baltic	25
Meeting of the States-General in France, 1789	25
Cessation of hostilities between Austria and Turkey, September, 1790	26
Storming of Ismail by Suwarrow, Christmas, 1790	26
Peace of Galatz between Russia and Turkey, August, 1791	27
General peace in eastern Europe, 1791	27
Progress of the Revolution in France, 1789-1791	28
Flight of the King, 1791	28
Declaration of Pilnitz, August, 1791	28
Significant coincidence of this date with Peace of Galatz	29
France declares war against Austria, April, 1792	29
Disorders in Paris, June-September, 1792	30
Suspension of the King, August, 1792	30
Battle of Valmy, September 20, 1792	30
Meeting of National Convention, September 22, 1792	31
Royalty abolished in France	31
Battle of Jemappes, November 6, 1792	31
The French occupy Austrian Netherlands and open the Scheldt	31
Decree of Fraternity, November 19, 1792	31
Decree extending the French system with their armies, December 15, 1792	32
Strained relations between Great Britain and France	32
Execution of Louis XVI., January 21, 1793	32
Dismissal of the French minister by the British court	34
France declares war against Great Britain and Holland, February 1, 1793	34

CHAPTER II.

The Condition of the Navies in 1793 — and especially of the French Navy.

	PAGE
Causes of the deterioration of the French navy after 1789	35
Ignorance of maritime conditions among French administrators	37
Value of the lessons derivable from this experience	38
Factors conditioning the effects of any form of military activity	38
The gun the one sea-weapon of the period in question	39
A ship is a mobile battery	39
It is handled by an organic body, whose members are mutually dependent	39
Necessity of special training to such an organization	40
Blindness of the French Legislature to these facts	41
Rise and growth of insubordination in the navy	41
The disturbances in Toulon, 1789	42
Maltreatment of Commodore D'Albert de Rions	43
Weakness of the National (Constituent) Assembly	43
The Nootka Sound trouble between Spain and Great Britain, 1790	44
France prepares to support Spain	45
De Rions ordered to command the Brest fleet	45
Mutiny in the Brest fleet	45
De Rions leaves the navy	46
His services and distinguished professional reputation	46
Disorders in the navy abroad	47
Disastrous effects upon the French colonies	48
Emigration of French naval officers	49
Reorganization of the navy by the Constituent Assembly, 1791	50
Previous measures of the monarchical government, 1786	51
Reorganization decrees of the Assembly, April, 1791	52
Essential spirit of this legislation	53
The Second (Legislative) Assembly lowers the qualifications for officers	54
Naval officers in the Reign of Terror	54
Further legislation by Third Assembly (National Convention), 1793	55
Results of the successive measures	56
Action of the Assemblies touching enlisted men	57
Singular arguments based on equality of rights	58
Extravagancies of the period	59

Direct results of these measures as shown in battle	60
Indirect effects of the laxness of the Assemblies upon discipline	60
Mutiny in the Brest fleet, 1793	62
Disorders in the Mediterranean fleet, 1792	63
Deterioration of the material of the navy	64
Misery of officers and seamen	64
Want of naval supplies and equipment	67
Effect of these disadvantages upon naval efficiency	68
Effect of naval inefficiency upon the general results of the war	68
Endurance and success of Great Britain due to her Sea Power	69
Condition of the British navy in 1793	69
Possesses a body of trained officers having a continuous tradition	69
Embarrassment of Great Britain for seamen	70
Condition and health of the crews	71
Mutinies in the British navy. How characterized	72
Character of the material in the British navy	73
Comparative force of the French and British navies	75
Numbers and condition of the Spanish navy	75
Inefficiency of its officers and seamen	76
Navies of Holland, Naples, and Portugal	78
Of Turkey and the Baltic States	78

CHAPTER III.

The General Political and Strategic Conditions, and the Events of 1793.

France declares war against Spain, March 7, 1793	79
Character of the governments arrayed against France	79
Mutual jealousy of Austria and Prussia	80
Attitude of the smaller German States	80
Military and naval situation of Spain	81
Policy of Great Britain	82
Attitude of Russia	82
Second Partition of Poland	82
Course of Sweden and Denmark	83
Internal dissensions and external dangers of Holland	83
Dutch colonies	83
Relations between Portugal and Great Britain	84
Attitude of the Italian States	84

CONTENTS.

	PAGE
Extent and disorganization of the Turkish Empire	85
Strategic importance of the Mediterranean islands	85
Their political distribution	86
Value of Malta and of Port Mahon	87
Corsica in the beginning of the French Revolution	88
Internal commotions in France	89
Reverses in Belgium and treason of Dumouriez	89
Reorganization of the Committee of Public Safety	90
Revolt of Lyon against the Convention	90
Fall of the Girondists	90
Risings of their followers throughout France	90
Siege of Lyon by Conventional troops	91
Toulon delivered to the British and Spanish fleets	92
French reverses on the eastern and northeastern frontiers	93
Desperate state of France	93
Mistakes of the allies	94
Energy of the Convention and its commissioners	94
Effect upon the armies	94
Failure to attain similar results in the navy	95
Causes of this failure	96
Naval unpreparedness of Great Britain in 1793	96
Difficulty in manning the fleet	96
Distribution of the British naval forces	96
Military and naval problem before Great Britain	97
Military value of insurrections in an enemy's country	98
Measures to compel the French navy to leave port	99
Difficulty of blockading French ports	99
Maritime claims of Great Britain	100
Military character of Lord Howe	101
His views of naval policy	101
Proper strategic use of the British fleet	102
Effects of inactivity upon a naval force	102
Successes of the French armies toward the close of 1793	103
Disasters of the Vendean insurgents	104
Fall of Lyon	105
The allies abandon Toulon, Dec. 19, 1793	105
Disadvantages of Toulon for the allies	106
End of the maritime year 1793	106

CHAPTER IV.

THE WEST INDIES, 1793–1810.

	PAGE
Present importance of the West India islands	109
Their value at the end of the eighteenth century	109
Control of a maritime region dependent upon the navy	110
Interests of Great Britain in the Caribbean Sea	110
Condition of Haiti	111
Relation of Haiti to the routes of commerce	112
Mistaken policy of the British in Haiti	113
Military and commercial value of the Lesser Antilles	114
Their political distribution in 1793	114
Naval weakness of Great Britain in that region	115
Expedition of Jervis and Grey in 1794	115
Capture of the French islands	115
The French retake Guadaloupe	116
Disastrous results to British possessions and commerce	117
Expedition of Christian and Abercromby, 1796	117
Its successes	118
Criticism of British military policy in 1794	119
Injury to Great Britain of Spanish and Dutch alliance with France	120
Capture of Trinidad by the British	121
Subsequent events in the West Indies	121

CHAPTER V.

THE NAVAL CAMPAIGN OF MAY, 1794, AND BATTLE OF THE FIRST OF JUNE.

Distress in France in 1793 and 1794	122
Food supplies ordered from the United States	123
Ships of war sent to convoy them to France	123
Squadrons of Nielly and Villaret sent to meet the convoy	124
Determination of British government to intercept it	125
Sailing of the Channel Fleet under Lord Howe	125
Howe meets the French fleet under Villaret Joyeuse, May 28	126
Partial engagement of May 28	127
Manœuvres of May 29	129
Partial engagement of May 29	130

	PAGE
Lord Howe breaks the French line	131
Villaret loses the advantage of the wind	131
Summary of the results of the two days' engagements	133
Merits of Howe's tactics	135
Strategic mistake by which Montagu's squadron was not on hand	135
Events of May 30 and 31	135
Preparations for battle, June 1	136
Character of Howe's attack	137
Opening of the battle	138
Howe's flag-ship again breaks the French line	139
General success of the first attack	140
The contest between the "Vengeur" and the "Brunswick"	140
Sinking of the "Vengeur"	143
Results of the encounter	144
Villaret's manœuvre to rescue his crippled ships	145
Howe's manœuvre to preserve his prizes	146
Incomplete results of the British victory	147
Physical prostration of Lord Howe	147
Tactical analysis of the action	149
Inferences deduced therefrom	152
Conduct of the French captains	153
Study of the strategic conduct of the two admirals	155
Howe's tactical success neutralized by strategic error	160
Termination of the campaign	161
Safe arrival of the convoy at Brest	161

CHAPTER VI.

The Year 1794 in the Atlantic and on the Continent.

Inaction of the British Channel fleet	162
Capture of the "Alexander," 74	162
Disastrous winter cruise of the French Brest fleet	163
Continued inactivity of the British Channel fleet	164
Howe leaves the command afloat	165
Succeeded by Bridport	165
Change in the British Admiralty	165
Little change of system	165
Dangers incurred by faulty dispositions	166
Reign of Terror in France	167
Fall of Robespierre, July 27, 1794	167
French successes on north-east frontier	168

	PAGE
Divergent retreat of Austrians and Anglo-Dutch	169
Conquest of Holland by the French	170
Establishment of Batavian Republic	170
Effect of this event upon the coalition	170
War between Great Britain and Holland	170
Fall of Dutch colonies	171
French successes on the Rhine and in the Pyrenees	171
Peace made with France by Prussia, Holland, and Spain	172
Treaties of Great Britain with Austria and Russia	172

CHAPTER VII.

THE YEAR 1795 IN THE ATLANTIC AND ON THE CONTINENT.

The year 1795 one of reaction in France	173
Reactionary measures	174
Counter-revolutionary disorders	175
Constitution of 1795	175
Dissolution of the National Convention	176
Six French ships-of-the-line transferred from Brest to Toulon	176
Action between Villaret Joyeuse and Cornwallis	177
Bridport's action off Île Groix	178
French adopt policy of commerce-destroying and withdraw their fleets from the ocean	179
Criticism of this decision	179
Military conclusions derivable from Napoleon's naval policy	180
Weakness of French military action in 1795	180
Serious reverses in Germany	181
Suspension of arms in Germany	182
Narrative shifts to the Mediterranean	183
Summary of results in 1795	183

CHAPTER VIII.

THE MEDITERRANEAN AND ITALY. — FROM THE EVACUATION OF TOULON IN 1793 TO THE BRITISH WITHDRAWAL FROM THAT SEA, IN 1796, AND BATTLE OF CAPE ST. VINCENT, IN FEBRUARY, 1797. — AUSTRIA FORCED TO MAKE PEACE.

Requirements of a base of operations	184
Policy and objects of Great Britain in the Mediterranean	185
Inadequacy of Gibraltar to these ends	185

CONTENTS.

	PAGE
Advantages of Corsica as a base	186
Expulsion of the French from Corsica	187
The crown of Corsica offered to the king of Great Britain	188
Strained relations between Paoli and the viceroy	188
French Toulon fleet puts to sea, in March, 1795	189
Action with the British Mediterranean fleet, March 14	190
Lethargy of Admiral Hotham	192
Losses in the two fleets	192
French re-enforced by a detachment from Brest	192
Disturbances in Toulon	193
Brush between the fleets off the Hyères Islands	194
Military events in Italy, 1795	195
Difficulty of suppressing coasting trade along the Riviera of Genoa	196
Sluggish movements of the Austrian general Devins	197
Decisive defeat of the Austrians at the battle of Loano	198
They retire across the Apennines	198
Criticism of the management of the British navy	199
Importance of Nelson's services	200
Commerce-destroying by the French	201
Admiral Jervis assumes command in the Mediterranean, and General Bonaparte in Italy	203
Professional Characteristics of Jervis	203
Disastrous results of Hotham's inactivity	207
Share of the French flotilla in maintaining Bonaparte's communications	207
Bonaparte's Italian campaign of 1796	208
Sardinia forced to peace	209
Successive defeats of the Austrians	210
Bonaparte occupies the line of the Adige, and blockades Mantua	210
Political results of the campaign	211
Naples abandons the Coalition, and the French occupy Leghorn	211
Consequent effects upon the British fleet	212
Bonaparte's designs upon Corsica	213
The British seize Elba	213
Offensive and defensive alliance between Spain and France	214
Singular conduct of Rear-Admiral Mann	214
Critical position of the British Mediterranean fleet	215
Ordered to evacuate Corsica	215
Junction of French and Spanish fleets	215
Jervis withdraws his fleet to Gibraltar	216
Policy of thus evacuating the Mediterranean	217
Influence of Naples upon Bonaparte's plans	218

	PAGE
Succession of disasters to Jervis's fleet	219
He repairs with it to Lisbon, January, 1797	219
Nelson's detached expedition to evacuate Elba	219
Events leading to the battle of Cape St. Vincent	220
Battle of Cape St. Vincent	221
Nelson's brilliant action	226
Merit of Sir John Jervis	228
Results of the battle	229
Sir John Jervis created Earl St. Vincent	229
Public depression in Great Britain at this time	230
Influence upon public feeling of the news of the battle	231
St. Vincent establishes the blockade of Cadiz	232
Critical condition of discipline in the British navy	232
Bonaparte's position in Italy	233
Capitulation of Mantua	233
Bonaparte advances through Carinthia into Austria	234
Preliminaries of peace signed at Leoben, April, 1797	234
Conditions, both open and secret	235
Austria treats alone, apart from Great Britain	235
Advantage to Great Britain from her Sea Power	236
Note, — incident of the mutinies of 1797 occurring in the fleet of Earl St. Vincent	236–239

CHAPTER IX.

THE MEDITERRANEAN IN 1797 AND 1798.

BONAPARTE'S EGYPTIAN EXPEDITION — THE RETURN OF THE BRITISH TO THE MEDITERRANEAN AND THE BATTLE OF THE NILE. — GREAT BRITAIN RESUMES CONTROL OF THE MEDITERRANEAN AND THE SECOND COALITION IS FORMED.

Negotiations for peace between Great Britain and France, 1796	240
The British envoy ordered to quit France	241
Difficulties between the United States and France	242
Death of Catharine II. of Russia and accession of Paul I.	243
Reactionary results of the French elections in 1797	243
Coup d'État of September 3–4, 1797	244
Reactionary members exiled from France	245
Renewed negotiations with Great Britain, 1797	245
The British envoy again dismissed	246
Bonaparte's Eastern projects	246

	PAGE
Insidious treatment of Venice	247
Nelson's expedition against Teneriffe	249
He is repulsed, loses his right arm, and returns to England	250
Peace of Campo Formio between France and Austria	250
Conditions of the peace	251
Venice ceases to exist, and France acquires the Ionian islands	251
Bonaparte leaves Italy and returns to Paris	252
Commands army intended to invade England	252
Difficulties of this enterprise	252
The expedition to Egypt determined in its stead	253
Absence of the British fleet from the Mediterranean in 1797	254
Nelson rejoins the fleet off Cadiz, April, 1798	256
Sent with three ships to watch the preparations in Toulon	256
Bonaparte sails with expedition for Egypt, May 19, 1798	256
Nelson joined by a re-enforcement of ten ships-of-the-line	257
Bonaparte seizes Malta, and sails again for Alexandria	257
Perplexity of Nelson as to the enemy's designs	258
Pursues to Alexandria, but fails to find the French	259
Cause of this disappointment	259
Retraces his steps to the westward	260
Bonaparte anchors off Alexandria, and at once disembarks troops	260
Nelson anchors at Syracuse, and again sails for Alexandria	261
Discovers the French fleet anchored in Aboukir Bay	261
Indecision and lethargy of the French admiral Brueys	262
Neglect of Bonaparte's orders	263
Description of Aboukir Bay	263
Brueys's inadequate preparations against attack	264
Comparison with those made by Hood in a like position	265
Battle of the Nile	266
Concentration upon the head of the French column	268
Grounding of the "Culloden"	269
Arrival of the British reserve and concentration on the French centre	270
The French flag-ship blows up	271
Only two French ships-of-the-line escape	271
Discussion of Nelson's claims to the credit of this action	273
Successes of Bonaparte in Egypt	277
Effect upon French troops of the battle of the Nile	277
Effect of the battle upon foreign powers	277
Aggressive action of France upon the continent of Europe	278
Intervention in Switzerland and Rome	279
Dissatisfaction of Naples and Austria	280
Hostile attitude of Paul I. of Russia	281

xviii CONTENTS.

	PAGE
Alliance between Russia and Austria	282
Effect of the tidings of the battle of the Nile	282
Influence of the battle in India	283
Nelson ordered to Naples	284
Blockade of Malta by the British	285
Disposition of the British Mediterranean fleet	286
Russo-Turkish attack upon the Ionian islands	286
Minorca captured by the British	287
Maritime results of the year 1798	287

CHAPTER X.

THE MEDITERRANEAN FROM 1799 TO 1801.

BONAPARTE'S SYRIAN EXPEDITION AND SIEGE OF ACRE. — THE INCURSION OF THE FRENCH BREST FLEET UNDER ADMIRAL BRUIX. — BONAPARTE'S RETURN TO FRANCE. — THE FRENCH LOSE MALTA AND EGYPT.

Bonaparte's hopes from the Egyptian expedition	288
Weakness of Egyptian institutions	289
Conquest of Upper Egypt	289
The Pasha of Syria advances against Egypt	290
Isolation of the French in Egypt	290
Consequent embarrassment of Bonaparte	291
Bonaparte hears of the Turkish preparations against him	292
Resolves to invade Syria	292
The French capture El Arish and advance to Acre	293
Character of Sir Sidney Smith, commanding the British squadron off Acre	294
His naval and diplomatic mission to the Levant	296
Annoyance thereby caused to Nelson and St. Vincent	297
Smith assumes command off Alexandria	298
Importance of Acre	299
Smith arrives at Acre from Alexandria	299
Captures a convoy with Bonaparte's siege train	300
Siege of Acre	300
Arrival of Turkish re-enforcements from Rhodes	301
Final assault by the French	302
They raise the siege and retreat to Egypt	302
Services of Sir Sidney Smith at Acre	303

	PAGE
The French fleet of twenty-five ships-of-the-line, under Admiral Bruix, escapes from Brest	304
Conduct of Lord Bridport	305
Excitement in Great Britain	306
Bruix appears off Cadiz, and enters the Mediterranean	307
Exposed position of the British naval detachments	308
Anxieties of Earl St. Vincent	309
Measures taken by him	309
Action of Nelson	310
Activity and sagacity shown by St. Vincent	311
The Spanish fleet leaves Cadiz and reaches Cartagena	312
St Vincent's health fails, and he gives up command to Keith	312
Bruix eludes Keith's pursuit and joins Spaniards in Cartagena	313
The allied fleets pass the Straits and reach Brest	316
Keith pursues to Brest and then goes to Torbay	316
Discussion of the French objects in this cruise	316
Conduct of the British admirals at the same time	318
The Turkish army lands in Aboukir Bay to attack the French	321
It is destroyed by Bonaparte	322
Bonaparte quits Egypt and returns to France	323
Criticism of the Egyptian expedition	324
Absolute control of the Mediterranean by the British navy	328
Surrender of Malta	330
Isolation of Egypt	330
Convention of El Arish for the evacuation of Egypt by the French	332
Ratification refused by British government, because unauthorized	333
Abercromby's expedition. Final loss of Egypt by the French	334
Assassination of Kleber	334

CHAPTER XI.

The Atlantic, 1796-1801. — The Brest Blockades. — The French Expeditions against Ireland.

The French resolution to depend upon commerce-destroying	335
Consequent effect upon naval war and upon the control of the sea	336
Resulting dispositions of French and British navies	337
Inefficient character of the blockade of Brest	338
Conditions of the maritime problem before Great Britain stated	339
Measures proper to be adopted	340
Mutual relations of the elements of a defensive system	341

	PAGE
Two aspects under which the military value of Brest should be considered	342
Description of the port and its surroundings	342
Strategic importance of the winds	344
Anchorages available to the British fleets as bases of operations against Brest	344
Theory of the Brest blockade	345
Fitness of the British bases relative to this theory	345
Policies of St. Vincent, Howe, and Bridport	346
Causes leading to the Irish expedition of 1796	347
Preparations for the expedition	348
Hoche appointed to command it	349
Villaret Joyeuse appointed to command the fleet	349
His distaste for the enterprise	349
He is superseded by Morard de Galles	350
Inefficiency of the French navy at this time	350
Departure of the expedition	351
Its dispersal on the night of starting	353
Reunion of the greater part of the ships	354
Absence of the two commanders-in-chief	354
The expedition reaches the coast of Ireland	355
Mishaps in Bantry Bay	356
The ships return to France	357
Shipwreck of the "Droits de l'Homme"	358
Misfortunes of the ship carrying Hoche and Morard	359
Inefficiency of the British dispositions against invasion	360
Analysis of these dispositions	361
Consequent impunity of the French	367
St. Vincent succeeds, in 1800, to the command of the Channel fleet	368
His strategic management of the general operations	369
His tactical dispositions to maintain the watch of the port	371
Dependence of the admiralty upon the commander-in-chief	373
St. Vincent's provisions in case of the blockade being forced	374
Decisive effects of the system introduced by him	375
Paralysis of Brest under this watch	376
Napoleon in consequence adopts Antwerp as his chief dockyard	377
Purposed expedition against Ireland from the Texel	378
Naval battle of Camperdown	378
Death of Hoche	378
The expeditions of 1798 against Ireland	379
Cessation of the attempts upon Ireland	380

LIST OF ILLUSTRATIONS.

VOLUME I.

MAPS AND BATTLE PLANS.

		PAGE
I.	Manœuvres of May 29, 1794, Figures 1 and 2	129
II.	Manœuvres of May 29, 1794, Fig. 3	131
III.	Battle of June 1, 1794	137
IV.	Map of Northern Italy	195
V.	Battle of Cape St. Vincent	223
VI.	Map of the Mediterranean	257
VII.	Coast Map, Alexandria to the Nile	263
VIII.	Battle of the Nile	267
IX.	Map of English Channel and North Sea	335
X.	Map of Brest and its Approaches	343

THE INFLUENCE OF SEA POWER

UPON THE

FRENCH REVOLUTION AND EMPIRE.

CHAPTER I.

INTRODUCTORY.

OUTLINE OF EVENTS IN EUROPE, 1783-1793.

THE ten years following the Peace of Versailles, September 3, 1783, coming between the two great wars of American Independence and of the French Revolution, seem like a time of stagnation. The muttering and heaving which foretold the oncome of the later struggle were indeed to be heard by those whose ears were open, long before 1793. The opening events and violences which marked the political revolution were of earlier date, and war with Austria and Prussia began even in 1792; but the year 1793 stands out with a peculiar prominence, marked as it is by the murder of the king and queen, the beginning of the Reign of Terror, and the outbreak of hostilities with the great Sea Power, whose stubborn, relentless purpose and mighty wealth were to exert the decisive influence upon the result of the war. Untiring in sustaining with her gold the poorer powers of the Continent against the common enemy, dogged in bearing up alone the burden of the war, when one by one her allies dropped away, the year in which Great Britain, with her fleets, her commerce, and her money, rose against the French republic, with its conquering armies, its ruined navy, and its bankrupt treasury, may well be taken as the beginning of that tremendous strife which ended at Waterloo.

To the citizen of the United States, the war whose results were summed up and sealed in the Treaty of Versailles is a landmark of history surpassing all others in interest and importance. His sympathies are stirred by the sufferings of the many, his pride animated by the noble constancy of the few whose names will be forever identified with the birth-throes of his country. Yet in a less degree this feeling may well be shared by a native of Western Europe, though he have not the same vivid impression of the strife, which, in so distant a land and on so small a scale, brought a new nation to life. This indeed was the *great* outcome of that war; but in its progress, Europe, India, and the Sea had been the scenes of deeds of arms far more dazzling and at times much nearer home than the obscure contest in America. In dramatic effect nothing has exceeded the three-years siege of Gibraltar, teeming as it did with exciting interest, fluctuating hopes and fears, triumphant expectation and bitter disappointment. England from her shores saw gathered in the Channel sixty-six French and Spanish ships-of-the-line,—a force larger than had ever threatened her since the days of the Great Armada, and before which her inferior numbers had to fly, for the first time, to the shelter of her ports. Rodney and Suffren had conducted sea campaigns, fought sea fights, and won sea victories which stirred beyond the common the hearts of men in their day, and which still stand conspicuous in the story of either navy. In one respect above all, this war was distinguished; in the development, on both sides, of naval power. Never since the days of De Ruyter and Tourville had so close a balance of strength been seen upon the seas. Never since the Peace of Versailles to our own day has there been such an approach to equality between the parties to a sea war.

The three maritime nations issued wearied from the strife, as did also America; but the latter, though with many difficulties still to meet, was vigorous in youth and unfettered by bad political traditions. The colonists of yesterday were thoroughly fitted to retrieve their own fortunes and those of their country; to use the boundless resources which Divine Providence had made ready to their hands. It was quite otherwise with France and Spain; while Great Britain, though untouched with the seeds of decay that tainted her rivals, was weighed down with a heavy feeling of overthrow, loss and humiliation, which for the moment hid from her eyes the glory and wealth yet within her reach. Colonial ambition was still at its loftiest height among the nations of Europe, and she had lost her greatest, most powerful colony. Not only the king and the lords, but the mass of the people had set their hearts upon keeping America. Men of all classes had predicted ruin to the Empire if it parted with such a possession; and now they had lost it, wrung from them after a bitter struggle, in which their old enemies had overborne them on the field they called their own, the Sea. The Sea Power of Great Britain had been unequal to the task laid upon it, and so America was gone. A less resolute people might have lost hope.

If the triumph of France and Spain was proportionate to their rival's loss, this was no true measure of their gains, nor of the relative positions of the three in the years after the war. American Independence profited neither France nor Spain. The latter had indeed won back the Floridas and Minorca; but she had utterly failed before Gibraltar, and Jamaica had not even been attacked. Minorca, as Nelson afterwards said, was always England's when she wanted it. It belonged not to this power or that, but to the nation that controlled the sea; so England retook it in 1798, when her fleets again entered the Mediterranean. France had gained even less than Spain. Her trading posts in India had been restored; but they, even more than Minorca, were defenceless unless in free communication with and supported by the sea power of the mother-country. In the West Indies she returned to Great Britain more than the latter did to her. "France," says a French historian, "had accomplished the duties of her providential mission" (in freeing America); "her moral interests, the interests of her glory and of her ideas were satisfied. The interests of her material power had been badly defended by her government; the only solid advantage she had obtained was depriving England of Minorca, that curb on Toulon, far more dangerous to us when in their hands than is Gibraltar."[1]

Unfortunately at this moment France was far richer in ideas, moral and political, and in renown, than in solid power. The increasing embarrassment of the Treasury forced her to stay her hand, and to yield to her rival terms of peace utterly beyond what the seeming strength of either side justified. The French navy had reaped glory in the five years of war; not so much, nearly, as French writers claim for it, but still it had done well, and the long contest must have increased the efficiency of its officers along with their growing experience. A little more time only was wanted for France, allied to Spain, to gain lasting results as well as passing fame. This time poverty refused her.

Spain, as for centuries back, still depended for her income almost wholly upon her treasure ships from America. Always risked by war, this supply became more than doubtful when the undisputed control of the sea passed to an enemy. The policy of Spain, as to peace or war, was therefore tied fast to that of France, without whose navy her shipping lay at England's mercy; and, though the national pride clung obstinately to its claim for Gibraltar, it was forced to give way.

[1] Martin, Histoire de France, vol. xix. p. 370.

Great Britain alone, after all her losses, rested on a solid foundation of strength. The American contest by itself had cost her nearly £100,000,000, and rather more than that amount had during the war been added to the national debt; but two years later this had ceased to increase, and soon the income of the State was greater than the outgo. Before the end of 1783, the second William Pitt, then a young man of twenty-four, became prime minister. With genius and aims specially fitted to the restorative duties of a time of peace, the first of British finance ministers in the opinion of Mr. Gladstone,[1] he bent his great powers to fostering the commerce and wealth of the British people. With firm but skilful hand he removed, as far as the prejudices of the day would permit and in the face of much opposition, the fetters, forged by a mistaken policy, that hampered the trade of the Empire. Promoting the exchange of goods with other nations, simplifying the collection of taxes and the revenue, he added at once to the wealth of the people and to the income of the State. Although very small in amount, as compared with the enormous figures of later years, the exports and imports of Great Britain increased over fifty per cent between the years 1784 and 1792. Even with the lately severed colonies of North America the same rate of gain, as compared with the trade before the war, held good; while with the old enemy of his father and of England, with France, there was concluded in 1786 a treaty of commerce which was exceedingly liberal for those days, and will, it is said, bear a favorable comparison with any former or subsequent treaty between the two countries. "In the course of little more than three years from Mr. Pitt's acceptance of office as First Lord of the Treasury," says the eulogist of his distinguished rival, Fox, "great commercial and financial reforms had been effected. . . . The nation overcoming its difficulties, and rising buoyant from depression, began

[1] Nineteenth Century Review. June, 1887, p. 922.

rapidly to increase its wealth, to revive its spirit, and renew its strength."[1]

Such was the home condition of the British people; but fully to appreciate the advantageous position to which it was rising, in preparation for the great conflict still unforeseen, it must be remembered that all things worked together to centre and retain the political executive power in the hands of Pitt. The feelings of the king, then a very real force in the nation; the confidence of the people, given to his father's son and fixed by the wisdom of his own conduct and the growth of the moneyed prosperity so dear to the British heart; the personal character of his only rival in ability, — all combined to commit the political guidance of the State to one man at the great crisis when such unity of action was essential to strength. Whether the great peace minister was equal to the wisest direction of war has been questioned, and has been denied. Certainly it was not the office he himself would have chosen; but it was a great gain for England that she was at this time able to give herself wholly to a single leader. He took office with a minority of one hundred in the House of Commons, held it for two months constantly out-voted, and then dissolving Parliament appealed to the country. The election gave him a majority of over a hundred, — a foretaste of the unwavering support he received from the representatives of the people during the early and critical years of the French Revolution, when the yet fluid opinions of the nation were gradually being cast and hardened into that set conviction and determination characteristic of the race.

How different the state of France is well known. The hopeless embarrassment of the finances, hopeless at least under the political and social conditions, the rapid succession of ministers, each sinking deeper in entanglements, the weak character of the king, the conflict of opinions, the

[1] Lord John Russell's Life of Fox, vol. ii. p. 137.

lack of sympathy between classes, all tending to the assembling of the Notables in February, 1787, and the yet more pregnant meeting of the States General, May 4, 1789, which was the beginning of the end. France was moneyless and leaderless.

But while the Western countries of Europe were by these circumstances disposed or constrained to wish for the continuance of peace, restlessness showed itself in other quarters and in ways which, from the close relations of the European States, disquieted the political atmosphere. The Austrian Netherlands and Holland, Poland and Turkey, the Black Sea and the Baltic, became the scene of diplomatic intrigues and of conflicts, which, while they did not involve the great Western Powers in actual war, caused them anxiety and necessitated action.

The Empress-Queen of Austria and Hungary, Maria Theresa, had died in 1780. Her son, the Emperor Joseph II., came to the throne in the prime of life, and with his head full of schemes for changing and bettering the condition of his dominions. In 1781, the weakness of Holland being plainly shown by her conduct of the war with Great Britain, and the other countries having their hands too full to interfere, he demanded and received the surrender of the fortified towns in the Austrian Netherlands; which, under the name of the "barrier towns," had been held and garrisoned by Holland since the Peace of Utrecht in 1713, as a bridle upon the ambition of France. At the same time the circumstances of the great maritime contest, which during the American Revolution covered all the seas of Europe, impelled every neutral nation having a seaboard to compete for the carrying trade. Holland for a time had shared this profit with the nations of the North; but when Great Britain, rightly or wrongly, forced her into war, the trade which had been carried on through Holland and her great rivers reaching into the heart of Germany, being denied its natural channel, sought a new one through the

Austrian Netherlands by the port of Ostend. The growth of the latter, like that of Nassau during the Civil War in the United States, was forced and unhealthy, — due not to natural advantages but to morbid conditions; but it fostered the already strong wish of the emperor for a sea power which no other part of his dominions could give.

This movement of Belgian commerce was accelerated by the disappearance of the British carrying trade. As in the days of Louis XIV., before he had laid up his ships-of-the-line, so in the American War the cruisers and privateers of the allies, supported by the action of the combined fleets occupying the British navy, preyed ravenously on British shipping. In the days of the elder Pitt it had been said that commerce was made to live and thrive by war; but then the French great fleets had left the sea, and British armed ships protected trade and oppressed the enemy's cruisers. Between 1778 and 1783 Great Britain was fully engaged on every sea, opposing the combined fleets and protecting as far as she could her colonies. "This untoward state of things reduced the English merchants to difficulties and distresses, with respect to the means of carrying on their trade, which they had never experienced in any other war. Foreign vessels were used for the conveyance of their goods, and the protection of a foreign flag for the first time sought by Englishmen."[1] The writer forgot the days of Jean Bart, Duguay-Trouin, and Forbin; we may profitably note that like conditions lead to like results.

Thus, while America was struggling for life, and the contests of England, France, and Spain were heard in all quarters of the world, Netherland ships showed abroad on every sea the flag of an inland empire, and Ostend grew merrily; but if the petty port and narrow limits thus throve, how should the emperor bear to see the great city of Antwerp, with its noble river and its proud commercial

---

[1] Annual Register, vol. 27, p. 10.

record, shut up from the sea as it had been since the Treaty of Westphalia? His discontent was deep and instant; but it was the misfortune of this prince that he took in hand more than his own capacity and the extent of his estates would let him complete. His attention being for the moment diverted to southeastern Europe, where Austria and Russia were then acting in diplomatic concert against the Porte, the question of Antwerp was dropped. Before it could be resumed, the Peace of Versailles had left Great Britain, France, and Holland — all so vitally interested in whatever concerned Belgium — free, though loath, to enter into a new contention. Matters having been for the time arranged with Turkey, the emperor again in 1784 renewed his demands, alleging, after the manner of statesmen, several collateral grievances, but on the main issue saying roundly that " the entire and free navigation of the Scheldt from Antwerp to the sea was a *sine qua non*" to any agreement.

The arguments — commercial, political, or founded on treaty — which were in this instance urged for or against the natural claim of a country to use a river passing through its own territory, to the sea that washes its shores, are not here in question; but it is important to analyze the far-reaching interests at stake, to note the bearing of this dispute upon them and so upon the general diplomacy of Europe, and thereby trace its intimate connection with that Sea Power whose influence upon the course of history at this period it is our aim to weigh. Though modified in expression by passing events, and even at times superficially reversed, like natural currents checked and dammed by contrary winds, these underlying tendencies — being dependent upon permanent causes — did not cease to exist during the storm of the Revolution. Ever ready to resume their course when the momentary opposition was removed, the appreciation of them serves to explain apparent contradictions, produced by the conflicts between transient necessity and enduring interests.

From that great centre of the world's commerce where the Scheldt, the Meuse, the Rhine, and the Thames meet in the North Sea, near the Straits of Dover, there then parted two principal lines of trade passing through European waters, — through seas, that is, along whose shores were planted many different powers, foreign and possibly hostile to each other. Of these two lines, one ended in the Baltic; the other, after skirting the coasts of France and the Spanish peninsula and running the gantlet of the Barbary corsairs, ended in the Levant or Turkish Seas. The great Empire of Russia, which only made itself felt in the sphere of European politics after the Treaty of Utrecht, in 1713, had since then been moving forward not only its centre, which bore upon the continent of Europe, but also both its wings; one of which touched and overshadowed the Baltic on the North, while the other, through a steady course of pressure and encroachment upon the Turks, had now reached the Black Sea. This advance had been aided by the fixedness with which France and England, through their ancient rivalry and their colonial ambitions, had kept their eyes set upon each other and beyond the Atlantic; but the Peace of Versailles forced the combatants to pause, and gave them time to see other interests, which had been overlooked through the long series of wars waged, between 1739 and 1783, over commerce and colonies. It was then realized that not only had Russia, in the past half-century, advanced her lines by the partition of Poland and by taking from Sweden several provinces on the Baltic, but also that she had so added to her influence upon the Black Sea and over the Turkish Empire by successive aggressions, wresting bits of territory and establishing claims of interference in behalf of Turkish subjects, as to make her practical supremacy in Eastern waters a possibility of the future.

The Western Question, as it may fitly be called, had been settled by the birth of a new nation, destined to greatness and preponderance in the western hemisphere; the Eastern Question, phrase now so familiar, soon loomed on the horizon. Was it to receive a like solution? Was a great nation, already close to the spot, to win a position of exceptional advantage for dominating in eastern waters as America must do in western? for it must be remembered that, although the Levant was then only the end of a European trade route, both the history of the past and the well understood possibilities of the future pointed to it as one of the greatest centres of commerce, and therefore of human interest and political influence, in the world. The Levant and Egypt had then, and still keep, the same interest that is now being felt in the Isthmus of Panama and the Caribbean; and it is hard to imagine a more threatening condition of naval power than the possession of the Black Sea and its impregnable entrance, by a vigorous nation, so close to the Eastern highway of the world. The position in 1783 was the more dangerous from the close alliance and respective abilities of the rulers of Austria and Russia; the cool-headed and experienced Catharine, through her influence on her weaker colleague, directing the resources of both empires in a path most favorable to Russia.

The tendency of Russian growth, and the historic events which marked its progress, were, of course, well enough known in England long before; but there is a difference between knowing facts and realizing their full meaning. Circumstances alter cases; and men's minds, when strongly bent one way, do not heed what is passing elsewhere. Hence, in 1785, we find the attitude of Great Britain toward Russia very different from that of fifteen years earlier, when the empress and the Porte were at war. In 1770, British officers commanded Russian fleets and ships, and a British admiral had leave to take a place in the Russian Admiralty, with the promise of his home rank being restored to him. The Czarina sent a fleet of twenty sail-of-the-line from the Baltic to the Levant. They stopped and refitted in Spithead; Russian soldiers were landed and camped ashore to refresh themselves; English sergeants of marines were employed to drill them; a Russian eighty-gun ship, flying the flag of an Anglo-Russian admiral, was docked in Portsmouth and cut down to improve her sailing qualities. Thus comforted and strengthened they sailed for the Mediterranean; and, receiving further damage from the poor seamanship of their crews, they were again fitted at Port Mahon,— then an English dockyard,— for action in the Levant.[1] When, among the hard knocks of the two following years, the Russians destroyed a Turkish fleet of fifteen ships-of-the-line in a port of Asia Minor, British lieutenants commanded the fire-ships, and a British commodore the covering squadron.

To us now, with our remembrance of Kars and Silistria, of the Crimea and Hobart Pasha, of Cyprus and Besika Bay, these things seem like a dream; and the more so, that the Mediterranean powers of the earlier day viewed the Russian approach with ill-concealed mistrust, and laid severe restrictions upon the use of their ports. But Turkey then, though a good friend to Great Britain, was a yet better friend to France; the Turkish alliance had been useful to the latter country by making diversion in her wars with Austria, Great Britain's natural ally; the French were the favored nation by Turkish commercial treaties, and a naval war in eastern waters could not but be injurious to their commerce. Difficulties about trade might even bring about a collision between France and Russia, which at least could do no harm to Great Britain at a time when her rival was known to be steadily building up her navy with a view to revenge past defeats; just as now she is thought to be looking for a day of reckoning with Germany. The Baltic trade was also of immense

---

[1] See Annual Register, 1769, pp. 2–4; 1770, pp. 27–41, 67, 71, 75.

value, and the friendship of Russia was necessary thereto. Altogether, in 1770, the Russian nation, notwithstanding the French leanings of the Czarina, was, upon the whole, the friend of Great Britain's friends, and the opponent of her enemies,— especially of the one traditional, or, as even generous Englishmen used to say, the *natural* enemy, France. Russia bore especially against Sweden, Poland, and Turkey; and these it was the consistent aim of the best school of French statesmen to court and strengthen.

But in 1785 a great change had taken place. The war of 1770 had planted Russia firmly on the Black Sea. The treaty of Kainardji in 1774 admitted her trade freely to the Mediterranean,— a privilege which other trading nations, in the narrow spirit of the day, considered their own loss. Russian frigates had entered the Dardanelles on their way to the Black Sea; and though the Porte, terrified at the consequences of its action, stopped them at Constantinople, the move was none the less significant. Then there had come, in 1774, the partition of Poland, universally condemned as unrighteous and dangerous to the balance of power, though submitted to by the other States. If Great Britain, though restless over this, saw still some compensation in the injury done to France by the weakening of her allies, and hugged herself with the belief that her insular position made the continental balance of less moment, she had had a severe reminder of Russia's growing strength and power to injure, in the Armed Neutrality of 1780. This unfriendly blow, aimed by a State she had looked upon as almost a natural ally, which she had so greatly helped but ten years before, and which had now chosen the moment of her direst straits to attack what she considered her maritime rights, probably completed the alienation, and opened the eyes of British statesmen to the new danger with which they were threatened by the position of Russia upon the Baltic and close to the Mediterranean.

France, also, had little less interest than England in this condition of things, and certainly felt no less. From the days of Henry IV. and Colbert, and even before, she had looked upon the Levant as peculiarly her own field, the home of a faithful ally, and the seat of a lucrative trade which was almost monopolized by her. Although so far foiled in India, she had not yet lost her hopes of overcoming and replacing the British hold upon that land of fabled wealth, and she understood the important bearing of the Levant and Egypt upon the security of tenure there. It need not then surprise us, in the great maritime war which we are approaching, to find Napoleon — for all his greatness, the child of his generation — amid all the glory and bewildering rush of his famous Italian campaign, planning conquest in Egypt and the East, and Nelson, that personification of the British sea power of his day, fighting his two most brilliant battles in the Levant and in the Baltic. Nor will we be unprepared to see an importance equal to that of Gibraltar and Mahon in former days, now attached to points like Malta, Corfu, Taranto, Brindisi, as well as to Sicily and Egypt, by the statesmen, generals, and admirals, whose counsels directed the military efforts of the belligerents. Many of these points had heretofore lain out of the field of action of the Western Powers, but the rising Eastern Question was bringing them forward.

Nor was it in the Levant alone that questions vitally affecting the rival States awaited solution. The trade interests of the Baltic, as the outlet through which great rivers and the products of immense regions found their way to the world beyond, made its control also an object of importance to both the chief parties in the coming struggle, — to Great Britain who strove to drive her enemy off the sea, and to France who wished to shut out hers from the land. But, besides its commercial importance, the secluded character of the sea, the difficulty of the approach, — aggravated by the severe climate, — and the immense preponderance in strength of Russia over Sweden and Denmark, made always possible an armed combination such as that of 1780, which was in fact renewed in 1800, seriously threatening the naval supremacy of Great Britain. Such a coalition it was vital to the latter to prevent, and most desirable to her enemy to effect. If formed, it was a nucleus around which readily gathered all other malcontents, dissatisfied with the harsh and overbearing manner in which the great Sea Power enforced what she considered her rights over neutral ships.

The nearness of England to the Baltic made it unnecessary to have naval stations on the way for the repair or shelter of her shipping, but it was most undesirable that the ports and resources of Holland and Belgium, lying close on the flank of the route, and doubly strong in the formidable outworks of shoals and intricate navigation with which nature had protected them, should be under the control of a great hostile power. Jean Bart, and his fellow-privateersmen of a hundred years before, had shown the danger to British shipping from even the third-rate port of Dunkirk, so situated. Where Dunkirk sent squadrons of frigates, Antwerp could send fleets of ships-of-the-line. The appearance of Russia, therefore, and her predominance on the Baltic, made weightier still the interest in the political condition of the Low Countries which, for generations past, Great Britain had felt on account of her commercial relations with them, and through them with Germany; an interest hitherto aroused mainly by the ambition of France to control their policy, if not actually to possess herself of a large part of their territory. She had to fear that which was realized under Napoleon,— the conversion of Antwerp into a great naval station, with free access to the sea, and the control of its resources and those of the United Provinces by a strong and able enemy.

Great Britain, therefore, had in 1781 seen with just apprehension the aggressive attitude of Joseph II. toward the Dutch, and the fall of the "barrier towns." It is true that these fortresses had ceased to afford much protection to Holland, owing to her military decline, but the event emphasized her exposure to France; while the power of Austria to defend her own provinces, or the Dutch, was notoriously less than that of France to attack, owing to the relative distance of the two from the scene, and the danger to troops, on the march from Austria, of being assailed in flank from the French frontier. Now, again, in 1784, she was forced to look with anxiety — less on account of Austria than of France — upon this raising of the question of the Scheldt. There was little cause to fear Austria becoming a great sea power now, when she had held the Netherlands three fourths of a century without becoming such; but there was good reason to dread that the movements in progress might result in increasing her rival's sea power and influence — perhaps even her territory — in the Low Countries. All these things did come to pass, though not under the dying monarchy.

It may be presumed that the wise Catharine of Russia, without in the least foreseeing the approaching French convulsion which shook her plans as well as those of other European rulers, realized the true relations between her country and the Western powers, when she so heartily supported the emperor in his claim for the free navigation of the Scheldt. There was no likelihood then, as there is little likelihood now, that Great Britain and France would act together in the Eastern Question, then too new to outweigh former prejudices or to unite old enemies. If the contention of Austria were successful, Russia would secure a friendly port in a region naturally hostile to her pretensions. If unsuccessful, as things then looked, the result would probably be the extension of French influence in the Netherlands and in the United Provinces; and French gain there meant gain of sea power, with proportionate loss of the same to Great Britain. The empress could still reckon on their mutual antagonism; while the British navy, and the way in which it was used in war, were more serious dangers to Russia than the French armies. Whatever her reasoning, there is no doubt that at this time her policy was drawing closer to France. The French ministers in the East mediated between her and the Sultan in the unceasing disputes arising from the treaty of Kainardji. A commercial treaty on most favorable terms was concluded with France, while that with Great Britain was allowed to lapse, and its renewal was refused during many years.

Such were the ambitions and the weighty solicitudes, well understood on all hands, which, during the eight years succeeding the emperor's demand for the opening of the Scheldt, underlay and guided the main tendencies of European policy, and continued so to do during the revolutionary wars. The separate events which group themselves round these leading outlines, up to the outbreak of war in 1793, can only be hastily sketched.

Notwithstanding the close family relationship between Louis XVI. and the emperor, the French government looked coldly upon the latter's action in the matter of the Scheldt. The long-standing struggle in the United Provinces between partisans of Great Britain and France was just now marked by the preponderance of the latter, and, consequently, of French influence. As Austria seemed resolved to enforce her claims by war, the king first offered his mediation, and, when that was unavailing, told the emperor he would interpose by arms. His troops were accordingly massed on the Belgian frontier. It was understood that the king of Prussia, who was brother-in-law to the stadtholder, would act with France. Russia, on the other hand, proclaimed her intention to support Austria. Sweden, as the enemy of Russia, began to put ships in commission and enlist soldiers; while from Constantinople came a report that, if war began, the sultan also would improve so good an opportunity of regaining what he had lately lost. While the quarrel about the Scheldt was thus causing complications in all quarters, an incident occurred upon the chief scene of trouble, which under such conditions might well have precipitated a general war. An Austrian brig was ordered to sail from Antwerp to the sea, to test the intentions of Holland. Upon passing the boundary she was fired upon and brought to by a Dutch armed ship. This happened on the 8th of October, 1784.

Yet after all war did not come, owing to Joseph's volatile attention being again drawn from the matter immediately in hand. He proposed to the elector of Bavaria to take the Netherlands in exchange for his electorate. This transfer, which by concentrating the possessions of Austria would greatly have increased her weight in the Empire, was resisted by the whole Germanic body with Frederic the Great at its head. It therefore came to naught; but the slackening of the emperor's interest in his Scheldt scheme promoted, under French auspices, a peaceful arrangement; which, while involving mutual concessions, left the real question substantially untouched. Its solution was not reached until the storm of the Revolution swept city and river into the arms of the French republic. This compromise was shortly followed by a treaty of the closest alliance between France and the United Provinces, engaging them to mutual support in case of war, fixing the amount of armed ships or men to be furnished, and promising the most intimate co-operation in their dealings with other States. This agreement, which, as far as compacts could, established French preponderance in the councils of Holland, was ratified on Christmas Day, 1785.

This treaty gave rise to serious and regretful consideration in Great Britain; but the growing financial embarrassment and internal disturbance of France were rapidly neutralizing her external exertions. The following years were marked by new combinations and alliances among

States. In 1786 Frederic the Great's death took away an important element in European politics. The quarrel between the two factions in Holland had reached the verge of civil war, when an insult offered by the French party to the wife of the stadtholder, sister to the new king of Prussia, led to an armed interference by this sovereign. In October, 1787, Prussian troops occupied Amsterdam and restored to the stadtholder privileges that had been taken from him. Even France had strongly condemned the act of those who had arrested the princess, and advised ample satisfaction to be given; but, nevertheless, when the French party appealed for aid against the Prussian intervention, she prepared to give it and notified her purpose to Great Britain. The latter, glad again to assert her own influence, replied that she could not remain a quiet spectator, issued immediate orders for augmenting her forces by sea and land, and contracted with Hesse for the supply of twelve thousand troops upon demand. The rapid success of the Prussians prevented any collision; but Great Britain had the gratification, and France the mortification, of seeing re-established the party favorable to the former.

In February, 1787, the Assembly of Notables, which had not met since 1626, was opened by Louis XVI. at Versailles. But the most striking event of this year was the declaration of war against Russia by Turkey, which determined no longer to wait until its enemy was ready before engaging in an inevitable conflict. The Turkish manifesto was sent forth August 24; Russia replied on the 13th of September.

The emperor, as the ally of Russia, declared war against Turkey on the 10th of February, 1788. Operations were carried on by the Austrians around Belgrade and on the Danube. The Russians, bent on extending their power on the Black Sea, invested Oczakow at the mouth and on the right bank of the Dnieper, — Kinburn on the left side having already been ceded to them by the treaty of Kainardji.

The czarina also decided to renew in the Mediterranean the diversion of 1770, again sending ships from the Baltic. When the distance and inconvenience of this operation, combined with the entire lack of any naval station in the Mediterranean, are considered in connection with the close proximity of Russia to that sea in mere miles, there will be felt most forcibly her tantalizing position with reference to commerce and sea power, to whose importance she has been keenly alive and to which she has ever aspired since the days of Peter the Great. It is difficult to understand how Russia can be quiet until she has secured an access to the sea not dependent upon the good-will of any other State.

Notwithstanding the many causes of displeasure she had given to Great Britain, Catharine went on with her arrangements as though assured of the good-will and help before received. Pilot boats were engaged to meet the ships in British waters, and take them to British dockyards. Under her orders, British merchants chartered eighteen large ships to convey artillery and stores after the fleet. All these arrangements were quietly frustrated by Pitt's ministry, which forbade seamen to serve in any foreign ships; and, upon the ground that the nation was to be strictly neutral, made the contractors renounce their engagements. Catharine then turned to Holland, which also refused aid, pleading the same purpose of neutrality. This concert of action between the two maritime States forced Russia to abandon so distant an expedition and illustrated the advantage she would have obtained from the emperor's claim to the Scheldt. It was at this time that the celebrated Paul Jones, who had distinguished himself by his desperate courage in the American Revolutionary War, took service in the Russian Navy and was given a high command; but his appointment so offended the British officers already serving in the fleet, whom their government had foreborne to recall, that they at once resigned. The Russians could not afford to lose so many capable men, and Jones was transferred from the Baltic to the Black Sea.

Soon a fourth State took part in the contest. On the 21st of June, 1788, Sweden advanced her troops into Russian Finland, and on the 30th war against her was declared by Russia. It now proved fortunate for the latter that she had not been able to get her fleet away from the Baltic. The fighting on land was there mainly confined to the north coast of the Gulf of Finland, while in the waters of the Gulf several very severe actions took place. These battles were fought not only between ships-of-the-line of the usual type, but by large flotillas of gunboats and galleys, and were attended with a loss of life unusual in naval actions.

War being now in full swing throughout the East, Great Britain and Prussia drew together in a defensive treaty, and were joined by Holland also, under the new lease of power of the stadtholder and British party. The quota of troops or ships to be furnished in case of need by each State was stipulated. The allies soon had occasion to act in favor of one of the belligerents. Denmark, the hereditary enemy of Sweden, and now in alliance with Russia, took this opportunity to invade the former country from Norway, then attached to the Danish crown. On September 24, 1788, twelve thousand Danish troops crossed the frontier and advanced upon Gottenburg, which was on the point of surrendering when the sudden and unexpected arrival of the king, in person and alone, prevented. There was not, however, force enough to save the town, had not Great Britain and Prussia interfered. The British minister at Copenhagen passed over hastily into Gottenburg, induced the Swedish king to accept the mediation of the two governments, and then notified the Danish commander that, if the invasion of Sweden was not stopped, Denmark would be by them attacked. The peremptory tone held by the minister swept away the flimsy pretext that the Danish corps was only an auxiliary, furnished to Russia in accordance with existing treaty, and therefore really a Russian force. There was nothing left for Denmark but to recede; an armistice was signed at once and a month later her troops were withdrawn.

The true significance of the alliance between the two Western Powers, to which Holland was accessory, is markedly shown by this action, which, while ostensibly friendly to Sweden, was really hostile to Russia and a diversion in favor of the sultan. Great Britain and Prussia, in consequence of the growing strength and influence of Russia in the Baltic, the Black Sea, and the Continent, and to check her progress, followed what was then considered to be the natural policy of France, induced by ties and traditions long antedating the existing state of things in Europe. Sweden then, and Turkey later, traditional allies of France, and in so far in the opposite scale of the balance from Great Britain, were to be supported by the demonstration — and if need were by the employment — of force. This was done, not because France was as yet less dreaded, but because Russia had become so much more formidable. It was again the coming Eastern Question in which, from the very distance of the central scene of action from Western Europe, and from the character of the interests and of the strategic points involved, Sea Power, represented chiefly by the maritime strength and colonial expansion of Great Britain, was to play the leading and most decisive part. It was the dawning of the day, whose noon the nineteenth century has not yet seen, during which Nelson and Napoleon, Mohammed Ali and Ibrahim Pasha, the Sultan Mahmond and the Czar Nicholas, Napier, Stopford, and Lalande in 1840, the heroes of Kars, Silistria, and the Crimea, and of the Russo-Turkish war of 1877, were to play their parts upon the scene.

But in the years after the Peace of Versailles this was a

new question, upon which opinions were unformed. It was true that, to quote from a contemporary writer, "England had had full leisure to ruminate upon, and sufficient cause to reprobate, that absurd and blind policy, under the influence of which she had drawn an uncertain ally, and an ever-to-be-suspected friend, from the bottom of the Bothnic Gulf to establish a new naval empire in the Mediterranean and Archipelago."[1] These meditations had not been fruitless, as was seen by the consistent attitude of Pitt's ministry at this time; but on the other hand, when it was proposed in 1791 to increase the naval force in commission, in order "to add weight to the representations"[2] being made by the allies to the belligerents,—in order, in other words, to support Turkey by an armed demonstration,—Fox, the leader of the Whigs, said that "an alliance with Russia appeared to him the most natural and advantageous that we could possibly form;"[3] while Burke, than whom no man had a juster reputation for political wisdom, observed that "the considering the Turkish Empire as any part of the balance of power in Europe was new. The principles of alliance and the doctrines drawn from thence were entirely new. Russia was our natural ally and the most useful ally we had in a commercial sense."[4] That these distinguished members of the opposition represented the feelings of many supporters of the ministry was shown by a diminished majority, 93, in the vote that followed. The opposition, thus encouraged, then introduced a series of resolutions, the gist of which lay in these words: "The interests of Great Britain are not likely to be affected by the progress of the Russian arms on the borders of the Black Sea."[5] In the vote on this, the minister's majority again fell to eighty, despite the arguments of those who asserted that

---

[1] Annual Register, 1788, p. 59.
[2] King's Message, March 29, 1781.
[3] Fox's Speeches (London, 1815), vol. iv. p. 178.
[4] Parl. Hist., vol. xxix. pp. 75-79.   [5] Annual Register, 1791, p. 102

"the possession of Oczakow by the empress would facilitate not only the acquisition of Constantinople, but of all lower Egypt and Alexandria; which would give to Russia the supremacy in the Mediterranean, and render her a formidable rival to us both as a maritime and commercial power." After making every allowance for party spirit, it is evident that British feeling was only slowly turning into the channels in which it has since run so strongly.

France, under the pressure of her inward troubles, was debarred from taking part with her old allies in the East, and withdrew more and more from all outward action. On the 8th of August, 1788, the king fixed the 1st of May, 1789, as the day for the meeting of the States General; and in November the Notables met for the second time, to consider the constitution and mode of procedure in that body, the representation in it of the Third Estate, and the vote by orders. They were adjourned after a month's session; and the court, contrary to the judgment of the majority among them, proclaimed on the 27th of December, 1788, that the representatives of the Third Estate should equal in number those of the two others combined. No decision was given as to whether the votes should be individual, or by orders.

Oczakow was taken by the Russians on the 17th of December, 1788, and during the following year the Eastern war raged violently both in the Baltic and in southeastern Europe. Turkey was everywhere worsted. Belgrade was taken on the 8th of October by the Austrians, who afterwards occupied Bucharest and advanced as far as Orsova. The Russians reduced Galatz, Bender, and other places. Besides losing territory, the Turks were defeated in several pitched battles. The conduct of the war on their part was much affected by the death of the reigning sultan.

The Swedish war was in its results unimportant, except as a diversion in favor of Turkey. To keep it up as such, subsidies were sent from Constantinople to Stockholm. Great Britain and Prussia were obliged again to threaten Denmark, in 1789, to keep her from aiding Russia. The British minister, speaking for both States, expressed their fixed determination to maintain the balance of power in the North. A defensive alliance was then formed between Russia and Austria on the one hand, and France and Spain on the other. The Bourbon kingdoms pledged themselves to a strict neutrality in the Eastern War as it then existed; but if Russia or Austria were attacked by any other State, they were to be helped, — Austria, by an army of sixty thousand men; Russia, by a fleet of sixteen ships-of-the-line and twelve frigates. The latter provision shows both the kind of attack feared by Russia and the direction of her ambition.

On the 4th of May of this year, 1789, the States General met at Versailles, and the French Revolution thenceforth went on apace. The Bastille was stormed July 14th. In October the royal family were brought forcibly from Versailles to Paris by the mob. The earlier events of the Revolution will hereafter be summarily related by themselves, before going on with the war to which they led. It will here be enough to say that the voice of France was now silent outside her own borders.

In 1790 the Eastern War was practically brought to an end. On the 31st of January a very close treaty of alliance was made between Prussia and the Porte, — the king binding himself to declare war at a set time against both Russia and Austria. The emperor died in February, and was succeeded by his brother Leopold, who was disposed to peace. A convention was soon after held, at which sat ministers of Austria, Prussia, Great Britain, and the United Provinces; the two latter acting as mediators because Prussia had taken such a pronounced attitude of hostility to Austria. A treaty was signed July 27, by which the emperor renounced his alliance with Russia. On September 20, he agreed to an armistice with Turkey; which, after long negotiation, was followed by a definitive peace, concluded August 4, 1791.

The Russian conflict with Turkey languished during the summer of 1790. Active operations began in October, and continued during a season whose severities the Russian could bear better than the Turk. The final blow of the campaign and of the war was the taking of Ismail by Suwarrow, a deed of arms so tremendous and full of horrors that a brief account of its circumstances is allowable even to our subject.

The town, which was looked on as the key of the lower Danube, was surrounded by three lines of wall, each with its proper ditch, and contained a garrison of thirteen thousand. Its population, besides the troops, was about thirty thousand. Owing to the season, December, Suwarrow determined not to attempt a regular siege, but to carry the place by assault, at any cost of life. Batteries were consequently put up in every available place, and as rapidly as possible, in order to prepare for and cover the attack. At five o'clock Christmas morning they all opened together, and, after a furious cannonade of two hours, the Russians moved forward in eight columns. After a three hours struggle the assailants were forced back; but Suwarrow, whose influence over his soldiers was unbounded, ran to the front, and, planting a Russian flag on one of the enemy's works, asked his men if they would leave it behind them. Through his efforts and those of the officers, the troops returned to the charge. The conflict, which must have resolved itself into a multitude of hand-to-hand encounters, lasted till midnight, when, after an eighteen hours fight, the third line of defence was carried and resistance ceased, though bloodshed continued through the night. It was computed at the time that thirty thousand Turks, including women and children, and some twenty thousand Russian soldiers died violent deaths during that Christmas day of 1790. Warlike operations continued during the spring, but preliminaries of peace between Russia and Turkey were signed at Galatz on the 11th of August, 1791.

This put an end to hostilities throughout the East, peace having been made between Russia and Sweden a year before, on August 11, 1790. The time of attack had been well chosen by the Swedish king, and had public opinion in Great Britain approached unanimity, a powerful lever would have been put in her hands to break down the Russian attack on Turkey by supporting the diversion in the North. The Russian and Swedish fleets were so evenly balanced that a small British division would have turned the scale, controlled the Baltic, and kept open the Swedish communications from Finland to their own coast. So far, however, was the nation from being of one mind that, as we have seen, the minister's majority steadily fell, and he probably knew that among those who voted straight, many were far from hearty in his support. Prussia also did not back Sweden as she should have done, after definitely embracing that policy, though she was both disconcerted and angered at the peace for which she had not looked. This irresolution on the part of the allied States limited their action to interposing between Sweden and Denmark, and prevented the results which might reasonably have been expected in the north, and yet more in the east of Europe; but it does not take from the significance of their attitude, nor hide the revolution in British statesmanship which marks the ten years now being treated.

The tendency thus indicated was suddenly, though only temporarily, checked by the Revolution in France. The troubles that had been so long fomenting in that country had, after a short and delusive period of seeming repose, begun again at nearly the very moment that the Eastern War was ending. This will be seen by bringing together the dates at which were happening these weighty events in the East and West.

It was on the 6th of October, 1789, that the king and royal family were brought from Versailles to Paris, unwilling but constrained. After this outbreak of popular feeling, comparative quiet continued through the last months of 1789 and all of 1790, during which were fought in the East the most important battles of the war, both in the Baltic and on the Danube, including the bloody assault of Ismail. During this time, however, Louis XVI. underwent many bitter mortifications, either intended as such, or else unavoidably humiliating to his sense of position. In June, 1791, he fled with his family from Paris to put himself in the care of part of the army stationed in eastern France under the Marquis de Bouillé and believed to be thoroughly trustworthy. Before reaching his destination he was recognized, and brought back to Paris a prisoner. The greeting of the royal family was significant of the change that had passed over the people within a few years, and which their unsuccessful flight had intensified. They were met by perfect silence, while some distance ahead of them rode an officer commanding the bystanders not to uncover. Despite the distrust it felt, the Constituent Assembly went on with the work of framing a constitution in which the king still had a recognized position, and which he formally accepted on the 14th of September, 1791. During that summer, peace was signed between Russia and Turkey, and a meeting was had at Pilnitz between the emperor and the king of Prussia, after which they put out their joint declaration that the situation in which the king of France found himself was an object of common concern to all the rulers of Europe; that "they hoped this common concern would lead them to employ, in conjunction with the two declaring sovereigns, the most efficacious means, relative to their forces, in order to enable the king of France to consolidate in the most perfect liberty, the basis of a monarchical government equally suitable to the rights of sovereigns and the welfare of the French nation."

The two princes ended by stating their own readiness to join in such united action with the force necessary to obtain the common end proposed, and that they would, meanwhile, give orders to their troops to be ready to put themselves in a state of activity.

The close coincidence in date of the Declaration of Pilnitz, August 27, 1791, with the Peace of Galatz, signed August 11, is curious enough for passing remark; the one formally opening the new channel of European interest and action, while the other marked the close of the old. The Declaration, however, was in the same line of effort that the new emperor had for some time been following. It met with a somewhat hesitating response. Russia and Sweden agreed to raise an army, which Spain was to subsidize; but Great Britain, under Pitt, declined to meddle in the internal affairs of another state.

The first National or, as it is conveniently called, Constituent Assembly, dissolved after framing a Constitution; and the following day, October 1, 1791, the second Assembly, known as the Legislative, came together. The Declaration of Pilnitz had strongly moved the French people and increased, perhaps unjustly, their distrust of the king. This change of temper was reflected in the Assembly. Strong representations and arguments were exchanged between the ministers of foreign affairs in Austria and France, through the ambassadors at either court; but in truth there was no common ground of opinion on which the new republic and the old empires could meet. The movements on either side were viewed with studied suspicion, and war was finally declared by France against Austria, April 20, 1792. The first unimportant encounters were unfavorable to the French; but more serious danger than that which threatened from without was arising within France itself. The king and the Assembly came into collision through the use by the former of his constitutional power of Veto. The agitation spread to the streets. On the 20th of June a deputation from the mob of Paris appeared before the Assembly, and asked permission for the citizens outside to defile before it, as a demonstration of their support. The extraordinary request was granted; and an immense crowd pressed forward, of people of all ages, armed with weapons of every kind, among which appeared a pike carrying the heart of a bull labelled an "Aristocrat's heart." From the Assembly the crowd went to the Louvre, and thence forced their way through the palace gates into the king's presence. The unhappy Louis bore himself with calm courage, to which perhaps he, at the moment, owed his life; but he submitted to put on the symbolic red cap, and to drink to the nation from a bottle handed him by a drunken rioter.

Little was left in life for a king thus humbled, and his final humiliation was close at hand. Prussia had not long delayed to act in concert with the emperor, after France declared war. On July 26, a month after the strange scene in the Tuileries, was issued an exposition of her reasons for taking arms; and at the same time the Duke of Brunswick, commander-in-chief of the allied armies, put forth a proclamation to the French framed in such violent terms as to stir to the utmost the angry passions of a frantic and excitable race. On the 10th of August the Paris mob again stormed the Tuileries, the king and royal family fled for safety to the hall of the Legislature, the Swiss Guards were killed and the palace gutted. The Assembly then decreed the suspension of the king; and on the 13th of August the royal family was removed to the Temple, the last home on earth for several of them.

On the 2d of September occurred the butcheries known as the September Massacres. To this date and this act is to be referred the great change in British feeling toward the Revolution. On the 20th the battle of Valmy, by some thought decisive of the fate of the Revolution, was won by the French. Though being otherwise far from a battle of the first importance, it led to the retreat of the allied forces and destroyed for a time the hopes of the royalists. Two days after Valmy met the third Assembly, the National Convention of terrible memory. Its first act was to decree the abolition of royalty in France; but the power that swayed the country was passing more and more to the mob of Paris, expressing itself through the clubs of which the Jacobin is the best known. The violence and fanaticism of the extreme republicans and of the most brutal elements of the populace found ever louder voice. On the 19th of November the Convention passed a decree declaring, "in the name of the French nation, that they will grant fraternity and assistance to all people who wish to recover their liberty; and they charge the executive power to send the necessary orders to the generals to give assistance to such people, and to defend those citizens who have suffered, or may suffer, in the cause of liberty." It was denied by the French diplomatists that there was any intention of favoring insurrections or exciting disturbances in any friendly country; but such intention is nevertheless fairly deducible from the words, and when a motion was made to explain that they were not so meant, the Convention refused to consider it. Mr. Fox, the ardent champion of the Revolution in Parliament, spoke of this edict as an insult to the British people.

Meantime the battle of Valmy had been followed by that of Jemappes, fought November 6. On the 14th the French army entered Brussels, and the Austrian Netherlands were rapidly occupied. This was instantly succeeded by a decree, dated November 16, opening the Scheldt, upon the express ground of natural right; the boisterous young republic cutting at one blow the knot which had refused to be untied by the weak hands of Joseph II. Decided action followed, a French squadron entering the river from the sea and forcing its way up, despite the protests of the Dutch officers, in order to take part in the siege of Antwerp. This was a new offence to the British Sea Power, which was yet further angered by a decree of December 15, extending the French system to all countries occupied by their armies. The words of this proclamation were so sweeping that they could scarcely but seem, to those untouched with the fiery passion of the Revolution, to threaten the destruction of all existing social order. The British ministry on the last day of the year 1792 declared that "this government will never see with indifference that France shall make herself, directly or indirectly, sovereign of the Low Countries, or general arbitress of the rights and liberties of Europe."[1]

While the Revolution was thus justifying the fears and accusations of those who foretold that it could not confine itself to the overturn of domestic institutions, but would seek to thrust its beliefs and principles forcibly upon other nations, the leaders were hurrying on the destruction of the king. Arraigned on the 11th of December, 1792, Louis XVI. was brought to trial on the 26th, sentenced to death January 16, and executed January 21, 1793. This deed brought to a decided issue the relations between France and Great Britain, which, from an uncertain and unsatisfactory condition, had become more and more embittered by the course of events ever since the November decree of fraternity. As far back as August 10, when the king was suspended, the British government had recalled its ambassador, who was not replaced; and had persisted in attributing to the French minister in London an ambiguous character, recognizing him only as accredited by the king who had actually ceased to reign — by a government which in fact no longer existed. Points of form were raised with exasperating, yet civil, insolence, as to the position which M. Chauvelin, the minister in question, actually occupied; and his office was not made more pleasant by the failure of his own government to send him new cre-

[1] Annual Register, 1793; State Papers, p. 118.

dentials. Papers written by him were returned by Lord Grenville, the foreign minister, because his claim to represent the French republic was not recognized; or, if accepted, they were only received as unofficial.

The letters thus exchanged, under forms so unsatisfactory, were filled with mutual accusations, and arguments marked by the brisk vivacity of the one nation and the cool aggressiveness of the other; but starting as they did from the differing bases of natural rights on the one hand, and established institutions on the other, no agreement was approached. The questions of the Scheldt, of the decree of fraternity, and of that extending the French system to countries occupied by their armies, were thus disputed back and forth; and to them were added the complaints of France against an Alien Act, passed by Parliament, January 4, 1793, laying vexatious restrictions upon the movements of foreigners arriving in Great Britain, or wishing to change their abode if already resident. This act M. Chauvelin rightly believed to be specially aimed at Frenchmen. It sprang from the growing apprehension and change of feeling in England; a change emphasized by a break in the Parliamentary Opposition, a large number of whom, in this same month of January, 1793, definitively took the step in which their great associate, Edmund Burke, had preceded them, broke their party ties, and passed over to the support of Pitt. The latter would seem to have become convinced that war was inevitable; that the question was no longer whether a nation should exercise a right of changing its institutions, but whether a plague should be stamped out before it had passed its borders and infected yet healthy peoples.

Things had come to this state when news reached London of the death sentence of the French king. M. Chauvelin had just received and presented credentials from the republican government. On January 20, the minister informed him that the king, under present circumstances, did not think fit to receive them, adding the irritating words: "As minister of the Most Christian King, you would have enjoyed all the exemptions which the law grants to public ministers, recognized as such; but as a private person you cannot but return to the general mass of foreigners resident in England."[1] On the 24th of January, the execution of Louis XVI. being now known, Lord Grenville wrote to him: "The King can no longer, after such an event, permit your residence here. His Majesty has thought fit to order that you should retire from the kingdom within the space of eight days, and I herewith transmit to you a copy of the order which His Majesty has given me to that effect."[1]

On the 1st of February, 1793, the French republic declared war against Great Britain and Holland. It was already at war with Austria, Prussia and Sardinia; while Russia and Sweden were avowedly unfriendly, and Spain almost openly hostile.

[1] Annual Register, 1793; State Papers, pp. 127, 128.

CHAPTER II.

The Condition of the Navies in 1793 — and especially of the French Navy.

BEFORE following the narrative of directly warlike action, or discussing the influence of the naval factor upon the military and political events, it is proper to examine the relative position, strength, and resources, of the rival nations, particularly in the matter of Sea Power, — to weigh the chances of the struggle, as it were, beforehand, from the known conditions, — to analyze and point out certain reasons why the sea war took the turn it did, in order that the experience of the past may be turned to the profit of the future.

First of all, it must be recognized that the problem to be thus resolved is by no means so simple as in most wars. It is not here a mere question of the extent, population, and geographical position of a country; of the number of its seamen, the tonnage of its shipping, the strength of its armed fleet; nor yet again, chiefly of the wealth and vigor of its colonies, the possession of good and well-placed maritime bases in different parts of the world; not even, at first hand, of the policy and character of its government, although it is undoubtedly true that in the action of French governments is to be found the chief reason for the utter disaster and overthrow which awaited the Sea Power of France. It was because the government so faithfully and necessarily reflected the social disorder, the crude and wild habits of thought which it was powerless to check, that it was incapable of dealing with the naval necessities of the day. The seamen and the navy of

France were swept away by the same current of thought and feeling which was carrying before it the whole nation; and the government, tossed to and fro by every wave of popular emotion, was at once too weak and too ignorant of the needs of the service to repress principles and to amend defects which were fatal to its healthy life.

It is particularly instructive to dwell upon this phase of the revolutionary convulsions of France, because the result in this comparatively small, but still most important, part of the body politic was so different from that which was found elsewhere. Whatever the mistakes, the violence, the excesses of every kind, into which this popular rising was betrayed, they were symptomatic of strength, not of weakness, — deplorable accompaniments of a movement which, with all its drawbacks, was marked by overwhelming force.

It was the inability to realize the might in this outburst of popular feeling, long pent up, that caused the mistaken forecasts of many statesmen of the day; who judged of the power and reach of the movement by indications — such as the finances, the condition of the army, the quality of the known leaders — ordinarily fairly accurate tests of a country's endurance, but which utterly misled those who looked to them only and did not take into account the mighty impulse of a whole nation stirred to its depths. Why, then, was the result so different in the navy? Why was it so weak, not merely nor chiefly in quantity, but in quality? and that, too, in days so nearly succeeding the prosperous naval era of Louis XVI. Why should the same throe which brought forth the magnificent armies of Napoleon have caused the utter weakness of the sister service, not only amid the disorders of the Republic, but also under the powerful organization of the Empire?

The immediate reason was that, to a service of a very special character, involving special exigencies, calling for special aptitudes, and consequently demanding special knowledge of its requirements in order to deal wisely with it, were applied the theories of men wholly ignorant of those requirements,— men who did not even believe that they existed. Entirely without experimental knowledge, or any other kind of knowledge, of the conditions of sea life, they were unable to realize the obstacles to those processes by which they would build up their navy, and according to which they proposed to handle it. This was true not only of the wild experiments of the early days of the Republic; the reproach may fairly be addressed to the great emperor himself, that he had scarcely any appreciation of the factors conditioning efficiency at sea; nor did he seemingly ever reach any such sense of them as would enable him to understand why the French navy failed. "Disdaining," says Jean Bon Saint-André, the Revolutionary commissioner whose influence on naval organization was unbounded, "*disdaining*, through calculation and reflection, *skilful evolutions*, perhaps our seamen will think it more fitting and useful to try those boarding actions in which the Frenchman was always conqueror, and thus astonish Europe by new prodigies of valor." [1] "Courage and audacity," says Captain Chevalier, "had become in his eyes the only qualities necessary to our officers." "The English," said Napoleon, "will become very small when France shall have two or three admirals willing to die." [2] So commented, with pathetic yet submissive irony, the ill-fated admiral, Villeneuve, upon whom fell the weight of the emperor's discontent with his navy: "Since his Majesty thinks that nothing but audacity and resolve are needed to succeed in the naval officer's calling, I shall leave nothing to be desired." [3]

It is well to trace in detail the steps by which a fine military service was broken down, as well as the results

---

[1] Chevalier, Mar. Fran. sous la République, p. 49
[2] Nap. to Decrès, Aug. 29, 1805.
[3] Troude, Batailles Nav., vol. iii. p. 370.

thus reached, for, while the circumstances under which the process began were undoubtedly exceptional, the general lesson remains good. To disregard the teachings of experience, to cut loose wholly from the traditions of the past, to revolutionize rather than to reform, to launch out boldly on new and untried paths, blind to or ignoring the difficulties to be met, — such a tendency, such a school of thought exists in every generation. At times it gets the mastery. Certainly at the present day it has unusual strength, which is not to be wondered at in view of the change and development of naval weapons. Yet if the campaigns of Cæsar and Hannibal are still useful studies in the days of firearms, it is rash to affirm that the days of sail have no lessons for the days of steam. Here, however, are to be considered questions of discipline and organization; of the adaptation of means to ends; of the recognition, not only of the possibilities, but also of the limitations, imposed upon a calling, upon a military organization, by the nature of the case, by the element in which it moves, by the force to which it owes its motion, by the skill or lack of skill with which its powers are used and its deficiencies compensated.

It is indeed only by considering the limitations as well as the possibilities of any form of warlike activity, whether it be a general plan of action, — as for instance commerce-destroying, — or whether it be the use of a particular weapon, — such as the ram, — that correct conclusions can be reached as to the kind of men, in natural capacities, in acquired skill, in habits of thought and action, who are needed to use such weapon. The possibilities of the ram, for instance, are to be found in the consequences of a successful thrust; its limitations, in the difficulties imposed by any lack of handiness, speed, or steering qualities in the ship carrying it, in the skill of the opponent in managing his vessel and the weapons with which he is provided for counter-offence. If these limitations are carefully considered, there will be little doubt how to answer the question as to the chance of a man picked up at hazard, untrained for such encounter except by years of ordinary sea-going, reaching his aim if pitted against another who has at least given thought and had some professional training directed to the special end.

Now the one sea-weapon of the period of the French Revolution was the gun; the cold steel, the hand-to-hand fight, commonly came into play only toward the end of an action, if at all. In naming the gun, however, it can by no means be separated from its carriage; using this word not merely in its narrow technical sense, but as belonging rightly to the whole ship which bore the gun alongside the enemy, and upon whose skilful handling depended placing it in those positions of advantage that involved most danger to the opponent and the least to one's self. This was the part of the commander; once there, the skill of the gunner came into play, to work his piece with rapidity and accuracy despite the obstacles raised by the motion of the sea, the rapid shifting of the enemy, the difficulty of catching sight of him through the narrow ports. Thus the skill of the military seaman and the skill of the trained gunner, the gun and the ship, the piece and its carriage, supplemented each other. The ship and its guns together formed one weapon, a moving battery which needed quick and delicate handling and accurate direction in all its parts. It was wielded by a living organism, knit also into one by the dependence of all the parts upon the head, and thus acting by a common impulse, sharing a common tradition, and having a common life, which, like all other life, is not found fully ripened without having had a beginning and a growth.

It would be foolish, because untrue, to say that these things were easy to see. They were easy to men of the profession; they were not at all easy to outsiders, apt to ignore difficulties of which they have neither experience

nor conception. The contempt for skilful manœuvres was
not confined to Jean Bon Saint-André, though he was unusually open in avowing it. But the difficulties none the less
existed; neither is the captain without the gunner, nor the
gunner without the captain, and both must be specially
trained men. It was not to be expected that the man
newly taken from the merchant vessel, whose concern with
other ships was confined to keeping out of their way, should
at once be fitted to manœuvre skilfully around an antagonist actively engaged in injuring him, nor yet be ready to
step at once from the command of a handful of men
shipped for a short cruise, to that of a numerous body
which he was to animate with a common spirit, train to
act together for a common purpose, and subject to a
common rigorous discipline to which he himself was, by
previous habit, a stranger. The yoke of military service
sits hard on those who do not always bear it. Yet the
efficiency of the military sea-officer depended upon his fitness to do these things well because they had been so
wrought into his own personal habit as to become a second
nature.

This was true, abundantly true, of the single ship in
fight: but when it came to the question of combining the
force of a great many guns, mounted on perhaps twenty-
five or thirty heavy ships, possessing unequal qualities, but
which must nevertheless keep close to one another, in certain specified positions, on dark nights, in bad weather,
above all when before the enemy; when these ships were
called upon to perform evolutions all together, or in succession, to concentrate upon a part of the enemy, to frustrate by well combined and well executed movements
attacks upon themselves, to remedy the inconveniences
arising from loss of sails and masts and consequent loss of
motive power, to provide against the disorders caused by
sudden changes of wind and the various chances of the
sea, — under these conditions, even one not having the

knowledge of experience begins to see that such demands can only be met by a body of men of special aptitudes and training, such as in fact has very rarely, if ever, been found in perfection, in even the most highly organized fleets of any navy in the world.

To these things the French National Assembly was blind, but not because it was not warned of them. In truth men's understandings, as well as their *morale* and beliefs, were in a chaotic state. In the navy, as in society, the *morale* suffered first. Insubordination and mutiny, insult and murder, preceded the blundering measures which in the end destroyed the fine *personnel* that the monarchy bequeathed to the French republic. This insubordination broke out very soon after the affairs of the Bastille and the forcing of the palace at Versailles; that is, very soon after the powerlessness of the executive was felt. Singularly, yet appropriately, the first victim was the most distinguished flag-officer of the French navy.

During the latter half of 1789 disturbances occurred in all the seaport towns; in Havre, in Cherbourg, in Brest, in Rochefort, in Toulon. Everywhere the town authorities meddled with the concerns of the navy yards and of the fleet; discontented seamen and soldiers, idle or punished, rushed to the town halls with complaints against their officers. The latter, receiving no support from Paris, yielded continually, and things naturally went from bad to worse.

In Toulon, however, matters were worst of all. The naval commander-in-chief in that port was Commodore D'Albert de Rions, a member of the French nobility, as were all the officers of the navy. He was thought the most able flag-officer in the fleet; he was also known and beloved in Toulon for his personal integrity and charitable life. After working his way with partial success through the earlier disorders, by dint of tact, concession, and his own personal reputation, he found himself compelled to send on shore from the fleet two subordinate officers who had excited mutiny. The men went at once to the town hall, where they were received with open arms, and a story before prevalent was again started that the city was mined and would be attacked the day or two following. Excitement spread, and the next day a number of people assembled round the arsenal, demanding to speak with De Rions. He went out with a few of his officers. The crowd closed round and forced him away from the gates. He went toward his house, apparently his official residence, the mob hustling, insulting, and even laying hands on his person. Having reached his home, the mayor and another city official came to him and asked forgiveness for the two culprits. He refused for a long time, but at length yielded against his judgment, — saying truly enough that such an act of weakness, wrung from him by the commune on the plea of re-establishing order, in other words of appeasing and so quieting the rabble, would but encourage new disorders and do irreparable wrong to discipline and the state.

It proved also insufficient to arrest the present tumult. An officer coming to the door was insulted and attacked. A rioter rushed at another, who was leaning over a terrace attached to the house, and cut his head open with a sabre. Then the windows were broken. The national guard, or, as we might say, the city militia, were paraded, but did no service. An officer leaving the house was attacked, knocked down with stones and the butts of muskets, and would have lost his life had not De Rions sallied out with thirty others and carried him off.

The national guard now surrounded the house, forbidding entry or withdrawal, and soon after demanded the surrender of an officer whom they accused of having ordered some seamen-gunners to fire on the mob. To De Rions's explanations and denials they replied that he was a liar, and that the officers were a lot of aristocrats who wished to assassinate the people. The commodore refusing to give up his subordinate, the guards prepared to attack them; thereupon all drew their swords, but the officer himself, to save his comrades, stepped quickly out and put himself in the hands of his enemies.

Meanwhile, the city authorities, as is too usual, made no effective interference. Part of their own forces, the national guards, were foremost in the riot. Soon after, De Rions was required to give up another officer. He again refused, and laid orders upon this one not to yield himself as the former had done. "If you want another victim," said he, stepping forward, "here am I; but if you want one of my officers, you must first pass over me." His manliness caused only irritation. A rush was made, his sword snatched from him, and he himself dragged out of the house amid the hoots and jeers of the mob. The national guards formed two parties,—one to kill, the other to save him. Pricked with bayonets, clubbed with muskets, and even ignominiously kicked, this gallant old seaman, the companion of De Grasse and Suffren, was dragged through the streets amid cries of "Hang him! Cut off his head!" and thrust into the common prison. Bad as all this was, there was yet worse. Any age and any country may suffer from a riot, but De Rions could get from the national authority no admission of his wrongs. The assembly ordered an investigation, and six weeks later made this declaration: "The National Assembly, taking a favorable view of the motives which animated M. D'Albert de Rions, the other naval officers implicated in the affair, *the municipal officers, and the National Guard*, declares that there is no ground to blame any one."[1] De Rions told his wrongs in words equally pathetic and dignified: "The volunteers," said he, "have outraged the decrees of the National Assembly in all that concerns the rights of the man and of the citizen. Let us not here be considered, if you will, as officers, and I myself

[1] Moniteur, Jan. 19, 1790, p. 82.

as the head of a respectable corps; see in us only quiet and well-behaved citizens, and every honest man cannot but be revolted at the unjust and odious treatment we have undergone."[1] His words were not heeded.

The Toulon affair was the signal for the spread of mutiny among the crews and the breaking-up of the corps of commissioned sea-officers. Similar incidents occurred often and everywhere. The successor of De Rions was also hauled by the mob to prison, where he remained several days. The second in command to him, a little later, was dragged to á gallows, whence he was only accidentally delivered. In Brest, a captain who had been ordered to command a ship on foreign service was assaulted as an aristocrat by a mob of three thousand people and only saved by being taken to prison, where he remained with nineteen others similarly detained. Orders to release them and prosecute the offenders were issued in vain by the cabinet and the king. "It was evident," says Chevalier, "that the naval officers could no longer depend upon the support of local authorities, nor upon that of the government; they were outlaws."[2] "Thenceforth," says another French naval historian, "if some naval officers were found sanguine enough and patriotic enough to be willing to remain at their post, they but came, on account of their origin and without further inquiry, to the prison and to the scaffold."[3]

In the fleets, insubordination soon developed into anarchy. In the spring of 1790 a quarrel arose between Spain and Great Britain, on account of the establishment of trading-posts, by British subjects, at Nootka Sound, on the northwest coast of America. These posts, with the vessels at them, were seized by Spanish cruisers. Upon news of the affair both nations made conflicting claims,

---

[1] Chevalier, Mar. Fran. sous la République, p. 11.
[2] Ibid., p. 12.
[3] Guérin, Histoire de la Marine, vol. iii. p. 156 (1st ed.).

and both began to arm their fleets. Spain claimed the help of France, in virtue of the still existing Bourbon Family Compact. The king sent a message to the Assembly, which voted to arm forty-five ships-of-the-line. D'Albert de Rions was ordered to command the fleet at Brest, where he was coldly received by the city authorities. The seamen at the time were discontented at certain new regulations. De Rions, seeing the danger of the situation, recommended to the Assembly some modifications, which it refused to make, yet, at the same time, took no vigorous steps to ensure order. On the same day that it confirmed its first decree, September 15, 1790, a seaman from a ship called the "Léopard," visiting on board another, the "Patriote," used mutinous language and insulted one of the principal officers. The man was drunk. The case being reported to the admiral, he ordered him sent on board the flag-ship. This measure, though certainly very mild, called forth great indignation among the seamen of the "Patriote." De Rions, hearing that mutiny was beginning, summoned before him a petty officer, a coxswain, who was actively stirring up the crew. He quietly explained to this man that the first offender had not even been punished. The coxswain, being insolent, was sent back, saying, as he went, "that it belonged to the strongest to make the law; that he was the strongest, and that the man should not be punished."

The next morning the admiral went to the "Patriote," mustered the crew, told them that the first offender had not been punished, but that the conduct of the coxswain had been so bad that he must be put in confinement. The crew kept silent so far, but now broke out into cries of "He shall not go." De Rions, having tried in vain to reestablish order, took his boat to go ashore and consult with the commandant of the arsenal. As he pulled away, several seamen cried out to her coxswain, "Upset the boat!"

Meanwhile a riot had broken out in the town against the

second in command at the dockyard, based upon a report
that he had said he would soon bring the San Domingo
rebels to order, if he were sent against them. This officer,
named Marigny, one of a distinguished naval family, only
escaped death by being out of his house; a gallows was
put up before it. These various outrages moved the National Assembly for a moment, but its positive action went
no further than praying the king to order a prosecution
according to legal forms, and ordering that the crew of the
Léopard, which ship had been the focus of sedition, should
be sent to their homes. D'Albert de Rions, seeing that he
could not enforce obedience, asked for and obtained his
relief. On the 15th of October this distinguished officer
took his final leave of the navy and left the country. He
had served at Grenada, at Yorktown, and against Rodney,
and when the great Suffren, bending under the burden of
cares in his Indian campaign, sought for a second upon
whom the charge might fitly fall, he wrote thus to the
minister of the day: " If my death, or my health, should
leave the command vacant, who would take my place? . . .
I know only one person who has all the qualities that can
be desired; who is very brave, very accomplished, full of
ardor and zeal, disinterested, a good seaman. That is
D'Albert de Rions, and should he be in America even, send
a frigate for him. I shall be good for more if I have him,
for he will help me; and if I die, you will be assured that
the service will not suffer. If you had given me him when
I asked you, we should now be masters of India."[1]

It was a significant, though accidental, coincidence that
the approaching humiliation of the French navy should
thus be prefigured, both ashore and afloat, both north and
south, on the Mediterranean and on the Atlantic, in the
person of its most distinguished representative. The incidents, however, though conspicuous, were but samples of
what was going on everywhere. In the West India colo-

[1] Troude, Batailles Nav. de la France, vol. ii. p. 201.

nies the revolutionary impulse transmitted from the mother-country had taken on a heat and violence of its own, characteristic alike of the climate and of the undisciplined temper of the colonists. Commotions amounting to civil war broke out, and both parties tried to command the support of the navy, even at the price of inciting mutiny. Here the Léopard, afterwards the centre of the Brest mutiny, first inhaled the germs of disorder. In July, 1790, the crew revolted, and deprived the captain of the command, to assume which, however, only one commissioned officer was found willing. The commandant of the naval station at the Isle of France, Captain McNamara, after once escaping threatened death, was enticed ashore under promise of protection, and then murdered in the streets by the colonial troops themselves. In the peninsula of India, Great Britain, being then at war with Tippoo Saib, undertook to search neutral vessels off the coast. The French commodore sent a frigate to convoy two merchant ships, and the attempt of the British to search them led to a collision, in which the French vessel hauled down her colors after losing twelve killed and fifty-six wounded. The significance, however, of this affair lies in the fact that when the commandant of the division announced that another such aggression would be not only resisted, but followed by reprisals, the crews of two ships told him they would not fight unless attacked. The officer, being thus unable to maintain what he thought the honor of the flag demanded, found it necessary to abandon the station.

Things abroad thus went on from bad to worse. Ships-of-war arriving in San Domingo, the most magnificent of the French colonies in size and fruitfulness, were at once boarded by the members of the party uppermost in the port. Flattered and seduced, given money and entertainment, filled with liquor, the crews were easily persuaded to mutiny. Here and there an officer gifted with tact and popularity, or perhaps an adept in that deft cajoling with

words which so takes with the French people, and of which
the emperor afterwards was so great a master, induced
rather than ordered his ship's company to do their duty up
to a certain point. As usual the tragedy of the situation
had a comical side. Three ships, one of the line, anchored
in San Domingo. The seamen as usual were worked upon;
but in addition two of the commanders, with several officers, were arrested on shore and, after being threatened
with death, were deprived of their commands by the local
assembly. The next day the crew of the ship-of-the-line
sent ashore to protest against the deprivation, which, they
observed, " was null and void, as to them alone (the crew)
belonged the right to take cognizance of and judge the
motives of their officers."[1] An admiral on the United
States coast was ordered by the French chargé d'affaires
to take his ships, two of-the-line and two frigates, and
seize the little islands of St. Pierre and Miquelon near
Newfoundland. A few days after sailing, the crews said
the orders were nonsense and forced the officers to go to
France.[2] No captain knew how long he would be in his
nominal position, or receive the obedience it claimed. " It
was not so easy," says a French historian, speaking of the
one who most successfully kept his dizzy height, " it was
not so easy for Grimouard to leave Port-au-Prince with his
flag-ship; he had to get the consent of a crew which was
incessantly told that its own will was the only orders it
should follow. In fifteen months Grimouard had not taken
a night's rest; always active, always on deck, reasoning
with one, coaxing another, appealing to the honor of this,
to the generosity of that, to the patriotism of all, he had
kept up on board a quasi-discipline truly phenomenal for
the times."[3] Later on, this same man lost his life by the
guillotine. Nothing more disastrous to the French colonies

---

[1] Guérin, Hist. Mar., vol. iii. p. 195 (1st ed.).
[2] Troude, Bat. Nav., vol. 2, p. 320.
[3] Guérin, vol. iii. p. 213.

could have happened than this weakening of the military authority, both ashore and afloat, for which the colonists were mainly answerable. The strife of parties, — at first confined to the whites, a very small minority of the population, — spread to the mixed bloods and the negroes, and a scene of desolation followed over all the islands, finding however its most frightful miseries and excesses in San Domingo, whence the whites were finally exterminated.

Such was the condition of anarchy in which the fleet was as early as 1790 and 1791, and to which the whole social order was unmistakably drifting. In the military services, and above all in the navy, where submission to constituted authority is the breath of life, the disappearance of that submission anticipated, but only anticipated, the period of ruin and terror which awaited all France. The weakness which prevented the executive and legislature from enforcing obedience in the fleet was hurrying them, along with the whole people, to the abysses of confusion; the more highly organized and fragile parts of the state first fell to pieces under the shaking of the whole fabric. After what has been said, little surprise will be felt that naval officers in increasing numbers refused to serve and left the country; but it is a mistake to say on the one hand that they did so from pure motives of opposition to the new order of things, or on the other that they were forced by the acts of the first, or Constituent, Assembly. Both mistakes have been made. Emigration of the nobility and of princes of the blood began indeed soon after the storming of the Bastille, but large numbers of officers remained attending to their duties. The Brest mutiny was fourteen months later, and complaints are not then found of the lack of officers.

After that event their departure went on with increasing rapidity. The successor of De Rions held his office but one week, and then gave it up. He was followed by a distinguished officer, De Bougainville. Aided by a temporary return to sober ideas on the part of the government and the town authorities, this flag-officer for a moment, by strong measures, restored discipline; but mutiny soon reappeared, and, from the complaints made by him later on, there can be little doubt that he must have asked for his detachment had not the fleet been disarmed in consequence of the ending of the Anglo-Spanish dispute. In the following March, 1791, Mirabeau died, and with him the hopes which the court party and moderate men had based upon his genius. In April the Assembly passed a bill re-organizing the navy, the terms of which could not have been acceptable to the officers; although, candidly read, it cannot be considered to have ignored the just claims of those actually in service. In June occurred the king's unsuccessful attempt at flight. On the first of July a return made of officers of the navy showed that more than three-fourths of the old corps had disappeared.[1] The result was due partly to royalist feeling and prejudice shocked; partly, perhaps, to distaste for the new organization: but those familiar with the feelings of officers will attribute it with more likelihood to the utter subversion of discipline, destructive to their professional pride and personal self-respect, and for which the weakness and military ignorance of the Constituent Assembly are mainly responsible.

It is now time to consider the plans upon which that Assembly proposed to re-create the navy, in accordance with the views popular at that day.

During the War of the American Revolution, the corps of naval officers had been found too small for the needs of the service; there was a deficiency of lieutenants and junior officers to take charge of the watches and gun-divisions. A systematic attempt was made to remedy this trouble in the future. By a royal decree, dated January 1, 1786, the navy was re-organized, and two sources of supply for officers were opened. The first was drawn

[1] Guérin, vol. iii. p. 153.

wholly from the nobles, the youths composing it having to show satisfactory proofs of nobility before being admitted to the position of *élèves*, as they were called. These received a practical and rigorous training especially directed to the navy; and, so far as education went, there is reason to believe they would have made a most efficient body of men. The second source from which the royal navy was to be supplied with officers was a class called volunteers. Admission to this was also restricted, though extended to a wider circle. There could be borne upon its rolls only the sons of noblemen, or of sub-lieutenants serving either afloat or in the dock-yards, of wholesale merchants, ship-owners, captains, and of people living " nobly." These, though required to pass certain examinations and to have seen certain sea-service, were only admitted to the grade of sub-lieutenant, and could be promoted no further except for distinguished and exceptional acts.[1]

Such was the organization with which, in 1791, a popular assembly was about to deal. The invidious privilege by which the naval career, except in the lower ranks, was closed to all but a single, and not specially deserving, class, was of course done away without question. There still remained to decide whether the privilege should in the future be confined to a single class, which should deserve it by giving all its life and energies to the career — whether the navy should be recognized as a special calling requiring like others a special training — or whether there was so little difference between it and the merchant service that men could pass from one to the other without injuring either. These two views each found upholders, but the latter prevailed even in the first Assembly; those who wished a wholly military service only succeeded in modifying the original scheme presented by the committee.

The new organization was established by two successive

---

[1] See Chevalier, Mar. Fran. sous la République, pp. 20-23.

acts, passed on the 22d and 28th of April, 1790.[1] Like the old, it provided two sources of supply ; the one from men specially trained in youth, the other from the merchant service. The former began in a class called *Aspirants*, three hundred of whom were in pay on board ships of war ; they were not then officers, but simply youths between fifteen and twenty learning their business. The lowest grade of officer was the *Enseigne ;* they were of two kinds, paid[2] and unpaid, the former being actually in the navy. The latter were in the merchant service, but susceptible of employment in the fleet, and, when so engaged, took rank with other *enseignes* according to the length of time afloat in national ships. Admission to the grade of paid, or naval, *enseigne* could be had between eighteen and thirty, by passing the required examination and proving four years service at sea, no distinction being then made in favor of those who had begun as *aspirants* or had served in the navy. Those passing for *enseigne* and wishing to enter the navy had a more severe and more mathematical examination, while, on the other hand, those who returned to the merchant service had to have two years longer service, six in all, one of which on board a ship of war. All *enseignes* twenty-four years old, and only they, could command ships in the foreign trade and certain parts of the home, or coasting, trade. By the age of forty, a definitive choice had to be made between the two services. Up to that time *enseignes* could pass for lieutenant, and there

---

[1] The decree of April 22 is in the Moniteur of the 23d. That of the 28th is not ; but it will be found in the "Collection Générale des Décrets rendus par l'Ass. Nat." for April, 1791.

[2] The word *entretenu*, here rendered "paid," is difficult to translate. The dictionary of the French Academy explains it to mean an officer kept on pay, without necessarily being employed. Littré says that an officer "non entretenu" is one not having a commission. The word carries the idea of permanence. By the decree of April 28, "enseignes non entretenus" had no pay nor military authority, except when on military service ; nor could they wear the uniform, except when so employed.

seems to have been no inducement to follow one branch of the sea service rather than the other, except this: that five-sixths of the lieutenant vacancies at any one time were to be given to those who had most service as *enseignes* on board ships of war. To pass for lieutenant at the mature age of forty, only two years of military sea service were absolutely required. Thenceforth the officer was devoted to the military navy.

The essential spirit and tendency of the new legislation is summed up in the requirements for the lieutenancy. Up to the age of forty, that is, during the formative years of a man's life, it was left to the choice, interest, or caprice of the individual, how he would pass his time between the two services. The inducements to stick to the navy were too slight to weigh against the passing inclinations of young or restless men. If the navy is the specialty that has been before asserted, there can be no doubt that this scheme was radically vicious. A period of commercial prosperity would have robbed it of its best men during their best years.

It is due to the Constituent Assembly to say that, while thus establishing the navy of the future on foundations that reason and experience have both condemned, it did not, as has sometimes been said, reject or drive away the able officers still in France; that is, by direct legislative act. Although the decree of April 22 abolished the existing corps of the navy, it provided also that the new organization should be constituted, "for this time only," by a selection made from the officers of the old service then available; from whom the higher grades, including lieutenants, were to be, as far as possible, filled. Those who were not so selected were to be retired with at least two-thirds of their present pay; and with the next higher grade, if they had served over ten years in the one they then held. Whatever dislike these officers may rightly have felt for the new organization, they personally lost little by it, unless not selected: but the failure on the part of the Assembly to realize the irreparable loss with which the country was threatened, — the unique value of a body of men already, and alone, fitted for the performance of very delicate duties, — and the consequent neglect to uphold and protect them, were as fatal in their results as though they had been legislated out of existence.

The second, or Legislative, Assembly during its year of existence made no radical changes in the organization it found; but the increasing want of officers led inevitably to lowering the qualifications exacted for the different grades, which was done by several acts. The National Convention went still farther in the same direction. January 13, 1793, immediately before the war with Great Britain, it decreed that rear-admirals might be taken from any captains whose commission dated back the month before. Merchant captains who had commanded privateers or ships in the foreign trade for five years, could be at once made post-captains. To be made lieutenant were needed only five years' sea-service, either in the navy or on board merchant ships. Decree now followed decree, all in the same direction, winding up on July 28 by authorizing the minister of marine, until otherwise ordered, to fill the places of flag and other officers from any grade and without regard to existing laws. Most of these measures were probably justified by stern and pressing necessity.[1]

The reign of terror was now at hand. The scourge fell upon the naval officers who had not fled the country as well as upon others. Grimouard, whose activity in the West Indies has been noted; Philippe d'Orléans, admiral of France, who had commanded the van at Ushant; Vice-Admiral Kersaint, who had stood in the foremost rank of revolutionists till the murder of the king; D'Estaing, also admiral of France, who had held high command with distinguished courage, if not with equal ability, in the war

[1] Troude, Bat. Nav., vol. ii. p. 260.

of American Independence, — perished on the scaffold. The companions of their glory had for the most died before the evil days. D'Orvilliers, De Grasse, Guichen, the first Latouche-Tréville, Suffren, La Motte Piquet, passed away before the meeting of the States-General.

Besides the judicial and other murders, the effect of the general suspiciousness was felt by the navy in new legislation of a yet more disastrous kind. By a decree of October 7, 1793, the minister of marine was to lay before the naval committee of the Assembly a list of all officers and *aspirants* whose ability or *civisme*, — *i. e.*, fidelity to the new order of things, — was suspected. This may have been well enough; but, in addition, lists of all officers and *aspirants* were to be posted in different places, and all people were invited to send in denunciations of those whom they believed to be lacking in ability or fidelity. These denunciations were to be passed upon by an assembly, made up of the general council of the Commune and all the seamen of the district. The decision was reached by majority of votes and forwarded to the minister, who was obliged to dismiss those against whom the charges were thus sustained.[1]

The navy being in this way purged, the vacancies were to be filled on a similar principle. The naval officers, merchant captains and other seamen of each district, who had qualified for *enseignes*, were to meet and name three candidates for each of the different vacancies. In the great want of officers then prevailing, some such system of nomination might have been very useful in lightening the immense burden resting on the minister; but it is obvious that the assemblies thus constituted were too numerous, too popular, too little fitted to carry on formal discussion, and too destitute of special technical knowledge, to be good judges. There was found here the same essential defect that underlay all the conceptions of the different assem-

[1] Troude, Bat. Nav., vol. ii. pp. 261, 262.

blies of the early republic: ignorant of, and therefore undervaluing, the high and special requirements of the naval profession, they were willing to entrust its interests and the selection of its officers to hands that could not be competent.

The result was depicted in a letter of Admiral Villaret Joyeuse, who was at once an officer of the old service, and yet had entered it from the auxiliary navy, having been captain of fireship; who, therefore, stood as nearly as possible between the two extremes of opinion. As a subordinate he had won the admiration of Suffren in the East Indies, and as admiral he commanded with honor the fleets of the Republic. He wrote: "The popular societies have been called on to point out the men having both seamanship and patriotism. The societies believed that it was enough for a man to have been long at sea to be a seaman, if he was besides a patriot. They did not reflect that patriotism alone cannot handle a ship. The grades consequently have been given to men without merit beyond that of having been much at sea, not remembering that such a man often is in a ship just as a bale is. It must be frankly said it is not always the man at once most skilful and patriotic that has had the suffrages of the societies, but often the most intriguing and the falsest,—he, who by effrontery and talk has been able to impose upon the majority."[1] In another letter he says: "You doubtless know that the best seamen of the different commercial ports kept behind the curtain in the beginning of the Revolution; and that on the other hand there came forward a crowd who, not being able to find employment in commerce, because they had no other talent than the phraseology of patriotism, by means of which they misled the popular societies of which they were members, got the first appointments. Experienced captains, who might have served the republic efficiently by their talents and skill

[1] Troude, Bat. Nav., vol. ii. p. 397.

have since then steadily refused to go to sea, and with inexcusable self-love still prefer service in the National Guard (ashore) to going to sea, where they say they would have to be under captains to whom they have often refused the charge of a watch. Hence the frequent accidents met with by the ships of the republic. Since justice and consequently talents are now (1795) the order of the day, and all France is now convinced that patriotism, doubtless one of the most necessary virtues in an officer of the government, is yet not the only one required to command armies and fleets, as was once claimed, you are quite right," etc.[1]

Enough has been said to show the different causes that destroyed the corps of French naval officers. Some of these were exceptional in their character and not likely to recur; but it is plain that even their operation was hastened by the false notions prevalent in the government as to the character and value of professional training, while the same false notions underlay the attempts both to fill the vacant places and to provide a new basis for the official staff of the future. The results of these mistaken ideas will be seen in the narrative; but it may be useful to give here the professional antecedents (taken from a French naval historian) of the admirals and captains in the first great battle of this war, June 1, 1794, by which time the full effect of the various changes had been reached. These three admirals and twenty-six captains of 1794 held in 1791 the following positions: the commander-in-chief, Villaret Joyeuse, was a lieutenant; the two other flag-officers, one a lieutenant, the other a sub-lieutenant; of the captains, three were lieutenants, eleven sub-lieutenants, nine captains or mates of merchant ships, one a seaman in the navy, one a boatswain, one not given.[2]

The action of the Assemblies with regard to the enlisted men of the fleet was as unreasonable and revolutionary as

[1] Troude, Bat. Nav., vol. ii. p. 396.
[2] Guérin, Hist. de la Mar., vol. iii. p. 411 (note). (Ed. 1848.)

that touching the officers. For twenty years before the
meeting of the States-General the navy had contained
nine divisions of trained seamen-gunners, numbering some
ten thousand men, and commanded, as in all services, by
naval officers. It is scarcely possible to over-rate the
value, in *esprit-de-corps* as well as in fighting effect, of
such a body of trained men. In 1792 these were replaced
by a force of marine artillerists, commanded by artillery
officers. The precise relation of these to the sea-officers
is not stated; but from the change must have sprung
jealousies harmful to discipline, as well as injury to the
military spirit of the naval officer. In 1794, these marine
artillerists, and also the marine infantry, were suppressed
on motion of Jean Bon Saint-André, so well known in connection with the French navy of the day. In his opinion,
endorsed by the vote of the National Convention, it savored
of aristocracy that any body of men should have an exclusive right to fight at sea. "The essential basis of our
social institutions," said he, "is equality; to this touch-
stone you must bring all parts of the government, both
military and civil. In the navy there exists an abuse, the
destruction of which is demanded by the Committee of
Public Safety by my mouth. There are in the navy troops
which bear the name of 'marine regiments.' Is this because these troops have the *exclusive privilege* of defending the republic upon the sea? Are we not *all* called
upon to fight for liberty? Why could not the victors of
Landau, of Toulon, go upon our fleets to show their courage to Pitt, and lower the flag of George? This right cannot be denied them; they themselves would claim it, were
not their arms serving the country elsewhere. Since they
cannot now enjoy it, we must at least give them the prospect of using it."[1]

"Thus," says a French writer, "a marine artillerist, a
soldier trained in the difficult art of pointing a gun at sea

[1] Chevalier, Mar. Fran. sous la Rép., p. 126.

and especially devoted to that service, became a kind of aristocrat."[1] None the less did the Convention, in those days of the Terror, vote the change. "Take care," wrote Admiral Kerguelen, "you need trained gunners to serve guns at sea. Those on shore stand on a steady platform and aim at fixed objects; those at sea, on the contrary, are on a moving platform, and fire always, so to speak, on the wing. The experience of the late actions should teach you that our gunners are inferior to those of the enemy."[2] The words of common sense could get no hearing in those days of flighty ideas and excited imaginations. "How," asks La Gravière, "could these prudent words draw the attention of republicans, more touched by the recollections of Greece and Rome than by the glorious traditions of our ancestors? Those were the days in which presumptuous innovators seriously thought to restore to the oar its importance, and to throw flying bridges on the decks of English ships of the line, as the Romans did on board the galleys of Carthage; candid visionaries, who with simplicity summed up the titles of their mission in words such as these, preserved among the archives of the Navy: 'Legislators, here are the outpourings of an ingenuous patriot, who has for guide no other principle than that of nature and a heart truly French.'"[3]

The effects of this legislation were soon seen in the fighting at sea. The British seventy-four, Alexander, fought three French ships of her own size for two hours; the average loss of each of the latter equalled that of the one enemy. In June, 1795, twelve French ships-of-the-line found themselves in presence of five British. There was bad management in more ways than one, but five of the French had three of the enemy under their fire for several hours; only thirteen Englishmen were hurt, and no ship

---

[1] Chevalier, Mar. Fran. sous la Rép., p. 126.
[2] Jurien de la Gravière, Guerres Mar., vol. i. p. 138 (1st ed.).
[3] Ibid., vol. i. p. 139 (1st ed.).

so crippled as to be taken. A few days later the same French fleet fell in with a British of somewhat superior force. Owing to light airs and other causes, only a partial engagement followed, in which eight British and twelve French took part. The whole British loss was one hundred and forty-four killed and wounded. Three French ships struck, with a loss of six hundred and seventy; and the nine others, which had been partially engaged, had a total of two hundred and twenty-two killed and wounded. In December, 1796, the British frigate Terpsichore met the French Vestale, of equal force. The latter surrendered after a sharp action of two hours, in which she lost sixty-eight killed and wounded against the enemy's twenty-two. This a French writer speaks of as a simple artillery duel, unmarked by any manœuvres. These are not instances chosen to prove a case, but illustrations of the general fact, well known to contemporaries, that the French gunnery was extremely bad. "In comparing this war with the American," says Sir Howard Douglas, " it is seen that, in the latter, the loss of English ships in action with French of equal force, was much more considerable. In the time of Napoleon, whole batteries of ships-of-the-line were fired without doing more harm than two pieces, well directed."

Nor was it only by direct legislation that the Assemblies destroyed the efficiency of the crews. The neglect of discipline and its bad results have before been mentioned. The same causes kept working for many years, and the spirit of insubordination, which sprang from revolutionary excess, doubtless grew stronger as the crews found themselves more and more under incapable officers, through the emigration of their old leaders. As they threw off wholesome restraint, they lost unavoidably in self-respect; and the class of men to whom the confusion of an ill-ordered ship was intolerable, as it becomes even to the humblest seaman who has been used to regularity, doubtless did as the merchant officers of whom Villaret Joyeuse wrote. They withdrew, under cover of the confusion of the times, from the naval service. "The tone of the seamen is wholly ruined," wrote Admiral Morard de Galles, on March 22, 1793, a month after the declaration of war with England: "if it does not change we can expect nothing but reverses in action, even though we be superior in force. The boasted ardor attributed to them" (by themselves and national representatives) "stands only in the words 'patriot,' 'patriotism,' which they are ever repeating, and in shouts of 'Vive la nation! Vive la République!' when they have been well flattered. No idea of doing right or attending to their duties." The government thought best not to interfere, for fear of alienating the seamen. Morard de Galles's flag-ship, having carried away her head-sails in a storm, tried unsuccessfully to wear. "If I had had a crew such as we formerly had," wrote the admiral to the minister, "I would have used means which would have succeeded; but, despite exhortations and threats, I could not get thirty seamen on deck. The army gunners and greater part of the marine troops behaved better. They did what they were told; but the seamen, even the petty officers, did not show themselves."[1]

In May, it being then open war, a mutiny broke out when the Brest squadron was ordered to get under way. To obtain obedience, the naval authorities had to call in the city government and the Society of Friends of Liberty and Equality. In June De Galles wrote again: "I have sailed in the most numerous squadrons, but never in a year did I see so many collisions as in the month this squadron has been together." He kept the sea until toward the end of August, when the fleet anchored in Quiberon Bay, seventy-five miles southeast of Brest. The Navy Department, which was only the mouthpiece of the Committee of Public Safety, directed that the fleet should

[1] Chevalier, Mar. Fran. sous la Rép., pp. 51, 52.

keep the sea till further orders. On the 13th of September, news reached it of the insurrection of Toulon and the reception there of the English fleet. Deputations from different ships came to the admiral, headed by two midshipmen, who demanded, with great insolence of manner, that he should return to Brest, despite his orders. This he firmly refused. The propositions of one of the midshipmen were such that the admiral lost his temper. "I called them," says he, "cowards, traitors, foes to the Revolution; and, as they said they *would* get under way, I replied (and at the instant I believed) that there were twenty faithful ships which would fire on them if they undertook any movements without my orders." The admiral was mistaken as to the temper of the crews. Next morning seven ships mast-headed their top-sails in readiness to sail. He in person went on board, trying to bring them back to obedience, but in vain. To mask his defeat under a form of discipline, if discipline it could be called, he consented to call a council of war, made up of one officer and one seaman from each ship, to debate the question of going back to Brest. This council decided to send deputies to the representatives of the Convention, then on mission in the department, and meanwhile to await further orders from the government. This formality did not hide the fact that power had passed from the commander-in-chief appointed by the State to a council representing a military mob.[1]

The deputies from the ships found the commissioners of the Convention, one of whom came to the fleet. Upon consultation with the admiral, it appeared that twelve ships out of twenty-one were in open mutiny, and four of the other nine in doubt. As the fleet needed repairs, the commissioner ordered its return to Brest. The mob thus got its way, but the spirit of the government had changed. In June the extreme revolutionary party had gained the

[1] Chevalier, Mar. Fran. sous la Rép., pp. 97-101.

upper hand in the State, and was no longer willing to allow the anarchy which had hitherto played its game. The Convention, under the rule of the Mountain, showed extreme displeasure at the action of the fleet; and though its anger fell upon the admirals and captains, many of whom were deprived and some executed, decrees were issued showing that rank insubordination would no longer be tolerated. The government now felt strong.

The cruise of Morard de Galles is an instance, on a large scale, of the state to which the navy had come in the three years that had passed since mutiny had driven De Rions from the service; but it by no means stood alone. In the great Mediterranean naval port, Toulon, things were quite as bad. "The new officers," says Chevalier, "obtained no more obedience than the old; the crews became what they had been made; they now knew only one thing, to rise against authority. Duty and honor had become to them empty words." It would be wearisome to multiply instances and details. Out of their own country such men were a terror rather to allies than foes. An evidently friendly writer, speaking of the Mediterranean fleet when anchored at Ajaccio in Corsica, says, under date of December 31, 1792: "The temper of the fleet and of the troops is excellent; only, it might be said, there is not enough discipline. They came near hanging one day a man who, the following day, was recognized as very innocent of the charge made against him by the agitators. The lesson, however, has not been lost on the seamen, who, seeing the mis-steps into which these hangmen by profession lead them, have denounced one of them."[1] Grave disorders all the same took place, and two Corsican National Guards were hanged by a mob of seamen and soldiers from the fleet; but how extraordinary must have been the feelings of the time when a critic could speak so gingerly of, not to say praise, the temper that showed itself in this way.

[1] Chevalier, p. 42.

While the tone and the military efficiency of officers and crew were thus lowered, the material condition of both ships and men was wretched. Incompetency and disorder directed everywhere. There was lack of provisions, clothing, timber, rigging, sails. In De Galles's fleet, though they had just sailed, most of the ships needed repairs. The crews counted very many sick, and they were besides destitute of clothing. Although scurvy was raging, the men, almost in sight of their own coast, were confined to salt food. Of the Toulon squadron somewhat later, in 1795, we are told almost all the seamen deserted. "Badly fed, scarcely clothed, discouraged by constant lack of success, they had but one thought, to fly the naval service. In September, ten thousand men would have been needed to fill the complements of the Toulon fleet."[1] The country was ransacked for seamen, who dodged the maritime conscription as the British sailor of the day hid from the press-gang.

After the action called by the British the Battle of L'Orient, and by the French that of the Île de Groix, in 1795, the French fleet took refuge in L'Orient, where they remained two months. So great was the lack of provisions that the crews were given leave. When the ships were again ready for sea "it was not an easy thing to make the seamen come back; a decree was necessary to recall them to the colors. Even so only a very small number returned, and it was decided to send out singly, or at most by divisions, the ships which were in the port. When they reached Brest the crews were sent round to L'Orient by land to man other ships. In this way the fleet sailed at different dates in three divisions."[2] In the Irish expedition of 1796, part of the failure in handling the ships is laid to the men being benumbed with cold, because without enough clothes. Pay was constantly in arrears. The

---

[1] Chevalier, Rép. p. 219.
[2] Troude, Bat. Nav., vol. ii. p. 423.

seamen, whatever might be their patriotism, could not be tempted back to the discomforts and hardships of such a service. Promises, threats, edicts, were all of no avail. This state of things lasted for years. The civil commissioner of the navy in Toulon wrote in 1798, concerning the preparations for Bonaparte's expedition to Egypt: "Despite the difficulties concerning supplies, they were but a secondary object of my anxiety. To bring seamen into the service fixed it entirely. I gave the commissioners of the maritime inscription the most pressing orders; I invited the municipalities, the commissioners of the Directory, the commanders of the army, to second them; and to assure the success of this general measure, I sent with my despatches money to pay each seaman raised a month's advance and conduct money. The inveterate insubordination of seamen in most of the western ports, their pronounced aversion to the service, making almost null the effects of the maritime commissioners, I sent a special officer from the port, firm and energetic," to second their efforts; "at length after using every lawful means, part of the western seamen have repaired to this port. There are still many stragglers that are being pursued unremittingly."[1]

The chief causes for this trouble were the hardships and the irregularity of pay, with the consequent sufferings to their families. As late as 1801, Admiral Ganteaume drew a moving picture of the state of the officers and men under his command. "I once more call your attention to the frightful state in which are left the seamen, unpaid for fifteen months, naked or covered with rags, badly fed, discouraged; in a word, sunk under the weight of the deepest and most humiliating wretchedness. It would be horrible to make them undertake, in this state, a long and

[1] Letter of the Ordonnateur de la Marine, Najac; Jurien de la Gravière, Guerres Mar. (4th ed. App.).

doubtless painful winter cruise."[1] Yet it was in this condition he had come from Brest to Toulon in mid-winter. At the same time the admiral said that the officers, receiving neither pay nor table money, lived in circumstances that lowered them in their own eyes and deprived them of the respect of the crews. It was at about this time that the commander of a corvette, taken by a British frigate, made in his defence before the usual court-martial the following statement: "Three fourths of the crew were sea-sick from the time of leaving Cape Sepet until reaching Mahon. Add to this, ill-will, and a panic terror which seized my crew at the sight of the frigate. Almost all thought it a ship-of-the-line. Add to this again, that they had been wet through by the sea for twenty-four hours without having a change of clothes, as I had only been able to get ten spare suits for the whole ship's company."[2] The quality of the crews, the conditions of their life, and the reason why good seamen kept clear of the service, sufficiently appear from these accounts. In the year of Trafalgar, even, neither bedding nor clothing was regularly issued to the crews.[3]

Surprise will not be felt, when human beings were thus neglected, that the needs of the inanimate ships were not met. In the early part of the war it is not easy to say whether the frequent accidents were due to bad handling or bad outfit. In 1793, the escape of six sail-of-the-line, under Admiral Van Stabel, from Lord Howe's fleet, is attributed to superior sailing qualities of the hulls and the better staying of the masts.[4] The next year, however, the commissioner of the Convention who accompanied the great ocean fleet, Jean Bon Saint-André, tried to account for the many accidents which happened in good weather

[1] Chevalier, Mar. Fran. sous le Consulat, p. 47.
[2] Ibid., p. 49.
[3] Troude, Bat. Nav., vol. iii. p. 337.
[4] La Gravière, Guerres Mar., p. 51.

by charging the past reign with a deliberate purpose of destroying the French navy. "This neglect," wrote he, "like so many more, belonged to the system of ruining the navy by carelessness and neglect of all the parts composing it."[1] It was well known that Louis XVI. had given special care to the material and development of the service; nor is it necessary to seek any deeper cause for the deterioration of such perishable materials than the disorders of the five years since he practically ceased to reign. From this time complaints multiply, and the indications of the entire want of naval stores cannot be mistaken. To this, rather than to the neglect of the dockyard officials in Brest, was due the wretched condition of the fleet sent in December, 1794, by the obstinacy of the Committee of Public Safety, to make a mid-winter cruise in the Bay of Biscay, the story of whose disasters is elsewhere told.[2]

The expedition to Ireland in 1796 was similarly ill-prepared; and indeed, with the British preponderance at sea hampering trade, the embarrassment could scarcely fail to grow greater. Spars carried away, rigging parted, sails tore. Some ships had no spare sails. This, too, was a mid-winter expedition, the squadron having sailed in December. In 1798 the preparation of Bonaparte's Egyptian expedition at Toulon met with the greatest difficulty. The naval commissioner showed much zeal and activity, and was fearless in taking upon himself responsibility; but the fleet sailed for an unknown destination almost without spare spars and rigging, and three of the thirteen were not fit for sea. Two had been condemned the year before, and on one they did not dare to put her regular battery. In January, 1801, a squadron of seven sail-of-the-line left Brest under Admiral Gantcaume, having the all-important mission of carrying a reinforcement of five thousand troops to the army in Egypt. Becoming discouraged, whether rightly or wrongly, after entering the Mediterra-

[1] Chevalier, Rép., p. 132.   [2] See Chapter VI.

nean, the admiral bore up for Toulon, where he anchored after being at sea twenty-six days. Here is his report of his fleet during and after this short cruise: "The 'Indivisible' had lost two topmasts and had no spare one left. The trestle-trees of the mainmast were sprung and could not support the new topmast. The 'Desaix' had sprung her bowsprit. The 'Constitution' and the 'Jean-Bart' were in the same condition as the 'Indivisible,' neither having a spare main-topmast after carrying away the others. Both the 'Formidable' and the 'Indomptable,' on the night we got under way, had an anchor break adrift. They had to cut the cable; but both had their sides stove in at the water-line, and could not be repaired at sea. Finally, all the ships, without exception, were short of rope to a disquieting extent, not having had, on leaving Brest, a single spare coil; and the rigging in place was all bad, and in a state to risk every moment the speed and safety of the ships."[1] It will be unnecessary to quote more of these mishaps, in which lack of skill and bad equipment each bore its part; nor need we try to disentangle the one cause from the other.

Enough has now been said to show the general state of the French navy in the last ten years of the eighteenth century. The time and space thus used have not been wasted, for these conditions, which continued under the empire, were as surely the chief cause of the continuous and overwhelming overthrow of that navy, as the ruin of the French and Spanish sea-power, culminating at Trafalgar, was a principal factor in the final result sealed at Waterloo. Great Britain will be seen to enter the war allied with many of the nations of Europe against France. One by one the allies drop away, until the island kingdom, with two-fifths the population of France and a disaffected Ireland, stands alone face to face with the mighty onset of the Revolution. Again and again she knits the coalitions,

[1] Chevalier, Mar. Fran. sous le Consulat, p. 43.

which are as often cut asunder by the victorious sword of the French army. Still she stands alone on the defensive, until the destruction of the combined fleets at Trafalgar, and the ascendency of her own navy, due to the immense physical loss and yet more to the moral annihilation of that of the enemy, enable her to assume the offensive in the peninsula after the Spanish uprising, — an offensive based absolutely upon her control of the sea. Her presence in Portugal and Spain keeps festering that Spanish ulcer which drained the strength of Napoleon's empire. As often before, France, contending with Germany, had Spain again upon her back.

There still remains to consider briefly the state of the other navies which bore a part in the great struggle; and after that, the strategic conditions of the sea war, in its length and breadth, at the time it began.

The British navy was far from being in perfect condition; and it had no such administrative prescription upon which to fall back as France always had in the regulations and practice of Colbert and his son. In the admiralty and the dockyards, at home and abroad, there was confusion and waste, if not fraud. As is usual in representative governments, the military establishments had drooped during ten years of peace. But, although administration lacked system, and agents were neglectful or dishonest, the navy itself, though costing more than it should, remained vigorous; the possessor of actual, and yet more of reserved, strength in the genius and pursuits of the people, — in a continuous tradition, which struck its roots far back in a great past, — and above all, in a body of officers, veterans of the last, and some of yet earlier wars, still in the prime of life for the purposes of command, and steeped to the core in those professional habits and feelings which, when so found in the chief, transmit themselves quickly to the juniors. As the eye of the student familiar with naval history glances down the lists of admirals and captains in 1793, it recognizes at once the names of those who fought under Keppel, Rodney, and Howe, linked with those who were yet to win fame as the companions of Hood, Jervis, Nelson, and Collingwood.

To this corps of officers is to be added, doubtless, a large number of trained seamen, who, by choice, remained in the navy under the reduced peace complement; a nucleus round which could be rapidly gathered and organized all the sea-faring population fit for active service. The strength of Great Britain, however, lay in her great body of merchant seamen; and the absence of so many of these on distant voyages was always a source of embarrassment when manning a fleet in the beginning of a war. The naval service was also generally unpopular with the sailor; to whom, as to his officer, the rigid yoke of discipline was hard to bear until the neck was used to it. Hence, in the lack of any system similar to the French maritime inscription, Great Britain resorted to the press; a method which, though legally authorized, was stained in execution by a lawlessness and violence strange in a people that so loved both law and freedom. Even so, with both press-gang and free enlistment, the navy, as a whole, was always shorthanded in a great war, so that men of all nations were received and welcomed; much very bad native material was also accepted. "Consider," wrote Collingwood, "with such a fleet as we have now, how large a proportion of the crews of the ships are miscreants of every description, and capable of every crime. And when those predominate what evils may we not dread from the demoniac councils and influence of such a mass of mischief." [1]

The condition of the seamen on board left much to be desired. The pay had not been increased since the days of Charles II., although the prices of all the necessaries of life had risen thirty per cent. The exigencies of the

[1] Collingwood's Correspondence, p. 48. (First American from fourth London edition.)

service, combined with the fear of desertion, led to very close enforced confinement to the ship, even in home ports; men were long unable to see their families. The discipline, depending upon the character of the captain, too little defined and limited by law, varied greatly in different ships; while some were disorganized by undue leniency, in others punishment was harsh and tyrannical. On the other hand, there was a large and growing class of officers, both among the sterner and the laxer disciplinarians, who looked upon the health and well-being of the crew as the first of their duties and interests; and better sanitary results have perhaps never been reached, certainly never in proportion to the science of the day, than under Jervis, Nelson, Collingwood, and their contemporaries, in fleets engaged in the hardest, most continuous service, under conditions of monotony and isolation generally unfavorable to health. Nelson, during a cruise in which he passed two years without leaving his ship even for another, often speaks with pride, almost with exultation, of the health of his crews. After his pursuit of Villeneuve's fleet to the West Indies, he writes: " We have lost neither officer nor man by sickness since we left the Mediterranean," a period of ten weeks. The number of men in his ships must have been near seven thousand. Both French and Spaniards of the fleet he pursued were very sickly. " They landed a thousand sick at Martinique, and buried full that number during their stay."[1] Collingwood writes: " I have not let go an anchor for fifteen months, and on the first day of the year had not a sick-list in the ship — not one man."[2] And again a year later: " Yet, with all this sea-work, never getting fresh beef nor a vegetable, I have not one sick man in my ship. Tell that to Doctor ———." " His flag-ship had usually eight hundred men: was, on one occasion, more than a year and a half without

---

[1] Nelson's Dispatches, vol. vi. p. 480.
[2] Collingwood's Correspondence, pp. 265, 266.

going into port, and during the whole of that time never had more than six, and generally only four, on her sick-list."[1] Such results show beyond dispute that the crews were well clothed, well fed, and well cared for.

Amid ship's companies of such mixed character, and suffering during the early years of the war from real and severe grievances, it was to be expected that acts of mutiny should occur. Such there were, rivalling, if not surpassing, in extent, those which have been told of the French navy. They also received intelligent guidance at the hands of a class of men, of higher educational acquirements than the average seaman, who, through drunkenness, crime, or simple good-for-nothingness, had found their way on board ship. The feature which distinguished these revolts from those of the French was the spirit of reasonableness and respect for law which at the first marked their proceedings; and which showed how deeply the English feeling for law, duty and discipline, had taken hold of the naval seamen. Their complaints, unheeded when made submissively, were at once allowed to be fair when mutiny drew attention to them. The forms of discipline were maintained by men who refused to go to sea before their demands were allowed, unless "the enemy's fleet should put to sea;"[2] and respect to officers was enjoined, though some who were obnoxious for severity were sent ashore. One very signal instance is given of military sympathy with obedience to orders, though at their own expense. A lieutenant, having shot one of several mutineers, was seized by the others, who made ready to hang him, and he stood actually under the yard-arm with the halter round his neck; but upon the admiral saying he himself was responsible, having given orders to the officer in accordance with his own from the Admiralty, the seamen stopped, asked to see the orders,

[1] Collingwood's Correspondence, p. 208.
[2] Brenton's Naval History, vol. i. p. 415. (Ed. 1823.)

and, having satisfied themselves of their terms, abandoned their purpose.

Captain Brenton, the naval historian, was watch-officer on board a ship that for many days was in the hands of mutineers. He says, " The seamen, generally speaking, throughout the mutiny conducted themselves with a degree of humanity highly creditable, not only to themselves, but to the national character. They certainly tarred and feathered the surgeon of a ship at the Nore, but he had been five weeks drunk in his cabin and had neglected the care of his patients; this was therefore an act which Lord Bacon would have called 'wild justice.' The delegates of the 'Agamemnon'" (his own ship) " showed respect to every officer but the captain; him, after the first day, they never insulted but rather treated with neglect; they asked permission of the lieutenants to punish a seaman, who, from carelessness or design, had taken a dish of meat belonging to the ward-room and left his own, which was honestly and civilly offered in compensation."[1] Still, though begun under great provocation and marked at first by such orderly procedure, the fatal effects of insubordination once indulged long remained, as in a horse that has once felt his strength; while the self-control and reasonableness of demand which distinguished the earlier movements lost their sway. The later mutinies seriously endangered the State, and the mutinous spirit survived after the causes which palliated it had been removed.

In meeting the needs of so great and widely scattered a naval force, even with the best administration and economy, there could not but be great deficiencies; and the exigencies of the war would not permit ships to be recalled and refitted as often as the hard cruising properly required. Still, by care and foresight, the equipment of the fleet was maintained in sufficient and serviceable condition. In the year 1783 a plan was adopted " of setting apart for every

[1] Brenton's Naval History, vol. i. p. 455.

sea-going ship a large proportion of her furniture and stores, as well as of stocking the magazines at the several dockyards with imperishable stores."[1] The readiness thus sought was tested, and also bettered, by the two partial armaments of 1790 against Spain and of 1791 against Russia; so that, when orders to arm were received in 1793, in a very few weeks the ships-of-the-line in commission were increased from twenty-six to fifty-four, and the whole number of ships of all sizes from one hundred and thirty-six to over two hundred. The same care and foresight was continued into the war. It was as much an object with Great Britain to hinder the carriage of naval stores from the Baltic to France as to get them herself, and there was reason to fear that her seizure of ships so laden and bound to France would, as before, bring on trouble with the northern States. "In 1796 the quantity of naval stores remaining on hand was too small to afford a hope of their lasting to the end of the war; but the government, foreseeing that a rupture must ensue, provided an abundant supply of materials for naval equipment; ship timber was imported from the Adriatic, masts and hemp from North America, and large importations were made from the Baltic. The number of British ships which passed the Sound in one year was forty-five hundred, chiefly laden with naval stores, corn, tallow, hides, hemp, and iron. At the same time the most rigid economy was enforced in the dockyards and on board ships of war."[2]

A bare sufficiency — to be eked out with the utmost care, turning everything to account, working old stuff up into new forms — was the economic condition of the British cruiser of the day. Under such conditions the knack of the captain and officers made a large part of the effi-

---

[1] James' Nav. Hist. vol. i. p. 53 (ed. 1878). This system had been adopted in France a century before by Colbert (Revue Mar. et Coloniale, September, 1887, p. 567).

[2] Brenton's Nav. Hist., vol. ii. p. 105.

ciency of the ship. "Some," wrote Collingwood, "who have the foresight to discern what our first difficulty will be, support and provide their ships as by enchantment; while others, less provident, would exhaust a dockyard and still be in want." Of one he said: "He should never sail without a storeship in company;" while of Troubridge Nelson wrote that "he was as full of resources as his old 'Culloden' was of defects." A lieutenant of the day mentions feelingly the anxieties felt on dark nights and in heavy weather off the enemy's coast, "doubting this brace or that tack," upon which the safety of the ship might depend. The correspondence of Nelson often mentions this dearth of stores.

The condition of the two navies in these various respects being as described, their comparative strength in mere numbers is given by the British naval historian James, whose statement bears every mark of careful study and accuracy. After making every deduction, the British had one hundred and fifteen ships-of-the-line, and the French seventy-six, when war was declared. The number of guns carried by these ships was respectively 8718 and 6002; but the author claims that, in consequence of the heavier metal of the French guns, the aggregate weight of broadside, undoubtedly the fairest method of comparison, of the line-of-battle in the two navies was 88,957 pounds against 73,957, — a preponderance of one sixth in favor of Great Britain.[1] This statement is explicitly accepted by the French admiral, La Gravière,[2] and does not differ materially from other French accounts of the numerical strength of that navy at the fall of the monarchy.

The navy of Spain then contained seventy-six ships-of-the-line, of which fifty-six were in good condition.[3] Particular and detailed accounts are wanting, but it may safely be inferred from many indications scattered along

---

[1] James' Nav. Hist., vol. i. pp. 57, 58.
[2] Guerres Mar., vol. i. p. 49 (1st ed.).   [3] James, vol. i. p. 55.

the paths of naval records that the valid strength fell very, very far below this imposing array of ships. The officers as a body were inexpert and ignorant; the administration of the dockyards partook of the general shiftlessness of the decaying kingdom; the crews contained few good seamen and were largely swept out of the streets, if not out of the jails. "The Spaniards at this time," says La Gravière, "were no longer substantial enemies. At the battle of St. Vincent there were scarcely sixty to eighty seamen in each ship-of-the-line. The rest of the crews were made up of men wholly new to the sea, picked up a few months before in the country or in the jails, and who, by the acknowledgment of even English historians, when ordered to go aloft, fell on their knees, crying that they would rather be killed on the spot than meet certain death in trying so perilous a service." [1]

"The Dons," wrote Nelson in 1793, after a visit to Cadiz, "may make fine ships, — they cannot, however, make men. They have four first-rates in commission at Cadiz, and very fine ships, but shockingly manned. I am certain if our six barges' crews, who are picked men, had got on board of one of them, they would have taken her." "If the twenty-one ships-of-the-line which we are to join off Barcelona are no better manned than those at Cadiz, much service cannot be expected of them, although, as to ships, I never saw finer men-of-war." [2] A few weeks later he fell in with the twenty-one. "The Dons did not, after several hours' trial, form anything that could be called a line-of-battle ahead. However, the Spanish admiral sent down two frigates, acquainting Lord Hood that, as his fleet was sickly nineteen hundred men, he was going to Cartagena. The captain of the frigate said 'it was no wonder they were sickly *for they had been sixty days at sea.*' This speech appeared to us ridiculous, for, from the circumstance of our having been longer than that time at

---

[1] Guerres Mar., vol. i. p. 164 (note).   [2] Nels. Disp. i. 309-311.

sea do we attribute our getting healthy. It has stamped with me the measure of their nautical abilities; long may they remain in their present state."[1] In 1795, when Spain had made peace with France, he wrote, " I know the French long since offered Spain peace for fourteen ships-of-the-line fully stored. I take for granted not manned, as that would be the readiest way to lose them again." " Their fleet is ill-manned and worse officered, I believe; and besides they are slow." " From the event of Spain making peace much may be looked for,—perhaps a war with that country; if so, their fleet (if no better than when our allies) will be soon done for."[2]

Captain Jahleel Brenton, a distinguished British officer of that day, being in Cadiz on duty before the war, sought and obtained permission to return to England in a Spanish ship-of-the-line, the " St. Elmo," with the express object of seeing the system of their service. He says, " This ship had been selected as one in the best state of discipline in the Spanish navy to be sent to England. She was commanded by Don Lorenzo Goycochea, a gallant seaman who had commanded one of the junto ships destroyed before Gibraltar in 1782. I had, during this voyage, an opportunity of appreciating Spanish management at sea. When the ship was brought under double-reefed topsails, it was considered superfluous to lay the cloth for dinner; I was told by the captain that not one officer would be able to sit at table, all being sea-sick, but that he had ordered dinner to be got ready in his own cabin for himself and me. It was the custom in the Spanish navy for the captain and officers to mess together in the ward-room. We had thenceforth a very comfortable meal together whenever the weather prevented a general meeting. As the safe arrival of this ship was deemed of great importance (she carried the Nootka Sound indemnity money), she had on board an English pilot to enable her to approach the coast

[1] Nels. Disp., i. p. 312.   [2] Ibid., ii. pp. 70, 77, 241.

of England in safety. A few nights before our arrival at
Falmouth, the ship, having whole sails and topping sails,
was taken aback in a heavy squall from the northeast,
and I was awoke by the English pilot knocking at my
cabin door, calling out, 'Mr. Brenton! Mr. Brenton! rouse
out, sir; here is the ship running away with these Spaniards!' When I got on deck I found this literally the
case. She was 'running away' at the rate of twelve knots,
and everything in confusion; she was indeed, to use the
ludicrous expression of a naval captain 'all adrift, like a
French post-chaise.' It required some hours to get things
to rights."[1]

Napoleon, in 1805, ordered Admiral Villeneuve to count
two Spanish ships as equal to one French; and the latter
certainly were not equal, ship for ship, to the British. It
is only fair to add that he said of the Spanish crews,
speaking of Calder's action, that they fought like lions.

Holland, first the ally and afterwards the enemy of
Great Britain in the war, had forty-nine ships-of-the-line,
but, owing to the shoalness of her waters, they were mostly
of light burden; many would not have found a place in a
British line-of-battle. The frigates were also of small
force. The condition of the ships being, besides, bad, the
Dutch navy was not an important factor on either side.[2]

Portugal and Naples had, the one six, the other four,
ships-of-the-line, which, during the early years of the war,
offered a respectable support to the British Mediterranean
fleet;[2] but the advance of the French under Bonaparte
into the two peninsulas reduced these States to neutrality
before the end of the century.

The fleets of the Baltic powers and of Turkey played no
part in the war which would, at this time, require a particular consideration of their strength.

---

[1] Life of Sir Jahleel Brenton.
[2] James' Nav. Hist., vol. i. p. 54. (Ed. 1878).

CHAPTER III.

THE GENERAL POLITICAL AND STRATEGIC CONDITIONS, AND THE EVENTS OF 1793.

THE declaration of war against Great Britain was followed, on the part of the National Convention, by an equally formal pronouncement against Spain, on the 7th of March, 1793. Thus was completed the chain of enemies which, except on the mountain frontier of Switzerland, surrounded the French republic by land and sea.

It is necessary to summarize the political and military condition, to take account of the strategic situation at this moment when general hostilities were opening, in order to follow intelligently the historical narrative of their course, and to appreciate critically the action of the nations engaged, both separately and, also,—in the case of the allies,—regarded as a combined whole.

The enemies of France were organized governments, with constitutions of varying strength and efficiency, but all, except that of Great Britain, were part of an order of things that was decaying and ready to vanish away. They belonged to, and throughout the Revolutionary and Napoleonic wars were hampered by, a past whose traditions of government, of social order, and of military administration, were violently antagonized by the measures into which France had been led by pushing to extremes the philosophical principles of the eighteenth century. But while thus at one in abhorring, as rulers, a movement whose contagion they feared, they were not otherwise in harmony. The two most powerful on the continent, Austria and Prussia, had alternately, in a not remote past, sided with France as her ally; each in turn had sustained open and prolonged hostilities with the other, and they were still jealous rivals for preponderance in Germany. They entered the present war as formal allies; but were unable, from mutual distrust and their military traditions, to act in concert, or to take advantage of the disorganized condition into which France had fallen, and from which the despotism of the Convention had not yet raised her. Divergent lines of operations were imposed upon them, not by military expediency, but by the want of any unifying motive which could overcome their divergent ambitions. The smaller States of Germany followed the two great powers, seeking each from day to day its own safety and its own advantage in the troubled times through which Europe was passing. Several of them had associations with France as a powerful neighbor, who in the past had supported them against the overbearing pretensions of the great German monarchies. With the Convention and its social levelling they could have no sympathy, but when a settled government succeeded the throes of the Revolution the old political bias asserted itself against the more recent social prejudice, and these weaker bodies again fell naturally under French control.

Spain under good government has, and at that crisis still more had, a military situation singularly fitted to give her weight in the councils of Europe. Compact and symmetrical in shape, with an extensive seaboard not deficient in good harbors, her physical conformation and remoteness from the rest of the Continent combined to indicate that her true strength was to be found in a powerful navy, for which also her vast colonial system imperiously called. Her maritime advantages were indeed diminished by the jog which Portugal takes out of her territory and coast line, and by the loss of Gibraltar. Lisbon, in the hands of an enemy, interposes between the arsenals of Ferrol and

Cadiz, as Gibraltar does between the latter and Cartagena. But there was great compensation in the extent of her territory, in her peninsular formation, and in the difficult character of her only continental frontier, the Pyrenees. Her position is defensively very strong; and whenever events make France the centre of European interest, as they did in 1793, and as the genius of that extraordinary country continually tends to make her, the external action of Spain becomes doubly interesting. So far as natural advantages go, her military situation at the opening of the French revolution may be defined by saying that she controlled the Mediterranean, and menaced the flank and rear of France by land. Despite Gibraltar, her action was to determine whether the British navy should or should not enter the Mediterranean — whether the wheat of Barbary and Sicily should reach the hungry people of southern France — whether the French fleet should leave Toulon — whether the French army could advance against the Germans and Piedmont, feeling secure as to the country behind it, then seething with revolt. The political condition of Italy, divided like Germany into many petty States, but unlike Germany in having no powerful centres around which to gather, left to Spain, potentially, the control of the Mediterranean. These advantages were all thrown away by bad government and inefficient military institutions. The navy of Spain was the laughing-stock of Europe; her finances depended upon the colonies, and consequently upon control of the sea, which she had not; while, between an embarrassed treasury and poor military administration, her army, though at first under respectable leadership, made little impression upon the yet unorganized levies of France, and an abject peace soon closed an ignominious war.

The path of Great Britain, as soon as she had determined to enter the war, was comparatively clear, being indicated alike by the character of her military strength and by her history during the past century. Since the days of Charles II. she had been at times the ally, at times the enemy, of Austria, of Prussia, and of Holland; she had, in her frequent wars, found Spain at times neutral, at times hostile, in neither case a very powerful factor; but, under all circumstances, France had been her enemy, sometimes secret, usually open. Steeped in this traditional hostility, both the British government and nation with single eye fastened upon France as the great danger, and were not diverted from this attitude of concentrated purpose by any jealousy of the more powerful among their allies. Spain alone might have been an unwelcome rival, as well as a powerful support, upon the watery plain which Great Britain claimed as her own dominion. Spanish ships of war were numerous; but the admiralty soon saw that the Spanish navy, from the poor quality of its officers and men, could not seriously menace British preponderance upon the ocean, although at times it might be an awkward embarrassment, and even more so as a suspicious ally than as an open foe. The co-operation of the two navies, however, at the opening of the war effectually secured for the time the control of the Mediterranean and of the approaches to southern France.

Russia, although declaring openly against the French Revolution, took no active part in the early military operations, except by a convention made with Great Britain on the 25th of March, 1793, to interdict the trade of France with the Baltic in grain and naval stores, as a means of forcing her to peace. Russia was then busily engaged with her projects against Poland, and a few days later, on the 9th of April, 1793, an imperial ukase was issued incorporating parts of that kingdom with the empire. This, with the Prussian decree of March 25, consummated the second partition of Poland, — the result of a series of aggressions by the two powers that had extended over the past two years, and the intermediate step to the final partition in 1795.

The smaller European States trimmed their course as best they could in the great convulsion which, far beyond most wars, left little room for neutrality. Sweden and Denmark strove hard to keep out of the turmoil and to retain the commercial advantages reaped by neutral flags in maritime wars. Their distance from the scene of the earlier strifes, and the peninsular position of Sweden, enabled them long to avoid actual hostilities; but the concurrence of Russia with Great Britain, in the latter's traditional unwillingness to concede neutral claims, deprived the smaller Baltic powers of the force necessary to maintain their contentions. Holland, as of old, was divided between French and British parties; but the latter, under the headship of the House of Orange, in 1793, held the reins of government and directed the policy of the State in accordance with the treaty of defensive alliance made with Great Britain in 1788. The ultimate policy of the United Provinces depended upon the fortune of the war. As France or her enemies triumphed, so would the party in the State favorable to the victor be retained in, or restored to, power. Neutrality was impossible to an open continental country, lying so near such a great conflagration; but, not to speak of the immediate dangers threatened by the attitude of the French Convention and its decrees of November 19 and December 15, Holland, with her vast colonial system, had more to fear from the navy of Great Britain, which had no rival, than from the armies of France which, in 1793, were confronted by the most powerful military States in Europe. At this time the United Provinces held, besides Java and other possessions in the far East, various colonies in the West Indies and South America, the island of Ceylon and the Cape of Good Hope. The last two alone Great Britain has finally retained; but all of them, as years went by, passed by conquest into her hands after Holland, in 1795, became the dependent of France.

Portugal retained her traditional alliance with Great Britain, and so became a point of supreme importance when the secession of Spain to France compelled the British navy to leave the Mediterranean. The formal connection between the two countries was for a short time severed by the genius and power of Napoleon; but, at the uprising of Spain in 1808, the old sentiment, unbroken, resumed its sway, and Portugal became the base of the British army, as in an earlier day she had been the secure haven of the British fleet.

In northern Italy the extent of Piedmont and its contiguity to the Austrian duchies of Milan and Mantua gave the means of forming a powerful focus of resistance to their common enemy, the French republic, around which the smaller Italian States might feel secure to rally; but the sluggishness and jealousies of the two governments prevented the vigorous, combined action which alone could cope with the energy impressed by the Convention upon its men. In the centre of the peninsula, the Pope inevitably threw his immense spiritual influence, as well as such temporal power as he could exercise, against the revolution; while, in the south, the Bourbon kingdom of the Two Sicilies, with its capital at Naples, was chiefly controlled by the queen, herself a sister of Marie Antoinette. The military strength of this kingdom, like that of Spain, was rendered contemptible by miserable administration, and was further neutralized by its remoteness from the seats of actual war; but the bias of the monarchy was undoubted. Like all weak and corrupt governments, it shuffled and equivocated under pressure and was false when the pressure was removed; but, so far as it could, it favored the allied cause and was a useful base to the British fleet in the Mediterranean.

In the eastern Mediterranean, the Turkish empire was not then the element of recognized critical hazard to the whole European system which it has since become; but its territorial limits were far wider than they now are. Extending on the north to the Save and the Danube, Turkey held also beyond the river Wallachia and Moldavia to the banks of the Dniester, and, on the south, the present kingdom of Greece. The islands of the Archipelago, with Crete and Cyprus, also belonged to her. Syria and Egypt likewise acknowledged the authority of the Porte, but in both the submission yielded was only nominal; the former, under Djezzar Pasha, and the latter, under the Mamelukes, were practically independent countries. At the outbreak of the French Revolution Turkey had sunk to the lowest pitch of disorganization and impotence; and her rulers, keenly feeling her condition and her danger from Russia, sought to avoid entanglement in the troubles of western Europe, from which their great enemy kept itself free. In this they were successful until Bonaparte, by his attack upon Egypt, forced them from their security and aroused Great Britain and Europe to their common interest in the East.

The islands of the western Mediterranean had not only the importance common to all members of that geographical family in naval wars, nor yet only that due to their intrinsic values. In so narrow a sheet of water each possessed an added strategic weight due to its nearness, either to some part of the mainland or to some one of the maritime routes traversing the sea. The influence thus exerted would fall naturally into the hands of the nation which, by controlling the water, controlled the communications of the island; but this statement, though generally true, is subject to limitations. The narrowness of the belts of water, or, to use the military phrase, the shortness of the communications from land to land, made evasion comparatively easy. No navy, however powerful, can with certainty stop an intercourse requiring only a night's run, and which, therefore, can be carried on by very many small vessels, instead of having to be concentrated into a few large ones; and this was doubly true in the days of sail, when the smaller could have recourse to the oar while the larger lay becalmed. Thus the British found it impossible to prevent French partisans from passing into Corsica in 1796, when the victories of Bonaparte had placed the French army in Leghorn; and at a later day the emperor succeeded, though with infinite trouble, in sending re-enforcements and supplies from southern Italy to his garrison in Corfu, upon which his far-reaching genius hoped, in a distant future, to base a yet further extension of power in the East. These instances, however, were but the exception, and on the small scale demanded by the other conditions; for the garrison of Corfu was few in number, and the French found the Corsicans friendly. As the communications lengthened, the influence of Sea-Power asserted itself. It was found impossible to relieve Malta, or even to extricate the large vessels blockaded there; and the French army in Egypt remained isolated until forced to surrender, despite the efforts, the uncontrolled power, and the strong personal interest of Bonaparte in the success of an occupation for which he was primarily responsible. So also the narrow strip which separates Sicily from Italy withstood the French arms; not because it was impossible to send many detachments across, but because, to support them in a hostile country, with such insecure communications, was an undertaking more hazardous than was justified by the possible advantages.

The political distribution in 1793 of the islands of the western Mediterranean was as follows. The most eastern, known as the Ionian islands, extending southward from the entrance of the Adriatic along the coast of Greece, from Corfu to Cerigo, were in possession of Venice. When the ancient republic fell before the policy of Bonaparte, in 1797, the islands passed to France and began that circulation from owner to owner which ended in 1863 with their union to Greece. Sicily formed part of the kingdom of the Two Sicilies. It became the refuge of that monarchy from the arms of France, and, by its fertility and the use of its ports, was a resource to Great Britain throughout the Napoleonic period. Malta was still in the hands of the Knights of St. John. Of immense military importance, from its geographical position and intrinsic strength, its transfer, through the medium of France, into the hands of the greatest of naval powers was due to Bonaparte. It is, perhaps, the greatest of Mediterranean strategic positions, Egypt being rather interoceanic than Mediterranean; but, being of scant resources, its utility is measured by the power of the fleet which it subserves. Its fate when in the hands of France, the history of Port Mahon in the hands of Great Britain, nay, even the glorious and successful resistance of Gibraltar, give warning that the fleet depends less upon Malta than Malta upon the fleet.

Sardinia gave its name to the kingdom of which Piedmont, forming the Italian frontier of France, was the actual seat, and Turin the capital. Amid the convulsions of the period, the royal family, driven from the mainland, found an obscure refuge in this large but backward island. France could not touch it; Great Britain needed nothing but the hospitality of its harbors. In Maddalena Bay, at its northern extremity, Nelson found an anchorage strategically well-placed for watching the Toulon fleet, and possessing that great desideratum for a naval position, two exits, one or other of which was available in any wind. The Balearic islands were in the hands of Spain. The maritime importance of the other members of the group was dwarfed by that of Minorca, which contained the harbor, exceptionally good for the Mediterranean, of Port Mahon. Like Malta, though not to the same extent, the fate of Port Mahon depends ultimately upon the sea. The British took possession of the island in 1798, but restored it at the peace of Amiens. In the later hostilities with Spain, from 1804 to 1808, they appear not to have coveted it. Maddalena Bay, though a less agreeable and convenient anchorage than Mahon, is far better fitted for prompt military movement, the prime requisite in the clear and sound judgment of Nelson.

Of the greater islands there remains to give account only of Corsica. This was a recent acquisition of France, received from Genoa in 1769, somewhat contrary to the wish of the people, who would have preferred independence. They were certainly not yet assimilated to the French, and there existed among them a party traditionally well-inclined to Great Britain. The preponderance of this or of the other national preference would be decisive of the final political connection; for if the British navy did control the surrounding sea, it was unable, as before said, entirely to isolate the island and so to compel an unwilling submission. On the other hand, France could not introduce any considerable body of troops, in the face of the hostile ships; and her standard, if raised, would depend for support upon the natives. In 1793, there was at the head of affairs the old leader of the struggle for independence, Paoli, who had passed many years in exile in England and had been recalled to the island by the National Assembly; but the excesses of the later days had shaken his allegiance to France, and the commissioners sent by the Convention into Corsica made themselves obnoxious to him and to the people. Denounced by the republicans of Toulon, Paoli was summoned to the bar of the Convention in April, 1793. The Revolutionary Tribunal had then been constituted, the Reign of Terror was begun; and Paoli, instead of complying, summoned the deputies from all the cities and communes of Corsica. These met in May and sustained him in his opposition; the revolt spread through the island, and the Commissioners with their handful of adherents were shut up in a few of the coast towns.

Amid these surroundings stood, in the spring of 1793, the terrible and awe-inspiring figure of the French Revolution. The Corsican revolt against the Convention reflected but faintly the passions agitating that body itself, and which were rapidly dividing all France into hostile camps. The four months following the execution of the king were one long strife between the party of the Gironde and the Jacobins; but the revolutionary fury demanded an expression more vigorous and more concentrated than could be had from a contest of parties in a popular assembly. The Girondists, men of lofty sentiment rather than of energetic action, steadily lost ground in the capital and in the legislative body, though retaining the allegiance of the provinces, with which they were identified. Embittered words and feelings took material shape in acts as violent as themselves. On the 9th of March was decreed the Revolutionary Tribunal, the great instrument of the Terror, from whose decisions there was no appeal. On the 13th of the same month, La Vendée rose for its long and bloody struggle in the royal cause. On the 18th, the Army of the North, which only four weeks before had invaded Holland, was signally defeated at Neerwinden, and its general, Dumouriez, the victor of Valmy and Jemappes, the most successful leader the war had yet produced, was forced to retreat upon France. On the 30th, he evacuated the Austrian Netherlands, the prize of the last campaign, and his army took positions within the frontiers, upon which the enemy advanced. On the 1st of April, Dumouriez, long since violently dissatisfied with the course of the Convention, arrested the four commissioners and the minister of war that had been sent to his headquarters. The next day he delivered them to the Austrians; and on the 4th, finding that the blind attachment of his army could no longer be depended upon, he completed his treason by flying to the enemy.

While disorganization, treason, and fear were spreading throughout France, from the capital to the frontiers, and seemed about to culminate in universal anarchy, an important measure was adopted, destined eventually to restore discipline and order, though at the expense of much suffering. On the 6th of April the Committee of Public Safety was reconstituted. Composed previously of twenty-five members who met in open session, it was now reduced to nine, a more manageable body, who sat in secret. To it was given authority over the ministers, and it was empowered to take all measures necessary for the general defence. The republic was thus provided with an efficient, though despotic, executive power which it had before lacked. The creature of the Convention, it was destined soon to become its master; being, as a French historian has aptly termed it, "a dictatorship with nine heads."

Time was still needed for the new authority to make itself felt, and the strife between the parties waxed more and more bitter. On the 15th of April the city of Lyon demanded permission to investigate the conduct of the municipality appointed by the Jacobin commissioners. The request, being denied, became the signal for civil war. On the 26th of May the "sections" of the city rose against the mayor. At the same time the scenes in Paris and in the Convention were becoming more and more tumultuous, and on the 31st the sections of the capital also rose, but against the Girondists. After two days of strife in the streets and in the legislative halls, the Convention decreed the arrest, at their own houses, of thirty-two members of the party. Thus, on the 2d of June, 1793, fell the Girondists, but their fall was followed by the revolt of their partisans throughout France. Marseille, Toulon, Bordeaux and Lyon all declared against the Convention; and movements in the same direction were manifested in Normandy and Brittany. In the western provinces, however, the attempts at resistance were chilled among the republicans by the proximity of the royalist insurrection in La Vendée. They were forced to reflect that armed opposition to the Convention, even as mutilated by the events of June 2, was a virtual alliance with royalism. In Bordeaux, likewise, the movement, though prolonged for some weeks, did not take shape in vigorous action. Words, not arms, were the weapons used; and the Girondist representatives were forced to fly the very department from which they took their name.

In the east and south conditions were far more threatening. The rising of the sections in Lyon had been followed by fighting in the streets on the 29th of May, and the triumphant party, after the events of June 2, refused to acknowledge the Convention. The latter sought to gain over the city peaceably; but its overtures were rejected, a departmental army was formed, and the leading member of the Jacobin party formally tried and executed. The Lyonnese also stopped supplies being carried to the Army of the Alps. On the 12th of July a decree was issued to reduce the place by force. The troops of the Convention appeared before it in the latter part of the month; but resistance was firm and well organized, and the siege dragged, while at the same time the departments of the south in general rejected the authority of the central government. The two seaboard cities, Marseille and Toulon, entered into correspondence with Lord Hood, commanding the British fleet, who arrived off the coast of Provence in the middle of August, 1793. The party of the Convention, favored by that want of vigor which characterized most of the measures of their opponents, got possession of Marseille before the treason was consummated; but in Toulon, which had long suffered from the violence of a Jacobin municipality, the reaction swung to the opposite extreme. A movement, beginning in honest disgust with the proceedings in Paris and with the conduct of the dominant party in their own city, insensibly carried its promoters further than they had intended; until a point was reached from which, before the savage spirit of the capital, it became dangerous to recede. Long identi-

fied with the royal navy, as one of the chief arsenals of
the kingdom, there could not but exist among a large class
a feeling of loyalty to the monarchy. Submissive to the
course of events so long as France had a show of government,
now, in the dissolution of civil order, it seemed
allowable to choose their own path.

With such dispositions, a decree of the Convention
declaring the city outlawed enabled the royalists to guide
the movement in the direction they desired. The leading
naval officers do not appear to have co-operated willingly
with the advances made to the British admiral;
but for years they had seen their authority undermined
by the course of the national legislature, and had become
accustomed to yield to the popular control of the
moment. The news of the approach of the Conventional
army, accompanied by the rush into the place of terror-stricken
fugitives from Marseille, precipitated Toulon
into the arms of Great Britain. The sections declared
that the city adopted the monarchical government as
organized by the Constituent Assembly of 1789; proclaimed
Louis XVII. king; ordered the disarmament of
the French fleet in the port, and placed in the hands
of the British admiral the works commanding the harbor.
Lord Hood undertook that the forts and ships
should be restored unharmed to France, when peace was
made. On the 27th, the British and Spanish fleets anchored
in the outer harbor of Toulon, and the city ran up
the white flag of the Bourbons. There were in the port
at the time of its delivery to the British admiral thirty
ships-of-the-line of seventy-four guns and upward, being
rather more than one third the line-of-battle force of the
French navy. Of these, seventeen were in the outer harbor
ready for sea. There were, besides, twenty-odd frigates
or smaller vessels.

While one of the principal naval arsenals of France, and
the only one she possessed on the Mediterranean, was thus

passing into the hands of the enemy, disasters were accumulating on her eastern borders. On the 12th of July, the fortified town of Condé, on the Belgian frontier, surrendered. This was followed on the 28th by the capitulation of the first-class fortress of Valenciennes in the same locality, after six weeks of open trenches. These two prizes fell to the allied Austrians, British and Dutch, and their submission was followed by an advance of the combined armies and retreat of the French. Shortly before, on the 22d of July, Mayence, a position of the utmost importance on the Rhine, had yielded to the Prussians; and here also the enemy advanced into the Vosges mountains and toward the upper Rhine, the French receding gradually before them. The great inland city of Lyon was at the same time holding out against the central government with a firmness which as yet needed not the support of despair. In its resistance, and in the scarce smothered discontent of the southern provinces, lay the chief significance and utility of the British hold on Toulon. As a point upon which insurrection could repose, by which it could be supported from without, Toulon was invaluable; but with rebellion put down, surrounded by a hostile army and shut up to itself, the city would become a useless burden, unbearable from the demands for men which its extended lines would make. Had La Vendée rested upon a Toulon, the task of the republic would have been wellnigh hopeless.

Among these multiplied disasters, with the Sardinians also operating on the Alpine frontier and the Spaniards entering their country by the eastern Pyrenees, France was confronted in every quarter by disciplined armies to which she could as yet oppose only raw and ragged levies. She found her safety in the stern energy of a legislature which silenced faction by terror, in her central position, which of itself separated from one another many of the centres of disturbance, and in the military policy of the allies, which increased instead of seeking to diminish the dissemination of force which was to some extent unavoidable. The Spaniards could not combine with the Sardinians, Toulon could not help Lyon, La Vendée had to stand apart from all the others; but in the east it was possible for the Austrians, Prussians and British to direct against the forces standing between them and Paris a combination of effort which, in the then condition of the French army, might have been irresistible. Instead of so doing, the Austrians and British on the northeastern frontier decided, early in August, to cease their advance and to separate; the Austrians sitting down before Le Quesnoy, and the British undertaking to besiege the seaport of Dunkirk. On the Rhine, the mutual jealousies of Austria and Prussia, and the sluggish movements of routine generals, caused a similar failure to support each other, and a similar dilatory action.

The opportunities thus lost by the allies, and the time conceded to the French, were improved to the full by the Committee of Public Safety and by the commissioners sent from the Convention to the head-quarters of every army. Men, for the most part, without pity as without fear, their administration, stained as it was with blood, was effectual to the salvation of France. From the minister in the cabinet to the general in the field, and down to the raw recruit forced from his home, each man felt his life to depend upon his submission and his activity. In the imminent danger of the country and the hot haste of men who worked not only under urgent pressure, but often with a zeal as blindly ignorant as it was patriotic, many blunders and injustices were committed; but they attained the desired end of impressing the resistless energy of the Convention upon each unit of the masses it was wielding. If ever, for good or ill, men had the single eye, it was to be found in the French soldiers of 1793, as they starved and bled and died that the country might live. Given time,— and the allies gave it, — units animated by such a spirit, and driven forward by such an impetus as the Committee knew how to impart, were soon knit into an overpowering organism, as superior in temper as they were in numbers to the trained machines before them.

Where there was conscious life to feel enthusiasm or fear, the contagion of the rulers' temper caught; but the fiery spirit of the Convention could not possess the stately ships of war that floated in the ports of the republic, nor make them yield, to the yet unskilled hands of the new officers, the docile obedience which their old masters had commanded from those beautiful, delicately poised machines. It was a vain hope to conjure victory at sea by harsh decrees,[1] pitched in unison to the passions of the times, but addressed to men whose abilities did not respond to their own courage nor to the calls thus made upon them. To the inexperience of the officers was added the further difficulty of the indiscipline of the crews, that had increased to a ruinous extent during the four years' paralysis of the executive government. With the triumph of the Jacobin party had now come a unity which, however terrible, was efficient. In September, 1793, in the mutiny of the Brest fleet in Quiberon Bay, the seamen again prevailed over their officers, and even over the commissioner of the Convention; but it was the last flagrant outburst. The past weakness of other authorities had played into the hands of the Mountain; now that the latter was supreme, it resolutely enjoined and soon obtained submission. Years of insubordination and license had, however, sapped the organization and drill of the crews; and the

---

[1] For example, that any captain surrendering to a force less than double his own should suffer death; and if of a ship-of-the-line, to any number of enemies unless the vessel was actually sinking. The same fate awaited him who, in a fleet action, allowed the line to be broken. So also the decree not to give quarter. See Chevalier, Mar. Fran. sous la Rép., p. 128; Guérin, Hist. de la Mar., vol. iii. p. 395.

new officers were not the men to restore them. The Convention and its commissioners therefore lacked the proper instruments through which they could impart direction as well as energy to the movement of the fleet. Ships were there and guns, men also to handle the one and fight the other; but between these and the government was needed an adequate official staff, which no longer existed. The same administrative weakness that had allowed discipline to perish, had also entailed upon the naval arsenals the penury of resources that was felt everywhere in the land. From all these circumstances arose an impotence which caused the year 1793 to be barren of serious naval effort on the part of France.

Great Britain herself was in this first year of war unprepared to take a vigorous initiative. In 1792 she had in commission at home but twelve ships-of-the-line, and but sixteen thousand seamen were allowed for the fleet. Not till December 20, six weeks only before the declaration of war, did Parliament increase these to twenty-five thousand, a number less than one fourth that employed in the last year of the American war. In the Mediterranean and in the colonies there was not then present a single ship-of-the-line, properly so called. Fortunately, of the one hundred and thirteen actually borne on the roll of the line-of-battle as cruising ships, at the beginning of 1793, between eighty and ninety were reported in good condition, owing to the two alarms of war in 1790 and 1791; and provident administration had kept on hand in the British dock-yards the necessary equipments, which had disappeared from those of France. More difficulty was experienced in manning than in equipping; but at the end of 1793, there were eighty-five of the line actually in commission. From twenty to twenty-five were allotted to the Channel fleet, cruising from thence to Cape Finisterre, under the command of Lord Howe; a like number to the Mediterranean under Lord Hood; and from ten to twelve to the West Indies. A reserve of twenty-five ships remained in the Channel ports, Portsmouth and Plymouth, ready for sea, and employed, as occasion demanded, for convoys, to fill vacancies of disabled ships in the cruising fleets, or to strengthen the latter in case of special need.

The mobilization of the fleet, though energetic when once begun, was nevertheless tardy, and Great Britain had reason to be thankful that years of civil commotion and executive impotence had so greatly deteriorated the enemy's navy, and also, at a critical moment, had thrown so large a portion of it into her hands at Toulon. With a widely scattered empire, with numerous exposed and isolated points, with a smaller population and an army comparatively insignificant in numbers, war with France threw her — and must inevitably always throw her — at first upon the defensive, unless she could at once lay her grasp firmly upon some vital chord of the enemy's communications, and so force him to fight there. She could not assume the offensive by landing on French soil. No force she could send would be capable of resisting the numbers brought against it, much less of injuring the enemy; nor should the flattering hopes of such a force serving as a nucleus, round which to crystallize French rebellion, have been suffered to delude her, after the bitter deceptions of the recent American struggle. What hopes had not Great Britain then based upon old loyalty, and upon discontent with the new order of things! Yet, though such discontent undoubtedly existed — and that among men of her own race recently her subjects — the expeditions sent among them rallied no decisive following, kindled no fire of resistance. The natives of the soil, among whom such a force appears, either view it with jealous suspicion or expect it to do all the work; not unfrequently are both jealous and inactive. It is well, then, to give malcontents all the assistance they evidently require in material of war, to keep alive as a diversion every such focus of trouble, to secure wherever possible, as at Toulon, a fortified port by which to maintain free entrance for supplies to the country of the insurgents; but it is not safe to reckon on the hatred of the latter for their own countrymen outweighing their dislike for the foreigner. It is not good policy to send a force that, from its own numbers, is incapable of successful independent action, relying upon the support of the natives in a civil war. Such support can never relieve such expeditions from the necessity, common to all military advances, of guarding their communications while operating on their front; which is only another way of saying again that such expeditions, to be successful, must be capable of independent action adequate to the end proposed. Risings, such as occurred in many quarters of France in 1793, are useful diversions; but a diversion is only a subordinate part in the drama of war. It is either a deceit, whose success depends rather upon the incapacity of the opponent than upon its own merits; or it is an indirect use of forces which, from their character or position, cannot be made to conduce directly to the main effort of the enterprise in hand. To enlarge such diversions by bodies of troops which might be strengthening the armies on the central theatre of war is a mistake, which increases in ever greater proportion as the forces so diverted grow more numerous.[1]

[1] The Peninsular War, so brilliant in many of its features and in the end so triumphantly successful, has some analogies to the smaller expeditions here criticised, and may be thought to refute the remarks in the text. The analogy, however, fails in some very decisive points. The landing and base of operations at Lisbon were in the territory of an ally of long standing; the projected advance was into a country in general insurrection against *foreign* rule; above all, the position of Lisbon and its distance from France imposed upon the French, in case they advanced against it in great force as they did in 1810, a long and very difficult line of communication, while the British had the sea open. Toulon, in 1793, was disadvantageous to the British as compared with Lisbon in 1809, because farther from England and in France. For remarks on Peninsular War see note at end of this chapter.

Offensive action of this character was therefore forbidden to Great Britain. To use small bodies for it was impolitic; and large bodies she had not to send. To strike a direct blow at France, it was necessary to force her to come out of her ports and fight, and this was to be accomplished only by threatening some external interests of vital importance to her. Such interests of her own, however, France had not. Her merchant shipping, in peace, carried less than one third of her trade, and was at once hurried into her ports when war began. Her West India colonies had indeed been valuable, that of Haiti very much so; but the anarchy of the past four years had annihilated its prosperity. There remained only to strike at her communications, through neutrals, with the outside world, and this was to be accomplished by the same means as most surely conduced to the defence of all parts of the British empire, — by taking up positions off the French coast, and drawing the lines as closely as the exigencies of the sea and the law of nations would permit. If possible, in order to stop commerce by neutral vessels, a blockade of the French coast, similar to that of the Southern Confederacy by the United States, would have been the most suitable measure to adopt; but the conditions were very different. The weather on the coast of the Southern States is much more moderate; the heaviest gales blow along shore, whereas, in the Bay of Biscay, they blow dead on shore; and there was almost everywhere good, sometimes even sheltered, anchorage, which was not generally to be had on the coast of France. Finally, while steam certainly helps both parties, the inside and the out, the latter profits the more by it, for he can keep in with the shore to a degree, and for a length of time, impossible to the sailing ship; the necessity of gaining an offing *before* a gale comes on, and the helpless drifting during its continuance, not existing for the steamer.

Despite, therefore, the decisions of the courts, that a

blockade was not technically removed when the ships maintaining it were driven off by weather, a blockade of the whole French coast does not seem to have been contemplated by the British ministry. Its offensive measures against French commerce were consequently limited to the capture of property belonging to French subjects, wherever found afloat, even under neutral flags; and to the seizure of all contraband goods destined to France, to whomsoever they belonged. Both these were conceded to be within the rights of a belligerent by the United States and Great Britain; but the latter now endeavored to stretch the definition of contraband to a degree that would enable her to increase the pressure upon France. She claimed that naval stores were included in the category, — a position the more plausible at that time because, the French merchant ships being unable to go to sea, the stores must be for the navy, — and further, that provisions were so. Though these arguments were hotly contested by neutrals, the British navy was strong enough to override all remonstrances; and the dearth of provisions did force the Brest fleet out in 1794, and so led directly to the first great naval battle of the war.

It cannot be considered a satisfactory result, nor one evincing adequate preparation, that the Channel fleet, to which belonged the protection of the approaches to the Channel, — the great focus of British trade, — to which also was assigned the duty of watching Brest, the chief French arsenal on the Atlantic, did not get to sea till July 14, and then only to the number of fifteen ships-of-the-line. A French fleet of similar size had sailed from Brest six weeks before, on the 4th of June, and taken a position in Quiberon Bay, off the coast of La Vendée, to intercept assistance to the insurgents of that province. The command of the Channel fleet was given to Lord Howe, an officer of very high character for activity and enterprise in previous wars, but now in his sixty-eighth year. Age had in no sense dulled his courage, which was as steadfast and well-nigh as impassive as a rock, nor impaired his mental efficiency; but it may be permitted to think that time had exaggerated and hardened a certain formal, unbending precision of action which distinguished him, and that rigid uniformity of manœuvre had become exalted in his eyes from a means to an end. This quality, however, joined to an intimate knowledge of naval tactics, eminently fitted him for the hard and thankless task of forming into a well-drilled whole the scattered units of the fleet, which came to him unaccustomed, for the most part, to combined action.

Lord Howe brought also to his command a strong predisposition, closely allied with the methodical tendency just noted, to economize his fleet, by keeping it sparingly at sea and then chiefly for purposes of drill and manœuvre. Its preservation in good condition was in his eyes a consideration superior to taking up the best strategic position; and he steadily resisted the policy of continuous cruising before the ports whence the enemy must sail, alleging that the injury received in heavy winter weather, while the French lay at anchor inside, would keep the British force constantly inferior. The argument, though plausible and based on undoubted facts, does not justify the choice of a position clearly disadvantageous with reference to intercepting the enemy. War presents constantly a choice of difficulties, and when questions of material come in conflict with correct strategic disposition they must give way. The place for the British fleet, as reflection shows and experience proved, was before the hostile arsenals; or, allowably, if such a position could be found, in a port flanking the route along which the enemy must pass. For the Channel fleet no such port offered; and in keeping it at Spithead, far in rear of the French point of departure, Howe exposed himself to the embarrassment of their getting away while he remained in ignorance of the fact until too late to intercept, and with imperfect knowledge in what direction to follow. The only solution of the difficulty that the British government should have adopted was to maintain a reserve of ships, large enough to keep the necessary numbers of efficient vessels cruising in the proper station. The experience gained by such constant practice, moreover, improved the quality of the men more than it injured the ships. Historically, good men with poor ships are better than poor men with good ships; over and over again the French Revolution taught this lesson, which our own age, with its rage for the last new thing in material improvement, has largely dropped out of memory.

The embarrassment arising from the British fleet being in a Channel port received singular, perhaps even exceptional, illustration in the French expedition against Ireland in 1796. It has been said that that expedition would have succeeded in landing its force had it had steam; it would be more just to say that it would never have come so near succeeding had the British fleet been cruising in the station which strategic considerations would prescribe.[1] There is also a certain indefinable, but real, deterioration in the *morale* of a fleet habitually in port, compared with one habitually at sea; the habit of being on the alert and the habit of being at rest color the whole conduct of a military force. This was keenly realized by that great commander, Lord St. Vincent, and concurred with his correct strategic insight to fix his policy of close-watching the enemy's ports. "I will not lie here," he wrote from Lisbon in December, 1796, "a moment longer than is necessary to put us to rights; for you well know that inaction in the Tagus must make us all cowards."[2] Doubtless this practice of lying at anchor in the

---

[1] For the strategic discussion of the British naval dispositions on the occasion of the Irish Expedition of 1796, see Chapter XI.

[2] Brenton's Life of St. Vincent, vol. i. p. 295.

home ports contributed to the impunity with which French cruisers swept the approaches to the Channel during much of 1793 and 1794.

The policy of Lord Howe combined with the crippled state of the French navy to render the year 1793 barren of striking maritime events in the Atlantic. In the interior of France and on her frontiers, amid many disasters and bloody tyranny, the saving energy of the fierce revolutionary government was making steady headway against the unparalleled difficulties surrounding it. After the ill-judged separation of the British and Austrians in August, the latter had succeeded in reducing Le Quesnoy, which capitulated on the 11th of September; but there their successes ended. Carnot, recently made a member of the Committee of Public Safety and specially charged with the direction of the war, concerted an overwhelming attack upon the British before Dunkirk, and raised the siege on the 9th of September; then, by a similar concentration upon the Austrians, now engaged in besieging Maubeuge, he caused their defeat at the battle of Wattignies, October 16, and forced them to retreat from before the place. In the northeast, both the allies and the French went into winter quarters early in November; but the prestige of a resistance that grew every day more efficient remained with the latter. On the eastern frontier also, after protracted fighting, the year closed with substantial success for them. The Prussians of the allied forces in that quarter retreated from all their advanced positions into Mayence; the Austrians retired to the east bank of the Rhine. Each of the allies blamed the other for the unfortunate issue of the campaign; and the veteran Duke of Brunswick, commanding the Prussians, sent in his resignation accompanied with predictions of continued disaster. At the same time the king of Prussia began to manifest the vacillating and shameless policy which made his country the byword of Europe during

the next twelve years, and betrayed clearly his purpose
of forsaking the coalition he had been so forward in forming. On the Spanish frontiers, the fortune of war was
rather against the French, who were embarrassed by the
necessity of concentrating all the force possible upon the
siege of Toulon; the recovery of that port being urgently
required for the national honor, as well as for the maritime
interests of the republic in the Mediterranean.

It was, however, in restoring internal submission and
asserting the authority of the central government that
the most substantial results of 1793 were attained. The
resistance of the Vendeans, long successfully protracted
through the blunders and lack of unity among the republican leaders, began to yield, as more concentrated
effort was imparted by the reconstituted Committee of
Public Safety. After the battle of Cholet, October 16,
the insurgents, routed and in despair, determined to leave
their own country, cross the Loire, and march into Brittany. They traversed the latter province slowly, fighting
as they went, and on the 12th of November reached Gran-
ville on the Channel coast, where they hoped to open
communications with England. Their assault on the town
failed, and as the hoped-for ships did not arrive, they
started back for La Vendée; but as a coherent body they
never recrossed the Loire, and a pitched battle, fought
December 22, at Savenay, on the north bank, completed
their dispersion. The embers of the civil war continued
to burn in La Vendée and north of the Loire during the
following year; but as a general insurrection, wielding
large bodies of fighting men, it had ceased to be formidable to the nation and wrought its chief harm to the
province which supported it.

The great stronghold of resistance in the east, Lyon,
fell on the 9th of October. Despite the disaffection which
had existed in the south and east, the commissioners of
the government were able, without opposition, to collect

round the city a body of men sufficient, first, to cut off its communications with the surrounding country, and, finally, to carry the works commanding the place. A spirit of discontent so feeble as to acquiesce tamely in the reduction of one of its chief centres gave no hope of support to any efforts made through Toulon by the allied forces; and the capitulation of Lyon showed that the port was not worth the cost of keeping, and at the same time released a large number of men to give activity to the siege. Toward the end of November, over twenty-five thousand republican troops were collected round the place. On the night of the 16th of December, the forts on a promontory commanding the anchorage for fleets were carried by assault. A council of war among the allies decided that the ships could not remain, and that the garrison could not hold out with its communications to the sea cut off. It therefore determined to evacuate the place, and on the 19th the British and Spaniards departed. Before sailing, an attempt was made to destroy both the dock-yard and all the French ships that could not be taken away; but the danger threatening from the commanding positions that had now fallen to the enemy was so great, the necessity for quick departure so urgent, and so much had consequently to be done in a very limited time, that the proposed destruction was but imperfectly effected. Of twenty-seven French ships-of-the-line still in Toulon, nine were burned and three accompanied the retreat. The remaining fifteen constituted the nucleus of a powerful force, and most of them appear in the fleet which went with Bonaparte to Egypt and was there destroyed by Nelson in 1798.[1]

The loss of Toulon, after the extravagant hopes excited by its surrender, gave rise to much complaint in England.

---

[1] Of the thirty ships-of-the-line in Toulon when occupied by the allies, three or four had been sent to Rochefort without guns, carrying French prisoners whom it was inconvenient to keep.

It is improbable, however, that its retention, even if feasible, would have been beneficial. The expenditure of men and money necessary to hold a seaport surrounded by enemy's territory, and commanded by a long line of heights which had to be occupied, would have been out of proportion to any result likely to follow. The communications, being by sea only, would ultimately depend upon Great Britain as the power best able to insure them and most interested in a naval position; and the distance to England was great. The utter lack of dependence to be placed upon local discontent, as an element in the usefulness of Toulon to the allied cause, had been shown by the failure to support Lyon and by the tame submission made in the southern provinces to the petty Conventional army sent against them. The country, moreover, was in 1793 wasted by dearth; and had there been in Toulon an allied force large enough to advance, it would have had to depend absolutely upon immense accumulations of food in the port. So great was the scarcity, that the French at one time thought of abandoning the siege on that account. In short, Toulon had, for the British, the disadvantage of great distance, far greater than Gibraltar, without the latter's advantages of strategic position and easy defence; and its occupation by them would have caused jealousy among the Mediterranean powers and introduced more discord into a coalition already mutually suspicious.

From Toulon Hood retired to Hyères Bay, a sheltered roadstead a few miles east of Toulon, where the end of the year found him still lying. Lord Howe took the Channel fleet into port in the middle of December, and there remained until the following May. Thus ended the maritime year 1793.

NOTE (to page 98). The Peninsular War, in its inception, was justified, not because the odds were favorable, but because there was a "fighting" chance of great results; just as there was at Toulon, where the attempt failed. The distinguished historian of that war claims that the British wrought the work of deliverance; and, after making every allowance for national prejudice, which in his case was certainly not undiscriminating, the general failure, except where the British arms were felt, may be taken to establish a fact which the disorganized state of Spain herself would alone render probable. The course of war in the west of the peninsula, where the British were, shows conclusively the limitations imposed upon the military enterprises of a state having a relatively small army with a great navy. Having landed in April, 1809, Wellesley, notwithstanding his genius and brilliant successes, notwithstanding the state of the peninsula, and notwithstanding, also, the immense length and difficulty of the French lines of communication, was still, in March, 1811, shut up within the lines of Torres Vedras; that is, he was simply holding on at Lisbon, unable to keep the country against the French. In external appearance, the military situation was just the same as at the beginning. The reasons for holding on were the same in character as in 1809; but the chances of success had become distinctly greater, owing to political and economical considerations, and to the extreme care and foresight by which the British leader had made his position round Lisbon inexpugnable. Nevertheless, the retreat and ultimate disaster of the French were due to the military difficulties of their enterprise, well understood and carefully improved by Wellington, and to the unmeasured political combinations of the emperor, — not to the power of the British army in Portugal, which, though admirable in quality and leadership, was very inferior in numbers. In the last analysis it was the emperor's Continental System, directed against the Sea Power of England, which gave to the army of England in the Peninsula the opportunity by which alone the weaker force can profitably assume the offensive. It is not a lessening, but a heightening, of the merit of the great Englishman, to say that he had the genius to foresee that the opportunity, though distant, must come, and the courage to hold on till it came.

It is instructive to note the essential military resemblances between the British invasion of the Peninsula, which was finally crowned with success, and Napoleon's projected invasion of England, which came to nought. In the one case, a navy supreme on the ocean and a small military force; in the other, an unrivalled army, and a navy very inferior because of its quality. In each, the chances were largely against success. In each, the enterprise, strictly offensive in character by the inferior force, hinged upon the occurrence of the favorable opportunity, which it was the part of the of fence to contrive and of the defence to prevent. That there was, in both cases, a long waiting of nearly equal duration is a fortuitous coincidence; but the attitude of unremitting watchfulness and constant readiness, in a skilfully chosen position, is the distinctive characteristic imposed upon the inferior force which hopes to escape from a mere defensive posture, and, by striking a blow, to make itself felt in the lists of war. The opportunity never came to Napoleon, because the British leaders never took their eyes off his fleet, upon which his profound combinations depended as an arch upon its keystone. It came to Wellington because the emperor turned his attention from the Peninsula, of whose troubles he was weary, and opposed inadequate means and divided commands to a single alert enemy.

CHAPTER IV.

The West Indies, 1793-1810.

AMONG the leading objects contemplated by the British ministry in this war was the control of the East and West Indies, particularly of the latter, as among the most important sources as well as markets of British trade. In the present day, the value of the West India islands, and of all positions in the Caribbean Sea, is chiefly military or maritime; due less to the commerce they maintain than to their relations, as coaling ports or fortified stations, to the commercial routes passing through that region. It is scarcely necessary to add that whatever importance of this character they now possess will be vastly increased when an interoceanic canal is completed. During the French revolution, however, the islands had a great commercial value, and about one fourth the total amount of British commerce, both export and import, was done with them. This lucrative trade Great Britain had gathered into her hands, notwithstanding the fact that other nations owned the largest and richest of the islands, as well as those producing the best sugar and coffee. The commercial aptitudes of the British people, the superior quality of their manufactures, their extensive merchant shipping and ingenious trade regulations, conspired to make it the interest of the foreign colonists to trade with them, even when by so doing the laws of their own governments were defied; and to a great extent the British free ports engrossed the West Indian trade, as well as that to the adjacent South and Central American coasts, known as the Spanish Main.

In war, the control of a maritime region depends upon naval preponderance. When the opposing navies are of nearly equal strength, it is only by open battle, and by the reduction of one to a state of complete inferiority, that control can be asserted. If the region contested be small and compact, as, for instance, the immediate approaches to the English Channel, the preponderance of the fleet alone will determine the control and the safety of the national commerce within its limits; but if it be extensive, the distance between centres great, and the centres themselves weak, the same difficulties arise that are felt in maintaining order in a large and sparsely settled territory on land, as has till very lately been the case in our western Territories. In such circumstances the security of the traveller depends upon the government putting down nests of lawlessness, and establishing, at fitting stations, organized forces, that can by their activity insure reasonable safety in all directions.

In the War of the French Revolution, it soon, though not immediately, became evident, that the British navy could everywhere preponderate in force over its enemy; but it could not be omnipresent. The Caribbean Sea offered conditions peculiarly favorable to marauders, licensed or unlicensed; while its commercial value necessitated the preservation, and, as far as possible, the monopoly, of so fruitful a source of revenue. The presence of hostile cruisers not only inflicted direct loss, which was measured by their actual captures, but, beyond these, caused a great indirect injury by the friction and delays which the sense of insecurity always introduces into commercial transactions. The ideal aim of the British ministry was to banish the enemy's cruisers absolutely from the region; but, if this was impossible, very much might be effected by depriving them of every friendly anchorage to which they could repair to refit or take their prizes, — in short, by capturing all the French islands. This would put an end to the myriads of very small craft, which, being able to keep the sea but for a few days, depended absolutely upon a near base; and would greatly cripple the operations of the larger vessels by throwing them, for supplies and refuge, upon the United States, which then extended a benevolent partiality to French cruisers and their prizes.

The French islands had vividly reflected during the past four years the movements and passions of the mother-country; but only in Haiti did the turbulence, extending through all classes of society until it ended in a servile insurrection, result in destroying the control of the home government. The disorder, amounting often to anarchy, which prevailed through the French part of the island, somewhat simplified the problem before Great Britain. It was the only base of operations to the westward then available for French cruisers; and, though too large to admit the thought of conquest under the climatic conditions with the force that could be spared for such an attempt, it was possible, without serious opposition, to occupy many of the ports commanding the principal trade routes. Such occupation deprived the enemy of their use, converted them into harbors of refuge for British commerce, and made them centres for the operations of British cruisers. Unfortunately the government, misled by the representations of French planters who saw their property threatened with destruction, conceived the hope of an easy conquest, or rather transfer of allegiance in the colony. In pursuance of this idea, several places were taken into possession, being either delivered or captured with an ease that showed how readily, in the then disorganized state of the island, most of the sea-ports could have been secured; but the motive being conquest, and not merely maritime control, the choice of objectives was decided by political or military, instead of maritime, considerations. The expected local native support followed the general rule noted in the last chapter, and proved futile; while yellow fever wasted the troops condemned to excessive exertion and exposure in so sickly a clime.

Had simple maritime advantages guided the British counsels, it would have been sufficient to note that Jamaica was the great centre of British interests in the western Caribbean; that outward-bound ships, entering the Caribbean through the eastern, or Windward, Islands, ran down with the trade wind along the south side of Haiti, where were two harbors, Aux Cayes and Jacmel, favorable as bases for privateers; and that the homeward trade passed through the Windward Passage, between Haiti and Cuba, which was flanked by two Haitian ports, Tiburon to the south and Môle St. Nicolas on the north. These four were, therefore, particularly dangerous to British trade, and consequently, so far as position went, particularly advantageous if in British occupation. It is true that the topographical conditions of the ground about a sea-port in an enemy's country may make the occupation very hazardous, except by the employment of more men than can be had; as was the case at Môle St. Nicolas, where the fortifications of the place itself were commanded by the surrounding heights. Yet it remained in the hands of the British from 1793 to 1798; and it may be believed that their interests would have been well served by strongly garrisoning these ports.[1]

---

[1] The author is keenly aware that this policy, of garrisoning several somewhat separated ports, is seemingly inconsistent with sound military principles as to concentration, as well as with what he himself has elsewhere said about the proper dispositions for maintaining military control of a maritime region. It is, therefore, well to explain that those principles and dispositions apply where the belligerent navies are so far equal as to create a real struggle. This was not the case in the French Revolution. Great Britain had undisputed naval supremacy in the West Indies, and the question before her was, not to beat the enemy's fleet, but to secure her own commercial routes. To this end it was necessary to disseminate, not concentrate her ships, and to provide them with convenient centres of refuge and supply along the routes. The case was analogous to the police arrangements of a city. In ordinary quiet

At the least they would so be lost to French cruisers. Instead of this, with the idea of conquest, the wholly insufficient forces sent were pushed down to the bottom of the bight of Gonaives, and the southern coast of the island was left in the enemy's hands. It is not desirable to give in detail the history of these petty military operations, nor of the civil commotions with which they were connected. Suffice it to say, that the course of events finally threw the government into the hands of a pure negro, Toussaint L'Ouverture. He continued to hold it till the Peace of Amiens, in 1802; and with him the British, in 1798, concluded a treaty by which they finally abandoned the island. Though the scheme of conquest had failed, their interference had opened the country to British trade and caused the loss of Haiti to France, by contributing to the rise of Toussaint, the negro most capable of leading his race. He still professed fidelity to the mother-country, but he acted as one possessing independent power. The British, by the treaty, recognized the island as a neutral territory, and Toussaint, on his part, permitted them as well as neutral ships to trade with it.[1] He also prohibited the sailing of privateers from ports of Haiti, as they seriously interfered with its commerce.[2] Under his strong and wise administration the prosperity of the island greatly revived, though without attaining the proportions of former days.

The islands known as the Lesser Antilles, which extend from Porto Rico in a southerly direction to Trinidad and form the eastern boundary of the Caribbean, are, from their small size, much more dependent than is Haiti or Cuba upon the control of the sea. Though the aggregate commercial value of the whole group was far inferior to

times the police are distributed to cope with individual offenders; when a mob gathers and threatens the peace they are concentrated in large bodies.

[1] Macpherson's Annals of Commerce, vol. iv. p. 454.
[2] Ardouin, Études sur l'Hist. de Haiti, vol. iv. p. 45.

that of the French part alone of Haiti, they had a distinct
military advantage which made them, in that point of
view and to the West Indies, more important than Haiti
itself. They were to windward of the whole Caribbean
with reference to the trade winds, which blow unceasingly
from east to west; and hence were much nearer in time,
that supreme factor in military combinations, to the great
western islands than the latter were to them. The same
circumstance of the trade wind threw them across the
path of vessels bound from Europe to all parts of the
Caribbean, and thus facilitated the intercepting of supplies essential to the support and industries of the islands,
for much of which they depended upon the mother-coun-
tries.

The largest, by far, of these islands, Trinidad, belonged
in 1793 to Spain, at that time the ally of Great Britain.
Its nearness to the South American continent gave it, as
a distributing centre, marked commercial advantages, of
which the unenterprising Spaniards made little use; but,
as the trade winds blow from the north of east, it was not
favorably placed for a naval station. The two next in size,
and among the most fertile, Guadaloupe and Martinique,
were French islands. Being in the centre of the chain
and to leeward of none, except the outlying English Barbadoes, they were admirably situated for military control,
and the strategic advantage of position was supplemented
by the defensive strength of Fort Royal (now Fort de
France), the principal harbor of Martinique; which was
then, as it is now, by far the most powerful naval position
in the eastern Caribbean. Besides them, France owned
Santa Lucia, next south of Martinique, and Tobago. The
military importance of these islands, combined with a
distinct though minor commercial value, and the experience in past wars of the injury done to British commerce
by privateering based upon them, made their reduction
advisable to Great Britain; to whom belonged most of

the other Lesser Antilles as well as the trade of the Caribbean. One of the first acts of the war, before sending a vessel to the Mediterranean or increasing the Channel fleet, was to despatch a squadron of seven sail-of-the-line to the West Indies, where there were at that time, except a few small cruisers, but two fifty-gun ships, one at Jamaica and one to windward, — a thousand miles apart. No fact shows more strongly how unprepared Great Britain was for war than the naval destitution of this region, at a time when France had three or four ships-of-the-line continually in her colonies. This British squadron sailed under the command of Admiral Gardner on the 24th of March, 1793; and there was a strong expectation that Martinique and Guadaloupe, which had hoisted the old royal standard of France upon learning the deposition of Louis XVI., would place themselves under British protection. This hope was disappointed, they having already resumed their republican allegiance, and Gardner returned to England in the fall, leaving a part of his squadron behind.

It was then decided to reduce the French islands by force, and on the 26th of November Sir John Jervis, afterwards Earl St. Vincent, sailed with a small force of ships-of-war carrying seven thousand troops destined for this service. Reaching Barbadoes in January, the expedition appeared off Martinique on the 5th of February, 1794, and after a series of successful operations the island capitulated on the 22d of March. A detachment was next sent against Santa Lucia, which was surrendered on the 4th of April. On the 10th of the same month the combined naval and military forces anchored off Guadaloupe, and on the 20th this island, with its off-lying dependencies, Marie-Galante, Desirade and the Saints, also submitted. Tobago having been seized with slight resistance in April, 1793, Great Britain was now in possession of all the hostile Windward Islands, except the petty St. Martin, part of which belonged

to France. A considerable detachment of troops was next
sent to Mole St. Nicolas to assist the undertaking against
Haiti: a reduction of the force in the Windward Islands
which led to disastrous consequences, felt throughout the
war by the islands and commerce of Great Britain. For
on the 3d of June, when the British commanders had
departed leaving a garrison in Guadaloupe, there appeared
off the coast a division of ships, two being frigates and the
others transports, which had left France in April, before
the loss of the colonies was known. Landing without
opposition, they established themselves firmly and gained
possession of half the island before Jervis and Grey could
appear. The struggle continued with varying fortunes
during the following six months, but the British continually lost ground and wasted with yellow fever. This dire
disease told likewise severely on the new French arrivals,
but these found a native creole population of nearly six
thousand, the larger part of whom were faithful to the
republic; whereas their enemies, out of a total original
force of seven thousand, had, besides losses in battle and by
disease, been obliged to spare garrisons for the captured
islands and a detachment to Haiti. These causes alone
would seem sufficient to account for the recapture of the
island: but the utmost credit must at the same time be
allowed to the French officers concerned, and especially to
the commissioner of the Convention, Victor Hugues, who
accompanied the expedition. This man, who had at Rochefort filled the rôle of public accuser, which in Paris gained
for Fouquier Tinville a hideous immortality, seems to have
embodied in himself the best and worst features of the men
of the Terror, whose fate he escaped by leaving France
betimes. In his report to the Convention he boasted of
having put to death twelve hundred royalists in Guadaloupe. This horror partakes doubtless of the evident exaggerations discernible in the French accounts of a military
operation which, not so adorned, would have been brilliant

enough. Hugues's brutality is unquestionable, but to it he joined the vigor, audacity, and unscrupulous determination to succeed which carried the French armies to victory in all parts. The British were forced to evacuate their last port in Guadaloupe on the 10th of December, 1794.

Upon receiving news of Hugues's success the Directory hastened to send re-enforcements, and on the 6th of January, 1795, a number of ships-of-war and transports reached Guadaloupe and landed troops variously stated at fifteen to twenty-five hundred. Hugues, who had meantime organized a respectable territorial army, used the land and naval forces now at his disposal with great energy. Santa Lucia was retaken on the 19th of June, and insurrection fomented and maintained in Dominica, St. Vincent and Grenada, among the negroes, aborigines and old French inhabitants, to the great distress of the British. National vessels and privateers, having once more a secure base of operations, swarmed throughout the seas and inflicted great losses on the trade. All this disaster, which continued throughout the year, arose from not having quite enough men in Guadaloupe to put Hugues down before he had a foothold; and the British government was now compelled to send a far larger force to repair in part an evil, which a smaller number, at the proper moment, would have wholly prevented.

The disastrous result of the campaign of 1794 in Belgium and Holland, resulting in the conquest of the latter by the French, the overthrow of the House of Orange, and the alliance of Holland with France under a republican government, had both released the British troops employed on the Continent and thrown open the Dutch colonies to British attacks. Sir Ralph Abercromby, who had distinguished himself in the recent operations, was appointed to the command in the eastern Caribbean, and sixteen thousand troops were assigned to the expedition, which was to be convoyed by eight ships-of-the-line under Admiral Christian.

They were to have sailed in September for a campaign in the drier and cooler winter months; but the usual difficulty in moving large bodies, particularly of sailing ships, delayed their departure until the 15th of November. Two days later the Channel was swept by a gale of hurricane violence, which caused the loss of many ships and lives, and forced all that survived to return to Portsmouth, a single transport alone reaching the destination at Barbadoes. On the 3d of December a second start was made, but almost equal bad fortune was met. After battling the ocean for seven weeks, Christian and Abercromby returned to England with part of the convoy, the remainder finding their way by driblets to Barbadoes; several, however, were taken by Hugues's cruisers. Abercromby then took passage in a frigate, reaching the island on the 17th of March, 1796; and was followed by the admiral, who arrived on the 21st of April with a fleet of transports. Santa Lucia was at once attacked, and on the 25th of May the French garrison capitulated. On the 11th of June, St. Vincent, and a few days later Grenada, which were in possession rather of insurgents than of enemies, likewise submitted. Prior to the arrival of Admiral Christian, Abercromby had sent a detachment of twelve hundred men against the Dutch colonies on the mainland, Demerara, Essequibo, and Berbice, which surrendered without resistance in April and May, and were laid open to British trade.

Great Britain had now resumed tranquil possession of all the eastern islands, except Guadaloupe. The strong organization which this had received from Hugues, and the re-enforcements that had been thrown in, indicated that prolonged operations would be needed to effect its subdual. The sickly rainy season was at hand, during which also hurricanes prevail, so that all reasons combined to postpone the attempt to the healthier months,—a decision which was amply justified by the great mortality from yellow fever which ensued among the troops, despite all the immunity from exposure that care and the cessation of campaigning could give. By the time that operations could begin, Spain had declared war against Great Britain; and the prospect of easily seizing her large and far more valuable islands diverted attention from Guadaloupe. The latter continued throughout this and the following war, until 1810, a thorn in the side of British trade. The recapture of Guadaloupe by the French, and the consequent evils, remain a pregnant warning against the folly of sending a boy to do a man's work; but underlying that miscalculation appears to have been the fatal error of relying upon local support to troops inadequate by themselves to the task before them. Desirous of doing many things at once, the British government easily accepted the assurances of a few royalists, as to the political dispositions of a most excitable and changeable race and the re-enforcements that could be raised among them. It was an exact repetition of the blunder which led to the invasion of the Southern colonies during the American Revolution; and the gist of the mistake is in the dependence upon unorganized forces to supplement the weakness of the organized force, which is not by itself alone sufficient to its undertaking.

It will not be denied that at times a diversion under such conditions may be attempted, if it does not take away force needed for serious enterprises. Upon this ground may perhaps be justified the attempted French invasion of Ireland in December, 1796, which, though on a somewhat larger scale, essentially resembled the expedition of Jervis and Grey against the West Indies. It also depended upon a local rising in favor of an insufficient force, upon the support of practically unorganized masses without military antecedents; but it was undertaken at a period when the tide of affairs elsewhere was running strongly in favor of France, and, whatever hopes may have been entertained of possible ultimate results, was essentially a diversion. The immediate aim was not a direct gain to France, but an

indirect advantage, by accumulating embarrassments for
Great Britain. A state entirely inferior at sea could not
count upon lasting military control of a large island with
an alien population; but it could hope that the insurrection
of Ireland, concurring with disaster upon the Continent,
might force a disadvantageous peace upon the arch enemy.
The conquest of the smaller Antilles, on the contrary, was
not properly a diversion, but an object of real importance
to a great British interest. It was feasible for the greater
naval power to take and hold them, being small; and their
tenure, by relieving the navy of part of its work, would
have facilitated the protection of Jamaica and its trade, as
well as the general control of the western Caribbean.
Haiti was too large and too populated for conquest; but
its power for injury could have been confronted with more
substantial force had Guadaloupe remained a British
garrison.

The alliance of Spain and Holland with France much
increased the difficulties of Great Britain, by throwing
open their colonial ports to French privateers. The extensive
sea-coasts of Cuba and Haiti became alive with them.
In 1807 it was estimated that there were from two to three
hundred depending upon these two islands, and unfitted,
from their size, to go far from them.[1] The number testifies
to the extent and value of British trade in that sea,
although the privateer did not confine his depredations to
the enemy, but preyed lawlessly on neutrals as well. The
same authority illustrates the annihilation of French and
Spanish commerce by stating that not more than two or
three British privateers were sailing from Jamaica.

General Abercromby went for a short time to Europe in
the fall of 1796. Upon his return a strong military and
naval expedition was sent against Trinidad, but did not
meet the resistance expected from the size and importance
of the island. It capitulated on the second day, February

---

[1] Account of Jamaica, London, 1808, pp. 51, 52.

18, 1797, and with it the Spaniards lost four ships-of-the-line. Thence Abercromby moved, in April, against Porto Rico; but upon reconnoitring, the defences were found too strong, and the troops were re-embarked after losing two hundred men. This ended the colonial expeditions in the West Indies for the first war. Quiet possession was taken of the Dutch colonies of Surinam and Curaçoa in 1799 and 1800; and in 1801, when Sweden and Denmark became involved in hostilities with Great Britain, their West India islands were also given up without resistance, but no further fighting took place.

NOTE. As it does not enter into the author's plan to give in detail the naval history after Trafalgar, it may be well to state here, in brief, the subsequent events in the West Indies. At the Peace of Amiens in 1801, Great Britain restored all her West India conquests except the Spanish Trinidad. When war broke out again in 1803, Tobago, Santa Lucia, Demerara, Essequibo, and Berbice were at once seized without difficulty, as was Surinam in 1804. There matters rested till 1807, when Curaçoa and the Danish islands fell, followed in 1809 by Martinique, and in 1810 by Guadaloupe. Spain having become again the ally of Great Britain in 1808, the latter had now no open enemy in the Caribbean; but the long habits of lawlessness left numerous pirates infesting Cuba, whom the weak Spanish government failed to control.

CHAPTER V.

The Naval Campaign of May, 1794, and Battle of the First of June.

THE pressure of the allied armies upon all her frontiers, combined with the British mastery of the sea, had thrown France largely upon her own resources during the year 1793; while the distracted condition of the country and a bad harvest had united to cause a scarcity of bread-stuffs, which threatened a famine, with all its consequences of sufferings to the army and the people, and inevitable increase of disturbance and sedition.

The eyes of the government had therefore turned beyond the sea to the United States, and its representatives there had been directed to accumulate a quantity of provisions to be shipped to France. It was intended to despatch these in a great convoy, to be protected on the voyage by a force of ships-of-war; while its approach to the shores of Europe would be covered by a sortie of the great fleet from Brest and Rochefort, to occupy the attention of, and, if necessary, forcibly to contest the control of the sea with, the British navy. Experience had not yet corrected the sanguine confidence of the republican government, based upon the wordy enthusiasm of the crews, nor taught it that, with the departure of the trained officers and the spread of license among the men, the navy had ceased to be the strong power which had faced Great Britain with success in the war of the American Revolution. The very measures which had most contributed to destroy its efficiency became, in the excitement and ignorance of the times, the sure gage of victory.

The convoying squadron of two ships-of-the-line and three smaller vessels sailed from Brest for the United States in December, 1793, under the command of Rear-Admiral Van Stabel, an active and judicious officer. On the 12th of February it anchored in Chesapeake Bay, and sailed again for France on the 11th of April. The merchant ships under its charge numbered one hundred and thirty,[1] among them being many laden with produce from the French West India islands, which, not venturing to make the passage home direct and unattended, for fear of British cruisers, had collected at Hampton Roads to await the time of sailing. It seems somewhat remarkable that the British government, which was fairly well informed as to the designs of the French, should not have attempted to intercept the convoy at its port of departure. That is the point at which a great maritime expedition, whether purely military or otherwise, can usually be most effectually watched; and in this case the more so, because, if the convoy had eluded the blockading squadron, the latter, few in number and homogeneous, could easily have outstripped the unwieldy multitude and again awaited it off its port of arrival. The success of this mass of merchantmen in escaping the numerous enemies that attended it off the coast of France is a striking illustration of the uncertainties of commerce-destroying, and of the chances that favor the safe arrival of a body of ships when the enemy is in doubt as to their exact destination.

The French minister to the United States, M. Genêt, had written home that he would forward a part of the convoy, under the care of two small ships of war, as soon as possible. With the idea that these might have sailed before Van Stabel reached America, a force of five ships-of-the-line with some lighter vessels was directed to protect their arrival. This squadron accordingly sailed from Brest under the command of Rear-Admiral Nielly, on the

---

[1] Troude, Bat. Nav., vol. ii. p. 326.

10th of April.[1] It had been preceded by a light division, whose mission was to meet the convoy and inform the officer in charge that Nielly would await him a hundred leagues west of Belle-Isle.

Later news corrected the expectations based upon Genêt's first despatches, and as the close approach of summer made it more easy for the British fleet to maintain its position in the Bay of Biscay, and consequently increased the dangers through which the convoy must pass, the French government determined to send out all the available ships in Brest. On the 16th of May the great fleet, comprising twenty-five ships-of-the-line, one of which carried one hundred and twenty guns and three others one hundred and ten, sailed under the command of Rear-Admiral Villaret Joyeuse. A representative of the National Convention, charged with duties resembling those of the representatives present with the armies in the field, embarked on board the flag-ship, "La Montagne." This magnificent vessel, called under the monarchy the "États de Bourgogne," now bore the name of the terrible party dominant in the National Convention. These were still the days of the Terror, and Robespierre had yet two months to live when the fleet sailed from Brest. The admiral's orders were to cruise in the same station that had already been assigned to Nielly, with whom he was expected to form a junction, and to protect the approach of the convoy at all hazards, but not to fight unless essential to secure that end, to which all other objects were subordinated. The time of waiting was to be utilized for fleet manœuvres, in which the representative and admiral had too much reason to fear that the captains were unskilled.

The anxiety of the French government about the convoy, and the embarrassment which would be caused by its loss, were obvious incentives to the British authorities

---

[1] Troude, Bat. Nav., vol. ii. p. 327. James says May 6.

to do all in their power to intercept it. The Channel fleet, so called from the ports upon which its operations were based, had returned from its cruises of the previous year in December, and had since then remained at anchor, repairing and refitting for the next year's work. Its commander, Lord Howe, as has before been said,[1] was averse from keeping the sea in winter with the heavy ships. According to his system of warfare, the fleet should be anchored at some convenient point on the Channel coast, and depend upon frigates stationed before the French ports to bring it word of the enemy's movements. Had, however, the expected convoy in 1794 sailed from America as soon as it was expected to do, it would have reached its own ports before the British had left their anchors.

On the 2d of May the Channel fleet, numbering thirty-four ships-of-the-line and attended by fifteen frigates and smaller ships-of-war, sailed from Spithead. It had under its charge one hundred and forty-eight sail of merchantmen, bound to Newfoundland and to the East and West Indies. Upon arriving two days later off the Lizard, a promontory near the south-west extremity of England and a hundred miles due north of the Island of Ushant, Howe detached eight ships-of-the-line to accompany the convoy to the latitude of Cape Finisterre, on the north-west coast of Spain. After performing this service, six, under Admiral Montagu, were to cruise between Cape Ortegal and the latitude of Belle-Isle, to intercept the convoy from America. The width, over two hundred miles, of the belt of ocean to be covered by these six ships with their accompanying frigates, taken in connection with the chances which night and fog might give the French convoy for passing unobserved, illustrates the comparative disadvantages of lying in wait at the supposed point of arrival, instead of at the known port of departure, for a body of vessels whose precise destination is in doubt.

[1] See *ante* p. 101.

Howe, with the twenty-six ships remaining to him, steered directly for Ushant, reconnoitred Brest, and, having ascertained that the bulk of the French fleet was still in port, proceeded to cruise in the Bay of Biscay, moving backward and forward across the probable track of the expected convoy. On the 19th of May he again looked into Brest, and found that the French had sailed. The same evening a frigate from Montagu joined him, requesting a re-enforcement, as the rear-admiral had learned from a captured vessel that Nielly's squadron was at sea, and that Van Stabel's force numbered four of the line. He consequently anticipated the possibility of falling in with nine ships-of-the-line, which would be too large a number for his own six to meet. As the frigate, of course, brought word where Montagu was to be found, Howe, knowing that the main French fleet was out, steered at once to join his subordinate; but ascertaining later, from passing vessels, that Villaret had been seen in a position and heading a course which would take him well clear of Montagu, he abandoned this purpose and went directly in pursuit of the enemy. The latter, by the information he received, numbered twenty-six ships-of-the-line, precisely equalling his own fleet.

A week, however, was to elapse before he found the French. On the morning of the 28th of May, the wind being then south by west, the lookout frigates signalled a strange fleet to windward. It proved to be that of Villaret, then steering north-north-east, nearly before the wind, in three columns. At the time of this meeting, Howe was running back to the eastward with a fair wind, having actually gone a hundred miles west of the enemy's rendezvous without finding him. The French admiral stood on until he could recognize the British, and then hauled to the wind, intending to form his line-of-battle on the port tack, heading west or a little south of it. The inexperience of the captains, of whom a large proportion had no naval training and had never commanded ships in a fleet, led to a long delay and a poor formation. Lord Howe, on the contrary, soon had his fleet in manageable condition, pressing to windward in two columns on the port tack, and with a flying squadron of four fast and handy seventy-four-gun ships well to the windward of the main body. The British fleet was now steering the same course as the French, to leeward, or north, of it, and at noon the distance between the main bodies was from nine to ten miles. The place of this first meeting was about four hundred miles west (and a little south) of the island of Ushant. There was a strong breeze and a moderately heavy sea.

Villaret soon found that the slowness of the formation, to facilitate which many of his ships had to heave-to,[1] was causing the line to set gradually to leeward, toward the British. Four also of his fleet were separated from the main body, being some distance astern and to windward, two of them slightly disabled. To approach these, and at the same time keep the advantage of the wind, he determined to put the fleet on the other tack. At ten minutes before two in the afternoon the French began tacking in succession, and by quarter past three were all on the starboard tack, heading now east-south-east toward the separated ships. Meantime, the British flying squadron, acting independently of the main body, but under orders to attack the enemy's rear, kept forcing to windward, and at a little after three o'clock one of them was able to open fire, just before the rear French ships went about. The main body tacked between three and four o'clock, and being now on the same course as the French, east-south-east, but entirely out of cannon-shot, carried a press of sail to overtake them.

[1] A ship is said to be hove-to when some of the sails are so arranged as to move her ahead and others to force her astern, — the result being that she remains nearly in the same spot, but drifts slowly to leeward.

The ships of the flying squadron, being handled for the most part with vigor and judgment, fulfilled Howe's purpose of making an impression upon the *rear* of the enemy's column. As soon as the attack became pronounced, one of the French one-hundred-and-ten-gun ships, the "Révolutionnaire," took the extreme rear, and upon her fell the brunt of the action, which lasted this day until after ten P. M.; daylight, at that time of the year and in that latitude, continuing till nearly then. The British advanced ships were joined after some time by two more from the main body, so that the "Révolutionnaire" had to encounter, first and last, some half-dozen hostile seventy-fours. No diagram of this day's fighting need be given. The reader has only to picture a long column of ships steering to the southward and eastward, its rear harassed by the repeated but irregular attacks of a superior hostile detachment.

The "Révolutionnaire" was nobly fought; and the concentration upon her, while eminently judicious, served to bring out vividly the advantage, which should never be forgotten, of one heavy ship over several smaller, even though the force of the latter may, in the aggregate, be much superior. The attacks this day made upon her were, from the nature of the case, not simultaneous. They resembled one of those elaborately combined movements in land warfare, whereby several separate columns are intended to be brought at the same time to the same point, but actually arrive one by one and are beaten off in detail. The result in the present instance was somewhat more fortunate. As darkness fell, Howe called off all but two of the assailants,— one having already been driven off,— in order to form his line for the night. The "Révolutionnaire" remained in hot action with a small seventy-four, the "Audacious," alone; for the comrade of the latter took no share. At ten P. M., having lost her captain and sixty-two men killed and eighty-six

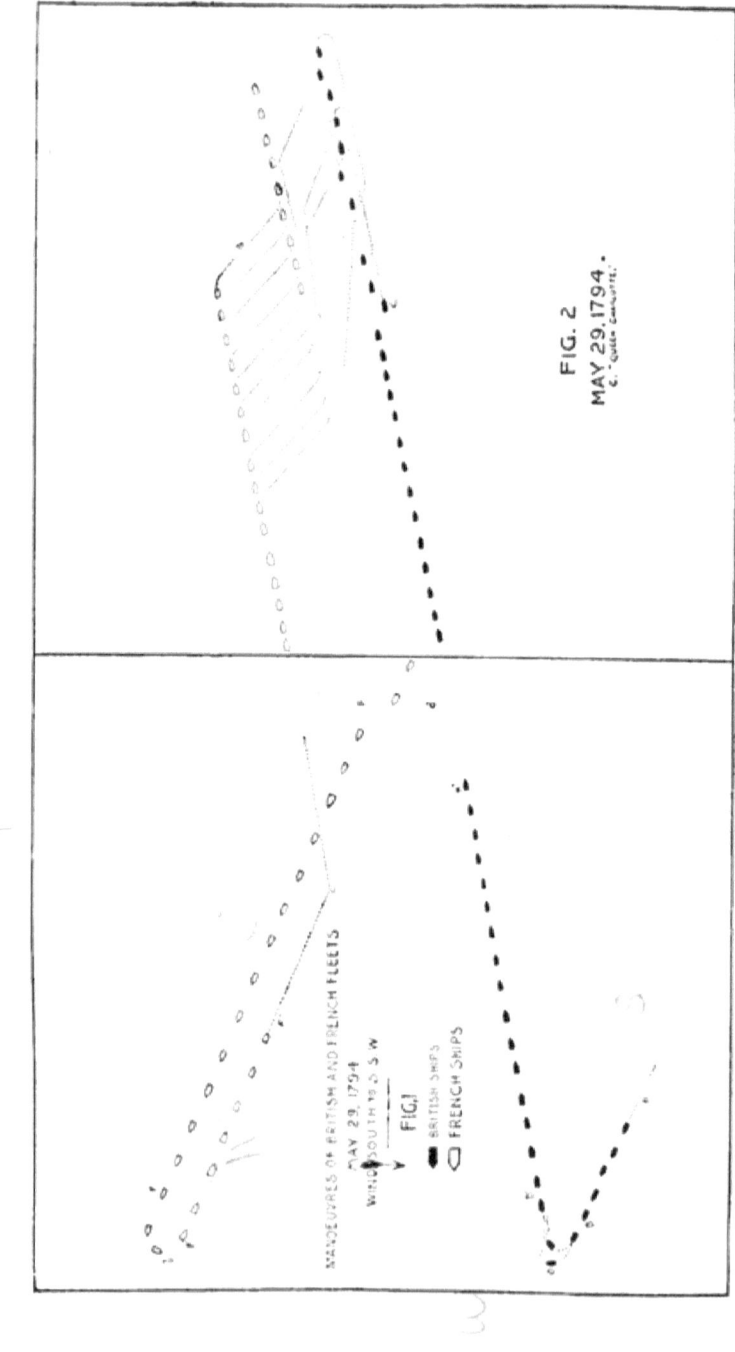

wounded, and with her mizzen-mast shot away, she wore out of action under charge of her fourth lieutenant, the three seniors having been killed or seriously hurt. Covered by the dark she passed to the northward, astern of the British fleet, her remaining masts falling soon after. The "Audacious" was so badly crippled that it took her long to get clear of the French line, and she was unable to rejoin her own that night. The next morning, finding herself isolated and in presence of some enemy's ships, she was forced to run before the wind and was permanently separated from the fleet. The two opponents passed within sight of each other the following day, but they were in no condition to resume the encounter, and both reached port without further injury.

During the short summer night the two fleets continued to run on parallel lines (May 29, Fig. 1. BB, FF,) southeast by east, being about three miles apart, the French bearing south from the British. The latter appear to have gained somewhat upon their less practised adversaries, so that at six o'clock Howe, ever intent upon getting to windward and thereby obtaining the opportunity to attack, directed his fleet to tack in succession (a), expecting that the van would on the new course pass near enough to the enemy's rear to exchange shots. After the evolution, the British were in column steering west (B'B'), the French still south-east by east. Villaret, seeing his rear threatened, wore his fleet in succession at quarter before eight (b), the van ships running down north-west by west (F'F') parallel to their previous course, toward the rear of their own column; upon reaching which the leading ship hauled to the wind again (c), followed by each of the others in order. These two manœuvres brought both fleets once more heading in the same direction, following parallel courses and abreast each other; the French still to windward, but having lost much of the distance which separated them from their enemies. A few shots had been

VOL. I.—9

exchanged, as Howe expected, between the British van and
the French rear as they passed on opposite tacks (Fig. 1, d).

Toward ten o'clock the French head ships ran down
toward the British van and opened fire at long range,
their centre and rear keeping out of action (May 29,
Fig. 2). The leading British ship, "Cæsar," failed to carry
sail enough, though repeatedly signalled to make more;
and in consequence those astern of her had also to shorten
sail, the flag-ship "Queen Charlotte" in particular being
forced to leeward by the necessity of backing a topsail to
keep in her station. At noon there was a brisk cannonade
between the two vans. Dissatisfied with this partial engagement, which, by crippling some of his ships, might put
out of his power to reach the enemy, Howe at noon signalled to tack again in succession, and to pass through the
French line. The "Cæsar," which should have begun the
manœuvre, made no reply, and it was necessary to repeat
the order. Shortly before one o'clock she wore instead of
tacking. The ships between her and the admiral also went
about; but none, save the "Queen," of ninety-eight guns,
second in the order, appears to have reached the hostile
line, except at its extreme rear. She passed alone, and
for a long time unsupported, along a considerable portion
of the enemy's order, which had now been re-established
by the centre and rear bearing down to support the van
(Fig. 2, a); but she was unable to break through, owing at
first to the closeness of the French ships to each other, and
afterwards to the injuries received from their successive
broadsides. The "Cæsar" kept so far from the wind as
to neutralize the admiral's purpose; and of the other van
ships all went to leeward of the French line, none breaking
through. So far, therefore, the general result was only to
bring confusion into the British order without attaining
the end which Howe desired. He therefore determined
to set the example, directed the flag-ship to be tacked
(Fig. 2, b), and stood under a press of sail toward the

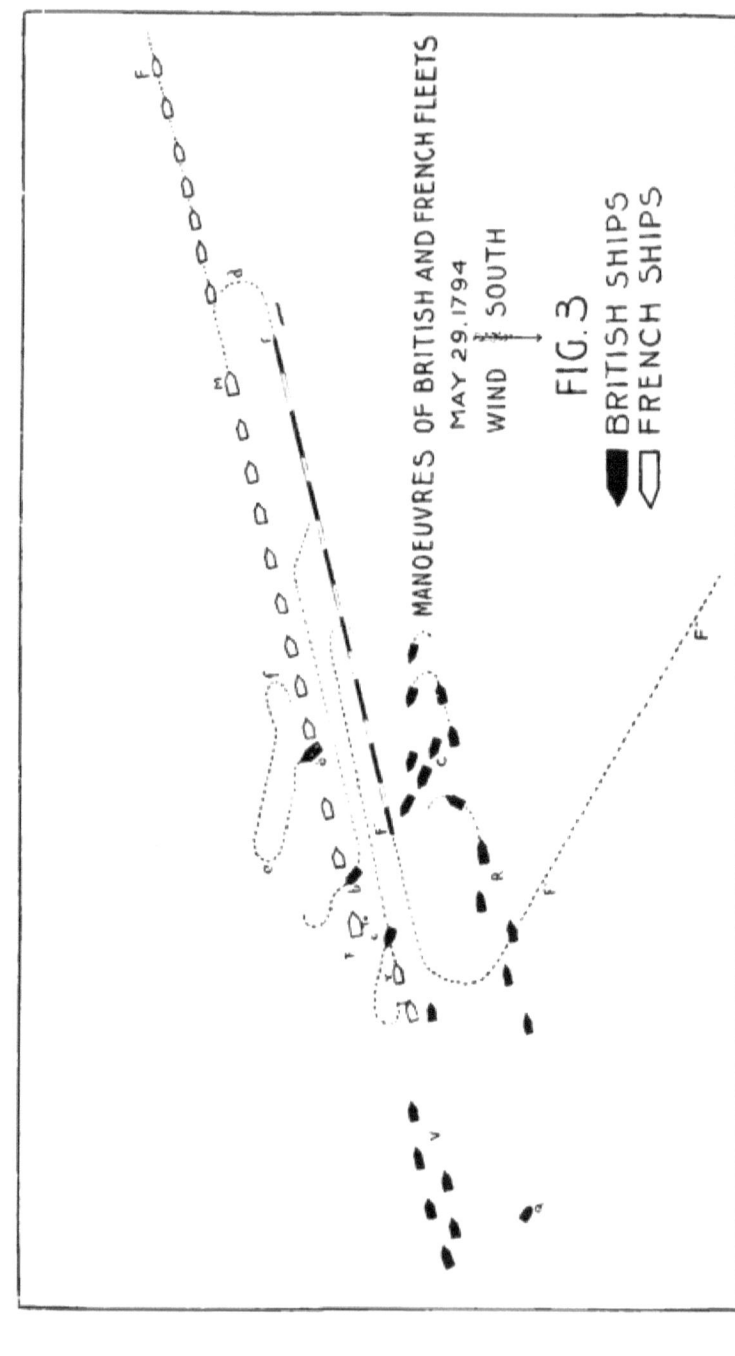

French line, closely followed by two others, the next ahead and next astern of him. The "Queen Charlotte," which had been tenth in the British column, reached the enemy at a point not far in rear of Villaret's flag-ship, and ran along the line (Fig. 3) till she came abreast of the sixth ship from the rear, astern of which she luffed through and gained to windward of the French (Fig. 3, a). One of her two followers passed through the second interval (b) behind that pierced by herself, and the other through the next (c), — that is, between the third and second vessel from the enemy's rear. The two remaining French ships, the "Indomptable" (I), of eighty guns, and the "Tyrannicide" (T), of seventy-four, were not only far astern but to leeward of their line. They were therefore easily to be reached by several of the British, who gradually encircled them.

With his rear thus for the third time threatened, and much more seriously than before, Villaret again made signal to wear in succession. The French van had by now become much separated from the rest of the fleet, and the leading ship was too disabled to go about. No other taking the initiative, the admiral, like Howe, was forced to set the example. The "Montagne" (M) wore out of line (d), and led down toward the two surrounded ships, with a signal flying to follow and form in her wake (F' F') without regard to usual station. This movement of Villaret not only tended to release the "Indomptable" and "Tyrannicide," but also threatened the "Queen" (Q), which had fallen to leeward disabled. Howe, after getting to windward and tacking (e), had endeavored to reach the "Terrible," of one hundred and ten guns, carrying the flag of the admiral commanding the French rear, which had been astern of the point at which the "Queen Charlotte" broke the line; but, while the "Charlotte" was putting about, the "Terrible" (Te) passed ahead and reached the centre of Villaret's column before Howe's ship could come up with her. For every reason, therefore, but especially for the safety of the "Queen," it became imperative for the British admiral to reverse his course. He therefore wore (f), gathering round him by signal all vessels within reach, and again stood east, toward the threatened ships of the two parties, — running in a column parallel to, but to windward of, that of the French admiral.

The "Queen," though much crippled, had, with her head to the eastward, passed astern of the two threatened French ships. These had suffered from the engagement, in passing, with the British van a few hours before, as well as with the flying squadron on the previous day; and the injuries then received had doubtless contributed to place them in the exposed and dangerous position they now occupied. The "Leviathan," seventy-four, attacked them to windward, the "Orion," of the same class, to leeward, and the latter was soon after re-enforced and replaced by the "Barfleur," of ninety-eight guns. No particular statement is given in the British narratives of other ships attacking these two, but several of those astern of the "Queen Charlotte," which could have reached no other of the French, lost killed and wounded, and it is probable that these shared in this encounter. The French accounts speak of their two vessels as "surrounded;" and Villaret wrote that their resistance "should immortalize their captains, Dordelin and Lamesle." They came out of the engagement of the 29th of May with only their lower masts standing; and the heavier of the two, the "Indomptable," was in such condition that Villaret thought necessary to send her to Brest that night, escorted by another of his fleet, which was thus dwindling piece-meal.

For the moment, however, the French admiral's manœuvre, well conceived and gallantly executed, rescued the endangered ships. The "Queen Charlotte" and her immediate supporters, after first tacking, had barely reached the rear of the French. As the latter continued to stand on, it was of course impossible for all the fifteen ships behind the British admiral to come up with them at once. In fact, the failure of the van to do its whole duty, combined with the remote position of the rear, — increased probably by the straggling usually to be observed at the tail of long columns, — had resulted in throwing the British order into confusion. "As the ships arrived," wrote Lord Howe in his journal, "they came up so crowded together as afforded an opportunity for the enemy to have fired upon them with great advantage." (Fig. 3, C, R.) "The British line was completely deformed," states one French authority. But, though disordered, they formed a large and dangerous body, all within supporting distance, — they had on their side the prestige of an indisputable, though partial, success, — they were flushed with victory, and it would appear that the French van had not yet come up. Villaret therefore contented himself with carrying off his rescued ships, with which and with the rest of his fleet he stood away to the northwest.

It is desirable to sum up the result of these two days of partial encounters, as an important factor in the discussion of the campaign as a whole, which must shortly follow. On the morning of May 28, the French numbered twenty-six ships-of-the-line [1] and were, when they first formed line, from ten to twelve miles to windward of the British, also numbering twenty-six. On the evening of May 29, in consequence of Howe's various movements and the course to which Villaret was by them constrained, — for he acted purely on the defensive and had to conform to the initiative of the enemy, — the French fleet was to leeward of the British. As Howe had succeeded within so short a time in forcing action from to leeward, there was every

[1] Villaret had been joined on the 19th of May by a ship-of-the-line, which had separated from Nielly's squadron; this raised his force from twenty-five to twenty-six.

reason to apprehend that from the windward position — decidedly the more favorable upon the whole, though not without its drawbacks — he would be able to compel a decisive battle, which the French naval policy proscribed generally, and in the present case particularly. Besides this adverse change of circumstance, the balance of loss was still more against the French. On the first day the "Révolutionnaire" on one side and the "Audacious" on the other had been compelled to quit their fleets; but the force of the latter was not over two thirds that of the former. By the action of the 29th the "Indomptable," of eighty guns, was driven from the French fleet, and the admiral thought necessary to send with her a seventy-four and a frigate. The "Tyrannicide," seventy-four, had lost all her upper masts; she had consequently to be towed by one of her consorts through the next two days and in the battle of the First of June. If Villaret had had any expectation of escaping Howe's pursuit, the presence of this disabled ship would have destroyed it, unless he was willing to abandon her. Besides the mishaps already stated, the leading ship, "Montagnard," had been so much injured in the early part of the engagement that she could not go about. Continuing to stand west, while the body of the fleet was running east to the aid of the "Indomptable" and "Tyrannicide," this ship separated from her consorts and was not able to regain them. To this loss of four ships actually gone, and one permanently crippled, may be added that of the "Audacieux," one of Nielly's squadron, which joined on the morning of the 29th, but was immediately detached to seek and protect the "Révolutionnaire." On the other hand, the British had by no means escaped unscathed; but on the morning of the 30th, in reply to an interrogatory signal from the admiral, they all reported readiness to renew the action, except one, the "Cæsar," which was not among the most injured. This ship, however, did not leave the fleet, and was in her station in the battle of the First.

The merit of Howe's conduct upon these two days does not, however, depend merely upon the issue, though fortunate. By persistent attacks, frequently renewed upon the same and most vulnerable part of the French order, he had in effect brought to bear a large part of his own fleet upon a relatively small number of the enemy, the result being a concentration of injury which compelled the damaged ships to leave the field. At the same time the direction of the attack forced the French admiral either to abandon the endangered vessels, or step by step to yield the advantage of the wind until it was finally wrested from him altogether. By sheer tactical skill, combined with a fine display of personal conduct, Howe had won a marked numerical preponderance for the decisive action, which he now had good reason to expect from the advantageous position likewise secured. Unfortunately, the tactical gain was soon neutralized by the strategic mistake which left Montagu's squadron unavailable on the day of battle.

Towards the close of the day the weather grew thick, and so continued, with short intervals of clearing, for the next thirty-six hours. At half-past seven the body of the French bore from the British flag-ship north-west, distant nine or ten miles; both fleets standing very slowly to the westward and a little northerly, with wind from the southward and westward. During most of the 30th, none of the British fleet could be seen from the flag-ship, but they all, as well as the French, kept together. On that day also, by a piece of great good fortune considering the state of the weather, Admiral Nielly joined Villaret with the three ships still under his command, as did also another seventy-four belonging to the Cancale squadron. These four fresh ships exactly replaced the four disabled ones that had parted company, and again made the French twenty-six to Howe's twenty-five.

About ten o'clock in the morning of May 31st, the fog lifted for a moment, allowing Howe to count twenty-seven sail of his ships and frigates; and, after again shutting down for a couple of hours, it finally dispersed shortly after noon. The French were then seen bearing from west to north-west. The British made sail in chase and by six P.M. had approached to within about three miles. They were not, however, able to reach the position Howe wished — abreast the enemy — early enough to permit the intended general engagement, unless by a night action; which for more than one reason the admiral was not willing to undertake. He therefore hauled again to the wind, heading to the westward in order of battle. The French had formed on a parallel line and were running in the same direction. During the night both fleets carried all the sail their masts would stand. In the morning the French, thanks to the better sailing of their vessels, were found to have gained somewhat on their enemies, but not sufficiently to avoid or postpone the battle, which they had been directed if possible to shun. Villaret therefore formed his fleet in close order, and stood on slowly under short canvas, which at once allowed irregularities in the order to be more easily corrected and also left the crews free to devote themselves exclusively to fighting the ships. Howe, by carrying sail, was thus able to choose his position prior to bearing down. Having reached it and formed his line, the French being now hove-to to await the attack, the British fleet was also hove-to, and the crews went to breakfast. At twelve minutes past eight it again filled-away by signal, and stood slowly down for the enemy (June 1, Fig. 1). The intention being to attack along the whole line, ship to ship, advantage was taken of this measured approach to change the place of the three-decked ships in the order, so that they should be opposed to the heaviest of the French. Lord Howe, who in the matter of drill was something of a precisian, is said to have rectified the alignment of his fleet more than once as it stood down; and, unless some such delay took place, it is difficult to reconcile the rate of

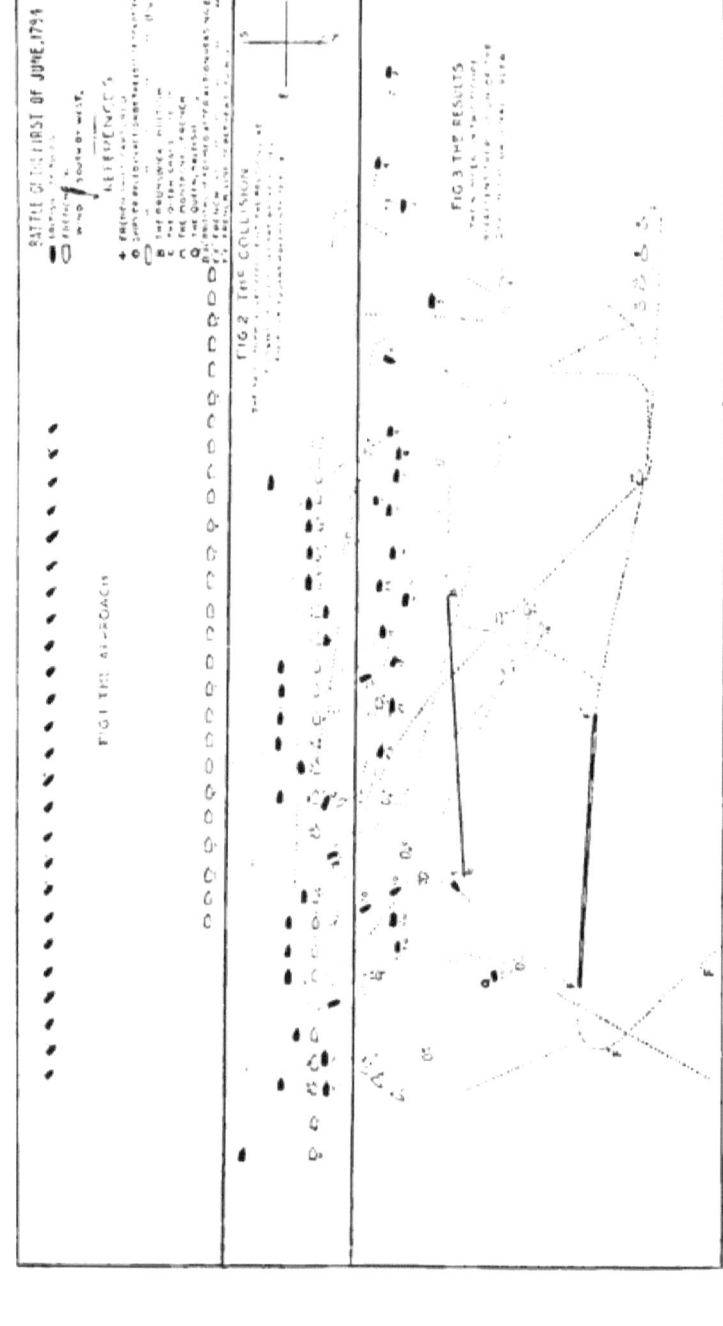

sailing of the ships with the time it took them to cover the ground. The combatants had a long summer's day before them, and such scrupulous care was not wholly out of place in an attack of the kind; for not only was it desirable that the shock should be felt everywhere at once, but ships in advance of the line would invite concentration of fire from the enemy, while those much in the rear would be embarrassed by smoke concealing the position it behooved them to take.

This difficulty from smoke was the more to be feared because Howe's plan, as communicated to the fleet by signal, was not merely to attack on the side from which he approached, but to pass through the intervals between the enemy's ships, and to engage them on the further, or lee, side. This method conferred the advantage of a raking fire[1] while passing through the line, and cut off the retreat of disabled enemies; for a crippled ship could only retire to leeward.[2] To carry out the design, however, required not only that the enemy should leave wide enough intervals, but also that the assailants should be able to see where the intervals were.

The British ships were steering each for its opposite in the enemy's order, heading about north-west; so that,

[1] A raking shot is one that passes from end to end, lengthwise, of a ship, instead of across, from side to side. It not only ranges through a greater space within, but attacks more vital parts, particularly about the stern, where were the rudder and the more important officers of a ship.

[2] Another advantage in engaging to leeward was that the lower-deck batteries, which contained the heaviest guns, were so near the water that a ship heeling over with a strong breeze could not always open her lee ports. The lee ship of two opponents, using her weather guns, would escape this inconvenience and have a proportionate advantage. On the First of June the weather was too moderate to affect the use of the lower-deck batteries; but on the 29th of May, the "Queen Charlotte," using her lee as well as her weather guns as she broke through the French line, had the lower deck full of water. One of her officers, Lieutenant (afterwards Admiral) Codrington, being knocked down by the recoil of a gun and thrown to the lee side of the deck, could, when leaning on his left arm, barely keep his head out of water. (Life of Admiral Codrington.)

as the French line was east and west, the approach was
not perpendicular but in a slanting direction. At twenty
minutes before nine, the formation was so accurate that
Lord Howe shut the signal book with an air of satisfaction, as though his work as admiral was done and all
that remained was to show the gallant bearing and example which had ever been associated with his name.
The gesture was, however, premature, and eccentricities
of conduct on the part of some captains compelled him
again to open the book and order them into their stations.
Shortly after nine o'clock the French van began firing.
The British ship "Cæsar," on the left flank of her line,
and therefore corresponding to the leader of the French,
instead of pressing on to her station for battle, hauled to
the wind and began firing while still five hundred yards
distant,— a position inconsistent with decisive results under the gunnery conditions of that day. Lord Howe, who
had not thought well of the captain of this ship, but had
permitted him to retain his distinguished position in the
order at the request of the captain of the "Queen Charlotte," now tapped the latter on the shoulder, and said,
"Look, Curtis, there goes your friend; who is mistaken
now?"

The rest of the fleet stood on. The "Queen Charlotte,"
in order to reach her position, had to steer somewhat more
to the westward. Either the French line had drawn a
little ahead, or some other incident had thrown this ship
astern of her intended point of arrival. Her course, therefore, becoming more nearly parallel to the enemy's, she
passed within range of the third vessel behind Villaret's
flag-ship, the "Montagne," her destined opponent. This
ship, the "Vengeur," opened fire upon her at half-past
nine. The "Queen Charlotte," not to be crippled before
reaching her place, made more sail and passed on. The
next ahead of the "Vengeur," the "Achille," also engaged
her, and to this the "Charlotte" replied at eight minutes

before ten. The assailant suffered severely, and her attention was quickly engrossed by the "Brunswick," the supporter of Howe's flag-ship on her starboard side, which tried to break through the line ahead of the "Achille."

The "Queen Charlotte" (June 1, Fig. 2, C) continued on for the "Montagne" (M). Seeing her evident purpose to pass under the stern, the captain of this ship threw his sails aback, so as to fall to the rear and close the interval. At the same moment the French ship next astern, the "Jacobin," increased her sail, most properly, for the same object. The two thus moving towards each other, a collision was threatened. As the only alternative, the "Jacobin" put her helm up and steered for the starboard, or lee, side of the "Montagne." At this moment the "Queen Charlotte" drew up. Putting her helm hard over, she kept away perpendicularly to the "Montagne," and passed under her stern, so close that the French flag brushed the side of the British ship. One after another the fifty guns of the latter's broadside swept from stern to stem of the enemy, -- three hundred of her crew falling at once, her captain among the number. The "Jacobin" having moved to the starboard side of the "Montagne," in the place the "Queen Charlotte" had intended to take, it was thought that the latter would have to go to leeward of both ; but, amid all the confusion of the scene, the quick eye of the gallant man who was directing her movements caught a glimpse of the "Jacobin's" rudder and saw it moving to change the ship's direction to leeward. Quickly seizing his opportunity, the helm of the British flag-ship was again shifted, and she came slowly and heavily to the wind in her appointed place, her jib-boom in the movement just clearing the "Jacobin," as her side a few minutes before had grazed the flag of the "Montagne." The latter, it is said, made no reply to this deadly assault. The "Jacobin" fired a few shots, one of which cut away the foretopmast of the "Queen Charlotte ;" and then, instead of imitating the latter's movement and coming to the wind again, by which the British ship would have been placed between his fire and that of the "Montagne," the captain weakly kept off and ran to leeward out of action.

By this time the engagement was general all along the line (Fig. 2). Smoke, excitement and the difficulties of the situation broke somewhat the simultaneousness of the shock of the British assault; but, with some exceptions, their fire from van to rear opened at nearly the same time. Six ships only passed at once through the enemy's line, but very many of the others brought their opponents to close action to windward. In this, the first pitched battle after many years of peace, there were found the inevitable failures in skill, the more sorrowful shortcomings of many a fair-seeming man. To describe minutely the movements of every ship would not tend to clearness, but to obscurity. For general impression of the scene at certain distinctive moments the reader is referred to the diagrams; in which, also, an attempt has been made to represent the relative motions of the ships in both squadrons, so far as can be probably deduced from the narratives. (See Figs. 2 and 3.)

There was, however, one episode of so singular, so deadly, and yet so dramatic an interest, occurring in the midst of this extensive *mêlée*, that it cannot be passed by. As long as naval history shall be written, it must commemorate the strife between the French ship "Vengeur du Peuple" and the British ship "Brunswick." The latter went into action on the right hand of the "Queen Charlotte;" its duty therefore was to pierce the French line astern of the "Jacobin." This was favored by the movement of the latter to support the "Montagne;" but, as the "Brunswick" pressed for the widened gap, the "Achille" made sail ahead and threw herself in the way. Foiled here, the "Brunswick" again tried to traverse the line astern of the "Achille," but the "Vengeur" now came up, and, as the "Brunswick" persisted, the two collided and swung side to side, the anchors of the British ship hooking in the rigging and channels of the French. Thus fastened in deadly embrace, they fell off before the wind and went away together to leeward (Fig. 2, B).

As the contact of the two ships prevented opening the lower ports as usual, the British crew blew off the lids. The "Vengeur" having already been firing from the side engaged, hers were probably open; but, owing to the hulls touching, it was not possible to use the ordinary sponges and rammers, with rigid wooden staves, and the French had no other. The British, however, were specially provided for such a case with sponges and rammers having flexible rope handles, and with these they were able to carry on the action. In this way the contest continued much to the advantage of the British on the lower decks, where the French, for the reason given, could use only a few of the forward and after guns, the form of a ship at the extremities causing the distance there between the combatants to be greater. But while such an inequality existed below, above the balance was reversed; the heavy carronades of the "Vengeur," loaded with langrage, and the superiority of her musketry, — re-enforced very probably by the men from the useless cannon below, — beating down the resistance of the British crew on the upper deck and nearly silencing their guns. The captain of the "Brunswick" received three wounds, from one of which he afterwards died; and a number of others, both officers and men, were killed and wounded. This circumstance encouraged the "Vengeur's" commander to try to carry his opponent by boarding; but, when about to execute the attempt, the approach of two other British ships necessitated calling off the men, to serve the guns on the hitherto disengaged side.

Meanwhile the "Brunswick's" crew maintained an unremitting fire, giving to their guns alternately extreme elevation and depression, so that at one discharge the shot went up through the "Vengeur's" decks, ripping them open, while at the other they tended to injure the bottom. The fight had thus continued for an hour when the "Achille," with only her foremast standing, was seen approaching the "Brunswick" on her port, or disengaged, side. The threatened danger was promptly met and successfully averted. Before the new enemy could take a suitable position, half-a-dozen guns' crews on each of the lower decks shifted to the side on which she was, and in a few moments their fire brought down her only remaining and already damaged mast. The "Achille" had no farther part in the battle and was taken possession of by the British a few hours later.

At quarter before one the uneasy motions of the two ships wrenched the anchors one after another from the "Brunswick's" side, and after a grapple of three hours they separated. The character of the contest, as described, had caused the injury to fall mainly upon the hulls and crews, while the spars and rigging, contrary to the usual result in so fierce an action, had largely escaped. As they were parting, the "Brunswick" poured a few final shots into the "Vengeur's" stern, injuring the rudder, and increasing the leaks from which the doomed ship was already suffering. Immediately afterwards the mizzen-mast of the British vessel went overboard; and, being already well to leeward of her own fleet and threatened by the approach of the French admiral, she stood to the northward under such sail as her spars would bear, intending to make a home port, if possible. In this long and desperate conflict, besides the injuries to be expected to hull and spars, the "Brunswick" had twenty-three of her seventy-four guns dismounted, and had lost forty-four killed and one hundred and fourteen wounded out of a crew of six hundred men.[1]

---

[1] A whimsical incident is told as occurring in this grim scene of slaughter and destruction. "The 'Brunswick' had a large figurehead of the Duke, with

Soon after the dismasting of the "Achille," the British ship "Ramillies," commanded by the brother of the "Brunswick's" captain, had been seen coming slowly down toward the two combatants. She arrived but a few moments before their separation, and, when they were far enough apart for her fire not to endanger the "Brunswick," she also attacked the "Vengeur," but not long after left her again in order to secure the "Achille." This fresh onslaught, however, brought down all the "Vengeur's" masts except the mizzen, which stood for half an hour longer. The French ship was helpless. With numerous shot-holes at or near the water line, with many of her port lids gone, she was rolling heavily in the waves, unsteadied by masts, and taking in water on all sides. Guns were thrown overboard, pumps worked and assisted by bailing, but all in vain, — the "Vengeur" was slowly but surely sinking. At half-past one the danger was so evident that signals of distress were made; but among the disabled or preoccupied combatants they for a long time received no attention. About six P.M., fortunately, two British ships and a cutter drew near, and upon learning the state of the case sent all their boats that remained unhurt. It was too late to save every survivor of this gallant fight, but nearly four hundred were taken off; the remainder, among whom were most of the badly wounded, went down with their ship before the British boats had regained their own. "Scarcely had the boats pulled clear of the sides, when the most frightful spectacle was offered to our gaze. Those of our comrades who remained on board the 'Vengeur du Peuple,' with hands raised to Heaven, implored with lamentable cries the help for which they could no longer hope. Soon disappeared

---

a laced hat on. The hat was struck off by a shot during the battle. The crew of the ship sent a deputation to the quarter-deck to request that Captain Harvey would be pleased to order his servant to give them his laced cocked-hat to supply the loss. The captain, with great good-humor, complied, and the carpenter nailed it on the Duke's head, where it remained till the battle was finished." (Barrow's Life of Howe.)

the ship and the unhappy victims which it contained. In the midst of the horror with which this scene inspired us all, we could not avoid a feeling of admiration mingled with our grief. As we drew away, we heard some of our comrades still making prayers for the welfare of their country; the last cries of these unfortunates were: 'Vive la République!' They died uttering them."[1] A touching picture of brave men meeting an inevitable fate, after doing all that energy and courage could to avoid it; very different from the melodramatic mixture of tinsel verbiage and suicide which found favor with the National Convention, and upon which the "Legend of the Vengeur" was based.[2] Of the seven hundred and twenty-three who composed her crew, three hundred and fifty-six were lost; two hundred and fifty of whom were, by the survivors, believed to have been killed or wounded in the three actions.

Long before the "Vengeur" and the "Brunswick" separated, the fate of the battle had been decided, and the final action of the two commanders-in-chief taken. It was just ten o'clock when the British flag-ship passed under the stern of the "Montagne." At ten minutes past ten the latter, whose extensive injuries were mainly to the hull, made sail in advance, — a movement which the "Queen

[1] Official narrative of the loss of the "Vengeur," by the survivors. Troude, Bat. Nav., vol. ii. p. 355.

[2] The speech of Barrère in the National Convention was as follows: "Imagine the 'Vengeur' ship-of-the-line pierced with cannon shot, opening in all directions, and surrounded by English tigers and leopards, a crew composed of wounded and dying men, battling against the waves and the cannon. All at once the tumult of the action, the fear of danger, the pain-stricken cries of the wounded cease; all mount or are carried upon deck. Every flag, every pennant is hoisted. Cries of 'Vive la République!' 'Vive la Liberté et la France!' are heard on all sides; it is the touching and animated spectacle of a civic festival, rather than the terrible moment of a shipwreck. For a moment they must have thought upon their fate. But no, citizens, our brothers thought no more upon that, they see only the English and their country. They choose rather to be engulfed than to dishonor her by a surrender. They hesitate not an instant. Their last prayers are for liberty and for the Republic. They disappear."

Charlotte," having lost both fore and main topmasts, was unable to follow. Many of the French ships ahead of the "Montagne" had already given ground and left their posts; others both before and behind her had been dismasted. Between half-past ten and eleven the smoke cleared sufficiently for Villaret to see the situation on the field of battle.

Ships dismasted not only lose their power of motion, but also do not drift to leeward as rapidly as those whose spars are up, but which are moving very slowly. In consequence, the lines having some movement ahead, the dismasted ships of both parties had tended astern and to windward of the battle. There they lay, British and French, pell-mell together. Of the twelve ahead of the French admiral when the battle began, seven had soon run out of action to leeward. Two of these, having hauled to the wind on the other tack, were now found to be astern and to windward of both fleets; to windward even of the dismasted ships. Of the rest of the twelve, one, having lost main and mizzen masts, was unavoidably carried to leeward, and the remaining four were totally dismasted. Of these four, three finally fell into the hands of the British. Of the thirteen ships astern of the "Montagne," six had lost all their masts, and one had only the foremast standing; the remaining six had their spars left in fairly serviceable condition, and had, some sooner and some later, retreated to leeward. Four of the dismasted ships in the rear, including among them the "Vengeur," were captured by the British.

When Admiral Villaret Joyeuse had recognized the situation, as thus briefly described, he directed the "Montagne" also to be headed to leeward, and made signals to gather the serviceable ships round the commander-in-chief. A column of twelve was thus formed (June 1. Fig. 3, F F') on the starboard tack, standing, that is, to the eastward again,—the "Montagne" leading and the rear being brought up by the "Terrible," the flag-ship of the second in command, which had only her foremast left and was therefore taken in tow by an uninjured seventy-four. Villaret considered it imprudent, if not impossible, to get far enough to windward to interpose in favor of the dismasted vessels. He determined, therefore, to place himself to leeward of them, in such position as to receive and cover those that could run down to him, or which his frigates could reach and tow away. In this manner the "Scipion," the "Jemappes," and the "Mucius," totally disabled, were restored to the French fleet between two and four o'clock. The last named had actually struck to a British ship, but had not been taken into possession. Villaret remained for some time, hove-to in this position, until satisfied that no more of the separated vessels could join him, and then made sail to the north-west (F″ F″).[1]

Lord Howe was unable to follow with his own ship the comparatively rapid movements of the French commander-in-chief. At eleven o'clock, however, a signal was made for those that could to close around the admiral, and the "Queen Charlotte" was with difficulty put on the other tack. Howe then led the column thus formed (B' B') to the eastward, a step that was necessary not only in order to cover dismantled British ships and secure the prizes, but also to relieve the "Queen," which was threatened by Villaret and in a critical situation. This ship, which had behaved with so much forwardness and gallantry in the British van on the 29th of May, had on the First of June been stationed in the rear. The antagonist which she attacked went away rapidly to leeward; and the "Queen," following with unrelenting ar-

---

[1] The French accounts state that he remained until eight P.M., during all which time he might have been attacked. The English on the contrary say that the whole French fleet was out of sight by quarter past six. The question is not material, for it is certain that Villaret did remain for some time, and that he would not have been attacked had he stayed longer.

dor, found herself at the end of the engagement again
between the lines, with a dismantled enemy, indeed, near
by, but with her own mainmast gone and other spars tottering. Eight of Villaret's column cannonaded her as
they passed, but without doing much harm, and Howe's
approach extricated her.

The escape of some of the French dismasted ships was
severely criticised at the time, and there was also an opinion that Howe should have renewed the attack after gathering about him his less injured vessels. There can be
little question that more promptitude and energy would
have secured some of the French that got away; many
competent eye-witnesses thought so, and much discontent
was openly expressed in the fleet. It is more doubtful
whether the admiral would have done well to order the
attack renewed. Several captains had behaved indiffer-
ently, either through lack of judgment or lack of nerve,
and the best were naturally among those whose ships, being well-placed and hard-fought, were now out of condition for fighting. A decisive practical reason for ceasing
the action is to be found in Howe's physical condition.
He was then sixty-eight years old; and, although possessed
of the calm, unworrying temper which bears responsibility
lightly, he had undergone great fatigue during the five
days of battle and chase, — his only resting-place from
the time the enemy was encountered being an arm-chair.
"When the report was brought to him," says the signal
lieutenant, "that the French fleet showed every symptom
of determination to sustain a battle, I watched his face
when he came to the quarter-deck to look at them: it expressed an animation of which, at his age, and after such
fatigue of mind and body, I had not thought it capable;"
but the reaction came possibly a little too soon for reaping
the full fruits of the victory. "He went to bed," wrote
the same officer, "completely done up after the action
of the First. We all got round him; indeed, I saved him

from a tumble; he was so weak that from a roll of the ship he was nearly falling into the waist. 'Why, you hold me up as if I were a child,' he said good-humoredly."[1] It is not surprising that, under such circumstances, he could not do all that a younger man might, nor that he yielded to the influence of his chief-of-staff, Sir Roger Curtis, a distinguished and gallant officer, but who appears to have been more impressed than was his superior by the disadvantages under which the British fleet labored.

Many years later, Admiral Stopford, who commanded a frigate in the action, made the following statement, which he allowed to be published: "Having observed the 'Marlborough' dismasted and surrounded by enemy's ships, I bore down and took her in tow, — which bringing me very near the 'Queen Charlotte,' I went on board for orders. The cool, collected manner in which I was received by Lord Howe, and the desire he expressed to get the ships set to rights to continue the action, showed that such was his intention; and for the purpose of exonerating Lord Howe's memory from the charges I have heard alleged against him for not following up his victory, I think it right to state that, when standing on the 'Queen Charlotte's' poop, close to Lord Howe, Sir Roger Curtis came up in haste and apparent perturbation, exclaiming, 'I declare to God, my Lord, if you don't assemble the fleet, they will turn the tables upon us.' I must confess that I did not see anything to warrant such an exclamation, except a French ship passing under the 'Queen Charlotte's' stern and firing a few guns into her. The admiral and Sir R. Curtis then retired to another part of the poop, and nothing more was done."[2]

The responsibility of a commander-in-chief is not affected by the advice given him by any subordinate, how-

---

[1] Life of Admiral (then Lieutenant) Codrington.

[2] Barrow's Life of Lord Howe, p 256 There are similar statements as to the bearing of Howe and Curtis made by Admiral Codrington.

ever high his reputation or confidential the relations between them; but in the state of bodily weakness from which Howe suffered, he must, for subsequent action, have depended largely upon Curtis, and it was probably well not to undertake an undeniable risk against the judgment of the officer who might be called upon to superintend the operation. The battle therefore terminated with the movement of the two commanders-in-chief, with their serviceable ships, to the eastward, through which three French vessels escaped, the "Queen" was extricated, and seven dismasted enemies were cut off by the British. At quarter past one the general firing ceased, though a few random shots continued to be exchanged by scattered vessels.

Such were the principal features of the battle of the First of June, 1794, which, being fought so far from any land,[1] has received no other distinctive name. It has not been thought desirable to attempt narrating, in words, the innumerable incidents of the fight. While avoiding a superfluity of details, however, a tactical analysis of the course of the action may be not uninteresting to the professional reader. The method of attack undertaken by Lord Howe, single ship against single ship, was identical with that employed on many previous occasions by British admirals, and is to be justified only by the evidence he had received, on the 28th and 29th of May, of the enemy's professional incompetency and indifferent gunnery. He was probably right in concluding, from the events of those days, as was decisively proved by the issue on June 1st, that the French line was at every point weaker than the ships he could thus bring against it. Under such conditions it may be permissible to the assailant to throw away the opportunity, which the offensive gives him, of combining an attack in superior force upon a part of the enemy's order. It is very possible that Howe might have reaped

---

[1] At noon of June 1, by the "Queen Charlotte's" log-book, the island of Ushant bore east one-half north, distant 429 miles.

better results by making such a combination, for the tactical inefficiency of the French fleet, which he had observed, assured him that it could not, in the moment of action, remedy any disadvantage under which he might place it; but, on the other hand, the drill of his own captains was not yet very good, nor were they all tried men upon whom he could depend. It was, therefore, not improbable that an attempt to execute a combination would result in a muddle, whereas he could count upon superior seamanship and superior gunnery, ship to ship, and the movement of approach which he made, though somewhat difficult in execution, is perfectly simple in idea. Upon the whole, weighing the pros and cons, it is the opinion of the author that Howe judged soundly in directing the simple attack that he did.[1]

It is instructive to observe that the results of the movement, though far more decisive in this than in previous battles, are, upon dissection, found to be closely analogous. The British fleet, in running down together, was ranged on a line parallel to the French, but steering a course

[1] The carelessness with which naval affairs are too often described by general historians may be illustrated by the account of this battle given by one of the most distinguished. "Lord Howe gained so decisive a success from the adoption of the same principles which gave victory to Frederic at Leuthen, to Napoleon at Austerlitz, and to Wellington at Salamanca, viz.: *to direct an overwhelming force against one half of the enemy's force*, and making the attack obliquely, keeping the weather gage of the enemy, to render it impossible for the ships to leeward to work up to the assistance of those engaged. By this means he reduced one half of the enemy's fleet to be the passive spectators of the destruction of the other. . . . Had he succeeded *in penetrating the line at all points*, or had his captains implicitly obeyed his directions in that particular, and engaged the whole to leeward, he would have brought twenty ships-of-the-line to Spithead." (Alison's "History of Europe.") How an attack upon one half of the line is consistent with penetrating the same line at all points does not clearly appear; but the statement concerning Lord Howe's principle of action on the 1st of June is absolutely contrary to all the facts, although Alison had James's painstaking work before him and refers to it frequently. His statement is that of Jomini's "Guerres de la Révolution Française;" but the latter author writes only as a military man, introduces naval matters merely incidentally, and was doubtless misled in the scanty information attainable when he wrote.

(north-west) that was oblique to its own front as well as to that of the enemy. The issue in every other instance had been indecisive, — scarcely ever was a ship taken or sunk. But while in this respect different, the experience of previous engagements was otherwise repeated. That flank of the assailant which in column had been the van came, as a whole, promptly and orderly into action, while delay and disorder, attended with imperfect execution, ensued in the rear. This feature of simultaneous fleet attacks was emphasized by the strenuous and brilliant efforts of three of the rear division, which prevented indeed a general failure there, but brought out all the more clearly how great the shortcoming would have been but for their exertions, unparalleled in former battles. The proportion of loss undergone in the different parts of the British column gives a fair measure of the vigor displayed by each. This test is indeed most misleading as a means of comparison between any two single ships. Instances can readily be chosen, from this very case, in which vessels skilfully placed and vigorously fought received less injury than others, which were badly handled and did little harm to the enemy; but when an average is taken of many ships, the specific causes of error in different directions tend to balance each other, and if the general conclusion is confirmed by the experience of other battles, it may be accepted with much confidence. Now, on the First of June, taking the total number of casualties in the British fleet, it will be found that in every hundred men killed the eight van ships lost forty-three, and in every hundred wounded forty-one; whereas the eight rear lost seventeen killed and twenty-two wounded, or rather less than half the proportion of the van. Nor does this tell the whole story, for four fifths of the entire loss of the rear fell upon the three vessels,[1] leaving but eight killed and thirty-three

---

[1] It is a curious coincidence, though not necessarily significant, that the number of men hit in each of these ships was nearly the same. The "Royal Sovereign" lost fifty-four, the "Queen" fifty-four, and the "Glory" fifty-two.

wounded to be divided among the remaining five; whereas, in the eight van ships, though there are marked individual differences, the loss is much more equally divided. The inference, were the truth not otherwise known, would amount almost to proof that the van ships went down in good order, attacked vigorously, and so afforded mutual support, whereas the rear, whatever the cause, did not impress themselves strongly on the enemy's line; while the exceptional casualties of the three which did their duty well indicate a lack of support from the others, which also appears to be confirmed by the ascertained facts.

When a result is thus reproduced in various battles, it cannot be attributed wholly to the fault of the captains. The exceptions to the rule on the First of June were not the rear ships which failed in gaining for themselves a fair share in the action, but those which succeeded in so doing. The cause of this usual result seems to be that the van ship is the pivot upon which the operation hinges, and in proportion as the distance from the pivot grows greater, irregularities become more frequent, while each one that occurs is propagated and increased, until at last, in a long line, an approach to disorder ensues. When this happens, the efficiency of each ship depends less upon her normal relations to the line than upon the initiative of her captain; and the differences between men, which had been controlled by the exigencies of the order, where it still existed, begin to tell. Short lines will suffer less than long ones from this cause; whence it follows that in a long line new pivots, or points of departure for the order beyond them, should be provided. On the 1st of June the "Queen Charlotte," by her steady action and the authority conveyed by the example of the commander-in-chief, served as such a pivot, and the conduct of the ships on her right was better than that of those on her immediate left, which were regulating their position by the van.[1] As it seems

---

[1] Brenton, in his naval history of Great Britain, tells an amusing story of the captain of one of the ships a little to Howe's left, which at once charac

probable, from the character of modern ships and weapons, that attacks will be made in a line of front, it is a matter of interest to naval officers to provide against this tendency to disorder and imperfect execution, which seems to inhere in the part of an order distant from the guide, or pivot.

The French line, by awaiting Howe's attack, laid itself open to any combination he might see fit to make, but the plan actually adopted threw the burden of resistance upon the individual captains, rather than upon the admiral. Whenever a ship was vigorously attacked by an enemy, her captain's task was simple, however arduous; nor does there seem to have been an instance of a French officer in this position failing to do his duty manfully. The superior gunnery of the British at this time, however, generally beat down the resistance of the opponent, and the latter then bore up and ran to leeward, unless his masts had been shot away, or unless the assailant by piercing the line had barred retreat. Thus the "Mucius," seventh in the line, was engaged to leeward by the "Defence." She tried, therefore, to escape by passing to windward of the British "Marlborough," next ahead, but fell on board of her and there lost all her masts. This circumstance of inferior gunnery, together with the fixed idea of keeping the line closed, appear to have governed the movements of the French ships after the battle joined. Now the duty of keeping the line closed is most important and essential to mutual support, but it is not paramount to every other consideration, particularly when an action, as this inevitably must, had passed into a *mêlée*; but the French captains, having few other ideas on fleet-fighting, clung to this one in its simplest form,—that of following close upon the heels of the next ahead. Thus the leading ship, "Convention," though not hotly attacked, wore out of the line and

terizes a type of officer and illustrates the above remark. He was, Brenton says, so occupied with preserving his station by the azimuth compass that he lost sight of his intended antagonist, and in the smoke never found him.

was closely followed by the "Gasparin," though the latter was vigorously engaged. The next five ships were hard pressed and fought manfully. The eighth, after a short engagement, ran to leeward and was followed by the three astern of her. This brings us to the twelfth, or nearly to the centre of the French line, and of the six that followed, down to and including the seventeenth, four were taken after a desperate resistance. The two that escaped were the flag-ship "Montagne," whose career has already been told, and the "Jacobin," next astern of her. The eighteenth, nineteenth, and twentieth seem to have received little injury, but yet ran to leeward; whether independently, or one following another, does not certainly appear. The remaining six suffered the fierce assault of the three of the enemy's rear, and four were reduced to such a condition that they must have been taken — and not two only of them — had the rest of the British division done their full duty.

Although the French officers, lacking both experience and instruction in fleet warfare, failed to do all they might in the battle, distinct misconduct by doing what should not have been done appears only in two cases. The first was the captain of the leading ship, for whose act in forsaking his post in the van no good reason appears. The second and much more serious fault was committed by the captain of the "Jacobin." The course of this officer in making sail to close upon the flag-ship, when the intention of the "Queen Charlotte" to pass between the two became evident, was perfectly proper. His keeping away, when collision with the "Montagne" threatened, was probably the only way of avoiding a disaster. Being thus forced to leeward of the line, he still retained the power of attacking the British ship to starboard, while she was, or should have been, engaged on the other side by the "Montagne." Instead of using this opportunity, Captain Gassin kept off and ran to leeward. This fault, grave in any case, was especially blameworthy in the next astern or next ahead of the commander-in-chief. Those were posts of peculiar honor, held by heavy vessels, chosen with the special object of supporting their leader and strengthening the part of the order in which he was. For Captain Gassin, personally, there may have been many excuses; but for the course of the ship, considered from a military and tactical point of view, no excuse whatever appears, for she suffered little in the fight. The void caused by the "Jacobin" was filled by the ships astern of her pressing up, and this forward movement, being transmitted to the end of the line, was partly the cause why the rear British ships did not reach their numerical opposite in the French order.

Some attention is due to the naval strategy, to the general conduct and results of this short maritime campaign, which covered only four weeks, — from the 16th of May, when Villaret sailed from Brest, to the 11th of June, when he again anchored just outside the port. In order to form a just opinion there must be considered the objects of each party, the forces at their control, and the measures pursued by them.

The object of the French was to insure the arrival of the convoy from America. For this purpose they had at sea, at the first, two detachments, — one of five ships-of-the-line under Nielly, the other of twenty-five under Villaret. The rendezvous for the two was the same, and the important point where their intended junction should take place was known to their admirals and unknown to the British. It may be again said that the instructions of the French government to its officers compelled the latter to avoid, if possible, any decisive engagement.

The object of the British was twofold: to intercept the expected convoy, and to bring the French fleet to battle. The two might, and did, interfere with each other, — might, by divergence of interest, prompt a separation of the force. Of the two, fighting the French fleet was indisputably the more important, and was doubtless so considered by Howe, in accordance with the usual British naval policy, which aimed at the destruction of the enemy's organized force afloat. The ships at his disposal, including Montagu's squadron, amounted to thirty-two of the line. He was ignorant of the rendezvous of the French fleets and of the exact course that would be followed by the convoy; but of both he could form approximate estimates.

From the 4th of May, when Montagu's squadron first separated, until the 19th, Howe supposed the French to be in Brest. On the latter day his lookouts reconnoitred the port for the second time, and he then learned that they had sailed. The same evening he was joined by a frigate from Montagu, bearing a request for a re-enforcement. Fearing that his subordinate might fall in with Villaret's greatly superior force, Howe next morning made all sail to join him; making a course of west by south, while the French had been steering west one-half south. On the 21st he fell in with and recaptured a number of Dutch ships, which had been taken by Villaret on the 19th. From the logs of these ships, the position and course of the French fleet two days before was ascertained; and Howe, concluding that they would not go near Montagu, who was well to the southward, dismissed the latter from his mind and devoted himself thenceforth to finding the enemy. This decision challenges criticism, because Montagu's orders were, if unsuccessful in finding the convoy, to abandon his cruise on the 20th and rejoin the admiral off Ushant. If he complied strictly with these instructions, he should not now have been very far from the main fleet.

Montagu, however, had seen reason for delaying some days on his cruising ground, and while thus waiting retook some of the Dutch prizes taken by Villaret and which had escaped recapture by Howe on the 21st. He then first learned of the French sailing, and at the same time that

Howe was in pursuit. Instead of making any attempt to rejoin his superior, or to take a position where he might further the general objects of the cruise, he on the 24th or 25th of May bore up for England and anchored at Plymouth on the 30th. The British naval historian, James, says this was done in compliance with the spirit of his orders. It would be more convincing to be told what was the letter of orders that could admit such a construction, and what the condition of his ships that could justify forsaking the field of action with so strong a detachment at such a critical moment. His decision, on whatever grounds made, seems not to have met the approval of the government, and orders were at once sent for him to sail immediately, accompanied by all the ships-of-the-line ready for sea at Plymouth. He accordingly did sail on the 4th of June with nine ships, and on the 8th reached the rendezvous appointed by Howe off Ushant, which was also the station indicated by the last instructions of the admiralty to him. On the 3d of June, the day before he left, the "Audacious" arrived, bringing the first tidings of the meeting of the fleets on the 28th of May, in which she had been disabled.

It appears from this account that neither Howe nor Montagu attached sufficient importance to the concentration of the British fleet. Howe's immediate pursuit might indeed be defended on the ground of the necessity to overtake Villaret, before he had effected his junction with Nielly; but, as both these admirals knew their rendezvous, while he did not, and as Villaret had three days' start, the chances all were that he would not come up before they met. Actually, one of Nielly's ships joined before Howe found him, another on the 29th, and the remainder on the 30th; thus neutralizing the advantages gained by the fine tactical efforts of the British admiral on the 28th and 29th. Had Montagu's six ships, however, come up, the full profit of the two previous days' fighting would have been preserved;

and it is hard to over-estimate the effect which they would have had upon the results, even if maintained simply as a reserve. To these considerations may be added the risk of missing both fleet and convoy, by going in search of them, instead of simply taking a position near which they must pass, and there uniting the British fleet. That this was very possible is shown by the facts of the chase. "On the 27th, at 9 A.M., having got a few leagues to the northward of the latitude in which he had reason to think Villaret was cruising, Lord Howe bore up and ran to the eastward, with the wind on the starboard quarter."[1] The fleet had been running on this course, with a fair and apparently fresh wind for twenty-one hours, when the French were first seen in the south-south-east. Although no precise data are at hand, it is reasonable to conclude from the above that Howe had gone over a hundred miles to the westward of the French rendezvous, which Villaret had reached a week before.[2] If in the meantime the convoy had appeared, as it perfectly well might, Villaret would at once have sailed for Brest, and the British admiral would not improbably have lost both fleet and convoy.

The question presented is purely strategic. It was certain that the French fleet, if undisturbed, would meet the convoy; therefore after it had sailed from Brest the two objects of the British were merged into one. There was no occasion thenceforth to remain divided into two detachments. For what point precisely the convoy would aim was not known, but Brest and Rochefort marked the two extreme points of the coast line, between which it would probably arrive. The approach of so large a body of ships, tied down to a common movement, is necessarily slow. It would be as ignorant of the point where the British would concentrate, as the latter were of the rendez-

---

[1] James, Nav. Hist., vol. i. p. 144. (Ed. 1878.)
[2] Troude says that he reached his station on the 21st of May. Bat. Nav., vol. ii. p. 330.

vous where the different French detachments were to meet. Fast single ships, well scattered to the westward, might reasonably be expected to meet it and to return to their main body in time to warn this where to look for the prey. That there were no difficulties in this line of action will not, certainly, be contended; but it was more sure and militarily sounder thus to concentrate the British force of thirty-two ships-of-the-line in a well chosen position, and with adequate lookouts, than to lead it hither and thither in search of the enemy's whereabouts. It is a singular and instructive fact that from first to last not a single British ship appears to have laid eyes on the convoy from America. Ships both of commerce and war, belonging to other bodies, were taken and retaken in the Bay of Biscay; but those coming from America wore invisible garments.

The strategic aim of the French admiral, after he had been so unfortunate as to be found by the British fleet, was to draw it away from the rendezvous appointed for the convoy. Both his orders and the tactical condition of his fleet forbade the attempt to secure this by bringing the enemy to battle. When first met, the French were to windward, south of the British. If they had been north, with the same advantage of the wind, the situation would have been most satisfactory to them; for the convoy was approaching from the west-south-west, and by retreating to the northward and westward Villaret would have led the enemy directly from the position endangering it. As things were, it was impossible to steer to the northward without bringing on the battle he had to avoid; and if defeated where he then was, the victorious fleet would be left too near the convoy. Villaret, therefore, kept the advantage of the wind and steered a west course, which diverged slowly from the convoy's path, and, if long enough continued, would allow it to pass out of sight. The slowness of this divergence, however, doubtless contributed to reconcile him to the loss of the weather gage on the 29th, and immediately upon finding himself north of the enemy he went to the northward and westward during the two following days.[1] The result was eminently successful. It is stated by the latest French authorities[2] that on the 30th the convoy passed over the ground where the partial engagement of the 29th was fought. If so, it must have been under cover of the dense fog which then prevailed, as the fleets had not moved very far.

It is impossible not to admire heartily the judicious and energetic measures by which Howe, on the 28th and 29th of May, succeeded in gaining the weather gage, while inflicting, at the same time, a heavy loss upon the enemy. Whatever judgment may be passed upon his tactics on the 1st of June,— and in the opinion of the writer they were the best adapted to the situation and to the condition of his fleet,— it cannot be denied that those of the preceding days were well conceived, and, on the part of the admiral, vigorously and gallantly executed. But the strategic mistake, or misfortune, wherever the fault lay, by which Montagu's detachment was absent, neutralized the tactical advantage gained; while the correct strategy of the French, which brought the two parts of their fleet within supporting distance of each other, restored the balance of strength. Thus was again confirmed the maxim of military writers, that a strategic mistake is more serious and far-reaching in its effects than an error in tactics.

After the two fleets separated each made the best of its

---

[1] Many years later Admiral Villaret was governor of Martinique. When that island was taken by the British in 1809, he went to England as a passenger in a ship commanded by Capt. E. P. Brenton. This officer in his naval history states that Villaret told him that Robespierre's orders were to go to sea, and that, if the convoy fell into Howe's hands, his head should answer for it. Therefore he avoided action so long, and endeavored to draw Lord Howe out of the track of the convoy. The loss of the ships taken was to him a matter of comparative indifference. "While your admiral amused himself refitting them, I saved my convoy, and I saved my head."

[2] Troude, Bat. Nav., vol. ii. p. 337. Chevalier, Hist. de la Mar. Fran. sous la Rép., p. 144.

way to a home port. Lord Howe waited until the morning of the 3d, securing and refitting his prizes and disabled ships, and reached Portsmouth on the 13th of June. Villaret Joyeuse went to Brest. On the morning of the 9th he fell in with Montagu's squadron, a little south of Ushant. The condition of the French, encumbered with injured ships, would have afforded an opportunity to a quick-moving fleet; but two of the British were excessively slow and the admiral did not dare approach a much superior force. Villaret pursued for a short distance, but, fearing to be drawn to leeward of his port in his crippled state, he soon gave over the chase. On the 11th of June, all his fleet anchored in Bertheaume roads, outside of Brest. Montagu, on the 10th, departed for England, a movement which finally closed the campaign on the part of the British. On the night of the 12th the French crews saw a number of lights in the Raz de Sein, the southern passage by which Brest is approached. They were those of the long-expected convoy. Admiral Van Stabel, fearing to find a hostile fleet before the usual and safer entrance, had steered for the Penmarcks, a rocky promontory thirty miles south of the port, and thence for the Raz de Sein. On the same day that Van Stabel made the land Montagu anchored in Plymouth. Two days later, June 14, the convoy and the remnant of Villaret's squadron entered Brest together. Thus ended the cruise, which was marked, indeed, by a great naval disaster, but had insured the principal object for which it was undertaken.

CHAPTER VI.

THE YEAR 1794 IN THE ATLANTIC AND ON THE CONTINENT.

WHILE the British ships engaged on the 1st of June were refitting, Admiral Cornwallis, on the 22d of the month, sailed in command of Montagu's division for a cruise to the westward, from which he returned to port on the 8th of July. With this short exception, both the Channel and the Bay of Biscay were left unguarded until the 3d of September, when Howe again sailed with thirty-four ships-of-the-line, five of which were Portuguese, returning on the 21st to Torbay after a tempestuous cruise. The fleet remained in port until November 8, when the "Canada" seventy-four arrived with the news that her consort, the "Alexander," of similar force, had been captured two hundred miles west of Ushant by a French division of five ships-of-the-line, from which she herself had escaped by better sailing. The British at once put to sea, but, it is needless to say, failed to find the French ships, which had cruised with impunity during their absence; and on the 29th the fleet anchored again at Spithead, a station so far to the eastward as to indicate little expectation of interfering with any of the operations of the enemy from Brest. There accordingly it remained until the 14th of the following February. The protection of commerce was entrusted to squadrons of frigates, whose young and enterprising commanders did much service by capturing or dispersing the French forces of a similar character.

The Committee of Public Safety determined to use the opportunity which was permitted them by the diligent care of the British admiral to economize his fleet. There were, at this time, in Brest and the other Biscay ports as many as forty-six ships-of-the-line, either afloat or building; whereas in the Mediterranean, in consequence of the disaster at Toulon, there were only fifteen. The Committee therefore decided to send six ships round, and Villaret Joyeuse was directed to sail with the entire Brest fleet, thirty-five in all, for the purpose of escorting this division clear of the Bay of Biscay; after which he was to cruise for a fortnight against British commerce. The destitution of the Brest arsenal, however, still continued; for, with the enemy's command of the Channel, the naval stores of the Baltic could reach Brest only by going north of the British islands, and then running the risk of capture in the Atlantic by hostile cruisers. There had therefore been great difficulty in repairing the injuries received in the actions with Lord Howe, as well as in equipping the ships not then engaged. When the orders were received, vivid remonstrances were made, and the condition of the vessels fully represented to the Committee as being entirely unfit for a winter's cruise. Many masts wounded in the battle could not be replaced, the rigging was in bad condition, the crews were untrained. Several of the ships it was proposed to send were old and worn out; and so great was the dearth of provisions that only those for Toulon received enough for some months, the others for no more than four weeks.

Robespierre had fallen five months before, and the Reign of Terror was now over; but the Committee were still unaccustomed to admit objections, and did not find in their limited knowledge of sea matters any reason for recalling orders once given. On the 24th of December, 1794, the fleet began to leave Brest, and, in so doing, one of the largest, of one hundred and ten guns, was wrecked on a rock in the entrance. On the 29th the remaining thirty-four had cleared the harbor and anchored in the road outside, whence they sailed on the 30th. On the night

of January 1, 1795, a furious gale sprang up, followed
by a spell of violent weather. Two eighty-gun ships and
a seventy-four foundered, the crews being with difficulty
saved. Two yet larger, of one hundred and ten guns, had
seven feet of water in the hold and would have been lost
had the storm lasted for twenty-four hours longer. Another seventy-four had to be run on the coast to save the
lives of her people. In the midst of these difficulties, which
caused the separation of the fleet, it was necessary to transfer provisions from the Toulon division to the other ships,
an herculean undertaking, but imperative to keep the latter from starving. On the 2d of February the greater
part of the survivors again reached Brest; but some had
to scatter to other ports as the weather permitted. The
Toulon ships returned with the rest. This midwinter
cruise had cost the republic five ships-of-the-line; it
brought in one British corvette and seventy merchantmen
as prizes.

The stars, or rather the winds, in their courses had
fought for Great Britain; but in no wise did she owe anything to her own efforts. Not till the 14th of February
did the Channel fleet put to sea, nearly a fortnight after
the French had returned to Brest. Whatever may be said
of the inexpediency of exposing the heavy ships to winter
weather, it seems clear that the opposite system left the
enemy at perfect liberty to combine his movements; and
that there was little likelihood of these being made known
to the commander-in-chief in Torbay soon enough for him
to follow efficaciously. Howe himself felt this, and, from
instructions issued by him to Sir James Saumarez on the
15th of January, it would appear that this escape of the
French roused him for a moment to contemplate the close
watch off Brest, afterwards practised by Jervis and Cornwallis.[1] This was the last occasion on which the veteran
admiral actually went to sea in command of a fleet; al-

[1] Ross's Life of Saumarez, vol. i. p. 146.

though, from an apparent reluctance to try new men, the
government insisted upon his exercising a nominal charge
from quarters on shore. He was now in his seventieth
year and suffering from many infirmities. The command
afloat devolved upon a man not much younger, Lord Bridport, one of the naval family of Hood, but whose career
does not bear the impress of great ability which distinguished so many of its members. Immediately before this,
general dissatisfaction had caused a change in the Admiralty, over which, since 1788, had presided Pitt's elder
brother, the Earl of Chatham. He was succeeded, in
December, 1794, by Earl Spencer, a more vigorous and
efficient man, who remained First Lord until the fall of
Pitt's administration in 1801.

The new head, however, did not make any substantial
variation of system, calculated to frustrate the enemy's
naval combinations by the strategic dispositions of the British fleet. More activity was displayed by keeping a small
squadron of half a dozen ships-of-the-line constantly cruising in the soundings and to the westward, and the great
Channel fleet was more continuously at sea during the
summer months; but the close blockade of Brest was not
attempted, nor was Bridport the man to persuade the government to the measures afterwards so vigorously, and in
the main successfully, carried out by Lord St. Vincent,
both as successor to Bridport in the Channel fleet and sub-
sequently as First Lord of the Admiralty. To this faulty
policy contributed not a little the system of telegraphs,
adopted in 1795, by which communications were quickly
transmitted from height to height between London and
Portsmouth. This great improvement unfortunately confirmed the tendency of the Admiralty to keep the Channel
fleet at the latter point, regardless of the obvious, but un-
appreciated, strategic disadvantage of a position so far
east of Brest, with winds prevailing from the western quarters. To have the commander-in-chief just there, under

their own hand, to receive orders from them, seemed much safer than to put him and his fleet in a central position whence he could most certainly intercept or most rapidly follow the enemy, and then to trust to the judgment of a trained and competent sea-officer to act as the emergency required. The plan came near resulting very disastrously when the French attempted to invade Ireland; and would have done so, had not the elements again interfered to remedy the absence of the British fleet. "If," says Osler in his life of Lord Exmouth,[1] from whom he probably received the idea, "if Lord Bridport (in 1796) had been waiting at Falmouth, with discretionary powers, Sir Edward Pellew having been instructed to communicate directly with him, he might have sailed early on December 21st." (Pellew reached Falmouth from before Brest on the 20th) "and found the enemy in Bantry Bay, when perhaps not a ship would have escaped him. It is, however, to be remembered that, as the destination of the French armament was unknown to the last, the Admiralty might very properly determine that he should receive his final instructions from themselves, and therefore would keep the fleet at Spithead (Portsmouth) for the convenience of ready communication." But why! How could they in London judge better than a good admiral on the coast?

During the year 1794, now closing, the Revolution in France had been rapidly devouring its children. After the overthrow of the Girondists in June, 1793, the Terror pursued its pitiless march, sweeping before it for the time every effort made in behalf of moderation or mercy. The queen was put to death on the 16th of October, and her execution was followed on the 31st by that of those Girondists who had not deigned to escape from their accusers. Dissension next arose and spread among the now triumphant party of the Jacobins; resulting in March and April, 1794, in the trial and death of the Hébertists

[1] Page 140.

on the one side, and of Danton and his friends on the other. More and more power fell into the hands of the Committee of Public Safety, whose tokens to the world were Robespierre and his chief supporters, St. Just and Couthon, ruling the Convention which passively decreed their wishes, and, through the Convention, France. For three short months Robespierre now appeared as the master of the country, but was himself carried on and away by the torrent which he had done so much to swell. The exigencies and dangers of his position multiplied the precautions he deemed necessary to secure his authority and his safety; and the cold relentlessness of his character recognized no means so sure as death. On the 10th of June, by his sole authority, without the intervention of the Committee of Public Safety, he procured a decree modifying the procedure of the Revolutionary Tribunal, and suppressing the few checks that restrained its uncontrolled power. In the fourteen months preceding this decree 1256 persons had been by the tribunal condemned to death; in the six weeks that followed, until Robespierre himself fell, the executions were 1361.[1] So extreme an access of fury betokened approaching exhaustion; no society could endure the strain; the most violent and blood-thirsty, as well as the most timid, felt their own lives in danger. Bitter opposition to the dictator arose both in the Committee of Public Safety and in the Legislature. The doubtful struggle, between the prestige of his power and long continued success and the various passions of fear and vengeance animating his opponents, culminated in a violent scene in the Convention on the 27th of July. For some hours the issue was balanced, but in the end the arrest and trial of Robespierre and his chief supporters were decreed. The following day he, St. Just and Couthon, with some others of lesser note, died on the guillotine.

[1] Martin, Hist. de France depuis 1789, vol. ii. p 240.

No immediate change in the form of government ensued. The Committee of Public Safety, reconstituted, continued to exercise the executive functions which nominally depended upon the Convention; and the impulse which it had imparted to the soldiers and armies of France continued for a time to carry them resistlessly forward. But the delirious intensity of the popular movement had reached its climax in the three months' unrestrained power of Robespierre, with whose name it has been ever associated. Though the external manifestations of strength continued for a time unabated, the inner tension was relaxing. Weakness was about to succeed the strength of fever, to spread from the heart throughout the whole organism, and, by threatening social dissolution, to prepare the way for concentrated absolute power.

The onward swing of the French armies on the northeast still continued. The year 1794 had opened with the investment of Landrecy by the allies, and its surrender to them on the 30th of April. The French began their campaign with the plan, especially affected by Carnot in all his military combinations, of attacking at the same time both flanks of the allied Austrians, Dutch and English, concentrating at each extremity of the line a force greatly superior to the enemy before it. As Jourdan, commanding the French right, threatened the allied stronghold of Charleroi, he drew thither the greater effort of the allies, and Pichegru, on the left, found his task easier. Five times did Jourdan cross the Sambre to attack Charleroi, and four times was he compelled to re-cross; but on the fifth, before the allies could come up in sufficient force, the place capitulated, — the guns of the relieving force being heard just as the garrison was marching out. The following day, June 26, 1794, Jourdan fought and won the battle of Fleurus; the Austrians retreating upon Nivelles towards the future field of Waterloo. The allies on both flanks continued to fall back; Ostend and

Nieuport, ports on the North Sea facilitating communication with England, were successively surrendered, and Brussels uncovered. On the 10th of July Pichegru entered Brussels and formed his junction with Jourdan. On the 15th the allies lost Landrecy, the first and only prize of the campaign. On the same day the French attacked in force the centre of the allied line, where the Anglo-Dutch left touched the Austrian right. The former being gradually turned fell back, and the Austrians, finding their flank uncovered, did the same. From this time the allies retired in divergent directions, the Anglo-Dutch northeast toward Holland, the Austrians eastward toward Coblentz; thus repeating in retreat the unmilitary and ruinous mistake which had rendered abortive the offensive campaign of 1793.

The French advance was now stayed by the Committee of Public Safety, in deference to an emotion of patriotism, until the towns surrendered the year before should be retaken. On the 11th of August Le Quesnoy opened its gates, on the 27th Valenciennes, and on the 30th Condé. The siege corps now rejoined the armies in the field and the advance was resumed; Pichegru following the British and Dutch toward Holland, Jourdan, by a series of flank attacks which threatened the communications of the Austrians, forcing the latter from one position to another, until on the 5th October they recrossed to the east side of the Rhine, the French occupying Coblentz and Bonn on the west bank. The advance of Pichegru was marked by less of battle and more of siege than that of Jourdan, but was alike successful. By the middle of October his army had reached the Rhine; which in Holland divides into two branches, the Waal and the Leck, between which the enemy lay. A month later they had retreated beyond the latter, the French being for a moment stopped by the floating ice in the rivers; but the winter was one of unusual severity, and early in January the waters were frozen hard. On the 17th of January, 1795, the Prince of Orange left Holland for England, and on the 20th Pichegru entered Amsterdam. The provinces and cities everywhere declared for the French, and a provisional republican government was established; while the pursuit of the British troops was continued with unremitting diligence until they had escaped into German territory, whence they returned, in April, to England.

The occupation of Belgium and Holland by the French was in every way a matter of concern to the other European powers. It threatened Great Britain in the North Sea, where her flank had previously been strengthened by the Dutch alliance, and compelled her at once to weaken the Channel fleet by a detachment of five ships-of-the-line to confront the Dutch squadrons. The merchants of Holland being among the great money-lenders of Europe, large revenues were opened to the needy French; and the resources thus gained by them were by the same blow lost to the allies. Great Britain thenceforth had to bear alone the money burden of the war. But on the other hand the republican commissaries sucked like leeches the substance of the Dutch; and the sources of their wealth, commerce and the colonies, were at the same time threatened with extinction by the British sea power, whose immediate hostility was incurred by the change in their political relations. Within a month, on the 9th of February, orders were issued to arrest all Dutch ships at sea; temporary provision being made to restore neutral property found on board them, because shipped while Holland was an ally. Vigorous measures were at once taken for the seizure of the rich Dutch colonies in all parts of the world; and before the year 1795 closed, there passed into the hands of Great Britain the Cape of Good Hope, Malacca, all the Dutch possessions on the continent of India, and the most important places in Ceylon; the whole island submitting in 1796. Besides these, other colonies were taken in the farther East and in the West Indies. The Dutch navy remained inoffensively in its ports until the year 1797, with the exception of a small expedition that escaped from the Texel in February, 1796, prepared to retake the Cape of Good Hope. Unable to go through the English Channel, which was completely under the enemy's control, it passed north of the British Islands and eluded capture until Saldanha Bay, near the Cape, was reached. Upon hearing of its arrival the British admiral on that station sailed in pursuit, and, having a greatly superior force, received its instant surrender.

The success that followed the French standards in Belgium and Holland during 1794 accompanied the less striking operations on the Rhine and in the South. At the end of the year the Austrians and Prussians had abandoned the west bank of the river, except Luxembourg and the very important fortress of Mayence. Luxembourg also was closely invested, and capitulated in June, 1795. In the Pyrenees, the Spaniards were driven across the frontiers, and had, in the early autumn, established themselves in a strong entrenched camp at Figueras. On the 17th and 20th of November the French assaulted this position, and on the latter day drove the enemy from all their works round the place, forcing them to retreat upon Gerona. The garrison of Figueras, ten thousand strong, capitulated a week later, and the French then invested Rosas, which held out for two months longer; but the resistance of Spain was completely broken, and the further events of the war in that quarter are unimportant.

On the Italian frontier the year opened with substantial successes on the part of the French, who got possession of important mountain passes of the Alps; but progress here was stopped, in May, by reverses attending the operations on the Rhine, causing troops to be withdrawn from the Army of the Alps. The belligerents rested in the same relative positions during the remainder of 1794.

The important political results of the French military successes in the campaign of 1794 were demonstrated and sealed by treaties of peace contracted in 1795 with Prussia, Spain, and Holland. That with the latter power was one not only of peace, but also of alliance, offensive and defensive. The principal naval conditions were that the United Provinces should furnish twelve ships-of-the-line, with frigates, to cruise in the North Sea and Baltic, and should admit a French garrison into the important seaport of Flushing. This treaty was signed May 15, 1795. The Prussian treaty was concluded on the 5th of April. It stipulated, generally, the surrender of Prussian possessions on the left bank of the Rhine, and by a later agreement established a neutral zone in North Germany under Prussian guarantee. The treaty with Spain was signed at Basle on the 22d of July. It maintained the integrity of the Spanish possessions in Europe, but provided for the cession to France of Spain's part of Haiti.

On the other hand, Great Britain during the same year drew closer the ties binding her to her still remaining allies. An agreement was made in May with the emperor of Germany that he should provide not less than two hundred thousand men for the approaching campaign, while Great Britain was to pay a large subsidy for their support. This was followed by a treaty of defensive alliance, each government engaging not to make a separate peace. With Russia also was made a defensive alliance, and the czarina sent twelve ships-of-the-line to cruise with the British fleet in the North Sea.

CHAPTER VII.

THE YEAR 1795 IN THE ATLANTIC AND ON THE CONTINENT.

THE year 1795 was for France one of reaction and lassitude. The wave of popular ferment which had been rushing forward since the fall of the royalty, gathering strength and volume, and driving before it all wills and all ambitions, crested and broke in July, 1794. Like the breakers of the seashore, a part of the accumulated momentum was expended in a tumultuous momentary advance, of increased force but diminishing depth, and then recession followed. The forward and backward impulses met and mingled, causing turmoil and perplexing currents of popular feeling, but the pure republican movement had reached the highest point it was destined to attain. It had stirred France to its depths, and brought to the surface many a gem which under quieter conditions would have remained hidden from the eyes of men; but, in the confusion and paralysis which followed, these were left stranded and scattered, waiting for the master hand which should combine them and set each in its proper sphere for the glory of France.

The recoil which followed the death of Robespierre took shape in several ways, all tending at once to lessen the internal vigor of the government, and to deprive it of means hitherto possessed for external effort. The revulsion to mercy provoked by his bloody tyranny was accompanied by sentiments of vengeance against the men who were, or were supposed to be, identified with his policy. The indulgence extended to those before proscribed brought them back to France in numbers, clamorous for revenge. These

discordant sentiments, agitating the Convention as well as
the people, the provinces as well as Paris, shattered that
unity of purpose which had been the strength of the government after the fall of the Girondists, and during the
domination of the Jacobins. At the same time were re-
voked the measures by which the Revolutionary Government, living as it did from hand to mouth, had provided
for its immense daily necessities. The law of the Max-
imum, by which dealers were forbidden to charge beyond a
certain fixed price for the prime necessaries of life, was re-
pealed. The paper money, already depreciated, fell rapidly,
now that the seller could demand as much as he wished
for articles of universal consumption. The goverament,
obliged to receive the assignats at their face value in payment of dues, sought to meet its difficulty by increased
issues, which accelerated the decline. At the same time,
requisitions in kind having been suppressed, as part of the
reaction from a rule of force, supplies of all sorts were with
difficulty obtained. Distress, lack of confidence, abounded
in all directions; speculation ran riot, and the government,
having relaxed the spring of terror, that most powerful of motives until it becomes unendurable, found itself drifting into
impotence. These various measures were not completed
till near the end of 1794; and the evil effect was, therefore,
not immediately felt in the armies, — whose wants were
also in part supplied by liberal demands upon their new
allies in Holland. Boissi d'Anglas, in a speech made January 30, 1795, in the Convention, and adopted by that body
as voicing its own sentiments, declared that the armies
would demonstrate to Europe that, far from being ex-
hausted by the three years of war, France had only aug-
mented her resources. The year then opening was to
witness to the emptiness of the boast, until Bonaparte by
his military genius laid the Continent again at her feet.

The internal history of France during this year, though
marked by many and important events, can be briefly

summed up. The policy of reconciliation towards the classes who had most suffered under Jacobin rule was pursued by the government; but against the party lately dominant the reaction that set in was marked by many and bloody excesses. If in the North and West the insurgent Vendeans and Chouans accepted the proffered pardon of the Convention, in the South and East the reactionary movement produced a terror of its own; in which perished, by public massacre or private assassination, several thousand persons, many of whom had not been terrorists, but simply ardent republicans. In Paris, the Jacobins, though depressed and weakened by the loss of so many of their leaders, did not at once succumb; and the tendency to agitation was favored in that great centre by the poverty of the people and the scarcity of food. On the 1st of April, and again on the 20th of May, the halls of the Convention were invaded by crowds of men, women and children, demanding bread and the constitution of 1793. On the latter occasion a member of the Convention was shot while endeavoring to cover the president with his body, and the greater part of the deputies fled from the hall. Those who remained, belonging mostly to the old Mountain, voted certain propositions designed to calm the people; but the next day the crowd was driven out by the national guard from some sections of the city, and the reaction resumed its course with increased force and renewed thirst for vengeance. The deputies who had remained and voted the propositions of May 20 were impeached, and the arrest was ordered of all members of the Committees which had governed during the Terror, except Carnot and one other.

The following month, June, the project for a new constitution was submitted to the Convention, and by it adopted on the 22d of August. It provided for an Executive Directory of five members, and a Legislature of two Chambers; the upper to be called the Council of the Elders, the lower the Council of Five Hundred. To this scheme

of a constitution, the Convention appended a decree that
two thirds of the new Legislature must be taken from the
members of the existing Convention. The Constitution
and the decree were submitted to the country in September.
The Provinces accepted both, but Paris rejected the decree;
and the protest against the latter took form on the 4th
of October in the revolt of the Sections,—a movement of
the bourgeoisie and reactionists against the Convention,
which on this occasion fell back for support upon the party
identified with the Jacobins. The defence of the Hall of
Legislature and of its members was entrusted to Barras,
who committed the military command to General Bonaparte, from whose skilful dispositions the assault of the
Sections everywhere recoiled. On the 26th of October the
National Convention dissolved, after an existence of three
years and one month. On the 27th the new Legislature began its sittings; and the upper council at once elected the
Executive Directory. Among its five members was Carnot.

On the sea the year 1795 was devoid of great or even
striking events. On the 22d of February the six ships destined for Toulon, which had been driven back early in the
month with the rest of the Brest fleet, again set sail under
the command of Admiral Renaudin, and, although much
delayed by heavy westerly winds in the Atlantic, reached
their destination in safety early in April. Not an enemy's
ship was seen on the way. The Channel fleet had gone
back to Spithead as soon as Howe learned that the Brest
fleet had returned to port after the disastrous January
cruise; while in the Mediterranean the British, now under
Admiral Hotham, were at anchor in a roadstead of Corsica when Renaudin drew near Toulon. This made the
French in the Mediterranean twenty to the British thirteen. "What the new Lords of the Admiralty are after,"
wrote Nelson, "to allow such a detachment to get out
here, surprises us all."[1]

[1] Nels. Disp., ii., p 32.

Under the new admiralty small divisions of the Channel fleet continued to cruise to the westward or in the Bay of Biscay; but not until the 12th of June did the main body, under Lord Bridport, put to sea. Ten days later, numbering then fourteen sail-of-the-line, it fell in with Villaret's fleet of twelve ships close in with its own coast, about eighty miles south of Brest. This meeting was due to a succession of incidents which are worthy of narration, as showing the conditions of the war and the prostration of the French navy. The supplies of the squadron at Brest and L'Orient, as well as much of the local traffic of the country, were carried by small coasting vessels rather than by inland roads. A division of three ships-of-the-line was sent to protect a numerous convoy coming from Bordeaux. On the 8th of June these vessels encountered the British division of five ships cruising in the Bay of Biscay, which took from it eight of the convoy before they could escape under the land. When news of this reached Brest, Villaret was ordered to take the nine ships that alone were then ready for sea and join the other three. This junction was made, and on the 16th of June the twelve again fell in with the British five, which, after temporarily withdrawing, had returned to their cruising ground. Chase was of course given, and as two of the British sailed very badly there was a good prospect that either they would be taken, or the rest of the division compelled to come down to their aid; which, with the disparity of force, ought to result in the capture of the whole. The admiral, Cornwallis, behaved with the utmost firmness and coolness; but with such odds and the disadvantage of speed, no courage nor conduct can avert some disaster. The inefficiency and bad gunnery of the French saved their enemies. After a cannonade which lasted from nine in the forenoon of the 17th until six in the evening, one British ship had thirteen men wounded, and Villaret abandoned the pursuit.

Five days later Bridport's fleet was sighted, and the

French being inferior stood in for their coast, intending to anchor and await action under the island called Groix. The pursuit continued with light airs all day and night; but at daybreak of June 23 the fastest British were within three miles of the slowest of the French, which opened fire at six A. M. All Villaret's signals could not bring his fleet into line, nor induce the undoubtedly brave, but ill trained, men who commanded the faster ships to take station for the support of the slower. A desultory action continued till half-past eight, ending in the capture of three French vessels, the last hauling down her flag within a mile of Île Groix. Bridport then called his ships off. It is the opinion of French writers, apparently shared by English critics,[1] that if he had pursued energetically, the remainder of the enemy must either have been taken or run ashore to avoid that fate. As it was, Villaret was permitted to get into L'Orient without molestation, although to do so he had to wait till the tide served. Such was the extreme circumspection characterizing the early naval operations of the British, until Jervis and Nelson enkindled their service with the relentless energy of spirit inspired by Bonaparte on land. Those to whom St. Vincent and the Nile, Algesiras and Copenhagen, have become history, see with astonishment nine ships of capital importance permitted to escape thus easily from fourteen; forgetting the hold tradition has on the minds of men, and that it belongs to genius to open the way into which others then eagerly press. How the admiralty viewed Bridport's action may be inferred from his retaining command of the fleet until April, 1800. The ships that reached L'Orient had to remain till the winter, when they slipped back two or three at a time to Brest.

The disaster at Île Groix, with some similar small misfortunes in the Mediterranean,[2] accompanied as they were

---

[1] Chevalier, Mar. Fran. sous la Rép. p. 216. Life of Adm. Codrington, vol. i. pp. 36, 37.

[2] See *post*, Chap. VIII., Martin's actions with Hotham.

by evidences, too plain to be any longer overlooked, of the inefficiency both of officers and men in the French fleets, determined the government to abandon all attempt to contest the supremacy of the sea. To this contributed also the extreme destitution, in the dockyards, of all sorts of stores for equipment or provision. With the English Channel and the forests of Corsica in the hands of Great Britain, the customary sources of supply were cut off; and moreover the providing for the navy — not the most cherished of the national institutions — met with the same difficulty as was experienced by other branches of the public service in the depreciation of the assignats, with which alone naval administrators could pay contractors. At the end of 1795 twelve hundred francs in paper were worth scarce twenty in gold. Having accepted naval inferiority as a necessary condition, the Committee of Public Safety resolved to maintain the great fleets in the ports simply as a threat to the enemy, and to send to sea only small divisions to prey upon his commerce and to levy tribute upon his colonies.

From the end of 1795 forward, this policy prevailed and was finally accepted even by the emperor after several attempts, fruitless through the incompetence of his sea-officers, to realize on the sea that employment of great masses in which he so wonderfully excelled on land. The reluctance of his supreme genius to accede to this system of petty war may be accepted as testimony that on sea, as on shore, great results can only be expected by wielding great masses. Upon this conclusion history too has set its seal; for the squadron and division warfare of the French navy, seconded though it was by hosts of commerce-destroyers, public and private, produced practically no results, had absolutely no effect upon the issue of the war. On the other hand, that Napoleon, when convinced that he could expect nothing decisive from his fleet, accepted the use of it as a means of harassment or of diversion, must be received as a weighty indication of the naval policy suited to the inferior power. To assume a menacing attitude at many points, to give effect to the menace by frequent and vigorous sorties, to provoke thus a dispersion of the enemy's superior force, that he may be led to expose detachments to attack by greater numbers, — such must be the outline of conduct laid down for the weaker navy. But that such a course may be really effective, — that the inferior may, as in some of Bonaparte's wonderful campaigns, become ultimately superior, — there must be at some fitly chosen point of the sea frontier a concentrated body of ships; whose escape, if effected, may be the means of inflicting a great disaster upon the enemy by crushing one or more of the exposed fractions of his fleet. Unless there be such a central mass, mere dissemination is purposeless. Inferiority carried beyond a certain degree becomes impotence; nor will all the commerce-destroyers fancy can picture restore the balance to the nation hopelessly weaker in ships of the line-of-battle.

On land as well as on sea weakness was stamped on the military movements of the year 1795. Its diplomatic successes were due to the arms of 1794. Early in the year Pichegru was removed from Holland to the upper Rhine, being succeeded by Moreau. Between the armies commanded by these two lay that of the Sambre and Meuse, still under Jourdan, concentrated on the left bank of the Rhine between Dusseldorf and Coblentz. It was provided that, in case of the three armies acting together, the chief command should be with Pichegru. The removal of the restraint enforced by the Terror was evidenced in these Northern forces by the number of desertions during the severity of this unusual winter. In the army of Italy the case was even worse; and the frightful destitution of the soldiers, made known a year later in Bonaparte's celebrated proclamation upon taking command, led to even greater losses from the ranks. Toward the end of January seventeen thousand men were detached from this army to Toulon to take part in a projected invasion of Corsica. The expedition never sailed; but such was the horror inspired by the sufferings they had undergone that the hardiest soldiers forsook their colors, and of two fine divisions not ten thousand men rejoined the army.[1]

Under such conditions military operations could not but be sluggish; the genius of a Bonaparte was needed to supply the impetus which the emasculated central government could no longer impart. The great Carnot, also, had been removed from the direction of the war, March 4, 1795, under the law prescribing periodic changes of members in the Committee of Public Safety. The fall of Luxembourg, already mentioned, was obtained only by the slow process of blockade. Not till September, when the season was nearly over, did the French armies move; Jourdan and Pichegru being then directed to undertake a concerted invasion, from their widely separated positions, intending to form a junction in the enemy's country. Jourdan crossed the Rhine, advanced south as far as the Main, and invested Mayence, the Austrians retiring before him. Pichegru received the capitulation of Mannheim, which opened its gates upon the threat of bombardment without receiving a shot. He showed no vigor in following this success, and his dilatory ill-combined movements permitted the Austrian general, Clairfayt, to concentrate his armies in a central position between the Main and Mannheim, parting the two French leaders. The new direction of war, either through folly, or from sharing the growing inefficiency of the general government, had failed to accumulate the supplies of all kinds needed by the masses thus gathered in a wild and impoverished region. Clairfayt combined a powerful movement against the destitute and suffering army of Jourdan, compelling him to retreat and recross the Rhine. Leaving a corps of observation before him and holding Pichegru in

[1] Jomini, Guerres de la Rév., livre viii. p. 74.

check on the south, he then himself crossed the river at Mayence and assaulted vigorously the lines on the left bank with which the enemy during the past year had surrounded the place. The blockading forces were driven back in divergent directions; and the Austrians in increasing numbers poured into the country west of the river, separating Jourdan from Pichegru.

It was at this moment that the National Convention was dissolving and the Directory assuming the reins of government. Carnot became one of its five members. Impressed by the importance of retaining Mannheim, the loss of which was threatened by the recent reverses, he sent urgent orders to Jourdan to move south to the support of his colleague, using his own judgment as to the means. It was too late. The mingled weakness and ignorance of the preceding government had caused a destitution of means and an inferiority of force wholly inadequate to cope with the superior strategic position of the Austrian masses. Mannheim, which had surrendered on the 20th of September, was regained on the 22d of November by the Austrians, who at once re-enforced the troops on the west bank, acting against Pichegru, while Clairfayt pushed further back the other French army. With this success his brilliant operations closed for the year. The weather had become excessively bad, causing great sickness; and on the 19th of December he proposed an armistice, which Jourdan was only too glad to accept. The Austrians, who when the year opened were east of the Rhine, remained in force on the west bank, holding well-advanced positions based upon Mayence and Mannheim,—the two capital places for sustaining operations on either side of the river.

The suspension of arms lasted until May 30, 1796, when the French, having given the notification required by the terms of the armistice, again crossed the river and began hostilities. But, although great and instructive military events followed this new undertaking, the centre of interest had by this time shifted from the north and east to the Italian frontier of the republic, where the successes of Bonaparte enchained it until the Peace of Campo Formio dissolved the coalition against France. That dazzling career had begun which becomes, thenceforth until its close, the main thread of French history, to which other incidents have to be referred, and by following which their mutual relations are most easily understood. We have reached therefore the period when a naval narrative reverts naturally to the Mediterranean; for Bonaparte's Italian campaigns profoundly affected the political and maritime conditions in that sea. Upon it also he next embarked for the extraordinary enterprise, condemned by many as chimerical, and yet so signally stamped by the characteristics of his genius, in which he first came into collision with the Sea Power of Great Britain, destined to ruin his career, and with the great seaman in whom that Sea Power found the highest expression it has ever attained.

"During the year 1795," says the distinguished military historian of these wars, "France, after a twelvemonth of victory, came near losing all her conquests; threatened with a dangerous internal reaction, she only with difficulty succeeded in freeing herself from embarrassments and modifying the defects of her institutions. The next year we shall find her launched in a yet vaster career, by the great captain who so long presided over her destinies, who raised her to the pinnacle of glory by his victories, and thence plunged her to the abyss through disregard of justice and moderation."[1]

---

[1] Jomini, Guerres de la Rév., livre ix. p. 341.

CHAPTER VIII.

THE MEDITERRANEAN AND ITALY. — FROM THE EVACUATION OF TOULON IN 1793 TO THE BRITISH WITHDRAWAL FROM THAT SEA, IN 1796, AND THE BATTLE OF CAPE ST. VINCENT, FEBRUARY, 1797. — AUSTRIA FORCED TO MAKE PEACE.

AFTER the evacuation of Toulon, on the 19th of December, 1793, Lord Hood had taken his fleet to Hyères Roads, — an anchorage formed by the group of islands of the same name a few miles east of Toulon. There he remained during the greater part of January, revictualling his ships and considering what steps should next be taken to assure British interests in the Mediterranean.

It is essential to a fleet, as to an army, to have always near at hand depots of supplies, upon which it can depend to replace the consumption of the limited stores carried on board, and to which it can resort for refit. The way from the depots to the fleet, or the army, technically called the communications, should be such as can most easily be defended by the armed force itself, without impairing its liberty in movements necessary to obtain the objects of the war. In other words, this depot, or base, should be near the scene of operations and, when practicable, so situated that the fleet, while actively engaged, interposes directly or indirectly between it and the enemy. Nearness was doubly important in the days of sailing ships, whose movements depended upon the fickle element of the wind; for then a ship going in for refit not only took more time to perform the voyage, but also in returning made a heavier draft upon her resources, and consequently could remain a shorter period at the seat of war.

Toulon, while securely held, served as such a base; although, being exposed to overpowering attack from the land side, its situation called for excessive expenditure of effort. Toulon was, however, now lost, and the British were thrown back upon Gibraltar, at the very entrance of the Mediterranean, and nine hundred miles from the seat of hostilities, for a secure depot in which to land stores and a safe anchorage for transports and crippled ships-of-war.

Although the possession of a strong place, suited in itself for a base, may decide the character of operations projected, logically the necessary operations should first be determined, and the choice of the base be decided by them. In the Mediterranean, as elsewhere generally at this time, the policy of Great Britain was to control the sea for the protection of commerce, and to sustain on shore the continental powers in the war against France, — chiefly by money, but also by naval co-operation when feasible. To support the land warfare, her diplomatic negotiations strove to unite, in the general military effort, as many as possible of the small independent states into which Italy was divided, to promote among them unity of action, and to foster the sense of security, in taking a decided step against France, which they could only derive from the presence among them of a strong power, such as Great Britain showed in her fleet. Neither their traditions nor the character of their rulers enabled them to combine strongly as equals; nor, as has before been said, was there any one state so predominant as to give a nucleus around which the others could gather. The only possible centre was Great Britain, present as a power in her fleet. Moreover, if unable, as she proved, to stir them up to positive, harmonious, concerted action, it was her interest to impose upon them a benevolent neutrality towards herself and her allies, and to deter them from inimical measures into which they might otherwise be impelled by the demands of the republic and their fear of the French army. Friendly ports along the whole coast were essential for the security of her shipping and the promotion of her commerce. Finally, it must be added that the character of the shore between Nice and Genoa, interposing between the French and Austrian armies, particularly favored direct naval coöperation. The Maritime Alps and the Apennines, coming down close to the sea, left but a single narrow, and yet long, line of communications along the beach, traversed by a very bad road, in many parts under fire from the sea.[1] This condition made the armies using that line chiefly dependent for supplies upon coasters, whose movements ships-of-war could harass and impede,— though not, when sailing vessels, entirely stop.

Corsica, in its existing political conditions of revolt against France under the leadership of Paoli, appeared to offer the strategic situation which Hood was seeking. It was near and centrally placed with reference to the probable operations on shore; San Fiorenzo Bay, which became the chief anchorage for the fleet, being equidistant, about one hundred miles, from Nice and from Genoa. Leghorn also, one of the greatest depots of British trade in the Mediterranean and the seaport of Tuscany, over which Great Britain wished to enforce her influence, was but sixty miles from Cape Corso at the northern extremity of the island. All the trade with northern Italy had to pass close to Corsica, and was consequently exposed to capture if the seaports remained in French hands; especially as calms prevail around the island, facilitating the operations of row-galleys and neutralizing the powers of a sailing navy. Being an island, Corsica depended upon the control of the sea; and, though its size and rugged surface precluded conquest, there was believed to be a disposition to accept the protection of Great Britain as the only means of dispossessing the French troops, who

---

[1] L'horrible route de la Corniche sous le feu des cannonières anglaises. — JOMINI, *Guerres de la Rév.*, livre x. p. 62.

still held the seaports of San Fiorenzo, Bastia, and Calvi.

Sir Gilbert Elliott, who had been the Civil Commissioner of Great Britain in Toulon during the last month of its occupation, left Hyères Bay early in January to confer with Paoli, who had proposed the annexation of the island to the British crown. His enthusiastic reception by the people and the assurances of the Corsican chieftain convinced him that the measure was sincerely desired; and in consequence of his representations, Hood, on the 24th of January, sailed from Hyères with his whole fleet for San Fiorenzo Bay. The weather proving very tempestuous, and the three-decked ships, of which there were several, being ill-fitted to contend with it, the admiral was forced to take them to Porto Ferrajo in Elba, and to send against San Fiorenzo a detachment only. This appeared off the place on the 7th of February; and after a series of combined operations, in which the navy bore a very conspicuous share on land, the French evacuated the town and works on the 19th of the month, retreating upon Bastia. The admiral then urged an attack upon Bastia; but the general thought he could not spare enough men. Nelson, who had been blockading there for some time, strongly represented the feasibility of the enterprise; and, after a sharp altercation between the two commanders-in-chief, Hood determined to undertake the siege with the navy and the troops who were serving on board as marines. The landing began on the 3d of April; but the place held out till the 21st of May, when it capitulated. Calvi was next taken in hand, the operations beginning on the 19th of June, and ending with its surrender on the 10th of August. The whole island was thus freed from the presence of French troops,— a result due almost wholly to the navy, although the army bore a share in the operations at San Fiorenzo and Calvi. To the determination of Hood and the ardent representations of Nelson was due that Bastia was besieged at all; and, as thirty-five hundred regular troops then surrendered to an outside force of fourteen hundred seamen and marines, the opinion of Sir Gilbert Elliott that "the blockade of the port was the chief means of reducing it," can scarcely be disputed. At the siege of Calvi Nelson lost his right eye.

Between the siege of Bastia and that of Calvi, the General Assembly of Corsica met, and on the 19th of June, 1794, tendered the insular crown to the king of Great Britain. With the successful issue of the military operations, this political act consummated the possession of the island. But, to quote the words of Elliott, the claim to Corsica rested upon superior force,[1] and by that only could be asserted; and this superior force the British government failed to provide. The love of the people for Paoli, and the period of anxiety through which he and they had passed, caused the connection to be eagerly desired, and accepted with demonstrations of the warmest delight; but as security succeeded the sense of danger, the first-love between nations so radically distinct in temperament and institutions was followed by the symptoms attending ill-assorted unions. Still, with prompt action and strong garrisons, the benefit of the foreign occupation might have been manifest, dissatisfaction might have yielded to considerations of interest, and the island been retained. The British government acted slowly. Elliott had urged that authority should be sent him beforehand to take over the executive functions at once, as soon as the Act of Union passed; instead of which, Paoli was left for four months in his old position, and developed a jealousy of his destined successor not unprecedented in the heads of states. This feeling, which he held with Corsican intensity, communicated itself to his followers; and an inauspicious division of sentiment already existed when, in October, after an interval of four months, Elliott received his

[1] Life of Lord Minto, vol. ii. p. 274.

powers as viceroy. Paoli continued for a year longer to reside in Corsica, and up to the time of his departure was a cause of trouble to the viceroy, and so of strength to the partisans of France, who became numerous.

During the year 1794 the superior importance of the operations on the frontiers of Belgium and Germany, as well as in Spain, caused the French armies of Italy and the Alps to remain quiet, after some early successes which had placed in their hands the chief passes of the mountains and advanced their line on the coast as far as Vado, on the borders of Genoese territory. Early in 1795 a force of eighteen thousand men was detached to Toulon for the invasion of Corsica; but, although the French had in the port fifteen ships-of-the-line, they felt that neither the admiral nor the officers possessed the tactical skill necessary to handle the fleet in presence of an enemy of nearly equal force, if encumbered with a large body of transports. The case reproduced that of Conflans, when expected in 1759 to cover the French invasion of England. As a rule, in combined military and naval expeditions the fleet and the army should start together; but the tactical embarrassment of transports is indisputable. If the fleet cannot encounter the enemy successfully when not so hampered, it but encourages disaster to incur the meeting with them in company. Not improperly, in such a case of doubt, it was decided that the Toulon fleet should sail alone; and, accordingly, on the 2d of March, 1795, Admiral Martin put to sea with fifteen of the line, seven frigates, and five smaller vessels. Despite these respectable numbers, the efficiency of the force was poor. Out of twelve thousand officers and men on board the ships-of-the-line, seventy-five hundred had never before been to sea; and Martin reported that, deducting officers and petty-officers, he had but twenty-seven hundred seamen to man the fleet.[1]

Hood had gone home the previous November, expecting

[1] Chevalier, Mar. Fran. sous la Rép., p. 174.

to return; and the British were now commanded by Admiral Hotham. The latter had cruised off Toulon for three weeks in mid-winter, on account of the indications of the French coming out, and after a succession of most violent weather returned to San Fiorenzo Bay on the 10th of January. He sailed again, apparently about the 22d of the month, to cover a convoy expected from England, leaving in port the " Berwick," seventy-four; which, through the carelessness of her officers, had been permitted to roll her masts overboard at her anchors. After some more hard cruising, the fleet put into Leghorn on the 25th of February, leaving still in San Fiorenzo Bay the " Berwick," the delay in whose repairs can only be attributed to the penury of naval resources. The presence of the fleet in Leghorn was probably necessary both for its own supplies and to remind the wavering Tuscany of the power of Great Britain at her doors; but the " Berwick " incident served powerfully to illustrate the far-reaching effects of individual carelessness and the impolicy of exposing small detachments not covered, directly or indirectly, by the main body. On the 7th of March the French fleet came in sight of Cape Corso, and almost at the same moment discovered the " Berwick," which had only the previous day succeeded in leaving San Fiorenzo for Leghorn. Being still crippled, she was easily overtaken, and forced to surrender at noon.

The following day Hotham in Leghorn learned that the enemy had sailed, and the next morning at dawn put to sea in pursuit. On the 11th the two fleets came in sight of each other, the French far south and to windward of the British, out of gun-shot, and thus continued during the 12th. That night one of the French seventy-fours lost a topmast and parted company, reducing their numbers to fourteen. The following morning the " Ça-Ira," an eighty-gun ship, ran into her next ahead, losing both fore and main topmasts, and thus became the source of anxiety and danger which a crippled ship ever is in the fleet to which she belongs. As she dropped out of the line, a British frigate ran close to her on the side encumbered with the fallen spars, annoying her there for some time with comparative impunity, and was then succeeded by Nelson in the "Agamemnon," who hung about on her quarters until several ships bore down to her relief.

During the night the "Sans Culottes," of one hundred and twenty guns, the heaviest vessel in the French fleet, dropped out of the line to leeward, and in the morning was out of sight. The "Ça-Ira" was taken in tow by the "Censeur," seventy-four, and at daybreak these two were some distance from, and to the north-east of, their fleet. Both parties were at this time much scattered from the irregularities of the wind; but it shifting now to the northwest favored the British, and those nearest the separated ships speedily brought them to action. While this partial engagement was going on, both fleets shaped their course for the scene, the French intending to cover the "Censeur" and "Ça-Ira" by passing between them and the British, but owing to some misunderstanding this was not done. As the two vans went slowly by on opposite tacks, a sharp exchange of shots took place, in which the British, not being well closed up, were overmatched, and two of their number suffered severely; but as the French allowed the enemy to interpose between them and the disabled vessels, these were forced to surrender after a very gallant resistance, in which they lost four hundred men and were partially dismasted. Each fleet continuing its course in opposite directions, they soon separated and passed out of sight.

The baffling character of the wind, combined with the indifferent sailing qualities of the British three-deckers, deprive this action of any special tactical significance; and the very mediocre calibre of the two admirals was not calculated to overcome the difficulties they encountered. The numerous accidents in Martin's fleet, and the parting of the "Sans Culottes" at such a moment, show the indifferent character of the French captains, and probably justify the comment that Hotham owed his success to the initiative of the admirable officers under his command rather than to his own capacity. "I went on board Admiral Hotham," wrote Nelson, "as soon as our firing grew slack in the van and the 'Ça-Ira' and 'Censeur' had struck, to propose to him leaving our two crippled ships, the two prizes, and four frigates, and pursue the enemy; but he, much cooler than myself, said, 'We must be contented, we have done very well.' Admiral Goodall backed me; I got him to write to the Admiral, but it would not do; we should have had such a day as I believe the annals of England never produced."[1] "Admiral Hotham," says Chevalier,[2] "showed great circumspection. He probably did not appreciate the improvised fleets of the republic. To fight, there are needed ships in good condition, capable seamen, skilful gunners, and officers accustomed to order, to military dispositions, and to squadron manœuvres. These we did not have." "The enemy," wrote Nelson about the same fleet, a few months later, "are neither seamen nor officers."[3] The immediate consequence of this defeat was the abandonment of the projected expedition against Corsica.

After the battle a gale of wind forced the British into Spezia and caused the wreck of the "Illustrious," seventy-four, which, from injuries received in the action, was not able to keep off shore. This, with the capture of the "Berwick," equalized the losses of the two fleets. The French anchored in Hyères Bay, where they were rejoined by the "Sans Culottes," and on the 24th of March returned to Toulon. Admiral Renaudin's arrival from Brest[4] on the 4th of April raised the available force to nineteen or twenty ships-of-the-line; to which the enemy

---

[1] Nels. Disp., vol. ii. p. 26.   [2] Mar. Fran. sous la Rép., p. 186.
[3] Nels. Disp., vol. ii. p. 50.   [4] See *ante*, p. 176.

could now oppose only thirteen of their own and two Neapolitan. But, although the British were very destitute of material for necessary equipment and repair,[1] the superiority of organization, discipline, and officer-like training, allowed them little real cause for anxiety. In the month of May a Jacobin outbreak occurred in Toulon. The government had ordered Martin to take advantage of Renaudin's junction, and again to seek the enemy while thus superior. The mob raised the cry that as soon as the fleet sailed the enemies of the Revolution would enter the town and massacre the patriots. The seamen, except those belonging to the Brest squadron, left their vessels, under pretext of deliberating on the dangers of their country, and took part in all the street demonstrations. An expedition was even set on foot against Marseille; but the central government was getting stronger, or rather anarchy was becoming wearisome, and after a paltry engagement the Toulonese fell back upon their city and submitted. A great number of seamen, however, had deserted; and the necessity of recovering them delayed the departure of the fleet, which finally put to sea on the 7th of June with seventeen ships-of-the-line. The time for a favorable sortie was, however, past; the British having at last received a large re-enforcement.

After partially refitting in Spezia, Hotham took his fleet to San Fiorenzo, arriving there on the 30th of March. On the 17th of April he sailed again for Minorca, where he hoped to meet a re-enforcement and a much-needed convoy; but a succession of westerly winds caused the fleet to lose ground, instead of gaining, until the 27th, when it unexpectedly and most fortunately met a body of store-ships from Gibraltar. With these the admiral at once bore up for Leghorn, arriving there next day. Had the French in their own dockyards refitted as rapidly as the British did

---

[1] "We cannot get another mast this side of Gibraltar." (Nels Disp., May 4, 1795.)

in a foreign port, and gone to sea with the increase of
strength that Renaudin brought, they should have intercepted this important convoy, if they did not bring the fleet
to action. The correspondence of Nelson, still a simple
captain, testifies continually, in his own vivid style, to the
critical state of the campaign at this moment.

On the 8th of May Hotham sailed again for Minorca, and
continued to cruise off that island until the 14th of June,
when Rear-admiral Robert Mann joined him with a re-
enforcement from England of nine [1] ships-of-the-line, making the British superior in number as in quality to the
enemy. As a convoy was also expected, the fleet kept the
same station until it arrived on the 22d, when the whole
body sailed for San Fiorenzo, anchoring there June 29.
On the 4th of July Hotham sent Nelson with his own ship
and some smaller vessels to co-operate on the Riviera of
Genoa with the Austrian advance against the French ; but
the detachment fell in with Martin's fleet, and had to return to San Fiorenzo, being, says Nelson, " hard pressed "
by the enemy, who pursued until they saw the British fleet
at anchor. The latter weighed as soon as possible, but
did not come up with the French until the 14th, near the
Hyères Islands, where a trifling brush took place, resulting
in the capture of the " Alcide," seventy-four, which immediately after surrendering caught fire and blew up. This
small affair was the last in which Admiral Hotham was
directly concerned. Hood had been definitively relieved
of the Mediterranean command before he could sail from
England on his return ; and Hotham, weary of a burden
to which he felt himself unfitted and had proved himself
unequal, applied for relief, and struck his flag on the 1st
of November, 1795.

Prior to the naval brush off Hyères, little had been done
in Italy by the armies on either side. The French, whose
forces were far inferior to those of the allies and in a state

---

[1] James, vol. i. p 297. Nelson says six. (Nels. Disp., vol. ii. p 47.)

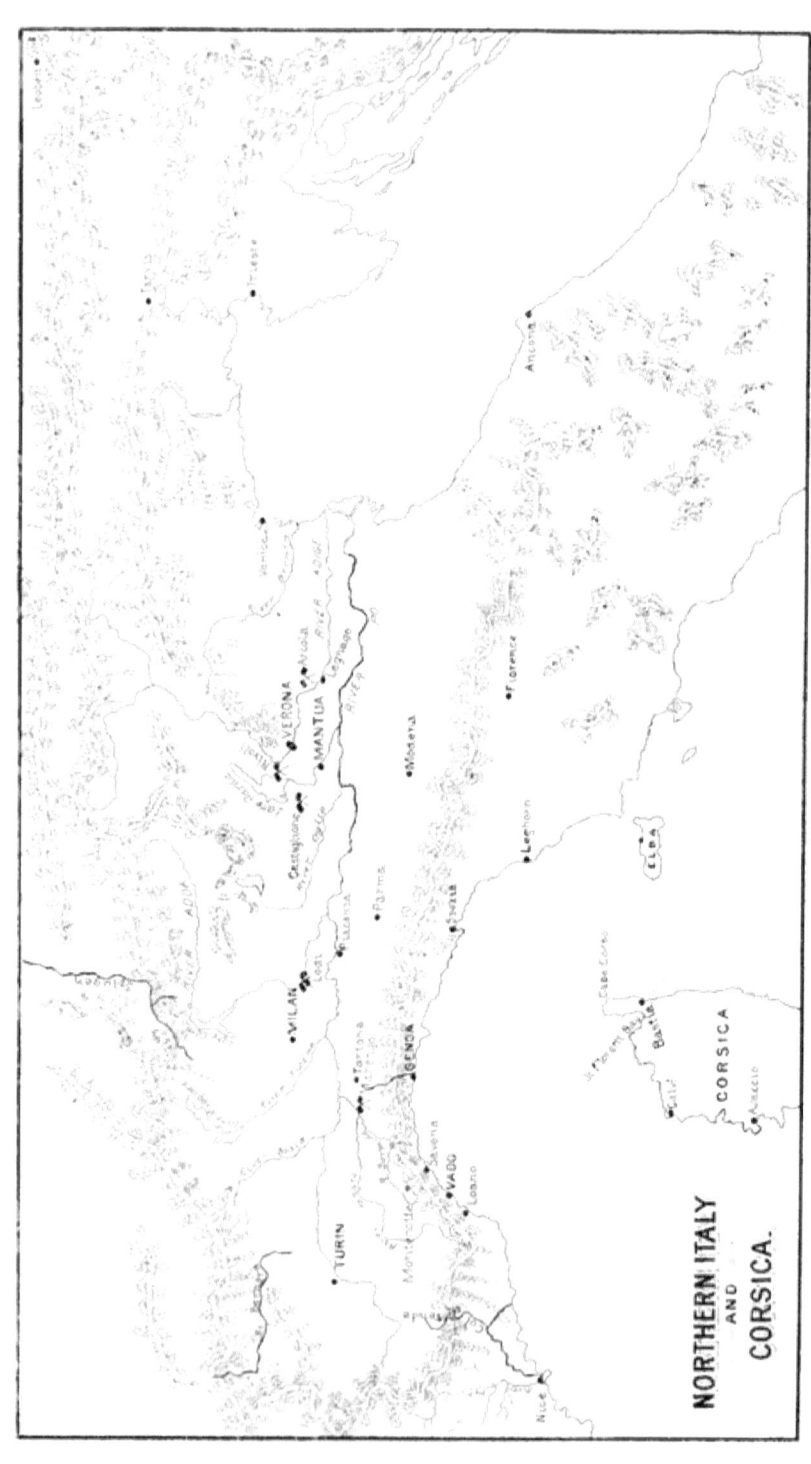

of great destitution, were compelled to stand on the defensive over a very long line, of which the advanced post on the sea was at Vado. The Austrians had imposed upon the Sardinians their own plan of campaign, which was to strike the extreme right of the French at Vado, and then drive them back along the Corniche, while the Sardinians attacked on the other flank through the passes of the Apennines up to the Col di Tende, where the Maritime Alps begin. The British fleet was to co-operate with the movement on the side of the sea, — a consideration which had much to do with determining the Austrian plan. By occupying Vado and the Riviera east of it, the coasting trade heretofore carried on from the ports of Genoa and Tuscany to southern France would be stopped; a matter of great consequence to the republic, as those departments only raised grain for three months' consumption and depended for the rest upon that which came from Barbary and Italy by way of Tuscany. With a British squadron at Vado, the populace of Provence, the navy at Toulon, and the army of Italy, would have to be supplied from the north of France by bad inland roads [1] Vado Bay was, moreover, the best anchorage between Nice and Genoa. Devins, the Austrian general, began his movement on the 13th of June, passing through Genoese territory against the protest of that neutral government. The French resisted sturdily; but the odds were too great, and by the end of June they had fallen back to a line extending from Borghetto on the sea to Ormea in the mountains, abandoning Vado and the intermediate coast towns. Devins now called on Hotham for naval support, and the British admiral detached Nelson, as has already been seen, to give it; but the encounter with the French fleet delaying his arrival for some days served Devins with a pretext for inaction. He employed the mean time in fortifying his position and improving the roads in his rear.

[1] Jomini, Guerres de la Rév., livre viii. p. 75.

On the 17th of July Nelson reached Genoa, took on board the British minister to that republic, and went to Vado, anchoring there on the 21st. He immediately conferred with Devins, who gave it as his opinion that the Austrians could not advance further until the French were compelled to retire by want of provisions, — a result he expected from the action of the navy. Nelson explained to the minister that the food supplies being carried in neutral vessels he was powerless to stop them; for he had stringent orders from the admiralty that no legal measures should be instituted against such, when arrested, until full particulars in each case had been sent to England and instructions had come back what to do. Meanwhile the cargoes, being perishable, would be spoiled. Such utterly inconsequent proceedings, though highly characteristic of the military action of cabinets, were most exasperating to a man of Nelson's temper, always prone to cut knots; but, as he was pecuniarily answerable and a poor man, he could not disregard them on his sole authority. The British ministers to Genoa and Sardinia both concurred in advising him to carry out Devins's wishes; and then Nelson, with the fearlessness of responsibility he always showed, — and sometimes out of, as well as in, season, — issued orders to his frigates to take every vessel bound to France or to ports within the French lines, to whatsoever nation it might belong. At the same time the general also sent out small cruisers; and it is roundly asserted by Jomini that he laid a tax on all coasting vessels brought in by them, forcing them to pay for a passport and appropriating the proceeds to himself. The utmost diligence, however, could not insure the interruption of a traffic carried on by very small vessels, having to make but short night runs close along a coast;[1] and Nelson's orders, while doubtless productive of some results in stopping large vessels from Tuscany and Algiers, could not prevent

---

[1] The effects were, however, very severely felt in France. (Corr. de Nap., vol. i., pp. 65, 79, 95.)

supplies getting in by Genoese coasters. The difficulty was increased by the fact that a number of the ports in rear of the French positions belonged to Genoa, and the inhabitants depended upon her for food. To turn a deaf ear to their cries of suffering, and to prevent supplies landed there being used by the French, were alike impossible.

These considerations should have led Devins to regard naval co-operation simply as the efforts of a light force, competent to harass, not to destroy, the enemy's communications; and should have induced him to force his own way, by early and vigorous action, while the French were inferior in numbers and before their positions became too strong. Instead of this, he used the Sardinians and British, not as allies, but as excuses for not moving; action of one kind or another on their part was necessary before he could advance. Thus the summer slipped away, the French busily strengthening their lines and bringing up the army of the Pyrenees to re-enforce that of Italy, after peace was made with Spain. Nelson was full of projects to embark a corps of Austrians, who should seize and occupy a coast position in rear of the French; but Devins only played with a proposition of which Jomini speaks with scant respect, and which was certainly open to the objection that, if carried out with adequate force, it divided the Austrian army. Nelson, it is true, guaranteed its retreat to his ships in case of need; but the Austrian, not unnaturally, preferred a less uncertain line. The British captain, who had at first felt respect for Devins's abilities, wrote on the 17th of September that it had for some time appeared to him " that the general intended to go no further than his present position, and meant to lay the miscarriage of his enterprise against Nice to the non-co-operation of the British fleet and the Sardinian army."[1] Whatever his purpose, Devins did not advance, but quietly awaited the French attack. Early in November a severe illness caused

[1] Nels. Disp., vol. ii. p. 84.

him to give up the command; and on the 23d of the month the enemy, under General Schérer, assaulted vigorously the centre of the allied position, where the Sardinians touched the Austrians. This point had always been weak, and after a short struggle was forced. The original intention of Schérer had been to turn, after piercing the centre, against the Sardinians, as Bonaparte did in the following year; but a very heavy fall of snow in the mountains decided him to swing round to the right, drive the Austrians back upon the coast, and, if possible, anticipate them upon their line of retreat to the eastward. In this he was not entirely successful; but the imminent danger forced the enemy to abandon all their line of works and fall back precipitately, with a loss of seven thousand men, killed, wounded and prisoners, besides their depots at Loano, Vado, and Savona. This action, which was a brilliant and decisive victory, is known as the battle of Loano. By the first of December the Austrians had recrossed the Apennines and were again in the positions from which they had set out the previous June.

The military plan and execution of the campaign by the land forces scarcely falls within the scope of the present work. An advance by the armies of a coalition, whose respective troops and lines of operation are separated by a chain of mountains, even of the height of the Apennines, with difficult communication across them, does not present a combination promising mutual support and probable success. To this disadvantage is to be added that of the long and narrow line by which all the Austrian supplies had to be forwarded; and which any successful advance would make yet longer and more difficult. On the other hand, the Austrians counted much upon the help that could be extended by the navy of Great Britain, in whose interest the occupation of the shore line was undertaken.[1] By

---

[1] The Austrian generals say, and true, they were brought on the coast at the express desire of the English to coöperate with the fleet, which fleet nor admiral they never saw. — *Nels. Disp.*, vol. ii. p. 213.

their advance they controlled Vado Bay, — the best anchorage between Villefranche (Nice) and Genoa; and their presence imposed a restraint upon the latter republic, whose attitude was largely determined by the comparative forces of the belligerents. Did then the British navy, under these circumstances, do all that it could have done to insure the success of the common cause?

The answer can scarcely be yes. Nelson, indeed, exerted himself with the energy that never failed him; but his correspondence shows that he did not think the force assigned him equal to its task. Could it then have been increased? The answer again is scarcely doubtful. The British fleet of the line was slightly superior in numbers to the French at Toulon, and far superior in the quality of its officers and men. It was doubtless embarrassed by numerous duties, — by those conflicting interests whose divergence imposes the great test of capacity upon a general officer. The French fleet at Toulon, co-operation with the Austrian advance, the protection of trade, the covering of Corsica, the political interests involved in controlling the action of the small Italian states, — all these cares fell upon the British admiral. Of these, the French fleet was the most important; but all other interests of Britain and her allies were better served by co-operation with the Austrian advance, — by victory in the field, — than by any dissemination of force for other purposes. A decisive Imperial success would have determined the policy of every state in the western Mediterranean and closed every port to French cruisers.

In short, offensive action, and not the merely defensive attitude maintained through the campaign, was here clearly indicated. Nelson intimates that the only course by which the navy could practically intercept the French communications was to enter the coasting ports and destroy the coasters. These little vessels defied detection on their voyages; only by chasing them into their nests could their wings be clipped. "A few days ago," he writes, "I scoured the coast between Monaco and Borghetto so completely, that although I was only able to take one ship loaded with corn, yet I forced the others into the Bay of Alassio, where they are so completely under the protection of formidable batteries *that not less than three sail-of-the-line* could attempt to take or destroy them. The number of vessels loaded and unloaded at those places is near one hundred, the greater part loaded with stores and corn for France."[1] Here was the strategic direction to be given to the British navy, after providing for the watch off Toulon. "You will now," wrote Nelson five years later to Lord Keith, "bear me out in my assertion, when I say that the British fleet could have prevented the invasion of Italy; and if our friend Hotham had kept his fleet on that coast, I assert, and you will agree with me, no army from France could have been furnished with stores or provisions; even men could not have marched."[2] If the fleet proved unequal to this task, final condemnation was passed on the allied plan of campaign, which was not in its conception characterized by sound military judgment. But Admiral Hotham, as Nelson said, had "no head for enterprise, perfectly satisfied that each month passes without any losses on our side."[3] Nelson never had under his orders any other ship-of-the-line than his own "Agamemnon;" and at the time of the decisive battle of Loano all his little squadron had been taken away except two, so that French gunboats harassed with impunity the left flank of the Austrians.[4] He himself at that critical moment had to remain in Genoa with the "Agamemnon," at the request of the Imperial minister, to prevent the crew of a French frigate then in port, supported as it would have

[1] Nels. Disp., vol. ii. p. 98 a. See also p. 110.
[2] Nels. Disp., June 6, 1800.
[3] Ibid., vol. ii., p. 64.
[4] For Nelson's complaints about the force under his command, see ibid., pp. 106–114.

been by French partisans, from seizing Voltri, — an important point upon the line of retreat of the Austrians, where a few resolute men could have stopped them until the pursuing army came up. To him alone was therefore attributed the escape of several thousand Imperial soldiers, among whom was the commander-in-chief himself.[1] Prior to the battle Genoa had permitted French intrigues and armed enterprises of this character to be concerted, almost openly, in her territories. This she would not have dared to do, had the British navy been present in force on the coast, acting under such a commander as Nelson; for the probabilities of final success would have been with the allies. In short, this campaign of the British fleet contributes another to the numerous lessons of history, upon the importance of having sufficient force at the decisive point and taking the offensive. It may be added that Hotham could better have spared ships to Nelson, if he had not thrown away his two opportunities of beating the Toulon fleet.

While Nelson was co-operating with the Austrians as far as his force admitted, the British fleet was generally cruising off Toulon, returning from time to time to San Fiorenzo or Leghorn for refit and stores. It was in this latter part of the year 1795 that the Directory, as will be remembered, decided to abandon the policy of fleet-fighting and to enter upon that of commerce-destroying, directed against exposed colonies of the enemy as well as against his trade afloat. Two squadrons, numbering in all seven ships-of-the-line and eight smaller vessels, were ordered fitted out at Toulon, which was with difficulty done for want of seamen. Since the action of July off Hyères, nearly all the sailors in Martin's fleet had deserted, disgusted with the bad food, scanty clothing, and constant disaster that were their portion. Enough, however, were at last gathered to man the ships selected; and on the 14th of Sep-

[1] Nels. Disp., vol. ii. p. 118.

tember six of the line and three frigates got away under the command of Captain Richery. It does not appear whether the British fleet was then at sea or at San Fiorenzo; but in either case it was at this port, and not until September 22d, that Hotham learned their escape. On the 5th of October this leisurely commander-in-chief sent Admiral Mann with six of the line in pursuit; but the French, having so great a start, could not be overtaken. They passed the Straits of Gibraltar early in October, bound to the British possessions in North America. On the 7th of the month, when a hundred and fifty miles west of Gibraltar, they fell in with an enemy's convoy of thirty-one merchant ships from the Levant, under the protection of three seventy-fours. Richery succeeded in capturing one of the latter, which had lost a topmast, and all the merchant ships except one. Having so valuable a booty, he decided to escort it into Cadiz, where he anchored on the 13th and was soon after found by Mann, whose arrival prevented his departure to fulfil his original mission. At about the same time some French frigates in the Atlantic took eighteen ships out of a Jamaica convoy. The other Toulon division, of one ship-of-the-line and six smaller vessels, cruised in the Levant; and, having made a number of prizes, returned safely to Toulon. Its commander, Captain Ganteaume, though undistinguished by any great achievements, was throughout his career remarkably fortunate in escaping the search of an enemy. It was he who commanded the flotilla on board which Bonaparte stole unseen through all the British cruisers, on his return from Egypt to France in 1799.

These results, coinciding so closely with the adoption of the new policy of commerce-destroying, confirmed the government in favor of this course, to which the French have always been strongly disposed. They hoped from it, to use the words of a representative in the Convention, "to force the English to a shameful bankruptcy;" what they obtained was the demoralization of their navy, the loss of the control of the sea and of their own external commerce, finally Napoleon's Continental System and the fall of the Empire.

The battle of Loano, decisive of the campaign of 1795, is yet more distinguished as marking the entrance upon the scene of two of the most remarkable figures in the war of the French Revolution. During the week after it was fought, Admiral Sir John Jervis, better known by his later title of Earl St. Vincent, arrived at San Fiorenzo, as the regular successor to Hood in the Mediterranean. During the winter Napoleon Bonaparte was chosen by the Directory to relieve Schérer in command of the Army of Italy.

The career and character of the youthful republican general are too well known, have been too often described, to be attempted by the author, from whose immediate theme, moreover, they stand apart. The personality of the already aged admiral, whose iron hands stamped his own image on the British navy and fashioned it into the splendid instrument with which the triumphs of Nelson were won, is, on the contrary, familiar to few except the students of naval history. Born in 1734, Sir John Jervis, when he assumed command of the Mediterranean fleet in his sixty-second year, had had no opportunity of distinguishing himself in the eyes of the world outside of the service to which he belonged. With the members of that service, however, he had long been a marked man. The child of a poor though well-born family, he had in early life, under the pressure of poverty, required of himself the same stern discipline and submission to the duty of the moment which he afterwards so rigorously exacted of others. Grave and unbending in his official relations, immovable as a rock when his determination was once formed, unrelenting almost to mercilessness in suppressing insubordination, then rife throughout the British navy, he had the high-bred polish of a man used to good society, and his demeanor was courteous, and, when occasion demanded, even courtly. A traveller by land as well as by sea, a constant and judicious reader, in a period when such habits were rarer than now among seamen, he was well informed in matters other than those relating merely to his profession. Of the latter, however, he was a master. His ship was the model of the British fleet during the American Revolution, and his high reputation drew to her quarter-deck youths from the best families of England, when they could obtain interest to get there. Yet no man was ever less swayed, in an age when social and political influence counted for so much, by any extrinsic claims of that character. Personal merit first, after that a family claim upon the navy, that a father or brother had given his life for the service,— nay, the very friendlessness of a deserving man,— such were the considerations that determined him in the use of patronage at his own disposal.

Yet, with all these strong attributes, capable too of a tenderness which could mourn long and deeply the loss of a valued comrade, the rule of Jervis was one of fear rather than love. It is impossible to criticise adversely measures whose extreme severity was justified, if not imperatively demanded, by the appalling crisis of the mutinies of 1797; impossible to withhold admiration, not unmingled with awe, from the impressive figure of the chief who stood unmoved and unyielding amid the smothered discontent, revolt threatening from below, the enemy's coast in sight from the deck, knowing that in every other fleet the crews had taken the ships from their officers, but determined it should not be so in the Mediterranean. Yet admiration is qualified by the feeling that to the ruthless temper of the man the position was not wholly displeasing, — that he was in his natural element when crushing opposition. A captain, who with great personal courage had quelled a rising in his ship, dragging the ringleaders with his own hands from among their followers, interceded on behalf of one of the condemned because he had previously borne a good character. "I am glad of it," replied Jervis; "hitherto we have been hanging scoundrels. Now men will know that no good character will atone for the crime of mutiny." In lesser matters, also, his tendency was to exaggerate restraint as well as punishment. "Where I would take a penknife," said Nelson, "Lord St. Vincent takes a hatchet."

With such characteristics, accompanied though they were by resolution and high professional accomplishments, it is not to be expected that the fire of genius will be found. Though not an ungenerous man, Lord St. Vincent lacked the sympathetic qualities that made Nelson at once so lovable and so great a leader of men. Escaping the erratic temper and the foibles of his great successor, upon whose career these defects have left marks ever to be regretted by those who love his memory, Jervis fell short too of the inspiration, of the ardor, which in moments of difficulty lifted Nelson far above the common plane of mankind, and have stamped his actions with the seal of genius. But after Nelson, Jervis, though of a different order, stands first among British commanders-in-chief. For inspiration he had a cool, sound, and rapid professional judgment; for ardor, a steady, unflinching determination to succeed; and these, joined to a perfect fearlessness of responsibility such as Nelson also showed, have won for him a place in the first rank of those chieftains, whether sea or land, who have not received the exceptional endowments of Nature's favorites. In the one general action which Fortune permitted to him, the battle of Cape St. Vincent, he illustrated these traits to a high degree; as Nelson then also showed that faculty of quick appreciation and instant action, in which all the processes of thought and will blend into one overpowering conviction and impulse that lesser men never know. Whether we consider the vastly superior numbers then deliberately engaged, the tactics of

the admiral on the battle-field, or his appreciation of the
critical position in which Great Britain then stood, Sir
John Jervis's conduct on that occasion must make the
battle of Cape St. Vincent ever illustrious among the
most brilliant sea-fights of all ages.

To these powerful elements of his nature, Jervis added
a capacity for comprehensive and minute attention to the
details of discipline, order and economy, without which
mere severity would become aimless and productive of
none but bad results. He was fortunate in finding among
the Mediterranean captains an unusual number of men of
consummate seamanship, energy and resources, in all the
vigor of a prime still youthful, who were only waiting for
a master-hand to combine and give direction to their abilities. With such a head and with such subordinates, the
British Mediterranean fleet soon became a model of efficiency and spirit, which was probably never equalled in the
days of sailing ships. Nelson so considered it; and the
old admiral himself bewailed its memory several years
later, when commanding the Channel fleet, and complained
testily of the "old women in the guise of young men,"
whom he found in charge of ships off Brest. As an administrator, when First Lord, the economy of Jervis became exaggerated into parsimony, and his experience of
the frauds connected with the dockyards of the day led
him into a crusade against them, which was both well
meant and necessary, but particularly ill-timed. It has
consequently left a stigma of failure upon his administration, which is due, however, not to his executive inefficiency, but to a misapprehension of the political signs of the
times. Absorbed in reform, and for it desiring quiet, he
saw only peace while the dark clouds of war were gathering thick on the horizon. Therefore the British navy,
well-worn by the first war, was not ready for that which
followed it in 1803.

Jervis's arrival in the Mediterranean was too late to

remedy the impending evils. It was a singular misfortune for Great Britain, that the interregnum between two such able men as Hood and Jervis should have coincided with the determination of the French to try the chance of battle with their Mediterranean fleet, and that the opportunities they lost should have fallen to so sluggish and cautious an admiral as Hotham. "To say how much we wanted Lord Hood on the 13th of July," wrote Nelson, "is to say, Will you have all the French fleet, or no action?"[1] Accepting this opinion in the light of Nelson's subsequent achievements, it may be permitted to think that, if not all the fleet, so many ships would have fallen as to have prevented the sailing of Richery's squadron and the consequent necessary detachment of Admiral Mann; while the loss of seamen captured would have seriously crippled the operations of the flotilla, which from Toulon supplied the Army of Italy with ammunition, artillery and stores. Light guns on mountain carriages could be carried along the Corniche; but at the opening of Bonaparte's operations all heavy guns, and artillery outfits of all kinds, had to be taken by sea from Nice to Savona.[2] The demands of this flotilla necessitated the laying up of the fleet,[3] — a matter of less consequence as the determination to resort to commerce-destroying had then been reached. The French navy therefore became, through the flotilla, a very important part of Bonaparte's communications; and it has already been pointed out that sailing ships could not break up, though they might much disturb, the voyages of the smaller vessels employed on a difficult coast, with batteries under which to take refuge.

After the battle of Loano, Nelson, whose occupation on the Gulf of Genoa was for the time over, went to Leghorn to refit his ship, then nearly three years in commission

---

[1] Nels. Disp., vol. ii. p. 63.
[2] Commentaires de Nap., vol. i. p. 112.
[3] Chevalier, Mar. Fran. sous la Rép. p. 251.

Not till January 19, 1796, did he join Jervis, who since his arrival on the station had, for the most part, remained in San Fiorenzo organizing his fleet. The new admiral showed him the same confidence as his predecessors, and sent him at once to his old station, with a light division, to prevent any small number of men making a descent upon Italy. A predominant idea, one might almost call it a fad, in Nelson's mind, was the landing of a body of men from ships in rear of the enemy. As has been seen, he was forward to recommend such an attempt to Devins, promising to support it with his squadron; and the intelligence concerning flat-boats and gun-boats prepared in the French ports suggested nothing to his mind so much as transporting troops to Tuscany, in rear of the Austrians, while the main French army operated in their front. Like Bonaparte, Nelson recognized the resources which the plains of Piedmont, Lombardy and Tuscany would offer to the needy enemy. He called them a gold mine; but he did not understand the weakness of the French in seamen, nor realize the improbability of Bonaparte's attempting such a use of his troops as would put them far out of mutual support and away from his own control. Certainly no indication of such a purpose is to be found in his correspondence or in the instructions of the Directory to him. On the contrary, he had strongly advised against a pet project of the Committee of Public Safety, early in 1795, to land an expedition in the papal states, — unless with control of the sea.[1]

Had the Austrians again advanced to the sea and occupied Vado, Jervis would undoubtedly have supported them and harassed the French to a very important extent. Nelson gave express assurances on that point.[2] Bonaparte, however, allowed him no opportunity. Leaving Paris on the 14th of March, 1796, the young general reached Nice

[1] Comment. de Nap., vol. i. p. 71.
[2] Nels. Disp., vol. ii. p. 128.

on the 27th of the month. On the 5th of April he moved his headquarters to Albenga, and on the 9th to Savona. On the 10th Beaulieu, the new Austrian general, began to move his left wing by the pass of La Bochetta, his right by that of Montenotte; the junction to be formed at Savona. Quick as lightning, Bonaparte struck at once where the Austrian right touched the Sardinian left. Blow followed blow upon the centre of the allies, and after six days' fighting their armies were definitively separated. Driving the Sardinians before him in unremitting pursuit, Bonaparte on the 28th granted an armistice, by which three of the principal fortresses of Piedmont were put into his possession and plenipotentiaries dispatched to Paris to treat for peace. This was concluded and signed on the 15th of May. Sardinia abandoned the coalition, surrendered the counties of Savoy and Nice, and yielded other conditions favorable to France, — particularly in the boundary lines traced on the crests of the mountains, where the commanding military positions were given to the republic. Thus the gates of Italy were forced; and Austria, stripped of her ally on shore and cut off from the British at sea, alone confronted Bonaparte.

The French were now in the plains of Piedmont, with Lombardy before them. Beaulieu, expecting an advance against Milan by the north bank of the Po, had withdrawn across that river, intending to dispute its passage. If forced, he would cover Milan by falling back successively upon the lines of the Sesia and the Ticino, tributaries of the main stream. Bonaparte, however, was not the man to attack an enemy in front and force him back along his natural line of retreat to his proper base. Weighing accurately the political and military conditions of the peninsula, he had fixed his eye upon the line of the Adige as that which he wished to reach and hold, and which, under all the circumstances, he believed he could master. The Adige flows from the Tyrol south along the east shore of

the Lake of Garda, then turns to the eastward and enters
the Adriatic between the Po and Venice. Occupying it, the
French army would cover all the valleys of the Po, lay
tribute upon their resources as well as upon those of the
small states south of the river, interpose between Austria
and southern Italy, and isolate Mantua, the enemy's great
stronghold. Making, therefore, a feint of following Beaulieu by the methodical front attacks expected by him,
Bonaparte pushed his main force stealthily along the south
bank of the Po. On the 7th of May the advance-guard
reached Piacenza, and crossed at once by boats. On the
9th a bridge was completed over the river, which at this
point is fifteen hundred feet wide and very rapid. Beaulieu's intended positions on the Sesia and Ticino were thus
turned, and the Austrians necessarily fell back to the line
of the Adda. On the 10th of May, just one month after
Beaulieu began his forward movements, the bridge of Lodi,
over the Adda, was carried; and the Austrians again fell
back to the Mincio, the outlet of the Lake of Garda, un-
covering Milan. On the 15th Bonaparte entered Milan in
triumph. Here he paused for ten days, and, after quitting
the place, had to return to punish a revolt which broke out
among the people; but on the 30th of May the French
crossed the Mincio, the Austrians retreating northward
toward the Tyrol, along the east shore of the Lake of
Garda.

This retrograde movement left Mantua to itself. On the
3d of June Bonaparte's headquarters were at Verona, — a
strongly fortified place bestriding the Adige, thus insuring
an easy transit to either side of the river, and which de-
rives further strategic importance from its topographical
position. A number of spurs run south from the Tyrol
along the Lake of Garda and fall into the plain at Verona,
which thus stands at the foot of the valleys formed by
them. On either side of this cluster of spurs lie the valleys of the Adige and the Brenta, the two probable lines

by which an Austrian attack would come. Verona, therefore, was a central point with reference to any offensive movements of the enemy, and became the pivot upon which Bonaparte's strategy hinged. On the 4th of June Mantua was blockaded. Having now compassed his first objective, Bonaparte passed temporarily from the offensive to the defensive, ceased his advance, and occupied himself with assuring the line of the Adige and pressing the siege of Mantua.

There remained only to realize the political advantages gained by his wonderful successes. The Duke of Parma had entered into a convention on the 9th of May, followed in the same course on the 17th by the Duke of Modena. On the 5th of June the Court of Naples, startled out of its dream of security, signed an armistice, withdrawing its troops from the coalition and its ships from the British fleet,— a precipitate abandonment of the common cause as ill-judged as it was cowardly. At that very moment the French leader was writing, " I see but one means not to be beaten in the autumn ; and that is, so to arrange matters that we shall not be obliged to advance into southern Italy." [1] The Pope still holding out, Bonaparte improved the time which the Austrians must need to prepare a new movement, by marching into the papal states a corps under Augereau, whom he followed in person. On the 19th Bologna was reached, and on the 24th the Pope signed an armistice. Coincidently with this advance, it was felt safe and opportune to send into Tuscany a division taken from the corps occupying Piedmont. This detachment entered Leghorn on the 28th of June, occupied the port despite the neutrality of Tuscany, drove out and broke up the great British commercial and naval interests centred there, and obtained a secure base for the intended attempt upon Corsica.

The failure of the Austrians to reach the coast, and their

[1] Corr. de Nap., vol. i. p. 465.

subsequent retreat, of course put an end to any direct cooperation between them and the British fleet. Jervis was forced to confine himself to watching the Toulon ships, — an operation conducted in the same spirit and on the same system which he afterwards imparted to the Brest blockade, and generally to that of all hostile arsenals. For over six months, from the beginning of April to the middle of October, he cruised with fifteen sail-of-the-line off the port; the heavy ships remaining some distance from it, but near enough to support a light division of three seventy-fours, which kept just out of range of the batteries, about two miles from the entrance. By unremitting care and foresight, the ships on this arduous service were provisioned, watered and repaired on the spot, without going into harbor. Nelson, as the year before, was actively employed in the Gulf of Genoa, harassing the coast communications, and was on one occasion fortunate enough to capture a convoy with guns and entrenching tools for the siege of Mantua. In the Adriatic, a few frigates and a flotilla of small vessels were engaged in protecting the Austrian communications by way of Trieste. Admiral Mann, with seven ships-of-the-line, was still off Cadiz, in the station assigned him by Hotham to watch Richery. Besides these strictly military operations, ships were called for in every direction to convoy trade, to cover the passage of storeships, and generally to keep the sea safe for unarmed British vessels, whether traders or government transports, upon whom depended the supplies of the fleet and those of Gibraltar drawn from Barbary. Between thirty and forty frigates and smaller vessels were thus occupied, and were found insufficient to meet the varied demands arising from the wide diffusion of British commerce and the activity of French cruisers.

Bonaparte's rapid successes and wide flight of conquest materially affected the British fleet; and the question of supplies became very serious with the ports of Tuscany

Naples and the Pope closed to its aid. Growing symptoms of discontent made the tenure of Corsica doubtful, with the French in Leghorn, and with Genoa tolerating their intrigues through fear of their armies. As early as May 20, immediately after entering Milan, Bonaparte had sent agents to Genoa to concert risings in the island; and in July he began to collect in Leghorn a body of Corsican refugees, at whose head he put General Gentili, also a native. The threatening outlook of affairs, and the submission of Tuscany to the violation of her neutrality by the French, determined the viceroy of Corsica to seize Elba, although a Tuscan possession. Nelson, with a small squadron, appeared before Porto Ferrajo on the 10th of July, and to a peremptory summons received immediate surrender. Being very small, Elba was more immediately under naval control than Corsica, and to hold it required fewer troops. In case of the loss of the larger island, it would still assure the British a base in the Mediterranean and continued control, so long as their fleet could assert predominance over those of their enemies.

Some doubt, however, was felt on this latter point. The attitude of Spain, far from cordial when an ally, had been cold as a neutral, and was now fast becoming hostile. The decrepit kingdom had a navy of over fifty sail-of-the-line; and, although its discipline and efficiency were at the lowest ebb, the mere force of numbers might prove too much for even Jervis's splendid fleet of only twenty-two, — seven of which were still before Cadiz, a thousand miles from the main body off Toulon. Foreseeing the approaching danger, Jervis, about the time Elba was seized, sent Mann orders to rejoin him: and accordingly, on the 29th of July, the blockade of Cadiz was raised. It was just in time, for on the 19th of August Spain, moved by the successes of Bonaparte and the French advance into Germany, — which had not yet undergone the disasters afterwards inflicted upon the separated armies of Jourdan and Moreau by the Archduke Charles, — had signed a treaty of offensive and defensive alliance with the republic. As soon as Mann's ships disappeared, Richery demanded the help of the Spanish fleet to cover his departure, and on the 4th of August sailed in company with twenty Spanish ships-of-the-line. These escorted him three hundred miles to the westward, and then returned to port, leaving the French to fulfil their original mission against British North America, after a detention of nearly ten months. Richery, who had been promoted to rear-admiral during this time, made his cruise successfully, harassed the fishing interests on the coasts of Newfoundland, captured and burned a hundred British merchant vessels, and got back to Brest in time to take part in the unfortunate expedition against Ireland, which sailed in December of this year.

Admiral Mann, though a brave and good officer, showed bad judgment throughout this campaign. Apparently, to use Napoleon's expression, "Il s'était fait un tableau" as to the military and naval situation; and to such a frame of mind the governor of Gibraltar, O'Hara, a pessimist by temperament,[1] probably was a bad adviser. In his precipitation to join the commander-in-chief, he forgot the difficulty about stores and left Gibraltar without filling up. Jervis consequently was forced to send him back at once, with orders to return as quickly as possible. On his way down, on the 1st of October, he was chased by a Spanish fleet of nineteen sail-of-the-line under Admiral Langara. His squadron escaped, losing two merchant vessels under its convoy; but, upon arriving in Gibraltar, he called a council of captains, and, having obtained their concurrence in his opinion, sailed for England, in direct disregard of the commands both of Jervis and the Admiralty. Upon his arrival his action was disapproved,[2] orders were sent him

---

[1] For O'Hara's characteristics, see life of Lord Minto, vol. ii. pp. 190, 195.
[2] See Nelson's Disp., vol. ii. p. 258, note.

The letter of the Admiralty to Admiral Mann may possess some interest as

to strike his flag and come ashore, and he appears never again to have been employed afloat; but, when it is remembered that only forty years had elapsed since Byng was shot for an error in judgment, it must be owned men had become more merciful.

Mann's defection reduced Jervis's forces by one third, at a time when affairs were becoming daily more critical. Not only did it make the tenure of the Mediterranean vastly more difficult, but it deprived the admiral of his cherished hope of dealing a staggering blow to the Spanish fleet, such as four months later he inflicted at Cape St. Vincent. After meeting Mann, Langara was joined by seven ships from Cartagena, and with this increase of force appeared on the 20th of October about fifty miles from San Fiorenzo Bay. Jervis had just returned there from off Toulon, having on the 25th of September received orders to evacuate Corsica,—an operation which promised to be difficult from lack of transports. On the 26th of October Langara entered Toulon, where the new allies had then thirty-eight ships-of-the-line collected.

During the summer months Nelson had blockaded Leghorn, after its occupation by the French; and this measure, with the tenure of Elba, seems to have effectually prevented

---

an example of the official correspondence of the day, as well as an expression of disapprobation too profound for reproach:—

Sir,—I have received and communicated to my Lords Commissioners of the Admiralty your letter to me of the 29th December, giving an account of your proceedings and of the severe [several?] occurrences which have taken place during your passage from Gibraltar, with the squadron under your command; and I have their Lordships' commands to acquaint you that they cannot but feel the greatest regret that you should have been induced to return to England with the squadron under your orders, under the circumstances in which you were placed.

I have their Lordships' further commands to acquaint you that orders will be to sent to you, either by this or to-morrow's post, to strike your flag and come on shore.   I am, &c.,

EVAN NEPEAN,
Secretary to the Admiralty

Tucker's St. Vincent, vol. i. p. 216.

any large body of men passing into Corsica. On the 18th
of September the little island of Capraja, a Genoese dependency and convenient refuge for small boats, was seized
for the same object. On the 29th, however, Nelson received orders from Jervis for the evacuation of Corsica, the
operations at Bastia being assigned to his special care. As
soon as the determination of the British was known, discontent broke out into revolt. Gentili, finding the sea clear,
landed on the 19th of October, pressing close down upon
the coast; and the final embarkation was only effected in
safety under the guns of the ships. On the 19th Nelson
took off the last of the troops, and carried them with the
viceroy to Elba, which it was intended still to hold. Jervis held on at San Fiorenzo Bay to the latest moment possible, everything being afloat for a fortnight before he left,
hoping that Mann might yet join, and fearing he might
arrive after the departure of the fleet. On the 2d of November provisions were so short that longer delay was impossible; and the admiral sailed with his whole force,
reaching Gibraltar, after a tedious voyage, on the 1st of December, 1796. During the passage, in which the crews were
on from half to one third the usual rations, Jervis received
instructions countermanding the evacuation, if not yet carried out. If executed, Elba was still to be held.

The policy of thus evacuating the Mediterranean admits,
now as then, of argument on both sides. The causes for the
vacillation of the British government are apparent. The
first orders to leave everything, Elba included, were dated
August 31. Generals Jourdan and Moreau were then far
in the heart of Germany; and the archduke having but
just begun the brilliant counter-move by which he drove
first one, and then the other, back to the Rhine, the effects
of this were in no way foreseen. From Italy the latest
possible news was of Bonaparte's new successes at Lonato
and Castiglione, and the fresh retreat of the Austrians.
The countermanding orders, dated October 21, were issued

under the influence of the archduke's success and of Wurmser's evasion of Bonaparte and entrance into Mantua; whereby, despite repeated defeats in the field, the garrison was largely increased and the weary work of the siege must be again begun. While Mantua stood, Bonaparte could not advance; and the Austrians were gathering a new army in the Tyrol. The British government failed, too, to realize the supreme excellence of its Mediterranean fleet and the staunch character of its leader. "The admiral," wrote Elliott[1] on the spot, "is as firm as a rock. He has at present fourteen sail-of-the-line against thirty-six, or perhaps forty. If Mann joins him, they will certainly attack, and they are *all* confident of victory." The incident of Mann's conduct, under these circumstances, is full of military warning. It is within the limits of reasonable speculation to say that, had he obeyed his orders, — and only extreme causes could justify disobedience, — the battle of Cape St. Vincent would have been fought then in the Mediterranean,[2] instead of in the Atlantic after the fall of Mantua, and would have profoundly affected the policy of the Italian States. With such a victory, men like Jervis and Elliott would have held on for further orders from home. "The expulsion of the English," wrote Bonaparte, "has a great effect upon the success of our military operations in Italy. We must exact more severe conditions of Naples. It has the greatest moral influence upon the minds of the Italians, assures our communications and will make Naples tremble even in Sicily."[3]

In the opinion of the author, Sir Gilbert Elliott expresses the correct conclusion in the words following, which show singular foresight as well as sound political

---

[1] Life of Lord Minto, vol. ii. p. 358.

[2] This was Jervis's opinion. (See Life of St. Vincent by Tucker, vol. i. p. 240; also Nelson's Dispatches, vol. ii. p. 294.)

[3] Napoleon's Correspondence, vol. ii p. 76. See also generally pp. 73–80. The relief obtained by Bonaparte from the departure of the British crops out on every page.

judgment: "I have always thought that it is a great and important object in the contest between the French republic and the rest of Europe, that Italy, in whole or in part, should neither be annexed to France as dominion, nor affiliated in the shape of dependent republics; and I have considered a superior British fleet in the Mediterranean as an essential means for securing Italy and Europe from such a misfortune."[1] Elliott's presentiments were realized by Napoleon at a later day; the immediate effect of the evacuation was indicated by a treaty of peace between France and Naples, signed October 10, as soon as the purpose was known. In 1796 the British fleet had been three years in the Mediterranean, and since the acquisition of Corsica had effected little. What was needed at the moment was not an abandonment of the field, but a demonstration of power by a successful battle. The weakest eyes could count the units by which the allied fleets exceeded the British; acts alone could show the real superiority, the predominance in strength, of the latter. That demonstrated, the islands and the remote extremities of the peninsula would have taken heart, and a battle in the Gulf of Lyon had the far-reaching effects produced by that in Aboukir Bay. At the time of the evacuation the three most important factors in the military situation were, the siege of Mantua, the Austrian army in the Tyrol, and, last but not least, the British fleet in the Mediterranean. This sustained Naples; and Naples, or rather southern Italy, was one of Bonaparte's most serious anxieties. Finally, it may be said that the value of Corsica to the fleet is proved by Nelson's preference of Maddalena Bay, in the straits separating Corsica from Sardinia, over Malta, as the station for a British fleet watching Toulon.

Immediately upon reaching Gibraltar, Jervis received orders to take the fleet to Lisbon, in consequence of a disposition shown by the allied French and Spanish govern-

[1] Life of Lord Minto, vol. ii p. 373.

ments to attack Portugal.¹ The limits of his command were extended to Cape Finisterre. Before sailing, he despatched Nelson up the Mediterranean with two frigates to bring off the garrison and stores from Elba, the abandonment of which was again ordered. On the 16th he sailed for Lisbon, arriving there on the 21st; but misfortunes were thickening around his fleet. On the 10th, at Gibraltar, during a furious gale, three ships-of-the-line drove from their anchors. One was totally lost on the coast of Morocco, and another struck so heavily on a rock that she had to be sent to England for repairs. Shortly after, a third grounded in Tangiers Bay, and, though repaired on the station, was unfit for service in the ensuing battle. A fourth, when entering the Tagus in charge of a pilot, was run on a shoal and wrecked. Finally, in leaving the river on the 18th of January, a ninety-eight-gun ship was run aground and incapacitated. This reduced the force with which he then put to sea to seek the enemy to ten ships-of-the-line.

Nelson, his most efficient lieutenant, was also nearly lost to him on that interesting occasion, when his fearlessness and *coup d'œil* mainly contributed to the success achieved. Sailing from Gibraltar on the 15th of December, he fought on the 20th a severe action with two Spanish frigates, which would have made a chapter in the life of an ordinary seaman, but is lost among his other deeds. His prizes were immediately recovered by a heavy Spanish squadron, but his own ships escaped. On the 26th he reached Porto Ferrajo, and remained a month. He was there joined by Elliott, the late viceroy of Corsica, who had been in Naples since the evacuation. General De Burgh, commanding the garrison, refused to abandon his post without specific orders from the government, and as

---

¹ The project of forcing the entrance to the Tagus by a squadron from Brest had been openly discussed in France. (Chevalier, Mar. Fran. sous la République, p. 258.)

Nelson had only those of Jervis, he confined himself to
embarking the naval stores. With these and all the ships
of war he sailed from Elba on the 29th of January, 1797.
On the 9th of February he reached Gibraltar; and thence,
learning that the Spanish fleet had repassed the Straits,
he hurried on to join the admiral. Just out of Gibraltar
he was chased by several Spaniards,[1] but escaped them,
and on the 13th fell in with the fleet. At 6 P. M. of that
day he went on board his own ship, the "Captain," seventy-four,
at whose masthead flew his broad pennant[2]
during the battle of the following day.

The meeting which now took place between the Spanish
and British fleets was the result of the following movements.
Towards the end of 1796 the Directory, encouraged
by Bonaparte's successes and by the Spanish alliance,
and allured by the promises of disaffected Irish, determined
on an expedition to Ireland. As the first passage of the
troops and their subsequent communications would depend
upon naval superiority, five ships-of-the-line were ordered
from Toulon to Brest. This force, under Admiral Villeneuve,
sailed on the 1st of December, accompanied by the
Spanish fleet of twenty-six ships, which, since October, had
remained in Toulon. On the 6th Langara went into Cartagena,
leaving Villeneuve to himself, and on the 10th the
French passed Gibraltar in full sight of the British fleet,
driving before the easterly gale, which then did so much
harm to Jervis's squadron and prevented pursuit. They

---

[1] An exciting incident occurred during this chase. In the height of it a
man fell overboard. A boat was lowered and picked him up; but the
enemy's ships were so close it became doubtful whether the British frigate
could afford to await her return. Nelson, always generous to the verge of
rashness, backed a topsail, saying "I won't let Hardy go," and succeeded in
carrying him off. The anecdote gains in interest when it is remembered that
Hardy, who was taken in the prize of December 20, had just been released
from Spain; and that, as captain of the flag-ship at Trafalgar, he was witness
of Nelson's fall and death-scene.

[2] The distinguishing flag which shows a commodore is on board the
ship.

did not, however, reach Brest soon enough for the expedition. The Spaniards remained in Cartagena nearly two months, during which time Admiral Cordova took command; but under urgent pressure from the Directory[1] they finally sailed for Cadiz on the 1st of February, passing the Straits on the 5th with heavy easterly weather, which drove them far to the westward. They numbered now twenty-seven ships-of-the-line.

Sir John Jervis, after leaving Lisbon on January 18, 1797, had convoyed to the westward some Portuguese merchant ships bound to Brazil, and then beaten back towards his station off Cape St. Vincent. On the 6th of February he was joined by a re-enforcement of five ships, which were sent from England as soon as the scare about Ireland had passed. With these fifteen he cruised off the Cape, knowing that he there must meet any squadron, from either the Mediterranean or the Atlantic, bound to Cadiz. At 5 A.M. of February 14, the frigate "Niger," which had kept sight of the Spanish fleet for some days, joined the admiral, and informed him that it was probably not more than ten or twelve miles distant, to the southward and westward. The wind, which had been strong south-easterly for several days, had changed during the night to west by south, enabling the Spaniards to head for Cadiz, after the weary battling of the past week; but this

---

[1] A favorite project with the Directory, as with Napoleon, was to mass the French and Spanish navies in one great body; as had several times been done under Louis XVI. during the American Revolution. Such a combination was hoped for the Irish expedition of 1796; and, though too late for that purpose, the movement from Cartagena to Cadiz was regarded by the Directory as a step toward uniting the fleets. This was one of the objects of Bruix's adventurous sortie from Brest in 1799, when he actually brought back to that port in his train fifteen Spanish ships,—nominal allies, actual hostages. The combination at Trafalgar is well known. Later on the Emperor sought to build up a patch-work fleet out of all the minor navies of the Continent, as he pieced together out of all the nations the immense army which was swallowed up in his Russian enterprise. But here, as usually, a homogeneous body, centrally placed, triumphed over an incongruous coalition.

otherwise fortunate circumstance became a very dangerous incident [1] to a large, ill-officered, and ill-commanded body of ships, about to meet an enemy so skilful, so alert, and so thoroughly drilled as Jervis's comparatively small and manageable force. At daybreak, about 6.30, the Spaniards were seen, stretching on the horizon from south-west to south in an ill-defined body, across the path of the advancing British. Their distance, though not stated, was probably not less than fifteen to twenty miles. The British fleet being close hauled on the starboard tack, heading from south to south by west, while the Spaniards, bound for Cadiz, were steering east-south-east, the two courses crossed nearly at right angles. At this moment there was a great contrast between the arrays presented by the approaching combatants. The British, formed during the night in two columns of eight and seven ships respectively, elicited the commendation of their exacting chief "for their admirable close order." [2] The Spaniards, on the contrary, eager to get to port, and in confusion through the night shift of wind and their own loose habits of sailing, were broken into two bodies. Of these the leading one, as all were sailing nearly before the wind, was most to leeward. It was composed of six ships, the interval between which and the other twenty-one was probably not less than eight miles. Even after the British fleet was seen, no attempt was for some time made to remedy this fatal separation; a neglect due partly to professional nonchalance and inefficiency, and partly to misinformation concerning the enemy's force, which they had heard through a neutral was only nine ships-of-the-line.[3]

---

[1] The stringent exactions of the close-hauled line-of-battle imposed upon a fleet, in the presence of an enemy, the tactical necessity of rectifying the order with any considerable change of wind, — an evolution whose difficulty increased in direct proportion to the number of the ships; and in a more than geometrical progression, when they were badly drilled.

[2] Tucker's Life of St. Vincent, vol. i. p. 255.

[3] James's Nav. Hist., vol ii. p. 37.

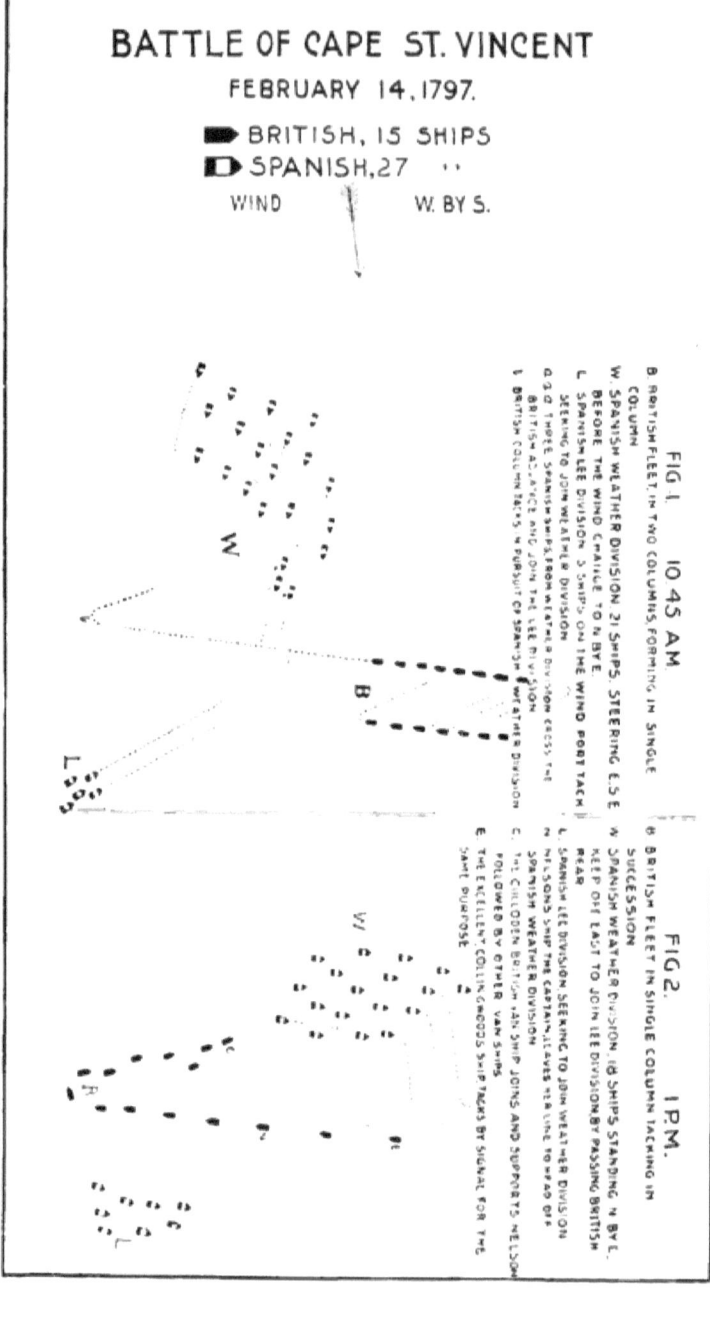

The weather being hazy and occasionally foggy, some time passed before the gradually approaching enemies could clearly see each other. At 9 A.M. the number and rates of the Spaniards could be made out from the masthead of the British flag-ship, so that they were then probably distant from twelve to fifteen miles. At half-past nine Jervis sent three ships ahead to chase, and a few minutes later supported them with three others. This advanced duty enabled these six to take the lead in the attack. About ten [1] the fog lifted and disclosed the relative situations. The British, still in two columns, were heading fair for the gap in the Spanish order. The six lee ships of the latter had realized their false position, and were now close to the wind on the port tack, heading about north-north-west, in hopes that they could rejoin the main body to windward, which still continued its course for Cadiz. Jervis then made signal to form a single column, the fighting order of battle, and pass through the enemy's line. It soon became evident that the lee Spanish ships could not cross the bows of the British. For a moment they wavered and bore up to south-east; but soon after five of them resumed their north-west course, with the apparent purpose of breaking through the hostile line whose advance they had not been able to anticipate.[2] The sixth continued to the south-east and disappeared.

The weather division of the Spaniards now also saw that it was not possible for all its members to effect a junction with the separated ships. Three stood on, and crossed the bows of the advancing enemy; the remainder hauled up in

---

[1] Nelson's Narrative. Dispatches, vol. ii. pp. 340, 343.

[2] James states that these ships first came to the wind on the starboard tack, heading as did the British, "as if intending to weather the whole British fleet." The superior speed and weatherliness of the Spanish ships, if well handled, might have enabled them very seriously to molest the British in their attack; but, from the whole conduct of the Spaniards on this day, it is probable that the movement, if made, was only one of the successive vacillations of men who had put themselves in a false position. (Vol. ii. p. 39.)

increasing disorder to the northward, steering a course
nearly parallel, but directly opposite, to the British, and
passing their van at long cannon shot. At half-past eleven
the "Culloden," Captain Troubridge, heading Jervis's
column, came abreast the leading ships of this body, and
opened fire. Sir John Jervis now saw secured to him the
great desire of commanders-in-chief. His own force, in
compact fighting order, was interposed between the fractions of the enemy, able to deal for a measurable time with
either, undisturbed by the other. Should he attack the
eighteen weather, or the eight lee ships, with his own fifteen? With accurate professional judgment he promptly
decided to assail the larger body; because the smaller, having to beat to windward, would be kept out of action longer
than he could hope if he chose the other alternative. The
decision was in principle identical with that which determined Nelson's tactics at the Nile. The signal was therefore made to tack in succession, in pursuit of the weather
ships. Troubridge, anticipating the order, had already
hoisted at the masthead his answering flag of recognition,
rolled up after the manner of the sea, needing but a turn
of the wrist to unloose it. Quick as the admiral's signal
flew the reply fluttered out, and the "Culloden's" sails
were already shaking as she luffed up into the wind.
"Look at Troubridge," shouted Jervis, in exultation: "he
handles his ship as if the eyes of all England were upon
him! and would to God they were!" The rear of the
Spaniards was just passing the "Culloden" as she thus
went round. Ship after ship of the British line tacked in
her wake and stood on in pursuit; while those still on the
first course, south by west, interposed between the two
Spanish divisions. Of these the lee, led by a hundred-gun
ship under a vice-admiral's flag, headed towards Jervis's
flag-ship, the "Victory," the seventh in the British order,
as though to go through the line ahead of her. The "Victory" was too prompt; and the Spaniard, to avoid colli-

sion, went about close under the British broadsides. In doing this he was exposed to and received a raking fire, which drove him out of action, accompanied by his consorts. The "Victory," which had backed a topsail a moment to aim more accurately, then stood on and tacked in the wake of the "Culloden," followed by the rest of the British column.

It was now nearly one o'clock. The action so far had consisted, first, in piercing the enemy's line, cutting off the van and greater part of the centre from the rear; and, second, in a cannonade between two columns passing on opposite parallel courses, — the Spanish main division running free, the British close to the wind. Naval history abounds in instances of these brushes, and pronounces them commonly indecisive. Jervis, who had seen such,[1] meant decisive action when he ordered the "Culloden" to tack and follow the enemy. But a stern chase is a long chase, and the Spanish ships were fast sailers. Some time must pass before Troubridge and his companions could overtake them; and, as each succeeding vessel of the British line had to reach the common point of tacking, from which the Spaniards were steadily receding, the rear of Jervis's fleet must be long in coming up. That it was so is proved by the respective losses incurred. It has, therefore, been suggested that the admiral would have done well to tack his whole fleet, or at least the rear ships together, bringing them in a body on the Spanish van. The idea is plausible, but errs by leaving out of the calculation the Spanish lee division, which was kept off by the British rear ships. Those eight lee ships are apt to be looked on as wholly out of the affair; but in fact it was a necessary part of Jervis's combination to check them, during the time required to deal with the others. Admiral Parker, commanding in the van, speaks expressly of the efforts made

---

[1] Notably in Keppel's action in 1778, in which he bore a distinguished part. See Mahan's Influence of Sea Power upon History, 1660–1783, p. 351.

by the Spanish lee division to annoy him, and of the covering action of the British rear.[1]

Thus, one by one, the British ships were changing their course from south by west to north-north-east in pursuit of the Spanish main division, and the latter was gradually passing to the rear of their enemy's original order. When they saw the sea clear to the south-east, about one o'clock, they bore up, altering their course to east-south-east, hoping to pass behind the British and so join the lee division. Fortunately for Jervis, Nelson was in the third ship from the rear. Having fully divined his chief's purpose, he saw it on the point of defeat, and, without waiting for orders, wore at once out of the line, and threw the "Captain," alone, in front of the enemy's leading ships. In this well-timed but most daring move, which illustrates to the highest degree the immense difference between a desperate and a reckless action, Nelson passed to the head of the British column, crossing the bows of five large Spanish vessels, and then with his seventy-four engaged the "Santisima Trinidad," of one hundred and thirty guns, the biggest ship at that time afloat. The enemy, apparently dashed by this act of extraordinary temerity, and as little under control as a flock of frightened sheep, hauled up in a body again to north-north-east, resuming what can only be described as their flight.

[1] "When the 'Prince George' tacked, the two three-deckers [of the Spanish lee division] tacked after us, and which the rest of the enemy's rear were about to do; but the commander-in-chief, with the ships of [our] centre and rear, following close, *covered us from their attack upon the rear of the ships with me*, and obliged them to re-tack . . . and effectually divided the enemy's fleet." (Sir William Parker's narrative of the conduct of the British van. Nelson's Dispatches, vol. ii. p. 473.) The gallant admiral's style is confused, but his meaning is clear enough after half a dozen readings. He must not be taken for the very distinguished officer of the same name, but of the next generation.

Both Parker and Nelson (Dispatches, vol. ii. pp. 340, 344) speak of the main Spanish division as "the van." In truth, when the "Culloden" interposed, the whole enemy's fleet were so nearly joined on the port tack as to seem in line, though disorderly and not quite connected.

Their momentary change of course had, however, caused a delay which enabled the British leaders to come up. Troubridge in the "Culloden" was soon right behind Nelson, to whom he was dear beyond all British officers, and three other ships followed in as close array as was consistent with the free use of their guns. The Spaniards, never in good order, lay before them in confusion, two or three deep, hindering one another's fire, and presenting a target that could not easily be missed. This closing scene of the battle raged round the rear ships of the Spanish main body, and necessarily became a *mêlée*, each British captain acting according to his own judgment and the condition of his ship. A very distinguished part fell to Collingwood, likewise a close associate of Nelson's, whose ship, the "Excellent," had brought up the rear of the order. Having, probably from this circumstance, escaped serious injury to her spars, she was fully under her captain's control, and enabled him to display the courage and skill for which he was so eminently distinguished. Passing along the enemy's rear, he had compelled one seventy-four to strike, when his eye caught sight of Nelson's ship lying disabled on the starboard side, and within pistol shot, of the " San Nicolas." a Spanish eighty ; " her foretopmast and wheel shot away, not a sail, shroud, or rope, left,"[1] and being fired upon by five hostile ships. With every sail set he pressed ahead, passing between the " Captain " and her nearest enemy, brushing the latter at a distance of ten feet, and pouring in one of those broadsides of which he used to assure his practised crew that, if they could fire three in five minutes, no vessel could resist them. The " San Nicolas," either intentionally or from the helmsman being killed, luffed and fell on board the " San Josef," a ship of one hundred and twelve guns, while the " Excellent," continuing her course, left the ground again clear for Nelson. The latter, seeing the " Captain " powerless for continued manœuvre,

[1] Nelson's Narrative, Dispatches, vol. ii. pp. 341, 345.

put the helm to starboard; the British ship came up to
the wind, fetched over to the "San Nicolas," and grappled
her. Nelson, having his men ready on deck, rushed at
their head on board the Spaniard, drove her crew below,
and captured her. The "San Josef," which was fast to
the "San Nicolas" on the other side, now opened a fire of
musketry; but the commodore, first stationing sentinels to
prevent the "San Nicolas's" men regaining their deck,
called upon his own ship for a re-enforcement, with which
he boarded the three-decker and carried her also. On her
quarter-deck, surrounded by his followers still hot from
the fight, he received the swords of the Spanish officers.

This dramatic ending to the distinguished part played by
him, and the promptitude of his previous action, by which,
while assuming a great responsibility, he saved the success
of the day, have made Nelson the most striking figure in
the battle of Cape St. Vincent; or, as it is sometimes
called, of St. Valentine's Day. This splendid movement of
his genius in no way detracts from the credit due to the commander-in-chief; as it was no lessening of Nelson's own
fame that the leader of the van at the Nile conceived on
the moment the happy thought of passing inside the French
line. To Jervis alone belongs the honor of attacking such
heavy odds, as well as of the correct and sufficient combination by which he hoped to snatch victory from superior
numbers. He was happy, indeed, in having such a lieutenant, so right a man in so right a place, and at so critical a
moment; but the whole responsibility and the whole original
plan was his, and no man can take it from him. To him,
too, was primarily due the admirable efficiency of his fleet,
which removed from his enterprise the reproach of rashness
to bestow upon it the praise of daring. A yet higher meed
of glory is due to this bold admiral. As the dull morning
light showed him the two fleets, he was heard to say, "A
victory is very essential to England at this moment."
Honor to the chief who can rise above his own anxieties

and his local responsibilities to think of the needs of his country, and who is willing to risk his own reputation to support her credit.

Four Spanish ships were now in the possession of the British, and the great "Santisima Trinidad" was without fore or mizzen mast,— some said she had struck; but the lee division of the enemy was at last coming up, and many of the weather were still uninjured. Jervis, therefore, about four in the afternoon formed his fleet in line on the starboard tack, interposing it between the enemy and his prizes. This ended the battle. It has been thought that further pursuit of a fleet so disgracefully beaten would have increased the British triumph; but Jervis was not the man to risk a substantial success, securely held, for a doubtful further gain. The victory essential to Great Britain was won; the worthlessness of the Spanish navy was revealed,— it could no longer be accounted a factor in the political situation. In the opinion of the author, Jervis was right not to expose this, the great and attained result of Valentine's Day, to those chances of mishap that cannot be excluded from the operations of war.

Among the numerous rewards bestowed for this action, the admiral was advanced to the peerage as Earl St. Vincent, while upon Nelson was bestowed the then distinguished honor of Knight of the Bath. On the 20th of February he was made a rear-admiral. The captains of the fleet received medals, and the senior lieutenant of each ship was promoted.

Jervis had well said that Great Britain was then in essential need of a victory; and never was one better timed for political effect. Deep gloom prevailed throughout the country, and in every quarter the horizon was black with clouds, when, on the 3d of March, the bearer of the dispatches reached the admiralty. Since Bonaparte had seized the line of the Adige and cut off Mantua, three distinct attempts had been made by the Austrians in superior force to dis-

lodge him and relieve the city; and in all three they had
been beaten with heavy loss. The news was but lately
come that Mantua had capitulated, leaving Bonaparte free
to assume the offensive and advance, as he shortly did.
The British fleet had been forced to abandon Corsica and
the Mediterranean. Peace negotiations, begun with the
republic, had ended by the British envoy being peremp-
torily ordered to leave France in forty-eight hours; and
although the government had not expected a favorable
issue, the effect on the people was disheartening. Consols
fell to 51, a depression greater than any reached during the
American Revolution.[1] The expedition of the French
against Ireland had indeed failed; but so little share had
the Channel fleet borne in their defeat, that the country
was forced to ascribe to the direct interposition of Divine
Providence a deliverance, which it would have preferred to
see wrought through the instrumentality of the navy. That
trusted arm of the national defence seemed palsied in every
quarter. Finally, among the greater of many discouraging circumstances, specie payments were stopped by the
Bank of England on the 26th of February, in obedience to
an order of the government. The profuse subsidies paid to
continental states, and the demands for coin to meet the expenses of the navy in all parts of the world, were the chief
causes of a drain against which the bank directors had frequently remonstrated during two years as threatening ruin.
To these causes for scarcity was added at this time another,
temporary in its character and arising in great part from
loss of confidence in the navy's efficiency,— the fear, namely,
of invasion. People had begun to call for and to hoard coin
against an evil day. Such was the outlook as Jervis's captain posted from Falmouth, where he landed, to London,
keeping the secret of his good news within his breast. The
frigate which had borne him went on to Plymouth with the
viceroy of Corsica, returning with his suite from his lost

[1] Annual Register, 1797, p. 148.

principality. When they landed on the 5th of March, news had just reached the town of the suspension of cash payments, and, as they told of the great achievement off Cape St. Vincent, people at first refused to believe that the tide had turned. They were expecting to hear of a junction between the French and Spanish fleets, and an approaching invasion. So great was the financial panic, that fifteen guineas were with difficulty collected among government officials to pay the expenses of Elliott's journey to London.[1]

The revulsion was great, and was proved by the profusion with which rewards were distributed. The Spanish navy had been but a bugbear, but as a bugbear it was great. The veil that covered its rottenness was stripped away, and at the same time were revealed to the nation, which feared it had no naval chiefs, the striking and brilliant figures of Jervis and Nelson. In vain did the Opposition, in the true spirit of faction, seek to turn men's eyes from the brilliant achievements of the warriors to the imbecility affirmed of the government, which had opposed fifteen ships to twenty-seven. Thinking men realized that the administration could not be held responsible for Mann's unauthorized return at Christmas-tide, nor for the extraordinary series of misfortunes by which five more of the Mediterranean fleet were in one short month incapacitated. They saw, too, that no popular government would have dared to replace Mann's ships so long as the fate of Ireland, then in the balance, was uncertain. But most men did not care to think. It was enough for them that fifteen British ships had dashed into the midst of twenty-seven enemies, had collared and dragged out four of the biggest and severely handled the rest. It was enough to hear that the crew of one British seventy-four, headed by a man whom few out of the navy yet knew, had, sword in hand, carried first a Spanish eighty and then another of one hundred and twelve

[1] Life of Lord Minto, vol. ii. p. 379.

guns. With such men to rule the fleet, and with Pitt at the
helm of state, they thanked God and took courage. Speculation is often futile; yet it is hard to see how the country
could have borne the approaching crisis of the mutinies,
on top of its other troubles, had not the fear of the Spanish
navy been removed and the hope of better naval leaders
been afforded. That the hope was well founded is no speculation. With St. Vincent began a series of victories and
achievements which have thrown the great deeds of earlier
years into undeserved obscurity.

Immediately after the battle the Spanish fleet entered
Cadiz, and Jervis returned to Lisbon to refit his ships. On
the 31st of March, having received further re-enforcements,
he left Lisbon with twenty-one ships-of-the-line and took
position off Cadiz, where the Spaniards had twenty-six of
the same class. After cruising for six weeks under sail, he
anchored the fleet for a long blockade, and this disposition
continued with little intermission for two years, — until
May, 1799, when the successful sortie of Admiral Bruix
from Brest, related in another place,[1] and the consequent
chase by the British blockading force, gave the Spaniards
the opportunity to slip out. This tedious watching was unfruitful in events of military interest; but the burden of
the commander-in-chief was increased by the spirit of
mutiny, rife throughout the whole period, which triumphed
temporarily in the Channel and North Sea fleets, and was
by Jervis kept down only by a stern vigilance of which few
but he were capable. Stamped out time and again by his
unflinching energy, it was continually renewed by the fresh
ships sent out from home, under officers of temper inferior
to his captains, and with seamen who knew not yet by experience the indomitable will which they sought to bend.
Execution followed execution; but never once did the old
man's courage quail nor his determination falter. Seaman
and officer alike were made to feel that while his flag flew

[1] See Chapter X.

his authority should prevail; and with such backing the officers showed themselves incapable of the weaknesses too often manifested in the home ports.[1] It is probable too that a strong nucleus of support existed among the crews that fought at St. Vincent, — due to admiration for the admiral himself, and for Nelson, Collingwood, Troubridge, Saumarez and others, who there distinguished themselves.

While these various events were transpiring at sea, from the evacuation of Corsica to the battle of St. Vincent, Bonaparte in Italy was still holding the line of the Adige and blockading Mantua. His posture therefore was essentially one of defence. The vigor and sagacity with which he resorted to offensive movements the instant the enemy drew down from the Tyrol to attack him, and the brilliant character of the victories won by him, obscure to most the fact that he was really on the defensive; holding on, amid risks and discouragements, to the conquests already made, and unable to attempt more until Mantua fell. The glories of Castiglione, Arcola, Rivoli, conceal this crucial feature of his situation, and the consequently important bearing of the presence of the British fleet, encouraging the dispositions of Naples and the Pope, which were distinctly hostile to the French. Nothing less than Bonaparte's energy and genius could have grappled successfully with such a situation; and his correspondence betrays his fear that, by the co-operation of the fleet, these dangers in the rear might become too great even for him. When Mantua capitulated on the 2d of February, Bonaparte turned first upon the Pope, whom he accused of violating the armistice concluded the previous June. His Holiness at once submitted, and on the 19th of February signed a peace, abandoning his right to his northern provinces, — Bologna, Ferrara and the Romagna, — and ceding to France, until the end of the war, Ancona, a good seaport on the Adriatic.

[1] For a striking incident of St. Vincent's energy in suppressing mutiny, see note at end of this chapter.

On the 10th of March, having completed all the dispositions that seemed necessary to secure his rear, Bonaparte advanced against the Austrians. The young Archduke Charles, whom the campaign of 1796 on the Danube had revealed to Europe as gifted with military talents of a very high order, had been sent to oppose him; but it was too late to resist on the plains of Italy, or even on the Italian side of the mountains. The French crossed the Tagliamento on March 16, and pushed up through the gorges of that stream and of the Isonzo into the eastern Alps. On the 23d Trieste was occupied. The Archduke retired continuously, barely disputing difficult positions with the enemy. His mind was fixed not to fight until he had drawn the French far into Germany, and had collected his own resources,—a decision whose wisdom Bonaparte sealed with his own commendation. "If the enemy had committed the folly of awaiting me," he wrote to the Directory, "I should have beaten them; but if they had continued to fall back, had joined a part of their forces from the Rhine, and had overwhelmed me, then retreat would have been difficult, and the loss of the Army of Italy might entail that of the republic. We must not shut our eyes to the fact that, though our military position was brilliant, we have not simply dictated the conditions."[1] Italy, too, was fermenting behind him. The moral effect, however, of this unopposed advance through the mountains of Carinthia brought the House of Austria to terms; and on the 18th of April preliminaries of peace were signed at Leoben, only sixty miles from Vienna. Though the formal treaty was not concluded until six months later, this transaction marked, for that time, the end of hostilities between Austria and France, which had then lasted five years,—from April, 1792, to April, 1797.

The preliminaries of Leoben stipulated a mutual cessation of hostilities between the republic and the emperor, and ex-

[1] April 19, 1797. Napoleon's Correspondence, vol. ii. p. 655.

tended this provision to all the states of the German Empire, as well as to the particular dominions of the emperor himself. Austria surrendered definitively the Netherlands (Belgium), and "recognized the limits of France as decreed by the laws of the French Republic." In this phrase was imbedded the rock upon which negotiations with Great Britain split. The republic, on its part, undertook to furnish to the emperor at the final peace a "just and suitable compensation" for the provinces he lost.

The "suitable compensation," thus mysteriously alluded to, was defined in the "secret preliminary agreements," contracted at the same moment. It was furnished by depriving the republic of Venice, with which Bonaparte had reasons for serious discontent, of all its possessions on the mainland of Italy, as well as of Istria and Dalmatia on the east coast of the Adriatic. The provinces thus taken were divided: Austria receiving all east of the Oglio and north of the Po, with Istria and Dalmatia. The country between the Oglio and the Adda, previously owned by Venice, was taken to constitute a new, independent republic; into which were also incorporated all possessions of Austria west of the Oglio conquered by the French in the recent campaign. This was to be known as the Cisalpine Republic. Thus the lords of the Adriatic were shorn of their glory, and brought to the brink of the precipice from which, six months later, at the final peace, the Corsican conqueror hurled them headlong. For the moment there were spared to them their ancient city and the Ionian Islands; and the legations of Bologna, Ferrara, and the Romagna, taken from the Pope, were given to them, — a like transient possession.

Such, in brief outline, were the principal terms of the preliminaries of Leoben. The great and significant feature does not ostensibly appear among the articles. Bonaparte, in diplomacy, had achieved the great end at which he aimed in his plans of campaign. He had separated his enemies. "The French Republic," wrote he, "in granting at Leoben preliminaries so advantageous to his Imperial Majesty, had as its principal end the conclusion of a *separate peace* with his Majesty, in order to be in a position to turn all its forces against England, and oblige her to a prompt peace." He alone made and signed the preliminaries, and this quotation gives the strategy and policy of his life in a nutshell.[1] The crucial fact at Leoben was that Austria then, as Sardinia a year before, treated alone, — without her ally. This Great Britain, to her honor, absolutely refused to do in 1796, and as long as her ally stood by her. There is, of course, a great difference between the position of a state which finds a victorious enemy in the heart of its territories, and that of an island empire; and great allowance must be made for Austria, even though the calm retrospect of history sees that she failed rightly to appreciate the extreme hazard of Bonaparte's situation. But this allowance merely emphasizes the important truth, that the imposing attitude maintained by Great Britain throughout this tremendous contest depended absolutely and wholly upon the control of the sea, — upon Sea-Power.

NOTE. — It now only remains to be seen how, when insubordination, and accompanied by villany of this magnitude, did make its open appearance, Lord St. Vincent dealt with it. A remarkable occasion will be mentioned, not indeed the first outbreak of mutiny, nor its last effort, but that one which excited the greatest sensation in the fleet, — that which came with most untoward circumstances, — that of which the enforcement of the penalty had, in Lord St. Vincent's opinion, the most salutary effect.

. . . .

No sooner had Sir Roger Curtis arrived, than applications came to the commander-in-chief for courts-martial on mutineers from three of those ships, — the "Marlborough," the "Lion," and the "Centaur." Selection will be made of the sequel to the "Marlborough."

As the squadron approached, and before the request for a court-martial, this ship being known to the commander-in-chief to have been among the most disorganized at Spithead, had been ordered to take her berth in the centre, at a small distance from the rest of the

[1] Napoleon's Correspondence, vol. iii. p. 346.

fleet. It, however, had so happened that a very violent mutiny in her had broken out at Beerhaven, and again during the passage, which had been suppressed by the officers, but chiefly by the first lieutenant. The very object too of this mutiny was to protect the life of a seaman who had forfeited it by a capital crime. A court-martial on the principal mutineers was immediately assembled; and one was no sooner sentenced to die than the commander-in-chief ordered him to be executed on the following morning, "*and by the crew of the 'Marlborough' alone, no part of the boats' crews from the other ships, as had been usual on similar occasions, to assist in the punishment,*"—his Lordship's invariable order on the execution of mutineers. On the receipt of the necessary commands for this execution, the captain of the "Marlborough," Captain Ellison, waited upon the commander-in-chief, and reminding his Lordship that a determination that their shipmates should not suffer capital punishment had been the very cause of the ship's company's mutiny, expressed his conviction that the "Marlborough's" crew would never permit the man to be hanged on board that ship.

Receiving the captain on the "Ville de Paris'" quarter-deck, before the officers and ship's company, hearkening in breathless silence to what passed, and standing with his hat in his hand over his head, as was his Lordship's invariable custom during the whole time that any person, whatever were his rank, even a common seaman, addressed him on service, Lord St. Vincent listened very attentively till the captain ceased to speak; and then, after a pause, replied,—

"What do you mean to tell me, Captain Ellison, that you cannot *command* his Majesty's ship the 'Marlborough'? for if that is the case, sir, I will immediately send on board an officer who can."

The captain then requested that, at all events, the boats' crews from the rest of the fleet might, as always had been customary in the service, on executions, attend at this also, to haul the man up; for he really did not expect the "Marlborough's" would do it.

Lord St. Vincent sternly answered: "Captain Ellison, you are an old officer, sir, have served long, suffered severely in the service, and have lost an arm in action, and I should be very sorry that any advantage should be now taken of your advanced years. That man *shall be* hanged, at eight o'clock to-morrow morning, *and by his own ship's company:* for not a hand from any other ship in the fleet shall touch the rope. You will now return on board, sir; and, lest you should not prove able to command your ship, an officer will be at hand to you who can."

Without another word Captain Ellison instantly retired. After he had reached his ship, he received orders to cause her guns to be housed and secured, and that at daybreak in the morning her ports should be lowered. A general order then issued to the fleet for all launches to rendezvous under the "Prince" at seven o'clock on the following morning, armed with carronades and twelve rounds of ammunition for service; each launch to be commanded by a lieutenant, having an expert and trusty gunners'-mate and four quartergunners, exclusive of the launch's crew; the whole to be under the command of Captain Campbell, of the "Blenheim." The written orders to the captain will appear in their place. On presenting them, Lord St. Vincent said, 'he was to attend the execution, and if any symptoms of mutiny appeared in the "Marlborough," any attempt to open her ports, or any resistance to the hanging of the prisoner, he was to proceed close touching the ship, and to fire into her, and to continue his fire until all mutiny or resistance should cease; and that, should it become absolutely necessary, he should even sink the ship in face of the fleet.'

Accordingly, at seven the next morning, all the launches, thus armed, proceeded from the "Prince" to the "Blenheim," and thence, Captain Campbell having assumed the command, to the "Marlborough."

Having lain on his oars a short time alongside, the captain then formed his force in a line athwart her bows, at rather less than pistol-shot distance off, and then he ordered the tompions to be taken out of the carronades, and to load.

At half-past seven, the hands throughout the fleet having been turned up to witness punishment, the eyes of all bent upon a powerfully armed boat as it quitted the flag-ship; every one knowing that there went the provost-marshal conducting his prisoner to the "Marlborough" for execution. The crisis was come; now was to be seen whether the "Marlborough's" crew would hang one of their own men.

The ship being in the centre between the two lines of the fleet, the boat was soon alongside, and the man was speedily placed on the cat-head and haltered. A few awful minutes of universal silence followed, which was at last broken by the watch-bells of the fleet striking eight o'clock. Instantly the flag-ship's gun fired, and at the sound the man was lifted well off; but then, and visibly to all, he dropped back again; and the sensation throughout the fleet was intense. For, at this dreadful moment, when the eyes of every man in every ship were straining upon this execution, as the decisive struggle between authority and mutiny, as if it were destined that the whole fleet should see the hesitating unwillingness of the "Marlborough's" crew to hang their rebel, and the efficacy of the means taken to enforce obedience, by an accident on board the ship the men at the yard-rope unintentionally let it slip, and the turn of the balance seemed calamitously lost; but then they hauled him up to the yard-arm with a run,—the law was satisfied, and, said Lord St. Vincent at the moment, perhaps one of the greatest of his life, "Discipline is preserved, sir!"

When the sentence was executed, and not any disturbance appeared, that it might be again made perceptible to all the fleet that abundant force had been provided to overpower any resistance which a line-of-battle ship could offer, Captain Campbell broke his line, and rowing down, placed his launches as close alongside the "Marlborough" as their oars would permit; and then re-forming them, resumed his station across her bows, continuing there until the time for the body's hanging having expired, it was taken down, sewed up as is usual in its own hammock with a shot, and was carried in one of the "Marlborough's" boats to half a mile from the ship, and sunk; upon which, Captain Campbell withdrew his force, and the "Marlborough's" signal was made to take her station in the line.

This was the fatal blow to the mutiny in the fleet before Cadiz; not that violent insubordination, treasonable conspiracies, and open resistances did not again and again occur, to be as often and as instantaneously quelled; for the ships were many that were sent out from England, several arrived in almost open mutiny, and they brought a profusion of infection to the rest. The dreadful sentence was again and again inflicted, and in all cases of insubordination the crews were invariably the executioners of their own rebels; but never again was the power of the law doubted by any one.— *Tucker's Memoirs of Earl St. Vincent*, vol. i. pp. 303–309.

CHAPTER IX.

THE MEDITERRANEAN IN 1797 AND 1798.

BONAPARTE'S EGYPTIAN EXPEDITION.—THE RETURN OF THE BRITISH TO THE MEDITERRANEAN AND THE BATTLE OF THE NILE.—GREAT BRITAIN RESUMES CONTROL OF THE MEDITERRANEAN, AND THE SECOND COALITION IS FORMED.

THE Preliminaries of Leoben silenced the strife of arms and permitted all eyes to turn to the field of diplomacy, upon which, for the twelve months following, the interest of Europe was chiefly fixed. Moreau and Hoche, commanding the two armies of France upon the Rhine, had crossed the river, to enter upon a campaign in Germany, at the very moment when Bonaparte was signing the articles. On the 22d of April, a courier, bearing news of the suspension of hostilities, arrived at the headquarters of each general, and put an immediate stop to their advance. War continued only upon the sea, between Great Britain and the nations allied with France against her.

The confidence of the Directory had grown with each successive victory of Bonaparte, and had induced a tone in their transactions with foreign governments which the latter looked upon as arrogant, if not presumptuous. Yielding to politic considerations of effect upon popular opinion, Pitt had sent to France, in October, 1796, a practised diplomatist, Lord Malmesbury, to treat for peace. The terms proposed by Great Britain were substantially a restitution of conquests on both sides. If France would give back to the emperor the Netherlands and Lombardy, Great Britain, who had lost nothing of her own, would return to

France her possessions in the East and West Indies, as well as in the Gulf of St. Lawrence, with the *status ante bellum* of the fisheries. As regards the colonies taken from Holland, the disposition would be to restore them, if the government of the stadtholder were replaced; but if the republic set up by the assistance of French arms were maintained, Great Britain and the emperor, from whom the former refused to dissociate herself, would insist upon indemnification elsewhere for the injury thus done to their political position in Europe. With these understandings as a basis, the British government would be willing to enter upon negotiations for a general peace; to which it expressly required that Russia and Portugal, as well as the emperor, should be admitted. The French government replied that Great Britain had no authority to speak here for her allies; and further, that to cede territory which had been incorporated by the edicts of the Convention, as the Netherlands had, was inconsistent with the organic law of the republic. This latter plea was treated by the British government as trifling; no negotiation to close a war could go on, if results, favorable to one party, were secluded from discussion by the *ægis* of its constitution. As the case stood, France and Great Britain were both conquerors; the chief allies of each were losers. Great Britain proposed that each should surrender its winnings for the benefit of its allies. France refused, because its conquests were now part of the national territory, and as such inalienable. Taking exception, moreover, to delays caused by Malmesbury's frequent references to his government for instructions, the Directory, on the 20th of December, ordered him to leave Paris, within the not very civil space of forty-eight hours.

Similar cavalier treatment was at the same time experienced by the United States. Our government, after the maritime war began, had frequent disputes with both belligerents, — concerning the treatment of American ships by the British and French cruisers, — the protection of enemies' goods by the neutral flag, — the stipulations of Jay's treaty of commerce and navigation, in 1794, regarded by France as unduly favorable to Great Britain, — and the attitude of the United States towards French privateers, which were at first allowed and afterwards forbidden to sell prizes in her ports. These difficulties were fundamentally due to the fact that, the United States having practically no navy, neither belligerent felt under any bonds to respect her rights. To Great Britain, however, friendly relations were important on account of trade interests; while France, having no merchant ships, found an advantage in using Americans as carriers, and their ports as bases from which her cruisers could harass British commerce. The former of these benefits Great Britain curtailed by the claim that enemy's goods were, by international law, seizable under a neutral flag. The United States admitted this, and also, in the interests of her own peace and neutrality, declined longer to favor French commerce-destroying. Mutual discontent followed, and resulted in the recall of the French embassy from America, in November, 1796. At the same time President Washington, being dissatisfied with Munroe, the minister at Paris, removed him. When the latter, on the 30th of December, took his leave, the President of the Directory made a speech, highly complimentary to him personally, but offensive to the United States government; and evinced, as President Adams justly said, " a disposition to separate the people of the United States from the government, and thus to produce divisions fatal to our peace." The same theory of the divergent interests of rulers and people, with which the French republic started on its self-imposed mission forcibly to regenerate ancient despotisms, was thus impartially applied to the free American people under the government of their chosen and beloved fellow-citizen, Washington. The Directory refused to receive Pinckney, the new envoy from the United States. He remained in Paris, unrecognized, for a month; but the morning after hearing of the victory of Rivoli, the Directory ordered him to leave France.

By a somewhat singular coincidence, while the republic was thus embroiling itself with the two chief maritime states, a change of rulers took place in Russia; which, if not strictly a maritime power, was yet well placed, through her preponderance on the Baltic, to affect the naval interests of the world. The Empress Catherine II. died on the 17th of November, 1796, when about to conclude an agreement with the courts of London and Vienna to abandon her rather passive attitude of hostility towards France, and send an army of sixty thousand men to the support of Austria. Her successor, Paul I., allowed this treaty to drop, and resumed a bearing of cold watchfulness, until Bonaparte, by the seizure of Malta, and the Directory by a threat of war if commerce were permitted between his empire and Great Britain, drove his half-insane temper into open hostilities. But this was a year later.

These events at the end of 1796 coincided in time with the close alliance of the republic with Spain and Holland and its formal treaties of peace with the Italian states. By these and by the preliminaries of Leoben were defined the external relations of France in April, 1797. At the same moment her internal condition became alarming. The time had come to choose new members to replace one third of each body of the legislature; and the elections, still influenced by the memory of the Terror, resulted in the return of so many reactionaries as to give these a majority in both houses, especially in the lower. The latter at once showed its spirit by electing for speaker, by a large majority, General Pichegru, who was in open quarrel with the Directory; and followed up this significant act by a series of measures calculated to thwart the executive power and enfeeble its action. The opposition between the legislature and the Directory grew more and more pronounced throughout the summer months; but the reactionists failed to read

aright the signs of the times. They allowed themselves, by
the machinations of the royalists and through injudicious
acts of their own, to seem enemies of republican government, which aroused the anxiety of Hoche, commanding
the army of the Sambre and Meuse; and they directly
brought into question the conduct of Bonaparte towards
Venice, thus stirring up the more personal and violent
enmity of the brilliant conqueror of Italy. The legislature
thus found itself opposed by the two generals who stood
highest in public esteem as essential to the safety of France,
and who, each according to his own nature, transmitted his
feelings to the troops under his command, and prepared
them for a *coup d'état*. Inflammatory speeches and toasts
prevailed throughout the armies, to which the republic was
dear rather as a name than as a reality, and they were
easily led to think that the two houses were contemplating
a return to royalty.

The majority of the Directory, half-believing the same
thing, and chafed by an opposition which seriously hampered the working of the government, were ready for violent
measures. Two of its members, however, were not prepared for such action; and one of these, Carnot, the
organizer of the republic's early victories, was then serving
his turn as president of the Directory. Unknown to him
the three plotters matured their scheme, and called upon
Bonaparte to send them Augereau, the most revolutionary
of the generals in Italy, to direct the troops in such forcible
proceedings as might be necessary. Upon his arrival he
was made commandant of the military division of Paris,
despite the opposition of Carnot. The latter's presidency
expired on the 24th of August, and he was succeeded by
one of the conspirators. On the night of September 3d Augereau surrounded the castle and garden of the Tuileries with
twelve thousand troops and forty cannon, driving out the
legislators who were then there, together with their guard.
The Directory ordered the arrest, by its own guard, of the two

members not in the plot. Carnot escaped into Switzerland ; but Barthélemi, their other colleague, was seized. The next day the members of the two houses who had not been imprisoned met and passed a resolution, invalidating a number of the recent elections, and exiling to Cayenne the two directors and fifty-three representatives. The legislature, thus purged, was brought into harmony with the executive. An address was next issued to the departments and to the armies, declaring that the country had been invaded and disorganized by the Counter-Revolution and that patriotism, with the social and public virtues, had taken refuge with the armies. "In this," says a republican historian, "there was unhappily some truth. The middle class had become reactionary or inert; the populace now intervened but little in political movements; active democracy scarcely showed itself out of the armies. But if armies can defend liberty, they cannot put it in practice and maintain its life when abandoned by civil society. The revolution just effected with the consent of the soldiery was leading to another revolution to be effected by and for the soldiers."[1] The 18th of Fructidor, 1797, was the logical forerunner of the 18th of Brumaire, 1799, when Bonaparte seized the reins of government.

The strife between the Directory and the legislature kept all Europe in suspense; for its result would profoundly affect the course of existing discussions. The emperor, repenting of his precipitation at Leoben, kept holding off from a final treaty, seeking to introduce Great Britain as a party to the deliberations. This Bonaparte indignantly refused; for it would defeat his principal aim of separate negotiations. Pitt, more desirous than before of peace, again sent Malmesbury. The Directory kept him dancing attendance at Lille, the appointed place of meeting, during its struggle with the Councils. It made several demands most unlikely to be conceded, and upon these prolonged a discussion, to

[1] Martin, Hist. de France depuis 1789, vol. ii. p. 479.

which the ministry, who now really wished a favorable termination, patiently submitted. A week after the *coup d'état* the French negotiators were recalled, and in their place were sent others, who immediately upon arrival demanded of the British ambassador whether he had " powers to restore to France and its allies *all* the possessions which since the beginning of the war have passed into the hands of the English." An answer was required in the course of the same day. Malmesbury coolly replied that he neither could, nor ought to, treat on any other principle than that of compensations. The French envoys then sent him orders from the Directory to return within twenty-four hours to his Court and get powers to make those restorations. This, of course, put an end to the conference, and the war went on for four years more.

During these eventful months Bonaparte, already the most influential man in the nation through his hold upon men's imaginations, was ripening projects deeply affecting the control of the sea and the future direction to be given the gigantic efforts of which France had shown herself capable. On the 5th of April, under his management, there had been concluded with the king of Sardinia, subject to ratification by the Directory, a treaty of offensive and defensive alliance, to which was prefixed a secret article ceding to France the island of Sardinia upon condition of compensation on the continent.[1] Soon after, however, events occurred which opened to his penetrating genius a more satisfactory combination. During his invasion of Carinthia the people in his rear, throughout the possessions of Venice on the Italian mainland, rose against the French, massacring several hundred soldiers who fell into their hands. This gave him a pretext for disposing of these territories, as already stated,[2] in the secret articles of Leoben, and at the same time drew from him the sinister prediction that the government of Venice, shut up to its

[1] Corr. de Nap., vol. ii. p. 590.   [2] See page 235.

small island, would not be of long duration.[1] On the 2d
of May, having returned to Italy, he issued a proclamation,[2] setting forth his many causes of complaint for the
commotions excited in his rear, endangering the army
"then plunged in the gorges of Styria." He ordered the
French minister to leave Venice, all Venetian agents to
quit Lombardy and the Venetian possessions, and the
French general to treat the troops of the republic as
enemies, and to tear down her standard throughout the
mainland.

This declaration of war was followed, on the 16th of
May, by the abdication of the ancient oligarchy in favor of
a provisional government, which requested the presence
of a French division in the city to maintain order during
the transition period. This Bonaparte granted, sending
five thousand men, and observing cynically in his despatch
to the Directory that it would thus be possible to avoid the
odium attendant upon the execution of the secret preliminaries with Austria, and at the same time to quiet the
clamors of Europe; since "it is apparent that the occupation is only temporary and at the demand of the Venetians
themselves."[3] Ten days later he despatched General Gentili, recalled from Corsica, to Corfu with some two thousand troops, directing him to secure his hold both upon
the islands and the Venetian squadron lying there, but always to act as though supporting the Venetian commissioners who were to accompany him. "If the islanders
incline to independence," wrote he, "flatter them, and talk
about Greece, Athens, and Sparta."[4] To the Venetian
government he wrote that the expedition was sent to second its commissioners; and on the same day to the Directory, that Corfu ought to be irrevocably possessed by the
French. "The island of Malta," he added, "is of the utmost importance to us. . . . Why should not our fleet

[1] Corr. de Nap., vol. ii. p. 622.   [2] Ibid., vol. iii. p. 21.
[3] Ibid., vol. iii. p. 73.   [4] Ibid., p. 89.

seize it before entering the Atlantic? That little island is
priceless to us. Secret articles with the king of Sardinia
stipulate for us the occupation of the little islands of San
Pietro. Now is the moment to fortify them;"[1] for the British Mediterranean fleet was before Cadiz, and the Channel
fleet in full mutiny.

Four months later Bonaparte again wrote, "With San
Pietro, Corfu, and Malta, we shall be masters of the whole
Mediterranean."[2] "The islands of Corfu, Zante, and
Cephalonia are of more consequence to us than all Italy.
If we had to choose, better restore Italy to the emperor
and keep the four islands. . . . The empire of the Turks
crumbles daily. The possession of the four islands will
enable us to sustain it, or to take our share. The time is
not far distant when we shall feel that, truly to destroy
England, we must take possession of Egypt. The vast
Ottoman Empire, which is perishing daily, puts on us the
obligation to take means for the preservation of our Levant
trade."[3] "If at the peace we have to consent to the cession of the Cape of Good Hope to England, we should
seize Egypt. That country has never belonged to a European nation. It does not now belong to the Grand Turk.
We could leave here with twenty-five thousand men, convoyed by eight or ten ships-of-the-line, and take possession
of it. I wish you would inquire, Citizen Minister, what
effect upon the Porte would result from our expedition to
Egypt."[4] "Our occupation of Corfu and the other islands
entails relations with the pashas of Albania. These are
well affected to the French. In vain should we seek to
sustain the Turkish Empire; we shall see its fall in our
day. Corfu and Zante give us mastery of the Adriatic
and the Levant."[5] In these quotations, which could be

[1] Corr. de Nap., May 26, 1797, vol. ii. pp. 86, 87.
[2] Ibid., Sept. 13, 1797, vol. ii. p. 392.
[3] Ibid., Aug. 16, 1797, vol. ii. p. 311.
[4] Bonaparte to Minister of Foreign Affairs, Corr., vol. iii. p. 392.
[5] Corr. de Nap., vol. iii. p. 313.

multiplied, is seen the genesis of the great Egyptian expedition, to which, until it was carried into effect, Bonaparte recurred again and again with the persistency characteristic of his conceptions.

While he was thus employed, on the one hand flattering Venice with the hope of continued national existence, and on the other treating with Austria for her extinction and a division of the spoil, in which France was to have the Ionian Islands and the Venetian navy,[1] — while Malmesbury was negotiating at Lille, and the Directory was in bitter conflict with the Councils, — there was painfully sailing for England, crippled and suffering, the man who was destined to dispel the gorgeous dreams of Eastern achievement which filled Bonaparte's brain, and to shatter the French navy, — the all-essential link which alone could knit together these diverse maritime possessions, the one foundation upon which stood the whole projected fabric of Mediterranean control. During the wearing times of the Cadiz blockade, Lord St. Vincent, aware how much the listlessness of such inactive service contributed to foment mutiny, endeavored ingeniously to contrive fighting to occupy the minds of the seamen. For that purpose, largely, he bombarded Cadiz; and for that purpose he sent Nelson, with a detached squadron, to seize the town of Santa Cruz in the Canary Islands by a sudden and vigorous assault, hoping

[1] "Upon reaching Venice, Commodore, you will call, in company with the commanding general and the Minister of France, on the provisional government. You will tell them that the conformity of principles existing between the French and Venetian republics, and the protection granted by us to them, exact the prompt equipment of their navy, in order to concert with us, to maintain the mastery of the Adriatic and the islands; that for this purpose I have sent troops to Corfu, to preserve it to the Venetian Republic; and that henceforth it is necessary to work actively to put their navy in good condition.

"You will get possession of everything under this pretext; having continually on your tongue the unity of the two republics, and using always the name of the Venetian Navy. . . . It is my intention to seize for the (French) Republic all the Venetian ships, and all the stores possible for Toulon." To Commodore Perrée, June 13, 1797. — *Napoleon's Correspondence*, vol. iii. p. 155. See also instructions to Admiral Brueys, ibid., p. 291.

also there to take the rich cargo of a galleon, laden on
account of the Court of Spain. The attack was made on
the night of July 24, with all the vigor to be expected of
Nelson, but under great disadvantage. It resulted in a
disastrous repulse with heavy loss; and the admiral himself suffered amputation of the right arm. It became necessary for him to go to England, where he remained
through a long and painful convalescence until the following April; when he again sailed to join the Mediterranean
fleet, arriving just in time to command the squadron sent
in pursuit of Bonaparte.

The dissensions which weakened the external action of
the French government having been silenced by the *coup
d'état* of September 4, Bonaparte rapidly drew to an end
the negotiations with Austria. On the 17th of October,
1797, he, as sole representative of France, signed the treaty
of Campo Formio; which followed the general lines of the
Leoben preliminaries, yet with important differences. The
dissimulation concerning Venice was thrown aside, and
the ancient state wholly disappeared. The city, with the
mainland as far as the Adige, were given to Austria.
West of the Adige, the old Venetian provinces went to the
Cisalpine Republic, which was also dowered with the papal
legations attributed for a brief moment to Venice. The
countries and islands east of the Adriatic which had belonged to her were divided at the Gulf of Drino. All inside
that point went to Austria; all outside, to France, which
thus became possessed of the desire of Bonaparte's heart,
Corfu and its sister islands, with some slight territory on
the adjacent mainland. The cession of the Netherlands to
France was confirmed, and provision was made for a Congress to be held at Rastadt for the pacification and rearrangement of the German Empire; for Bonaparte had
persisted in treating with the emperor on account only of
his own dominions, and apart from the rest of the empire.
By secret stipulations, the two great powers agreed to

support each other's demands and interests in the Congress; where France wished to secure a certain line of the Rhine, and Austria to indemnify herself, at the expense of some German minor states, for the losses undergone by the treaty.

The salient features of this treaty were therefore the cession of Belgium; the annihilation of Venice; the settlement of the Cisalpine Republic as a powerful dependency of France; the strengthening of the latter as a Mediterranean state by the gain of the Ionian Islands; and, finally, the loosing of her hands against Great Britain, which now stood without a strong ally in all Europe. Bonaparte justified his action to his critics on these grounds, but especially on account of the necessity of dealing with Great Britain single-handed. "When the Cisalpine has the best military frontier in Europe, when France gains Mayence and the Rhine, when she has in the Levant Corfu, extremely well fortified, and the islands, what more would you wish? To scatter our force, in order that England may continue to take from us, from Spain, from Holland, our colonies, and postpone yet further the restoration of our trade and our navy? . . . Either our government must destroy the English monarchy, or must expect itself to be destroyed by the corruption and intrigue of those active islanders. The present moment offers us a fine game. Let us concentrate all our activity upon the navy, and destroy England. That done, Europe is at our feet."[1] Thus did Bonaparte demonstrate that the scene of strife was to be transferred to the sea.

The Directory at once ratified the Treaty of Campo Formio, and named Bonaparte one of three plenipotentiaries to the Congress of Rastadt. The general remained in Italy for a month longer, organizing the new state, and distributing the army with a view to support the interests of France, while withdrawing some thirty thousand men for the in-

[1] Corr. de Nap., vol. iii. pp. 519, 529.

tended army of England. On the 17th of November he left
Milan, and on the 25th arrived at Rastadt. He remained
there, however, but a week; and then, apparently at the
call of the Directory,[1] started for Paris, which he reached
on the 5th of December. He was avowedly to command the
army of England, and during the two following months his
correspondence betrays no sign of any other purpose; his
orders to various subordinates, and especially to Berthier,
his celebrated chief-of-staff, at the time commanding in
Italy, abound with dispositions and instructions to transfer
troops thence towards the Channel. Particularly significant
of such intention were the orders sent from him to Admiral
Brueys, commanding the French division in Corfu, to start
for Brest,[2] — a mission which would make his force inaccessible for the Egyptian expedition. Too much stress, however, cannot be laid upon such indications coming from so
crafty a nature; and the first intimation of a change of
purpose has more the appearance of stripping off a mask
than of awakening from a dream. "Make what efforts we
will," wrote he to the Directory, on February 23, 1798,
"we shall not for many years acquire the control of the
seas. To make a descent upon England, without being
master of the sea, is the boldest and most difficult operation
ever attempted."[3] Most true, but not new. Nor was the
veil under which he covered his change of attitude very
difficult to pierce. On the 7th of February, 1798, he wrote
to the Minister of War that he was about to visit the Channel coast, near Dunkirk, sending Kleber and Desaix to
Havre and Brest. On the 12th from Dunkirk he sends
engineers to examine Boulogne, Etaples, Ambleteuse, and
Calais, — ports on which he, five years later, based his more
serious projects of invasion; and at the same time two
others are dispatched to Holland to demand help of various

[1] Corr. de Nap., vol. iii. p. 597.
[2] Ibid., vol. iii. p. 609 (Dec. 14, 1797).
[3] Ibid., p. 644 (Feb. 23, 1798).

kinds. The very next day, February 13, he sends orders to Toulon, in the name of the Directory, not only to hold on to the ships ordered for Brest, but to send despatch vessels in every direction to recall to Toulon all ships-of-war cruising in the Mediterranean.[1] Returning to Paris, he addressed a letter to the government, setting forth what needed to be done by the month of April in order to make the attempt upon Great Britain even possible,— a long array of requirements, which only he, if his heart were in the matter, was capable of accomplishing. He concluded by saying there were but three ways of reaching England. One was by direct invasion; the second, by an attempt upon Hanover and Hamburg,— the continental centres of her trade; the last, by an expedition to the Levant.

On the 5th of March Bonaparte communicated to the government a note containing the dispositions necessary for an expedition to seize Egypt and Malta. The same day the Directory issued a number of decrees, constituting a commission on the Coast Defences of the Mediterranean, under cover of which the needed preparations were to be carried on, and defining the various steps to be taken. The ships at Toulon were required to be ready for sea on the 4th of April. Admiral Brueys, who had been unable to sail for Brest on account of want of provisions, was on February 12 ordered to Toulon. He arrived there with his squadron on the 2d of April, and was appointed to command the naval part of the expedition, to consist of thirteen ships-of-the-line with smaller vessels. All arrangements were pushed with the greatest activity possible, though much retarded by the extreme want of naval stores, of provisions, and of money. Still greater difficulty was experienced from scarcity of sailors; the inducements offered by privateers having drawn away almost all the seamen of the republic, and landed great numbers of them in British prisons,— a sad result of the much-vaunted commerce

[1] Corr. de Nap., vol. iii. p. 643.

destroying. Through all, the pretence of invading England was maintained; and Bonaparte himself, to mislead opinion, stayed till the last moment in Paris. The Spanish fleet at Cadiz was, by the urgent demands of the Directory, made to assume positions which threatened an approaching departure, in order to fasten St. Vincent's ships to the port and foster in British minds the easily aroused fear of an invasion of Ireland. But measures so extensive could not long escape comment and suspicion. The actual intentions of the Directory were kept so impenetrably secret that, after the expedition sailed, the senior naval officer at Toulon wrote to the Minister of Marine, "I know no more of the movements of the squadron than if it did not belong to the republic:"[1] but it was not possible to conceal the patent fact that Marseille, Toulon, Genoa, Civita Vecchia, and Corsica were alive with hurried preparations for a great naval undertaking, whatever its destination might be. It was evident, therefore, that France was about to expose herself for a time upon the sea to the blows of Great Britain, and the ministry determined not to let such an opportunity slip.

During the year 1797 no British fleet, and, with the rare exception of one or two scattered cruisers, no British ship-of-war, had entered the Mediterranean. The gathering of the Spanish navy at Cadiz, and of the greater part of the French in Brest, with the apparent design to invade Ireland or England, had dictated the concentration of the British navy before those two ports; either immediately, as St. Vincent at Cadiz, or by the dispositions — less fitted to compass their purpose — of the Channel fleet, by which bodies of ships were gathered at points other than Brest, with the hope of combining them against any sortie from that port. Great Britain, during the time following St. Vincent's retreat from the Mediterranean, was in the position of a nation struggling for existence, — for so she felt

[1] Jurien de la Gravière, Guerres Maritimes (4th ed.), vol. i. p. 350.

it,[1] — which had been compelled to contract her lines through loss of force, due to the gradual submission of her allies to her enemies. To this had further conduced the threatening attitude of the Dutch navy in the Texel, requiring a strong North Sea fleet. To her other embarrassments had been added, in this year of distress, the extensive mutinies in the navy. Though appeased in some instances and quelled in others, the spirit which caused them still existed. Under these circumstances Bonaparte, in 1797, had met no naval obstacle to his plans for the control of the Mediterranean, which had, moreover, been so covert as to escape detection. Admiral Brueys had gone from Toulon to the Adriatic, remained there several months, and returned in peace; and all minor naval movements went on undisturbed. The destiny of Corfu was not revealed till the end of the year; the purpose to get hold of Malta, seriously entertained by Brueys at the instigation of Bonaparte,[2] never transpired; and the talk about the army of England combined with the actual positions of the allied fleets to retain the British in the same stations. Toward the end of 1797 several circumstances occurred to relieve the pressure. In October Admiral Duncan inflicted upon the Dutch fleet, off the Texel, a defeat so decisive and complete as to throw it out of the contest for a long time. Of fifteen ships opposed to him, nine were taken. The condition of the French fleet in Brest, if not accurately known to be as bad as Bonaparte represented it,[3] was still suffi-

---

[1] So moderate a man as Collingwood wrote (Jan. 26, 1798): "The question is not merely who shall be conqueror, . . . but whether we shall be any longer a people, — whether Britain is still to be enrolled in the list of European nations." — *Collingwood's Memoirs*.

[2] See Correspondence of Brueys with Bonaparte; Jurien de la Gravière, Guerres Maritimes (Appendix, 4th ed.).

[3] "There are fitting out at Brest but ten ships-of-the-line, which have no crews, and are still far from being in condition to keep the sea. . . . The expedition against England would appear not to be possible before next year" (Corr. de Nap., vol. iii p. 644, Feb. 23, 1798.) The British Channel fleet at this time numbered forty-seven of the line, exclusive of sixteen in the North Sea.

ciently understood. No attempt had been made during the summer or winter of 1797 to renew the Irish expedition; and when the opening spring of 1798 permitted the Channel fleet in a body to keep the sea, the ministry felt it safe to detach a force to the Mediterranean.

Sir Horatio Nelson sailed from England on the 10th of April, and joined the fleet off Cadiz on the 30th. Lord St. Vincent welcomed him gladly, and at once sent him with three ships-of-the-line to the Mediterranean, to watch the impending armament, and, if possible, learn its destination. Nelson left the fleet on the 2d of May, the day before Bonaparte quitted Paris. On the 17th, having been unavoidably delayed at Gibraltar, he was in the neighborhood of Toulon, and captured a French corvette just leaving port; from which he learned particulars as to the naval force of the enemy, but nothing as regarded its destination. On the night of the 20th, in a violent gale of wind, his own ship was dismasted and with difficulty saved from going ashore. By great exertions she was towed by her consorts into the San Pietro Islands, at the south end of Sardinia, where she anchored on the 23d. On the 19th Bonaparte had sailed with the Marseille and Toulon divisions of the expedition. He was to be joined on the way by the detachments from Genoa, Corsica, and Civita Vecchia, — the total number of troops amounting to between thirty and thirty-five thousand.

On the same day that Nelson parted from St. Vincent, May 2, the admiralty wrote to the latter that it was essential to send twelve ships-of-the-line into the Mediterranean to counteract the French armament; and that to replace them eight ships had been ordered from England. A private letter from the First Lord, by the same mail, authorized St. Vincent to take his whole force for this object, if necessary, but hoped a detachment would be sufficient. In the latter case, while the choice of its commander was left to the admiral, it was intimated that Nelson,

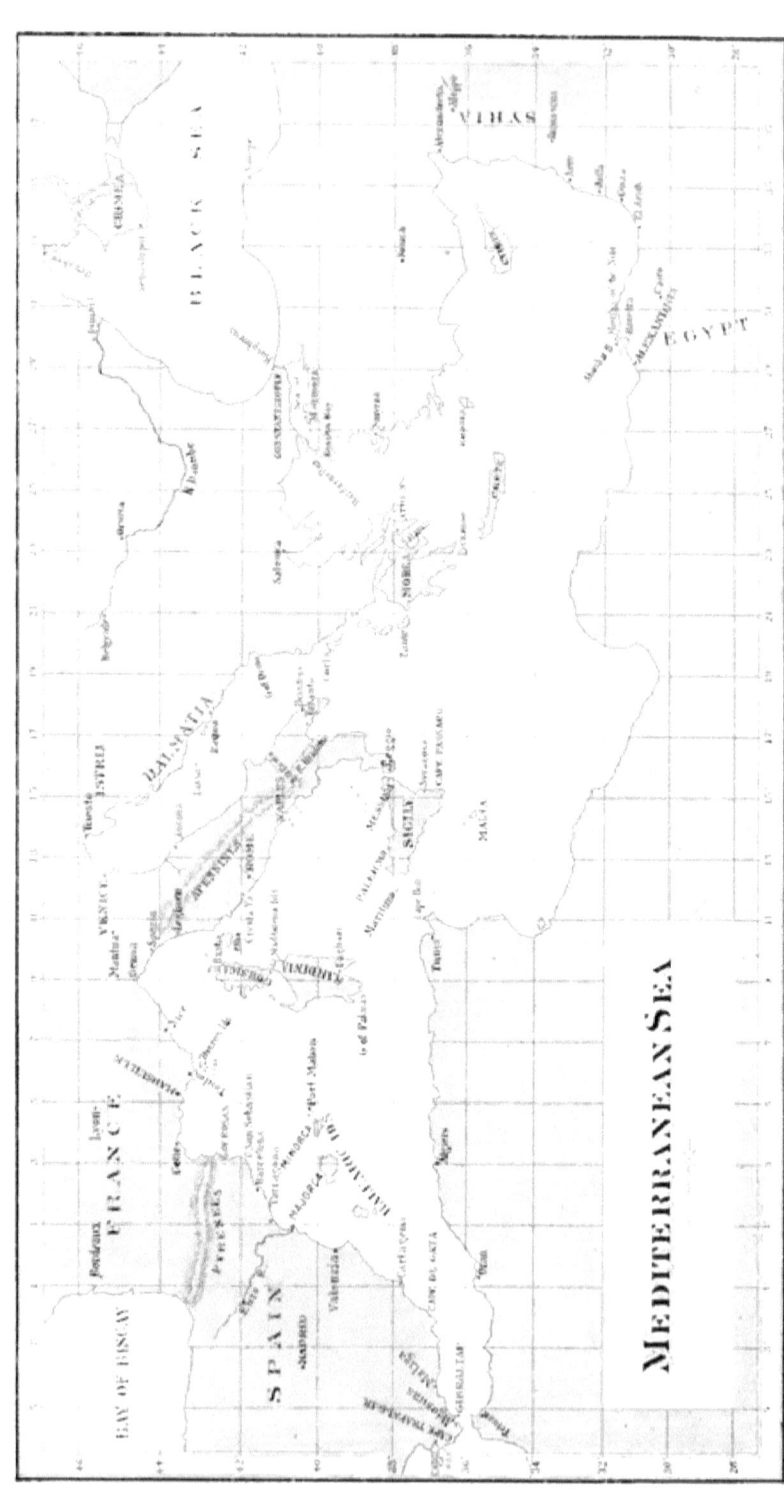

though junior to two other flag-officers, was by all means the proper man. Jervis had already made the same decision; and now at once told off and prepared the nine ships-of-the-line, forming the inshore squadron of the blockade, to start the moment the expected re-enforcement arrived. The junction of the latter with the main fleet was made May 24, out of sight of the port; and during the night Captain Troubridge sailed with the inshore ships, their places being taken by vessels similarly painted, so that no suspicion of the transaction might arise in Cadiz. On the 7th of June Troubridge joined Nelson, having picked up two more ships by the way; so that the British were now thirteen seventy-fours and one of fifty guns. By a very strange fatality, however, the frigates at first with Nelson had parted company the night his ship was dismasted, and had never rejoined. Troubridge brought only one little brig; and, as it was inadmissible to scatter the ships-of-the-line, the want of lookout vessels seriously affected all Nelson's movements in the long and harassing pursuit, covering nearly eight weeks, that lay before him.

After leaving Toulon, Bonaparte directed his force along the Gulf of Genoa, where, on the night of May 20, he experienced the same gale that dismasted Nelson. The next day the convoy from Genoa joined. Steering south along the east coasts of Corsica and Sardinia, the division from Corsica met him on the 26th off the south end of the island, but that from Civita Vecchia failed to appear. Here the French first heard that Nelson was in the Mediterranean with three ships, and expected ten more. Bonaparte then continued on for Malta, which he reached on the 9th of June, and found there the division from Civita Vecchia, thus bringing his whole force under his hand. The island was immediately summoned, and after a faint show of resistance capitulated on the 12th; the French fleet and convoy, numbering four hundred sail, entering the port of La Valetta on the 13th. Bonaparte remained the

VOL. I. — 17

time necessary to secure his conquest temporarily; then leaving a garrison of four thousand men, and notifying the Directory that at least four thousand more with ample supplies were needed, he sailed again on June 19 for Egypt.

The British fleet, after its junction, was becalmed for several days. It then made the best of its way round the north end of Corsica, and thence south between Italy and the islands. Not till June 14, off Civita Vecchia, was probable information received that the French had been seen ten days before off the south-west point of Sicily, steering to the eastward. As yet there was no certainty as to their destination, and Nelson had no light vessels for scouts. St. Vincent in his instructions had said, reflecting the ideas of the government, that the enemy's "object appears to be either an attack upon Naples or Sicily, the conveyance of an army to some part of Spain to invade Portugal, or to pass through the Straits with the view of proceeding to Ireland." The whole situation vividly illustrates the difficulty of pursuit by sea, and the necessity of stationing and keeping the detaining force near the point of the enemy's departure before he can get away. By whatsoever fault, certainly not that of Nelson or St. Vincent, the British fleet was a fortnight too late in entering the Mediterranean. It would have been yet more so, had the resources of the French dockyards answered to the spur of Bonaparte's urgency; but it is ill goading a starved horse.

An easterly course, however, with a fresh north-west wind, indicated that neither Spain nor the Atlantic was the destination of the French armament; and Nelson at once decided it must be Malta, to be used as a base of operations against Sicily. "Were I," said he, "the admiral of the fleet attending an army for the invasion of Sicily, I should say to the general: 'If you can take Malta, it secures the safety of the fleet and the transports, and your own safe retreat, if necessary;' *Malta is in the direct road to Sicily.*"[1] Pausing

---

[1] Nelson's Dispatches, vol. iii. p. 35.

a moment to communicate with Naples, he there heard, on the 17th of June, that the French had landed at Malta; and pushing on, received off Messina the news of its surrender. This was on the 20th, the day after Bonaparte sailed from the island for Egypt. On the 22d, off Cape Passaro, the south-east extremity of Sicily, a vessel was spoken, from which Nelson gained the information of Bonaparte's departure, supposed to be for Sicily; but he had meantime learned from Naples that the French had no intention of molesting any part of that kingdom. Utterly in the dark, and without frigates, he concluded, after weighing all the chances, that Egypt was the enemy's destination, and with a fair wind and a press of sail shaped his course for Alexandria. On the 28th the fleet came off the port, and sent a boat ashore. No French vessels had been seen on the coast.

This remarkable miscarriage, happening to a man of so much energy and intuition, was due primarily to his want of small lookout ships; and secondly, to Bonaparte's using the simple, yet at sea sufficient, ruse [1] of taking an indirect instead of a direct course to his object. This, however, in a narrow sea, with so numerous a body of vessels, would not have served him, had the British admiral had those active purveyors of information, those eyes of the fleet, which are so essential to naval as to land warfare.[2] On leaving Malta, Bonaparte directed the expedition to steer first for Candia. After a week's quiet navigation he was off the south side of the island, and on the 27th of June was joined by a frigate from Naples, to tell him of Nelson, with fourteen sail, being off that port ten days before. At

---

[1] Marmont attributes the approach to Candia to a wish to give the shelter of the island to the numerous coasters in the convoy. (Mémoires du Duc de Raguse, vol. i. p. 362.)

[2] Bonaparte in his preparations laid special stress on having enough small vessels. "It is indispensable to have with the squadron the greatest attainable number of corvettes and despatch vessels. Send orders to all the ports for all such to join the fleet." — Corr. de Nap., vol. iv. pp. 79, 80.

this moment the British admiral had already outstripped his chase. On the 25th the two fleets had been about sixty miles apart, the French due north of the British, steering in nearly parallel directions.[1] When Bonaparte knew that his enemy was somewhere near upon his heels, he again changed the course, ordering the fleet to make the land seventy miles west of Alexandria, and sending a frigate direct to the port to reconnoitre. On the 29th of June, the day Nelson sailed away from Alexandria, the light squadron signalled the coast, along which the fleet sailed till July 1st, when it anchored off the city. Determined to run no chance of an enemy's frustrating his objects, the commander-in-chief landed his army the same evening.

If, in this celebrated chase, Nelson made a serious mistake, it was upon his arrival at Alexandria. He had reasoned carefully, and, as the event proved, accurately, that the French were bound to Egypt; and had justly realized the threat to the British supremacy in India contained in such an attempt. Knowing the time when the French left Malta, as he did, and that they were accompanied by so great a train of transports, it seems a fair criticism that he should have trusted his judgment a little further, and waited off the suspected port of destination to see whether so cumbrous a body had not been outsailed by his compact, homogeneous force. He appears, on finding his expectations deceived, to have fallen into a frame of mind familiar to most, in which a false step, however imposed by the conditions under which it was taken, can be seen only in the light of the unfortunate consequences, and therein as-

---

[1] This statement is based on the plate in the "Commentaires de Napoléon," vol. ii. p. 190. There are evident inaccuracies in the British positions there given (e. g., for June 22, and in the approach to Alexandria); but that of the 25th seems probable. James states that on the night of June 22 the tracks of the two fleets crossed, but at a sufficient interval of time to prevent a meeting, — the more so as a constant haze prevailed. (Nav. Hist., vol. ii. p. 177.)

sumes the color of a fault, or at best of a blunder. "His active and anxious mind," wrote Sir Edward Berry, who, as captain of the flagship, was witness of his daily feelings, "would not permit him to rest a moment in the same place; he therefore shaped his course to the northward for the coast of Caramania."[1] His one thought now was to get back to the westward, taking a more northerly course on the return, so as to increase the chance of information. The fleet accordingly stretched to the northward until the coast of Asia Minor was made, and then beat back along the south shore of Candia, not seeing a single vessel until it had passed that island. On the 19th of July it reached Syracuse, whence Nelson wrote to the British minister at Naples that, having gone a round of six hundred leagues with the utmost expedition, he was as ignorant of the situation of the enemy as he had been four weeks before. The squadron now filled with water, which was running short, and on the 24th again sailed for Alexandria; the admiral having satisfied himself that the French were at least neither in Corfu nor to the westward. On the 1st of August the minarets of the city were seen, and soon after the port full of shipping, with the French flag upon the walls, but, to Nelson's bitter disappointment, no large ships of war. At one in the afternoon, however, one of his fleet made signal that a number of ships-of-the-line were at anchor in Aboukir Bay, twelve or fifteen miles east of Alexandria; and Nelson, prompt to attack as Bonaparte had been to disembark, gave slippery fortune, so long unkind, no chance again to balk him, but with a brisk breeze flew at once upon the foe.

Neither by the character of the anchorage nor by its own dispositions was the French fleet prepared for the attack thus suddenly, and most unexpectedly, precipitated upon it. Two days after the army landed, the commander-in-chief gave Admiral Brueys explicit and urgent orders at

[1] Narrative in Naval Chronicle, vol. i. p. 48.

once to sound the old port of Alexandria, and, if possible, take his ships in there; if not, and if Aboukir Bay would admit of defence at anchor against a superior force, he might choose a position there. Failing both, he was to go with his heavy vessels to Corfu.[1] That and the other Ionian Islands were within Bonaparte's district, by the decree of April 12 making him commander of the Army of the East. In a much later dispatch, which Brueys did not live to receive, he explains that it was indispensable to preserve the fleet from serious injury until the affair in Egypt was settled, in order to check any movement of the Porte; for, though the allegiance of the Mamelukes was but nominal, it was possible the Sultan might resent the French invasion. The justice of this cautious view was shown by the action of the Porte as soon as the destruction of the fleet became known. Brueys ordered the necessary soundings, and the report which he received on July 18, a fortnight before the battle, was favorable; with good weather it was possible to take the ships-of-the-line inside.[2] The admiral, however, was an invalid, and of a temper naturally undecided; unable to make a choice of difficulties, he hung on the balance and remained inactive, taking refuge in a persuasion that the British would not return. Bonaparte thought the same. "All the conduct of the English," wrote he on the 30th of July, "indicates that they are inferior in number, and content themselves with blockading Malta and intercepting its supplies." But the great soldier, prone as he always was to tempt fortune to the utmost for a great object, found in this opinion no reason for running unnecessary risks and

[1] Corr. de Nap., vol. iv, pp. 275–277.
[2] In a chart of the old port of Alexandria, made in 1802 by Major Bryce of the Royal Engineers, attached to Abercromby's expedition, it is said that not less than five fathoms will be found throughout the middle passage. The directions add that heavy ships cannot get out unless with good weather for warping. This was Brueys's great objection to entering, and it was well taken; but the alternative of destruction was worse.

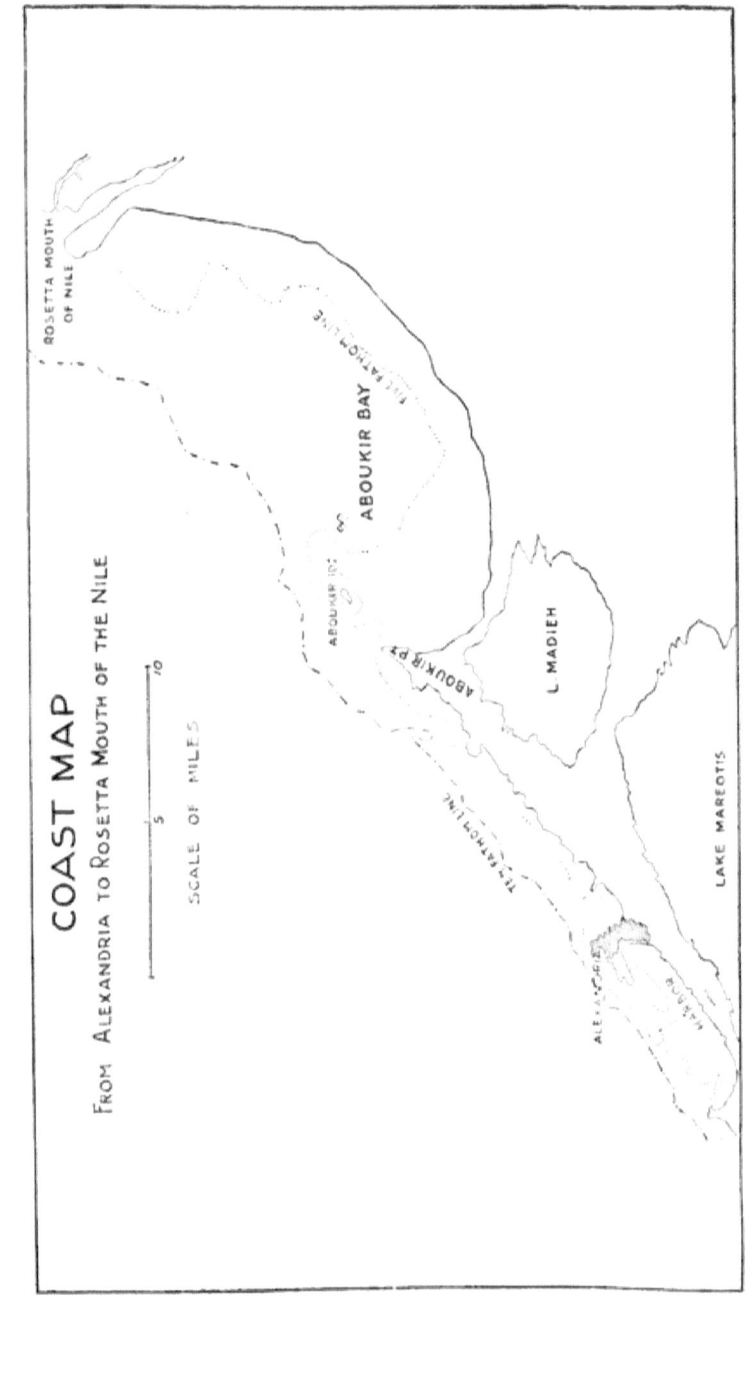

in the same breath insisted upon Alexandria or Corfu for the fleet. Brueys had taken his ships to Aboukir Bay on the 8th of July, and there remained. He had the orders of his commander; but the latter, at a distance and absorbed in the cares of his operations ashore, could not communicate to his vacillating subordinate the impulse of his own energy. All the work of the squadron proceeded listlessly; the belief that the British fleet would not return sapped every effort; carelessness, indiscipline and insubordination, among officers and men, caused constant complaint and trouble. In such delusion and lethargy went by the priceless days which were passed by Nelson in unresting thought and movement, in "a fever of anxiety"[1] that scarcely allowed him to eat or drink.

The Bay of Aboukir,[2] in the western portion of which the French fleet was anchored, and where was fought the celebrated Battle of the Nile, is an open roadstead, extending from the promontory of Aboukir, fifteen miles east of Alexandria, to the Rosetta mouth of the Nile. The distance between the two extreme points is about eighteen miles. In the western part, where the French were lying, the shore-line, after receding some distance from Aboukir Point, turns to the south-east and continues in that direction in a long narrow tongue of sand, behind which lies the shallow Lake Madieh. North-east from the point is a line of shoals and rocks, rising at two and a half miles' distance into a small island, then bearing the same name, Aboukir, but since known as Nelson's Island; beyond which the same stretch of foul ground continues for another mile and a quarter. Behind this four-mile barrier there is found fair shelter from the prevailing north-west summer wind; but as, for three miles from the beach, there were only four fathoms of water, the order of battle had to be established

---

[1] Nelson's Dispatches, vol. iii. p. 128.
[2] See Coast Map, Alexandria to Rosetta, and Plan of the Battle of the Nile.

somewhat beyond that distance. The north-western ship, which with the prevailing wind would be to windward and in the van, was moored a mile and a half south-east from Aboukir Island, in five fathoms of water.¹ This was scant for a heavy vessel, but it does not seem that she was carried as close to the shoal as she might have been. As the van ship in the column, she was on one flank, and that the most exposed, of the line-of-battle, whose broadsides were turned to the sea. She should, therefore, have been brought so near the shoal as not to leave room to swing, and there been moored head and stern. So placed, the flank could not have been turned, as it actually was. This was the more necessary because the few guns established by Brueys on the island were so light as to be entirely ineffective, in range and weight, at the distance between them and the flank they pretended to strengthen. They were a mere toy defence, as futile as the other general dispositions taken. This being so, it would seem that the frigates might have been placed along the shoal ground ahead, where the enemy's ships-of-the-line could not reach them, and thence have supported the flank ship. From the latter, the line extended south-east to, and including, the eighth in the order, when it turned a little toward the beach; making with its former direction a salient angle, but one very obtuse. The distance from ship to ship was about one hundred and sixty yards; from which, and from the average length of the ships, it may be estimated that the whole line from van to rear was nearly a mile and three quarters long. In case of expecting attack, a cable was to be taken from ship to ship to prevent the enemy passing through the intervals; and springs also were then to be put upon the cable by which each vessel was anchored.²

¹ Chevalier, Mar. Fran. sous la République, p. 365.
² A spring is a rope taken from the stern of a ship at anchor and fastened either to the riding cable or to an anchor suitably placed, so as to turn the broadside in the direction wished. Owing to the boats being away to get

It will be instructive to a professional reader to compare the dispositions of Admiral Brueys, in Aboukir Bay, with those adopted by Lord Hood in 1782, at St. Kitt's Island, when expecting an attack at anchor from a very superior force.[1] The comparison is historically interesting as well as instructive; for it has been said that Nelson framed his own plan, in the cogitations of his long chase, upon Hood's scheme for attacking the French fleet under Admiral DeGrasse while lying at the anchorage from which he first drove it, before occupying it himself. The parallel is quite complete, for neither at St. Kitt's nor Aboukir was the anchored fleet able to get substantial assistance from batteries. The decisively important points in such a disposition, as in any order of battle, land or sea, are — (1) that the line cannot be pierced, and (2) that the flanks cannot be turned. Hood thrust one flank ship so close to the shore that the enemy could not pass round her, and closed up his intervals.[2] Brueys left the same flank — for in both cases it was the van and weather ship — open to turning, with long spaces between the vessels. In his arrangement for the other flank, for the lee ships, Brueys was equally inferior. Hood threw his eight lee ships at right angles to the rest of the fleet, so that their broadsides completely protected the latter from enfilading fire. Brueys simply bent his line a little, with a view of approaching the rear to shoal water. Failing thus to obtain a fire at right angles to the principal line of battle, the rear did not contribute to strengthen that; while, not actually reaching to shoal water, it remained itself in the air, if attacked by the enemy in

water when Nelson appeared, to the failure of many of them to return, and to the rapidity with which the attack was made, these precautions were not carried out.

[1] Mahan's "Influence of Sea-Power upon History," pp. 469-478. Plates XVIII. and XIX.

[2] Letter of DeGrasse to Kerguelen, Jan. 8, 1783. Hood "ranged his vessels in very close order (*très-serrés*), and it was impossible to pass between the land and them, as I wished." — *Kerguelen's Guerre Maritime de* 1778, p. 259.

preference. This was the more singular, as Brueys had
expected the rear to be the object of the British efforts.
"I have asked," he wrote, "for two mortars to place upon
the shoal on which I have rested the head of my line; but
I have much less to fear for that part than for the rear,
upon which the enemy will probably bring to bear all their
effort."[1] Nelson, however, whether illumined by Hood's
example, through that historical study of tactics for which
he was noted, or inspired only by his own genius, had well
understood beforehand that, if he found the French in
such order as they were, the van and centre were at his
mercy; and he had clearly imparted this view to his captains. Hence, when the enemy were seen, he needed only
to signal "his intention was to attack the van and centre
as they lay at anchor, according to the plan before developed,"[2] and could leave the details of execution to his
subordinates.

The evening before the eventful first of August, as the
British fleet expected to make Alexandria the next day, the
"Alexander" and "Swiftsure" were sent ahead to reconnoitre. In consequence of this detachment, made necessary by
the want of frigates, these ships, when the main body at 1 P.M.[3]
sighted the French fleet, were considerably to leeward, and
did not get into action until two hours after their consorts.
As soon as the enemy were seen, the British fleet hauled
sharp up on the wind, heading about north-east, to weather
Aboukir Island and shoal; the admiral at the same time
making signal to prepare for action, anchoring by the stern.

---

[1] Letter of Brueys to Bonaparte, July 13, 1798; La Gravière, Guerres
Maritimes, vol. i. p. 367. This is a somewhat singular example of following
a rule, the principle of which is not grasped. The rear of a column of sailing
ships under way was the weaker end, because less easily helped by the van;
but in a column of ships at anchor, head to wind, the weather ships were incomparably more exposed, the lee having a very hard pull to get up to them.

[2] Narrative of Sir Edward Berry. See Naval Chronicle, vol. i. p. 52.

[3] James, ii. p. 177. The Vanguard's Journal, quoted by Sir Harris
Nicolas, Nelson's Disp. vol. iii. p. 49, says 4 P. M.

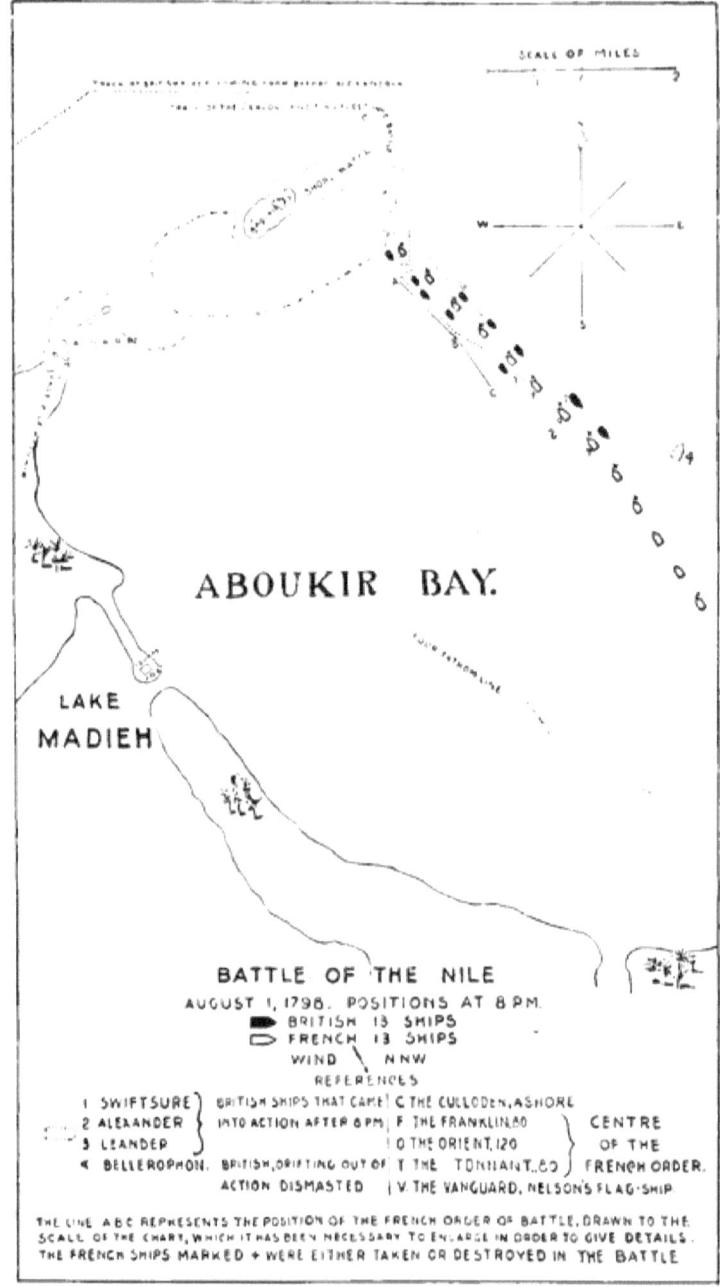

As they drew by the shoal, being in eleven fathoms,[1] Nelson hailed Captain Hood, of the "Zealous," and asked if he thought they were far enough to the eastward to clear it; for the only chart in the fleet was a rough sketch taken from a captured merchant vessel, and no British officer knew the ground. Hood replied that he would bear up, sounding as he went, so that the other ships keeping outside of him would be safe. Thus the fleet was piloted into action; one ship, the "Goliath," being ahead of the "Zealous," but on her outer bow, and the admiral very properly allowing others to pass him, until he was sixth in the order, so as to be reasonably certain the flag-ship would not touch the bottom. Captain Foley of the "Goliath," still keeping the lead, crossed ahead of the French column, over the ground left open by Brueys's oversight, intending to attack the van ship, the "Guerrier;" but the anchor hung for a moment, so that he brought up on the inner quarter of the second, the "Conquérant," while Hood, following close after, anchored on the bow of the "Guerrier." These two British ships thus came into action shortly before sundown, the French having opened fire ten minutes before. Five minutes later, just as the sun was sinking below the horizon, the foremast of the "Guerrier" went overboard. "So auspicious a commencement of the attack was greeted with three cheers by the whole British fleet."[2] The "Orion" followed with a much wider sweep, passing round her two leaders, between them and the shore, and anchored on the inner side of the fifth French ship; while the "Theseus," which came next, brought up abreast the third, having gone between the "Goliath" and "Zealous" and their antagonists. The "Audacious," the fifth of the British

---

[1] The ships-of-the-line needed nearly five fathoms in smooth water, more if there was much sea.

[2] James's Naval History, vol. ii. p. 184 (ed. 1878). In the main, the author has followed James in the details of this and other battles, though not without careful comparison with other sources of information accessible to him.

to come up, chose a new course. Steering between the
"Guerrier" and the "Conquérant," she took her place on
the bow of the latter, already engaged on the quarter by
the "Goliath." These five all anchored on the inner (port)
side of the French. Nelson's ship, the "Vanguard," coming
next, anchored outside the third of the enemy's vessels, the
"Spartiate," thus placed between her and the "Theseus."
The "Minotaur," five minutes later, took the outer side of
the fourth, heretofore without an opponent ; and the "Defence" attacked, also on the outer side, the fifth ship,
already engaged on her inner side by the "Orion." Five
French seventy-fours were thus in hot action with eight
British of the same size, half an hour after the first British
gun was fired, and only five hours from the time Brueys
first knew that the enemy were near.

This most gallant, but most unfortunate, man had passed
suddenly from a condition of indolent security face to face
with an appalling emergency. When Nelson's fleet was
first reported, numbers of men were ashore, three miles or
more away, getting water for the ships. They were recalled,
but most of them did not return. Brueys still cherished
the belief, with which indeed he could not have parted
without despair, that the enemy would not brave the unknown perils of the ground with night falling ; nor could
he tell their purpose until they had passed Aboukir Island
and opened the bay. A hurried council of senior officers
renewed the decision previously reached, to fight, if fight
they must, at anchor ; but Brueys betrayed the vacillations
of an unsteady purpose by crossing the light yards, a step
which could have no other significance than that of getting
under way. Still, he hoped for the respite of a night to
make the preparations so long neglected. Little did he
know the man whom England herself still hardly knew.
Without a moment's pause, without a tremor of uncertainty,
yet with all the precautions of a seaman, Nelson came
straight onward, facing with mind long prepared the diffi-

culties of navigation, the doubts and obscurity of a night action. Hurriedly the French prepare for battle; and, secure that the enemy will not dare go within the line, the batteries on that side are choked with the numerous encumbrances of ship economy, the proper disposal of which is termed "clearing for action."

For half an hour Brueys was a helpless and hopeless, though undaunted, spectator of an overwhelming attack, which he had never expected at all, delivered in a manner he had deemed impossible upon the part of his order he thought most secure. Soon he was freed from the agony of mere passive waiting by the opportunity to act. The "Bellerophon" and "Majestic," both seventy-fours, anchored outside and abreast, respectively, of the flag-ship "Orient," of one hundred and twenty guns, and of the "Tonnant," eighty, next astern. Darkness had just settled down upon the water as the arrival of these two ships completed the first scene of the tragedy; and the British vessels, which were fighting under their white ensign,[1] as more easily seen at night, now hoisted also four lanterns, horizontally arranged, whereby to recognize each other.

Meanwhile a woful mishap had befallen Nelson's chosen brother-in-arms, Troubridge. His ship, the "Culloden," had been some distance from the main body of the fleet when the latter rounded the shoal, and, doing her own piloting, ran upon its outer extremity at a quarter before seven. There she stuck, despite all the efforts of her most able commander, until two o'clock the next morning, when the

---

[1] Until after the middle of this century there were in the British navy three flags of the same general design, but with red, white, and blue grounds. Admirals were divided into three classes, of the Red, the White, and the Blue; and, according to their classification, ships under their immediate command showed the corresponding ensign. Nelson being at this time a rear-admiral of the Blue, his ships would usually carry the blue flag, almost invisible at night.

At the present day all British naval vessels wear the white flag, and merchant ships the red.

battle was over. There also, however, she served as a beacon to the two remaining ships, "Alexander" and "Swiftsure," who had to make the perilous passage in the dark. These vessels, with the "Leander," fifty, arriving after eight o'clock, at a critical moment of the battle, played the part of a reserve in a quarter where the British were meeting with disaster.

Neither the "Bellerophon" nor the "Majestic" was equally matched with the French ship opposed to it; but the "Bellerophon" especially, having to do with a vessel double her own force and having brought up fairly abreast, where she got her full fire, was soon nearly a wreck. In three quarters of an hour her main and mizzen masts were shot away, and in thirty minutes more, unable longer to endure her punishment, the cable was cut and she wore out of action. As she did so, the foremast also fell, and, with forty-nine killed and one hundred and forty-eight wounded, out of a ship's company of six hundred and fifty men, the "Bellerophon" drifted down the line, receiving the successive broadsides of the French rear. As she thus passed, without flag or light, the "Swiftsure" came up. Withholding his fire, Captain Hallowell hailed, and finding her to be a British ship, let go at once his anchor, bringing up on the starboard bow of the "Orient." Immediately afterwards the "Alexander" arrived and anchored on the port quarter of the three-decker, while the "Leander," with the discretion becoming her size, placed herself on the port bow of the "Franklin," the next ahead to the "Orient," in a position of comparative impunity, and thus raked both the French ships. The French centre was thus in its turn the victim of a concentration, similar to that with which the action began in the van, and destined to result in a frightful catastrophe.

At about nine in the evening the French flag-ship was observed to be on fire, from what cause has never been certainly known. The British guns, trained on the part in flames, helped to paralyze all efforts to extinguish them, and they gained rapidly. The brave and unfortunate Brueys was spared the sight of this last calamity. Already twice wounded, at half-past eight a cannon-ball carried away his left leg at the thigh. He refused to be taken below, and passed away calmly and nobly a few moments before the fire broke out. At ten the "Orient" blew up. Five ships ahead of her had already surrendered, and the eighty-gun ship "Franklin" also hauled down her flag before midnight.

Six of the French still had their colors flying; but either from their cables being cut by shot, or from the necessity of slipping to avoid the explosion of the "Orient," they had drifted far astern. The three in the extreme rear had been but slightly engaged; of the others, the "Tonnant" was totally dismasted, while the "Heureux" and "Mercure" had received considerable injury.[1] The following morning these vessels were attacked by some of the least injured of the British, with the result that the "Tonnant," "Mercure," "Heureux" and "Timoléon," the last of which had been the extreme rear, or flank, ship of the original order, ran ashore. There the three first named afterwards hauled down their flags, and the fourth was burned by her officers. The two other French ships, "Guillaume Tell" and "Généreux," escaped. The former bore the flag of Rear-Admiral Villeneuve, who had commanded the rear in this battle, and was hereafter to be commander-in-chief of the allied fleet at

[1] The first attack of the thirteen British ships (counting among them the "Leander," fifty,) was confined to the eight head ships of the French line, down to and including the "Tonnant." As these were one by one crushed, the British dropped down and engaged those in the rear, — but with a vigor necessarily diminished by the injuries they had themselves received, not to speak of the physical fatigue induced by the labor and excitement of the previous hours. Nevertheless the "Mercure," when she hauled down her flag, had lost one hundred and five killed and one hundred and forty-eight wounded, and had but six guns that could be used. The loss of the "Heureux" is not stated, but she had nine feet of water in her hold. (Chevalier, Mar. Fran. sous la Rép., pp. 376, 377.)

the memorable disaster of Trafalgar. His inaction on this occasion has been sharply criticised, both in his own time and since. Upon the whole, the feeling of later French professional writers appears to be that his courage, though unquestionable, was rather of the passive than the active type; and that in Aboukir Bay there was afforded him a real opportunity and sufficient time to bring the rear ships into action, which he culpably failed to improve.[1] Bonaparte, on the contrary, wrote to Villeneuve, soon after the battle, that "if any error could be imputed to him, it was that he had not got under way as soon as the 'Orient' blew up; seeing that, three hours before, the position Brueys had taken had been forced and surrounded." [2]

Such was, in its main outlines, the celebrated Battle of the Nile, the most complete of naval victories, and among the most decisive, at least of the immediate course of events. In it the French lost eleven out of thirteen ships-of-the-line[3] and thirty-five hundred men, killed, wounded, or drowned;[4] among them being the commander-in-chief and three captains killed, a rear-admiral and six captains wounded. The British loss was two hundred and eighteen killed — of which one captain — and six hundred and seventy-eight wounded, among whom was the admiral himself, struck in the head by a heavy splinter. The hurt, which he at first thought fatal, disabled him for the moment and seriously affected his efficiency for some days. "I think," wrote he, four weeks later, "that if it had pleased God I had not been wounded, not a boat would have escaped."[5]

[1] Jurien de la Gravière, Guerres Maritimes, vol. i. pp. 228-230; Chevalier, Mar. Fran. sous la République, pp. 386-388. A letter from Villeneuve, justifying his inaction, is to be found in the former work, p. 231, and in Troude, Batailles Navales, vol. iii. p. 121.

[2] Corr. de Nap., vol. iv. p. 520.

[3] The two that escaped were captured by Lord Nelson's squadron before July, 1800, when he resigned the Mediterranean command.

[4] Chevalier, p. 384.

[5] Nels. Disp., vol. iii. p. 10.

The particular circumstances under which the British attack was undertaken, the admirable skill as well as conduct shown by all the captains, and the thoroughly scientific character of the tactical combination adopted, as seen in its execution, unite with the decisiveness of the issue to cast a peculiar lustre upon this victory of Nelson's. Lord Howe, inferior to none as a judge of merit, said to Captain Berry that the Battle of the Nile " stood unparalleled and singular in this instance, that every captain distinguished himself."[1] It has been disputed how far belongs to the admiral the credit of the bold manœuvre, whereby the leading ship, passing ahead of the French line, showed to her successors the open path through which the operation of doubling on the enemy could be most effectually carried out. Into this discussion the author has no intention of entering, beyond noting an omission in the full treatment of the question made by the careful and laborious editor of Nelson's correspondence, Sir Harris Nicolas, who was not able to reach a decision.[2] In Ross's " Life of Admiral Saumarez" it is stated that, while discussing the various modes by which the enemy might be attacked, Saumarez offended Nelson by saying that he " had seen the evil consequences of doubling upon an enemy, especially in a night action;" and had differed with the admiral in the plan of attack, because " it never required two English ships to capture one French, and that the damage which they must necessarily do each other might render them both unable to fight an enemy's ship which had not been engaged."[3] Saumarez's objection, though not without some foundation, was justly over-ruled; but it could scarcely have been raised had Nelson never contemplated the precise method of doubling employed, — a British ship on each

---

[1] Nelson's Dispatches, vol. iii. p. 84.
[2] For this discussion see Nelson's Dispatches and Letters, vol. iii. pp. 62-65; also App. p. 474.
[3] Ross's Life of Saumarez, vol. i. p. 228.

VOL. I. — 18

side of a single enemy,— for in no other position could the
risk of mutual injury have been serious.

It is in entire keeping with Nelson's well-known character, that, after discussing all likely positions and ascertaining that his captains understood his views, he should with perfect and generous confidence have left all the details of immediate action with them. In the actual case he could not, without folly, have rigorously prescribed to Captain Foley what path to follow. Only the man on the "Goliath's" deck, watching the soundings, could rightly judge what must each instant be done; and it was no less a transcendent merit in Nelson that he could thus trust another, than that, with falling night and unknown waters, he could reach the instant decision to attack an enemy of superior force, in an order which he must have supposed to be carefully and rationally assumed. In fact, however, the operation of doubling on the enemy,— in contradistinction to doubling the head of the line,— was really begun by Nelson himself; for his ship was the first to anchor on the side opposite to that taken by her five predecessors. It was open to him to have followed them, for the same reasons that prompted Foley's action.[1] Instead of that, he deliberately anchored outside the third French ship, already engaged on the inside by the "Theseus;" thus indicating, as clearly as example can, what he would have those succeeding him to do. The first two French ships were already so engaged or crippled as to be properly passed. The fullest credit therefore can be allowed to Captain Foley for a military decision of a very high order, without stripping a leaf from Nelson's laurels.[2]

---

[1] Nelson's Disp., vol. iii.; Appendix, p. 474. Letter of Admiral Browne.

[2] The American novelist and naval historian, Fenimore Cooper, in the preface to the "Two Admirals," has attributed the whole tactical combination to the captains, on the authority of Captain Ball of the "Alexander," speaking to the late Commodore Morris of the United States Navy, who in turn was Cooper's informant. This constitutes a perfectly respectable oral tradition, coming through intelligent men of unquestioned integrity; but

"The boldness and skill of Admiral Nelson," says Captain Chevalier, "rose to a height which it would have been difficult to surpass."[1] "The action of Nelson," said Napoleon, "was a desperate action which cannot be proposed as a model, but in which he displayed, as well as the English crews, all the skill and vigor possible."[2] This sentence is susceptible of a double construction. The condemnation, if the words be meant as such, comes ill from the man who pushed on his desperate advance to Leoben in 1797, who at Marengo stretched his line till it broke, and who in 1798 ventured the Mediterranean fleet and the Army of Italy on the Egyptian expedition, with scarce a chance in his favor, except a superstitious reliance upon a fortune which did not betray him. The arrangements of Brueys being what they were, the odds were with the British admiral.

It has been said that, with better gunnery on the part of the French, disaster must have resulted to the attacking force; and precisely the same criticism has been applied to Trafalgar.[3] Now, putting out of consideration that Great Britain had at this date been for five years at war with France, and that British seamen had thus gained an

---

when opposed to the contemporary written statement of Captain Berry, Nelson's flag-captain, who had the fullest opportunity of knowing the facts, it becomes impossible to doubt that somewhere in the chain of witnesses there has been a misunderstanding. That Captain Foley conceived on the moment the plan he executed is perfectly credible; but that the whole body of captains were inspired to carry out, as by mutual consent, a combination of which there had been no previous mention, is a marvel of which Berry's account of Nelson's constant discussions and explanations with his officers effectually disposes. (See Narrative of an Officer of Rank, etc. Naval Chronicle, vol. i. p. 52.)

[1] Marine Françsons la République, p. 381.
[2] Commentaires de Napoléon, vol. ii p. 350.
[3] "Good gunners would assuredly have modified the issue of these sinister dramas, for they would have crushed the English fleet at the first act." (Jurien de la Gravière, Guerres Mar., vol ii. p. 225, 1st ed.). "If Nelson had led in upon an American fleet, as he did upon the French at the Nile, he would have seen reason to repent the boldness of the experiment." (Cooper, preface to "The Two Admirals.")

experience of French gunnery upon which Nelson could
reckon, the justice of this criticism further depends upon
the circumstances of the wind and the character of the approach. An attack made with a very light wind, leaving
the assailant long under the enemy's fire, or with a fresh
breeze on a course that lies close to the wind, thereby
bringing the greatest strain upon the spars, is a very different thing from one made with a good working breeze
well abaft the beam, which was the case at the Nile. One
cannot dogmatize on probabilities when, from the nature
of the case, there are few precedents on which to rest an
opinion. In bearing down against a fleet under way, of
which there are many instances, the experience in scarcely
any case was that so many spars were lost as to prevent
the assailant reaching the hostile line; and at the Nile,
once the anchor was down, the loss of a spar or two was
of little consequence. It seems altogether probable that,
had the French gunnery been much better than it was, the
British ships would yet have reached their station; and
once there, the tactical combination adopted would still
have given them the victory, though more dearly bought.
If, however, Brueys's arrangements had been more skilfully made, resembling those of Hood at St. Kitt's, and if
the French gunnery had been very good, it may safely be
conceded that the British admiral would have needed more
circumspection in making his attack. To say that under
totally different circumstances different results will obtain,
is a species of prophecy with which no one need quarrel.
If, in the shock of war, all things on both sides are exactly
equal, — if the two admirals, their captains and crews, the
ships of the fleets, the tactical arrangements, are equal,
each to each, — there can be no result. When inequality,
whether original or induced by circumstance, enters in any
one of these factors, a result will follow proportional to
the disparity. When this is great, the result will be great;
when small, small. At the Battle of the Nile, the differ-

ence in admirals, in captains, in crews, in gunnery, and in tactical combination, were all greatly against the French, and the result was a disaster more than usually complete.

During the month passed by Brueys in indolent security, Bonaparte had advanced steadily in his projected conquest of Egypt. On the 21st of July the battle of the Pyramids was fought, the next day Cairo submitted, and on the 25th the general-in-chief entered the city. Remaining there a few days to repose his troops and secure his position, he departed again on the 7th of August to complete the conquest of lower Egypt; leaving Desaix to take care of Cairo and prepare the corps destined for the subjugation of the upper Nile. By the 12th of August the Mamelukes, still under arms in the Delta, had been driven into the Isthmus of Suez, whence they retired to Syria; and there, on the borders of the desert, Bonaparte received from Kleber the news of the disaster in Aboukir Bay. Under this tremendous reverse he showed the self-control of which he was always capable at need. The troops gave way to despair. "Here we are," said they, "abandoned in this barbarous country, without communication with home, without hope of return." "Well," replied their general, "we have then laid on us the obligation to do great things. Seas which we do not command separate us from home; but no seas divide us from Africa and Asia. We will found here an empire."

The magical influence he exerted over the soldiers, most of whom had followed him to victory in Italy, restored their courage, and French lightheartedness again prevailed over despondency. The blow, nevertheless, had struck home, and resounded through the four quarters of the world. The Mamelukes, Ibrahim Bey in Syria, and Mourad Bey in upper Egypt, cast down by their reverses, were preparing to treat; upon the news of Nelson's victory they resumed their arms. The Porte, incensed by the invasion of Egypt, but still hesitating, notwithstanding the pressure

exerted by the ministers of Great Britain and Russia, took
heart as soon as it knew that the French fleet was no more.
Bonaparte had rightly warned Brueys that the preservation of his ships was necessary to hold Turkey in check.
The Sultan and his Pashas of Egypt and Syria rejected the
French advances. On the 2d of September a memorial
was sent to all the foreign ministers in Constantinople, expressing the surprise of the Porte at Bonaparte's landing,
and stating that a considerable force had been despatched
for Egypt to stop his progress. On the 11th of the month
war was formally declared against the French Republic.[1]

Throughout the year 1798 the state of affairs on the
continent of Europe had grown continually more threatening. The politico-military propagandism of the Revolution
had given birth to, and was now being replaced by, an aggressive external policy, to which the victories of Bonaparte gave increased vigor and extension. It became the
recognized, if not the avowed, aim of French diplomacy to
surround France with small dependent republics, having institutions modelled upon the same type as her own, with
all local powers merged in those of a central government.[2]
The United Provinces, in becoming a republic, had retained
their federal constitution; but in January, 1798, they underwent a revolution, promoted by the French Directory,
which did away the provincial independence inherited from
past ages. The Cisalpine Republic and Genoa had received a similar organization at the hands of Bonaparte.
In many of the cantons of Switzerland there were discontent and disturbance, due to the unequal political conditions of the inhabitants. The Directory made of this a
pretext for interference, on the plea of France being interested both in the internal quiet of a neighboring country
and also in the particular persons whose discontent was
construed as evidence of oppression. French troops en-

[1] Annual Register, 1798; State Papers, pp. 267-272.
[2] Martin, Histoire de France depuis 1789, vol. iii. p. 6.

tered Switzerland in January, 1798. The canton of Berne fought for its privileges, but was easily subdued; and a packed convention, assembled at Aaran, adopted for Switzerland a centralized constitution in place of the old cantonal independence. This was followed some months later, in August, 1798, by an offensive and defensive alliance between the Helvetian and French republics.

The invasion of Berne had had another motive than the political preponderance of France in the councils of her neighbors. The revenue of the Directory still fell far short of the expenditure, and money was particularly wanted for Bonaparte's approaching expedition. Seventeen million francs were found in the Bernese treasury and appropriated. Eighteen million more were raised by requisitions, and other cantons were drained in proportion.[1] The same motive contributed,[2] at the same instant, to the occupation of Rome, for which a more plausible pretext was found. In the papal states, as elsewhere throughout Europe, French agents had secretly stirred up a revolutionary movement. On the 28th of December, 1797, this party had risen in Rome, and a collision between it and the papal troops had occurred in the neighborhood of the French embassy. General Duphot, who was then residing there, was killed while attempting to interpose between the combatants. The French ambassador at once left the city; and the Directory, refusing all explanations, ordered Berthier, Bonaparte's successor in Italy, to advance. On the 10th of February he entered Rome, recognized the Roman Republic, which was proclaimed under his auspices, and forced the Pope to retire to Tuscany. It was owing to this occupation that a contingent of the Egyptian expedition embarked at Civita Vecchia, as the most convenient point.

Neither Naples nor Austria ventured on overt action in behalf of the Pope; but the dissatisfaction of both was extreme. Never under Bonaparte himself had French

[1] Martin, Hist. de France depuis 1789, vol. iii. p. 9.   [2] Ibid., p. 11.

troops come so near to the kingdom of the Two Sicilies, whose importance to the common cause of the Continent, from its geographical position, was perfectly understood. But while the situation of Naples at the far end of the peninsula made it a serious danger to the flank and rear of the French, when engaged with an enemy in upper Italy, its remoteness from support, except by way of the sea, was a source of weakness to a state necessarily dependent upon allies. This was especially felt in February, 1798, when the British fleet, after a year's absence, had as yet given no sign of returning to the Mediterranean, and the ships which accompanied Bonaparte to Egypt were still in Toulon. The latter would doubtless have been directed upon Naples, had Naples moved against Rome. The Bourbon kingdom therefore swallowed its vexation, but drew closer to Austria; which, in addition to the affront offered to the Pope, had its own motives for discontent in the occupation of Switzerland by the French, and in the changes introduced into the political complexion of the Continent by these aggressive actions of the republican government. The course of the Directory during the continental peace of 1797 and 1798 was closely parallel to that of Bonaparte four years later, which made impossible the continuance of the Peace of Amiens. With less ability and less vigor, there was the same plausible, insidious, steady aggression, under color of self-protection or of yielding to popular demand, which forced on the power of France at the expense of other states. An occurrence in Vienna at this moment came near to produce war and stop the Egyptian expedition. When Bonaparte entered Germany in April, 1797, the youth of Vienna had offered themselves in mass to defend the country. In April, 1798, the anniversary of the day was celebrated with a popular demonstration, which the French ambassador resented by hoisting the tricolor. The crowds in a rage broke into and sacked the embassy.[1] So

---

[1] Martin, Hist. de France depuis 1789, vol. iii. p. 16.

great was the excitement over this affair that the troops in Toulon and other ports were ordered not to embark, and Bonaparte himself was directed to go as plenipotentiary to Rastadt; but the emperor made explanations, and the incident passed. Still, as a French historian says, "things were getting spoiled between Austria and France."[1]

Russia at the same time was fairly forced from her attitude of reserve, maintained since the death of Catherine II., by the same policy which drove the United States into the *quasi* war of 1798 with France.[2] A decree of the French legislature had made lawful prize any neutral ship which had on board, not merely British property, but any goods of British origin, even though the property of a neutral. This was given a special application to the Baltic by a notification, issued January 12, 1798, that "if any ship be suffered to pass through the Sound with English commodities, of whatever nation it may be, it shall be considered as a formal declaration of war against the French nation."[3] Although immediately directed against Sweden and Denmark, as the two countries bordering the Sound, this was resented by the Czar, in common with all neutral governments; and on the 15th of May, he "ordered twenty-two ships-of-the-line and two hundred and fifty galleys to proceed to the Sound, to protect trade in general against the oppression of the Directory."[4]

Once enkindled, the violent and erratic temper of Paul I. soon rushed into extremes; and he received further provocation from the capture of Malta. When Bonaparte took possession of that island, he found there a treaty, just signed, by which the Czar stipulated a payment of four hundred thousand rubles to the Order, in which to the end of his days he preserved a fan-

---

[1] Martin, Hist. de France depuis 1789, vol. iii. p. 24.
[2] See *post*, Chapter XVII.
[3] Annual Register, 1798; State Papers, p. 237.
[4] Ibid. Martin, Hist. de France, vol. iii. p. 23.

tastic interest. As a measure of precaution, the French
general decreed that any Greeks in Malta or the Ionian Islands maintaining relations with Russia should be shot, and
Greek vessels under Russian colors sunk.[1] Hence the
members of the Order in Russia made, in August, a violent
protest against the seizure, throwing themselves upon the
Czar for a support which he eagerly promised.[2] He then
drew near to Great Britain, and offered to aid Austria with
troops. The emperor at first answered that nothing could
be done without Prussia; and the three governments then
applied themselves to obtain the accession of this kingdom to a new coalition. On the 19th of May — the very day,
it may be observed, that Bonaparte sailed from Toulon —
Austria and Naples signed a defensive alliance.[3] The con-
ferences at Rastadt, so far as the emperor was concerned,
were broken off on the 6th of July, although those with the
empire dragged on longer. The imperial envoy, Cobentzel,
at once went to Berlin, where he entered into cordial relations with the British and Russian plenipotentiaries. On
the 10th of August a convention was signed between the
two emperors, by which the Czar undertook to send thirty
thousand troops into Galicia to support the Austrian army.
Great Britain, as ever, was ready to help the cause with
ships and money. Prussia refusing to join, the Russian envoy took his leave, saying: " We will make war on France
with you, without you, or against you." [4]

On governments so prepared to be enkindled, yet hesitating before the prestige of French success and feeling the
mutual distrust inseparable from coalitions, the news of the
battle of the Nile fell like a brand among tinder. The
French fleet was not only defeated, but annihilated. The
Mediterranean from the Straits to the Levant was in the
power of the British navy, which the total destruction of its

---

[1] Corr. de Nap., vol. iv. pp. 226, 233.
[2] Annual Register, 1798; State Papers, p. 276.
[3] Martin, Hist. de France, vol. iii. p. 27.
[4] Ibid. pp. 24, 25.

enemy relieved from the necessity of concentration and allowed to disperse to every quarter where its efforts were needed. The greatest general and thirty thousand of the best troops France possessed, with numbers of her most brilliant officers, were thus hopelessly shut off from their country.

After the victory, conscious of its far-reaching importance, Nelson took measures to disperse the news as rapidly as his want of small vessels would permit. The "Leander" sailed on the 5th of August with the first despatches for Lord St. Vincent off Cadiz, but was on the 18th captured by the "Généreux," seventy-four, one of the two ships which had escaped from Aboukir Bay. To provide against such an accident, however, the brig "Mutine" had also been sent on the 13th to Naples, where she arrived on the 4th of September, bringing the first news that reached Europe, and which Nelson asked the British minister to see forwarded to all the other courts. The captain of the "Mutine" started the next day for England, by way of Vienna, and on the 2d of October, 1798, two full months after the battle, reached London with the first acounts.

Conscious of the effect which events in Egypt might have upon British influence in India, Nelson also sent a lieutenant, on the 10th of August, to make his way overland through Alexandretta and Aleppo to Bombay. This officer bore dispatches to the governor, informing him both of the landing and numbers of Bonaparte's expedition, and also of the fatal blow which had just befallen it. The news was most timely. The French had been actively intriguing in the native courts, and Tippoo Saib, the son and successor of Hyder Ali, Sultan of Mysore, their former ally in the days of Suffren, had openly committed himself to his father's policy. It was too late for Tippoo to recede, and he was erelong embarked in a war, which ended in April, 1799, in his death at the assault of Seringapatam and the overthrow of his kingdom; but on the other native states

the striking catastrophe produced its due impression. In
their operations against Tippoo the British were not embarrassed by troubles in other quarters.

"The consequences of this battle," sums up a brilliant
French naval writer, "were incalculable. Our navy never
recovered from this terrible blow to its consideration and
its power. This was the combat which for two years delivered the Mediterranean to the English, and called thither
the squadrons of Russia; which shut up our army in the
midst of a rebellious population, and decided the Porte to
declare against us; which put India out of the reach of our
enterprise, and brought France within a hair's-breadth of
her ruin; for it rekindled the scarcely extinct war with
Austria, and brought Suwarrow and the Austro-Russians to
our very frontiers."[1] Great Britain, the Sea Power so
often and so idly accused of backwardness in confronting
France, of requiring continental support before daring to
move, was first to act. Long before news of the battle, before even the battle was fought, or the alliance of Austria
and Russia contracted, orders had been sent to St. Vincent
to detach from Nelson's force to the support of Naples,
hoping there to start the little fire from which a great matter should be kindled. These "most secret orders"
reached Nelson on the 15th of August.[2] He had just
dispatched to Gibraltar seven of the British fleet with six
of the captured French vessels, the whole under charge of
Sir James Saumarez. Setting fire to the three other prizes,
he intrusted the blockade of Alexandria to Captain Hood,
with three ships-of-the-line, and with the three then remaining to him sailed for Naples on the 19th. From the
wretched condition of his division[3] the passage took over a

---

[1] Jurien de la Gravière, Guerres Maritimes, vol. i. p. 229 (1st ed.).

[2] Nelson's Dispatches, vol. iii. p. 105.

[3] This division consisted of the "Vanguard," flag-ship, which had not had
proper lower masts since she was dismasted immediately after entering the
Mediterranean (p. 256); the "Culloden," that had beaten heavily on Abou-

month; but on the 22d of September he anchored in the bay, where the renown of his achievement had preceded him.

On his way, Nelson had been informed that a Portuguese squadron, commanded by the Marquis de Niza, had entered the Mediterranean to support his operations. At his request this division, which had appeared off Alexandria on the 29th of August,[1] but refused to remain there, undertook the blockade of Malta, until such time as the repairs of the British ships should allow them to do so. The natives of the island had risen against the French on the 26th of August, and driven them from the open country into the forts of La Valetta. Niza took his station off the port, about the 20th of September, and on the 24th Sir James Saumarez appeared with his division and the prizes. The following day the two officers sent General Vaubois a summons to surrender, which was as a matter of course refused. Saumarez went on to Gibraltar; but before doing so gave the inhabitants twelve hundred muskets with ammunition, which materially assisted them in their efforts, finally successful, to deprive the enemy of the resources of the island. Nelson sent off British ships as they were ready, and himself joined the blockading force on the 24th of October, though only for a few days, his presence being necessary in Naples. The garrison was again by him formally summoned, and as formally rejected his offers. From that time until their surrender in September, 1800, the French were in strict blockade, both by land and water.

In October of this year Lord St. Vincent went to live ashore at Gibraltar, both on account of his health, and because there, being the great British naval station of the Mediterranean, he was centrally placed to receive information, to give orders, and especially to hasten, by his unflagging personal supervision, the work of supply and repair upon which

kir reef for seven hours during the battle; and the "Alexander," both masts and hull in very bad order.

[1] Corr. de Nap., vol. iv. p. 660.

the efficiency of a fleet primarily depends. The division
off Cadiz, numbering generally some fifteen of the line,
kept its old station watching the Spaniards, under the command of Lord Keith,— one of the most efficient and active
of the generation of naval officers between St. Vincent and
Nelson, to the latter of whom he was senior. Within the
Mediterranean Nelson commanded, under St. Vincent.
The blockade of Egypt and Malta, and co-operation with
the Austrian and Neapolitan armies in the expected war,
were his especial charge. He was also to further, as far
as in him lay, the operations of a combined Russian and
Turkish fleet, which had assembled in the Dardanelles in
September, 1798, to maintain the cause of the coalition in
the Levant. This fleet entered the Mediterranean in October; but instead of assuming the blockade of Alexandria
and the protection of the Syrian coast, it undertook the
capture of the Ionian Islands. All of these, except Corfu,
fell into its power by October 10; and on the 20th Corfu,
the citadel of the group, was attacked. Nelson saw this
direction of the Russo-Turkish operations with disgust and
suspicion. "The Porte ought to be aware," he wrote, " of
the great danger at a future day of allowing the Russians
to get a footing at Corfu." [1] " I was in hopes that a part
of the united Turkish and Russian squadron would have
gone to Egypt, — Corfu is a secondary consideration. . . .
I have had a long conference with Kelim Effendi on the
conduct likely to be pursued by the Russian Court towards
the unsuspicious (I fear) and upright Turk. . . . A strong
squadron should have been sent to Egypt to have relieved
my dear friend Captain Hood; but Corfu suited Russia
better." [2] At the same time Turkish troops, under the
pashas whose good dispositions Bonaparte had boasted,
swept away from France the former Venetian territory on
the mainland, acquired by the treaty of Campo Formio.

[1] Nels. Disp., vol. iii. p. 160.
[2] Ibid., p. 204.

While Bonaparte's Oriental castles were thus crumbling, through the destruction in Aboukir Bay of the foundation upon which they rested, — while Ionia was falling, Malta starving, and Egypt isolated, through the loss of the sea — the Franco-Spanish allies were deprived of another important foothold for maritime power. On the 15th of November Minorca with its valuable harbor, Port Mahon, was surrendered to a combined British military and naval expedition, quietly fitted out by St. Vincent from Gibraltar.

The year 1798 in the Mediterranean closed with these operations in progress. At its beginning France was in entire control of the land-locked sea, and scarcely a sail hostile to her, except furtive privateers, traversed its surface. When it closed, only two French ships-of-the-line fit for battle remained upon the waters, which swarmed with enemy's squadrons. Of these two, refugees from the fatal bay of Aboukir, one was securely locked in Malta, whence she never escaped; the other made its way to Toulon, and met its doom in a vain effort to carry relief to the beleaguered island.

CHAPTER X.

THE MEDITERRANEAN FROM 1799 TO 1801.

BONAPARTE'S SYRIAN EXPEDITION AND SIEGE OF ACRE. — THE INCURSION OF THE FRENCH BREST FLEET UNDER ADMIRAL BRUIX. — BONAPARTE'S RETURN TO FRANCE. — THE FRENCH LOSE MALTA AND EGYPT.

AFTER the destruction of his fleet, Bonaparte resumed the task of subduing and organizing Egypt, which had by that misfortune become more than ever essential to his projects. In the original conception of his eastern adventure the valley of the Nile had borne a twofold part. It was, in the first place, to become a permanent acquisition of France, the greatest of her colonies,— great not only by its own natural resources, susceptible as was believed of immense development, but also by its singular position, which, to a power controlling the Mediterranean waters, gave the military and commercial link between the eastern and western worlds. To France, bereft of the East and the West Indies, childless now of her richest colonies, Egypt was to be the great and more than equal compensation. But this first object obtained, though in itself a justification, was but the necessary step to the more dazzling, if not more useful, achievement of the destruction of the British power in India, and the creation there of an empire tributary to France. "Thus, on the one side Egypt would replace San Domingo and the Antilles; on the other, she would be a step towards the conquest of India."[1]

[1] Commentaires de Napoléon, vol. iii. pp. 19, 20.

Measured by the successes of a few handfuls of British in the empire of the Moguls, the army brought by Bonaparte into Egypt was more than able to subdue that country, and to spread far and wide the obedience to the French arms. Like the founders of the British Indian Empire, the French general found himself face to face, not only with military institutions incomparably weaker and less cohesive than those of Europe, but with a civil society — if such it can be called — from which the element of mutual confidence, and with it the power of combined resistance, had disappeared. The prestige of success, the knowledge that he could command the services of a body of men superior in numbers as in disciplined action to any aggregation of units that could be kept steadily together to oppose him, was sufficient to insure for him the supremacy that concentrated force will always have over diffused force, organized power over unorganized. In military matters two and two do not make four, unless they are brought together in concerted action. Unfortunately, at the very moment of the most brilliant demonstration of his genius and of the valor of his troops, there had fallen upon one part of his command a reverse more startling, more absolute, than his own victories, and inflicted by a force certainly not superior to the one defeated. The Orientals, who could count upon no sufficient stay in men of their own race, now saw hopes of succor from without. They were not disappointed. Again a British naval captain, in the moment of triumphant progress, stopped the advance of Bonaparte.

The autumn and early winter of 1798 were passed in the conquest and overrunning of upper Egypt by Desaix, who left Cairo for this purpose on the 25th of August, and in the settlement of the affairs of the lower Nile upon such a basis as would secure quiet and revenue during the absence of the commander-in-chief. An insurrection in Cairo in October, provoked partly by dissatisfaction with intended changes, partly by the rumor of the Porte having declared war upon France, gave Bonaparte in quelling it an opportunity to show the iron firmness of his grip, and afterwards to manifest that mixture of unrelenting severity towards the few with politic lenity towards the many, which is so well calculated to check the renewal of commotion.

In November, when the weather became cooler, a detachment of fifteen hundred men was sent to occupy Suez, and toward the end of December Bonaparte himself made a visit of inspection to the isthmus, by which he must advance to the prosecution of his larger schemes. While thus absent he learned, through an intercepted courier, that Djezzar, the Pasha of Syria, had on the 2d of January, 1799, occupied the important oasis of El Arish in the desert of Suez, and was putting its fort in a state of defence.[1] He at once realized that the time had come when he must carry out his project of advance into Syria, and accept the hostility of Turkey, which he had wished to avoid.

The singular position of isolation in which the French in Egypt were placed, by the loss of the control of the sea, must be realized, in order to understand the difficulties under which Bonaparte labored in shaping his course of action, from time to time, with reference to the general current of events. Separated from Palestine by two hundred miles of desert, and by a yet wider stretch of barren sand from any habitable land to the west, Egypt is aptly described by Napoleon himself as a great oasis, surrounded on all sides by the desert and the sea. The intrinsic weakness of the French navy, its powerlessness to command security for its unarmed vessels in the Mediterranean, had been manifested by the tremor of apprehension and uncertainty which ran through the officials at Toulon and in Paris, when, after the sailing of Bonaparte, they learned of

[1] Of all obstacles that can cover the frontiers of an empire, a desert like that of Suez is indisputably the greatest. It is easy to understand that a fort at El Arish, which would prevent an enemy from using the wells and encamping under the palm-trees, would be very valuable. — *Commentaires de Napoléon*, vol. iii. p. 16.

Nelson's appearance. The restless activity of the British admiral, and the frequent sight of his ships in different places, multiplied, in the imagination of the French authorities, the numbers of hostile cruisers actually on the sea.[1] A convoy of twenty-six large ships, for the completion of whose lading the expedition could not wait, lay in Toulon during the summer months, ready to sail; but no one dared to despatch them. From time to time during the outward voyage Bonaparte sent urgent messages for their speedy departure; but they never came.

If this fear existed and exercised such sway before the day of the Nile, it may be imagined how great was the influence of that disastrous tidings. Not only, however, did a moral effect follow, but the annihilation of the French fleet permitted the British cruisers to scatter, and so indefinitely increased the real danger of capture to French ships. Surrounded by deserts and the sea, the commander-in-chief in Egypt saw, on and beyond both, nothing but actual or possible enemies. Not only so, but being in utter ignorance of the attitude of most of the powers as well as of European events, he could not know what bad effect might result from action taken by him upon imperfect information. His embarrassment is vividly depicted in a letter dated December 17, 1798: "We are still without news from France, not a courier has arrived since July 6: this is unexampled even in the colonies."[2] The courier mentioned, leaving France in July, had reached Bonaparte on the 9th of September; but the vessel which brought him had been obliged to run ashore to escape the British cruisers, and only one letter from the Directory was saved.[3] The next tidings came on the 5th of February, when a Ragusan ship, chartered by two French citizens, succeeded in enter-

---

[1] For a graphic account of the anxieties of the French officers in Toulon, illustrated by letters, see Jurien de la Gravière's Guerres Maritimes (4th edition), pp. 352–362. (Appendix.)

[2] Corr. de Nap., vol. v. p. 276.

[3] Ibid., vol. iv., Letter to Directory, Sept. 8, 1798 (postscript).

ing Alexandria. "The news," he said, "is sufficiently
contradictory; but it is the first I have had since July 6."
He then first learned definitely that Turkey had declared
war against France.[1] His troops were at that moment in
the desert, marching upon Syria, and he himself on the
point of following them.

Up to that time Bonaparte had hoped to cajole the Porte
into an attitude of neutrality, upon the plea that his quarrel
was solely with the Mamelukes on account of injury done
by them to French commerce. On the 11th of December
he had sent to Constantinople a M. Beauchamp, recently
consul at Muscat, with instructions how to act in the twofold contingency of war having been declared or not. At
that time he expected that Talleyrand would be found in
Constantinople as Ambassador of France.[2] The news by
the Ragusan enlightened him as to the actual relations with
Turkey; but the disquieting rumors before received, coinciding with his ultimate purpose to advance upon India
through Syria, had already determined him to act as the
military situation demanded.[3] He had learned that troops
were assembling in Syria and in the island of Rhodes, and
divined that he was threatened with a double invasion, —
by the desert of Suez and by the Mediterranean Sea.
True to his sound and invariable policy, he determined to
use his central position to strike first one and then the
other, and not passively to wait on the defensive until a
simultaneous attack might compel him to divide his force.
During the violent winter weather, which would last yet for
six weeks or two months, landing on the Egyptian coast was
thought impracticable.[4] For that period, probably for

[1] Corr. de Nap., vol. v. pp. 385, 391, 392. It is interesting to note that
by this mail Bonaparte seems first to have heard the word "conscript," applied
to the system of which he later made such an insatiable use (p. 387).

[2] Instructions pour le citoyen Beauchamp, Corr. de Nap., vol. v. pp.
260–263.

[3] Commentaires de Napoléon, vol. iii. p. 24.

[4] The roadstead of Aboukir is not safe in winter. It can protect a squad-

longer, he could count upon security on the side of the sea. He would improve the interval by invading Syria, driving back the enemy there, breaking up his army, and seizing his ports. Thus he would both shut the coast to the British cruisers off Alexandria, which drew supplies from thence, and make impossible any future invasion from the side of the desert. He counted also upon the moral effect which success in Syria would have upon the negotiations with the Porte, which he conceived to be in progress.[1]

The first essential point in the campaign was to possess El Arish, just occupied by the troops of Djezzar. General Reynier advanced against it with his division on the 5th of February, 1799. The Turks were by him routed and driven from the oasis, and the fort besieged. Bonaparte himself arrived on the 15th, and on the 20th the garrison capitulated. The corps destined for the expedition, numbering in all thirteen thousand men, having now assembled, the advance from El Arish began on the 22d. On the 25th Gaza was taken. On the 3d of March the army encamped before Jaffa, and on the 7th the place was carried by storm. A port, though a very poor one, was thus secured. The next day there entered, from Acre, a convoy of Turkish coasters laden with provisions and ammunition, which fell a welcome prize to the French, and was sent back to Hayfa, a small port seven miles south of Acre, for the use of the troops upon arrival. On the 12th of March the army resumed its march upon Acre, distant about sixty miles. On the 17th, at five in the afternoon, a detachment entered and held Hayfa, to provide a place of safety for the flotilla,

ron during the summer. (Commentaires de Nap., vol. ii. p. 235.) In Abercromby's expedition, 1801, " all the pilots accustomed to the Egyptian coast declared that till after the equinox it would be madness to attempt a landing." (Sir R. Wilson's History of British Expedition to Egypt, 2d edition, p. 6.) The fleet then lay in Aboukir Bay from March 2 to March 8, before landing could be made.

[1] Corr. de Nap., vol. v, p. 402, where the reasons for the Syrian expedition are given categorically, and can probably be depended upon as truthful.

which, coasting the beach, slowly followed the advance of the troops. From Hayfa Bonaparte could see the roadstead of Acre, and lying there two British ships-of-the-line, the "Tigre" and the "Theseus," both under the command of Sir Sidney Smith, the captain of the former; who, as ranking officer on the spot, represented the naval power of Great Britain, about again to foil the plans of the great French leader.

Sir Sidney Smith, to whom now fell the distinguished duty of meeting and stopping the greatest general of modern times, was a man who has left behind him a somewhat singular reputation, in which, and in the records commonly accessible, it is not always easy to read his real character. He was not liked by St. Vincent nor by Nelson, and their feeling towards him, though much intensified by the circumstances under which he now came to the Mediterranean, seems to have depended upon their previous knowledge of his history. The First Lord, in assigning him to this duty, felt obliged to take an almost apologetic tone to Earl St. Vincent. "I am well aware," he wrote, "that there may perhaps be some prejudices, derived from certain circumstances which have attended this officer's career through life; but, from a long acquaintance with him personally, I think I can venture to assure your lordship that, added to his unquestioned character for courage and enterprise, he has a great many good points about him, which those who are less acquainted with him may not be sufficiently apprised of. I have no doubt you will find him a very useful instrument to be employed on any hazardous or difficult service, and that he will be perfectly under your guidance, as he ought to be."[1] In the concluding sentence Earl Spencer sums up Sir Sidney's real character, as far as it can be discerned in the dim light of the recorded facts — or rather in the false lights which have exaggerated some circumstances and distorted others. He

[1] Barrow's Life of Sir Sidney Smith, vol. i. p. 244.

was bold and enterprising to Quixotism; he was a most useful instrument; but so far from having no doubt, the First Lord must have had very serious, if unacknowledged, doubts as to how far he would be under the guidance of St. Vincent, or any one else, out of signal distance. A self-esteem far beyond what the facts warranted, a self-confidence of the kind which does not inspire confidence in others, an exaggerated view of his own importance and of his own services, which was apt to show itself in his bearing and words,[1] — such seem to have been the traits that alienated from Sir Sidney Smith the esteem of his contemporaries, until his really able, as well as most gallant, conduct at Acre showed that there was more in him than the mere vainglorious knight-errant. His behavior even there has been distorted, alike by the malevolence of Napoleon and by the popular adulation in Great Britain, which, seizing upon the brilliant traits of energy and valor he exhibited, attributed to him the whole conduct of the siege;[2] whereas, by entrusting the technical direction of the defence to an experienced engineer, he made proof of a wisdom and modesty for which few of his contemporaries would have given him credit. At this time Smith had received some severe snubbings, which, administered by men of the standing of St. Vincent and Nelson, could not be disregarded, and may have had a wholesomely sobering effect.

The circumstances of his coming to the Mediterranean

[1] The opinion of a French officer may be worth quoting. "Although every one knows what he is, I will nevertheless say a word about Sir Sidney Smith. He has something at once of the knight and of the charlatan. A man of intelligence, yet bordering upon insanity, with the ability of a leader, he has thought to honor his career by often running absurd risks, without any useful end, but only to be talked about. Every one ridicules him, and justly; for in the long run he is wearisome, though very original." (Mémoires du Duc de Raguse (Marmont), vol. ii p. 30.)

[2] The melodramatic painting of Sir Sidney Smith in the breach at Acre represents graphically the popular impression of his character. See frontispiece to Barrow's Life of Sir Sidney Smith.

were as follows. Having been a prisoner of war in Paris
for nearly two years, he escaped through the stratagem of
a French royalist, Phélippeaux, about a week before Bonaparte left the city for Toulon.[1] The incidents of his release were dramatic enough in themselves, and, in common
with all his adventures, were well noised abroad. He became a very conspicuous figure in the eyes of the government, and of the public outside the navy. In October,
1798, he was given command of the "Tigre," with directions to proceed to Gibraltar and put himself under St.
Vincent's orders. At the same time he was appointed
minister plenipotentiary to the Porte, being associated in
that capacity with his younger brother, Spencer Smith,
who was already ambassador at Constantinople; the object being that, with the diplomatic rank thus conferred,
he should be able to direct the efforts of the Turkish and
Russian forces in the Levant, in case the military officers
of those nations were of grade superior to his. This somewhat complicated arrangement, which presupposed in the
Turks and Russians a compliance which no British naval
officer would have yielded, was further confused by the instructions issued, apparently without concert, by the Foreign Office to Smith himself, and by the Admiralty to St.
Vincent. The latter clearly understood that Smith was
intended to be under his command only, and that merely
pro formâ:[2] but under no obedience to Nelson, although
his intended scene of operations, the Levant, was part of
Nelson's district. This view, derived from the Admiralty's
letter, was confirmed by an extract from the Foreign Office
instructions, communicated by Smith to Nelson, that "his
(Smith's) instructions will enable him to take the command of such of his Majesty's ships as he may find in

---

[1] Smith escaped from Paris on the 25th of April. Bonaparte left Paris
May 2; Nelson sailed from Cadiz on his great mission May 2,—a very
singular triple coincidence.

[2] Brenton's Life of Lord St. Vincent, vol. ii. p. 6; Barrow's Life of Sir
Sidney Smith, vol. i. p. 236.

those seas (the Levant) unless, *by some unforeseen accident*, it should happen that there should be among them any of his Majesty's officers of superior rank."[1]

Nelson, of course, was outraged. Here was intruded into his command, where he had achieved such brilliant success, and to the administration of which he felt fully equal, a man of indifferent reputation as an officer, though of unquestioned courage, authorized to act independently of his control, and, as it seemed, even to take his ships. He was hurt not only for himself, but for Troubridge, who was senior to Smith, and would, so Nelson thought, have done the duty better than this choice of the Government. The situation when understood in England was rectified. It was explained that diplomatic rank was considered necessary for the senior naval officer, in order to keep in the hands of Great Britain the direction of combined operations, essentially naval in character; and that Smith had been chosen to the exclusion of seniors because of his relationship to the minister at Constantinople, who might have felt the association with him of a stranger to be an imputation upon his past conduct. Meanwhile St. Vincent, indignant at what seemed to him Smith's airs, had sent him peremptory instructions to put himself under Nelson's orders. Thus, in the double character of naval captain and minister plenipotentiary to Turkey, Smith went up the Mediterranean; where he did first-rate service in the former capacity, and in the latter took some action of very doubtful discretion, in which he certainly did not trouble himself about the guidance or views of his naval superiors.

In compliance with orders from Lord St. Vincent, Nelson in January sent Troubridge with some bomb-vessels to Alexandria, to bombard the shipping in the port; after performing which service he was to turn over to Sir Sidney

---

[1] Nelson's Dispatches, vol. iii. p. 216. The Admiralty, upon remonstrance emphatically denied any such purpose. (Ibid., p. 335.)

Smith the blockade of Alexandria and the defence of the Ottoman Empire by sea, of which Nelson thenceforth washed his hands.[1] The bombardment was maintained during several days in February, doing but little harm; and on the 3d of March Sir Sidney, having made his round to Constantinople, arrived and took over the command. Troubridge left with him the "Theseus," seventy-four, whose captain was junior to Smith, with three smaller vessels; and on the 7th sailed to rejoin Nelson. This was the day that the French stormed Jaffa, and the same evening an express with the news reached the "Tigre." Smith at once sent the "Theseus" to Acre, with Phélippeaux, the French officer who had aided him to escape from Paris and had accompanied him to the East.

Of the same age as Bonaparte, Phélippeaux had been his fellow-pupil at the military school of Brienne, had left France with the royalists in 1792, and returned to it after the fall of Robespierre. He had naturally, from his antecedents, joined the party of reaction; and, after its overthrow in September, 1797, was easily moved to aid in Sir Sidney's escape from Paris. Accompanying him to England, he received from the Crown a colonel's commission. To the guidance of this able engineer the wisdom and skill of the defence was mainly due. Never did great issues turn on a nicer balance than at Acre. The technical skill of Phélippeaux, the hearty support he received from Smith, his officers and crews, the untiring activity and brilliant courage of the latter, the British command of the sea, all contributed; and so narrow was the margin of success, that it may safely be said the failure of one factor would have caused total failure and the loss of the place. Its fall was essential to Bonaparte, and his active, far-seeing mind had long before determined its seizure by his squadron, if the British left the Levant. "If any event drives us

---

[1] For Nelson's attitude until he received orders (Feb. 1, 1799) from St. Vincent to take Smith under his orders, see Dispatches, vol. iii. pp. 223, 224.

from the coast of Egypt," wrote Nelson on the 17th of December, 1798, "St. Jean d'Acre will be attacked by sea. I have Bonaparte's letter before me."[1] As the best port and the best fortress on the coast, Acre was the bridgehead into Palestine. To Syria it bore the relation that Lisbon did to the Spanish Peninsular War. If Bonaparte advanced, leaving it unsubdued, his flank and rear would through it be open to attack from the sea. If it fell, he had good reason to believe the country would rise in his favor. " If I succeed," said he at a late period of the siege, when hope had not yet abandoned him, " I shall find in the city the treasures of the Pasha, and arms for three hundred thousand men. I raise and arm all Syria, so outraged by the ferocity of Djezzar, for whose fall you see the population praying to God at each assault. I march upon Damascus and Aleppo. I swell my army, as I advance, by all malcontents. I reach Constantinople with armed masses. I overthrow the Turkish Empire. I found in the East a new and great empire which shall fix my place in posterity."[2] Dreams? Ibrahim Pasha advanced from Egypt in 1831, took Acre in 1832, and marched into the heart of Asia Minor, which the battle of Konieh soon after laid at his feet; why not Bonaparte? Damascus had already offered him its keys, and the people were eager for the overthrow of the pashas.

On the 10th of March Sir Sidney Smith himself left the blockade of Alexandria, and on the 15th anchored with the "Tigre" off Acre. He found that much had already been done, by Phélippeaux and the "Theseus," to make the obsolete fortifications more fit to withstand the approaching siege. Sending the "Theseus" now to cruise down the coast towards Jaffa, it fell to himself to deal the heaviest and most opportune blow to Bonaparte's projects. Some light coasters had sailed with a siege train from the Damietta

[1] Nels. Disp., vol. iii. pp. 204, 205.
[2] Mémoires de Bourrienne, vol. ii. pp. 243-245.

(eastern) mouth of the Nile, which the British never had
ships enough to blockade. On the morning of the 18th they
were seen approaching Acre, under convoy of a small corvette. The "Tigre" at once gave chase, and captured all but
the corvette and two of the coasters. The cannon that
should have been turned against the walls were landed and
served to defend them; while the prizes, receiving British
crews, thenceforth harassed the siege works, flanking the
two walls against which the attacks were addressed, and
enfilading the trenches. The French, having by this
mishap lost all their siege guns proper, had to depend upon
field-pieces to breach the walls until the 25th of April, when
half a dozen heavy cannon were received from Jaffa.[1] This
time was simply salvation to the besieged and ruin to the
assailants; for, in the interval, the skill of Phélippeaux
and the diligence of the men under him prepared the place
to withstand attacks which at an early period would have
caused its fall.

Into the details of this siege, petty in itself but momentous in its bearing upon events, it will not be expected that
this work shall enter. The crucial incident was the capture
of the siege train and the precious respite thus obtained.
Orders were indeed sent to Rear-Admiral Perrée to come
as speedily as possible, with his small squadron of three
frigates and two corvettes, to Jaffa and land guns; but
Alexandria was already blockaded, and, from the narrowness of the entrance, very difficult to leave in face of a foe.
On the 5th of April, however, the blockading force had to
go to Cyprus for water,[2] and on the 8th Perrée got away.

---

[1] "The siege of Acre lasted sixty-two days. There were two periods. The first from March 19 to April 25, thirty-six days, during which the artillery of the besiegers consisted of two carronades, 32 and 24 pound, taken from British boats, and thirty-six field guns. The second period was from April 25 to May 21, twenty-six days." (Commentaires de Napoléon, vol. iii., p. 63.) "During the latter period the park was increased by two 24-, and four 18-pounders." (Ibid, p. 82.)

[2] Nelson's Dispatches, vol. iii. p. 351.

On the 15th he landed at Jaffa six ship's guns, and so much ammunition as left his little squadron with only fifteen rounds. He then received orders to cruise to the westward of Acre and intercept the communications of the Turks with Candia and Rhodes. Returning from this duty on the 14th of May, he was seen and chased by the "Theseus." An accidental explosion on board the latter forced her to give over pursuit; but Perrée, recognizing the danger of capture, and being short of water and supplies, determined to go to France, as his instructions allowed in case of necessity. On the 17th of June, when only sixty miles from Toulon, he met a British fleet, by which all five vessels were taken.

On the 4th of May, when the besieged and besiegers had been mining, countermining, and daily fighting, for over six weeks — separated by but a stone's throw one from the other — a breach thought practicable by the French general was made, the mine for blowing in the counterscarp was finished, and a general assault was ordered for the 5th; but the engineers of the besieged countermined so industriously that by daybreak they had ruined the mine before being discovered. This caused the assault to be postponed to the 9th. On the 7th, towards evening, some thirty or forty sail were seen on the western horizon. They bore the long expected Turkish succors from Rhodes; whose commander even now had only been induced to approach by a peremptory exercise of Sir Sidney Smith's powers as British minister. Bonaparte saw that no more time could be lost, and ordered the assault at once; the weather being calm, twenty-four hours might still elapse before the re-enforcements could enter the place. Under a heavy fire from one side and the other, the attack was made; and in the morning the British seamen saw the French flag flying on the outer angle of one of the towers. It marked the high water of Bonaparte's Syrian expedition.

On the 8th the assault was renewed. As the French columns advanced, the Turkish ships were still detained in the offing by calms, and the soldiers were being brought ashore in boats, but still far from the landing. Then it was that Sir Sidney Smith, seeing that a few critical moments might determine the success or failure of his weary struggle, manned the boats of his ships, and pulling rapidly ashore led the British seamen, armed with pikes, to help hold the breach till the troops could arrive. The French carried the first line, the old fortifications of the town; but that done, they found themselves confronted with a second, which Phélippeaux, now dead, had formed by connecting together the houses and garden walls of the seraglio within. The strife raged throughout the day, with varied success in different quarters; but at nightfall, after a struggle of twenty-four hours, the assailants withdrew and Acre was saved. On the 20th the siege was raised, the French retreating during the night. Upon the 25th they reached Jaffa, and on the 29th Gaza. Both places were evacuated; and the army, resuming its march, next day entered the desert. On the 2d of June it encamped in the oasis of El Arish. The garrison of the fort there was re-enforced, the works strengthened with more artillery, and the place provisioned for six months. It was the one substantial result of the Syrian expedition, — an outpost which, like Acre, an invader must subdue before advancing. On the 7th, after nine days' march through the desert under the scorching heat of the June sun, the army re-entered Egypt. It had lost since its departure fifteen hundred killed or dead of disease, and more than two thousand wounded.

The reputation of Sir Sidney Smith with posterity rests upon the defence of Acre, in which he made proof of solid as well as brilliant qualities. Bonaparte, who never forgave the check administered to his ambition, nor overcame the irritation caused by sixty days fretting against an unexpected and seemingly trivial obstacle, tried hard to decry the character of the man who thwarted him. " Smith is a lunatic," he said, "who wishes to make his fortune and keep himself always before the eyes of the world. He is a man capable of any folly, to whom no profound or rational project is ever to be attributed."[1] "Sir Sidney Smith occupied himself too much with the detail of affairs on shore, which he did not understand, and where he was of little use; he neglected the maritime business, which he did understand, and where he had everything in his power." This accusation was supported by the circumstantial misstatement that six big guns, with a large quantity of ammunition and provisions, were landed by Perrée, undetected, seven miles from Smith's ships.[2]

That there was a strong fantastic and vainglorious strain in Smith's character seems certain, and to it largely he owed the dislike of his own service; but so far as appears, he showed at Acre discretion and sound judgment, as well as energy and courage. It must be remembered, in justice, that all power and all responsibility were in his hands, and that the result was an eminent success. Under the circumstances he had to be much on shore as well as afloat; but he seems to have shown Phélippeaux, and after the latter's death, Colonel Douglas, the confidence and deference which their professional skill demanded, as he certainly was most generous in recognizing their services and those of others. When the equinoctial gales came on he remained with his ship, which had to put to sea; an act which Bonaparte maliciously attributed to a wish to escape the odium of the fall of the place. Whether ashore or afloat, Smith could not please Bonaparte. The good sense which

---

[1] Corr. de Nap., June 26, 1799, vol. v. p. 617.

[2] Commentaires de Napoléon, vol. iii. pp. 81, 82. It is only fair to say that an attempt was made by Perrée a few weeks later to land ammunition back of Mt. Carmel, when he was discovered and chased off. (Barrow's Life of Sir Sidney Smith, vol. i. p. 300.) Napoleon may have confused the two circumstances. His own correspondence (vol. v., pp. 517, 518) contradicts the landing near Acre. The guns were put on shore at Jaffa and thence dragged to Acre.

defers to superior experience, the lofty spirit which bears
the weight of responsibility and sustains the courage of
waverers, ungrudging expenditure of means and effort, un-
shaken determination to endure to the end, and heroic
inspiration at the critical moment of the last assault, —
all these fine qualities must in candor be allowed to Sir
Sidney Smith at the siege of Acre. He received and
deserved the applause, not only of the multitude and the
government, but of Nelson himself. The deeds of Acre
blotted out of memory the exaggerated reports of the almost total destruction of the French fleet at his hands
when Toulon was evacuated; reports which had left upon
his name the imputation of untrustworthiness. But,
whatever the personal merits of Sir Sidney Smith in this
memorable siege, there can be no doubt that to the presence
of the British ships, and the skilled support of the British
officers, seamen, and marines — manning the works — is to
be attributed the successful resistance made by the brave,
but undisciplined Turks.

During the last days of the siege of Acre and while
Bonaparte was leading his baffled army through the sands
of the desert back into Egypt, the western Mediterranean
was thrown into a ferment by the escape of the French fleet
from Brest. This very remarkable episode, having led to
no tangible results, has been little noticed by general historians; but to the student of naval war its incidents are
most instructive. It is scarcely too much to say that never
was there a greater opportunity than that offered to the
French fleet, had it been a valid force, by the scattered condition of its enemies on this occasion; nor can failure
deprive the incident of its durable significance, as illustrat-
ing the advantage, to the inferior navy, of a large force
concentrated in a single port, when the enemy, though superior, is by the nature of the contest compelled to disseminate his squadrons. The advantage is greatest when the
port of concentration is central with reference to the

enemy's positions; but is by no means lost when, as was then the case with Brest, it is at one extremity of the theatre of war. It was a steady principle in the policy of Napoleon, when consul and emperor, to provoke dissemination of the British navy by threatening preparations at widely separated points of his vast dominions; just as it was a purpose of the British government, though not consistently followed, to provoke France to ex-centric efforts by naval demonstrations, menacing many parts of the shore line. The Emperor, however, a master of the art of war and an adept at making the greatest possible smoke with the least expenditure of fuel, was much more than a match in the game of deception for the unmilitary and many-headed body that directed the affairs of Great Britain.

Although in 1799 the Channel fleet had attached to it as many as fifty-one ships-of-the-line,[1] of which forty-two upon the alarm that ensued very soon got to sea,[2] Lord Bridport had with him but sixteen when he took command off Brest, on the 17th of April, relieving the junior admiral who, with eight or nine ships, had done the winter cruising. On the 25th Bridport looked into the port and saw there eighteen ships-of-the-line ready for sea. The wind being fresh at north-east, the British admiral stood out until he reached a position twelve miles west-south-west of Ushant Island. The entrance being thus clear and the wind fair, the French fleet, numbering twenty-five of the line and ten smaller vessels, slipped out that night under command of Admiral Bruix, then minister of marine, who, by his close official relations to the government, was indicated as a proper person to fulfil an apparently confidential mission, for which his professional ability and activity eminently fitted him.

Being bound south and the wind favoring, Bruix passed through the southern passage, known as the Passage du

---
[1] Schomberg's Naval Chronology. Appendix No. 374.
[2] Ibid. Appendix No. 376.

Raz,[1] distant thirty miles or more from the spot where Bridport had stationed his fleet, which consequently saw nothing, though it had great reason to suspect a movement by the French. At 9 A. M. on the 26th, however, a British inshore frigate caught sight of the enemy just as the last ships were passing through the Raz, and hastened toward her fleet. At noon she lost sight of the French, and an hour later, the signal being repeated from vessel to vessel, Bridport learned that the enemy were out. He at once made sail for Brest, assured himself on the 27th that the news was true, and then steered for Ireland to cover it from a possible invasion, sending at the same time warning to Keith off Cadiz and to St. Vincent at Gibraltar, as well as orders into the Channel ports for all ships to join him off Cape Clear. The whole south coast of England was at once in an uproar; but the government, knowing how scattered were the vessels in the Mediterranean, had a double anxiety. On the 6th of May, five ships-of-the-line sailed from Plymouth to join St. Vincent.[2] The rest of the Channel fleet got off as fast as they could to Bridport, who, in spite of the reports from merchant vessels that had seen the French to the southward, and steering south, refused to believe that Ireland was safe. In this delusion he was confirmed by a barefaced and much-worn ruse, a small French vessel being purposely allowed to fall into his hands with dispatches for Ireland. On the 12th of May there remained in Plymouth but a single ship-of-the-line, and that detained by sickness among the crew, — "a circumstance scarcely ever remembered before."[3] Despite this accumulation of force, it was not till June 1 that Bridport detached to the southward sixteen sail-of-the-line,[4] of which twelve went on to the Mediterranean.

[1] See map of Brest in next chapter.
[2] Naval Chronicle, vol. i. p. 537.
[3] Ibid., p. 539.
[4] Ibid., vol. ii p. 81. Osler's Life of Lord Exmouth, p. 191.

On the morning of the 3d of May Admiral Keith, off Cadiz, was joined by a British frigate chased the day before by Bruix's fleet, of which she had lost sight only at 4 P. M. The next morning the French appeared, twenty-four ships to the British fifteen, which were to leeward of their enemy. The wind, that had been blowing fresh from northwest since the day before, rapidly increased to a whole gale, so that though there were nineteen Spanish ships in Cadiz and twenty-four French outside, the British remained safe; and not only so, but by making it impossible for the French to enter without an engagement, prevented this first attempt at a junction. "Lord Keith," wrote St. Vincent, "has shown great manhood and ability, his position having been very critical, exposed to a hard gale of wind, blowing directly on shore, with an enemy of superior force to windward, and twenty-two ships-of-the-line in Cadiz ready to profit by any disaster that might have befallen him."[1] Bruix, who knew that his captains, long confined to port by the policy of their government, were not able to perform fleet manœuvres in ordinary weather, dared not attack on a lee shore with a wind that would tax all the abilities of experienced seamen.[2] He therefore kept away

[1] Brenton's Life of St. Vincent, vol. ii. p. 17.

[2] "Admiral Bruix, being able to rely more on the devotion of his captains than upon their exactitude and precision in manœuvring, took pains before sailing to lay down the duties of a captain under all circumstances; carefully refraining, however, from making a special application of these lessons to any one individual, that their self-love might not be wounded. This wise precaution did not prevent new mistakes, whose consequences would have been much aggravated had we been obliged, by meeting the enemy, to manœuvre either to avoid or compel action." (Journal of Captain Moras, special aide-de-camp to Admiral Bruix. La Gravière, Guerres Maritimes, vol. i. p. 373. Appendix, 4th edition.)

The gunnery, apparently, was equally bad. "I will cite only one fact to give an idea of the effects of our artillery. When Admiral Bruix was bringing to Brest the French and Spanish fleets, at least nine hundred guns were fired in very fine weather at an Algerian corsair without doing any harm. I do not believe that ever, in a combat of that kind, was so much useless firing done." (Article by "an officer of marine artillery;" Moniteur, 3 Fructidor, An 8 [Aug. 20, 1800].)

again to the south-east, determining to lose no time, but at
once to enter the Mediterranean; and the following day
Lord St. Vincent, gazing from the rock of Gibraltar through
the thick haze that spread over the Straits, saw, running
before the gale, a number of heavy ships which, from dispatches received the day before, he knew must be French.

The situations of the vessels in his extensive command,
as present that morning to the mind of the aged earl, must
be realized by the reader if he would enter into the embarrassment and anxiety of the British commander-in-chief,
or appreciate the military significance of Bruix's appearance, with a large concentrated force, in the midst of dispositions taken without reference to such a contingency.
The fifteen ships off Cadiz, with one then lying at Tetuan,
on the Morocco side of the Straits, where the Cadiz ships
went for water, were the only force upon which St. Vincent could at once depend, and if they were called off the
Spanish fleet was released. At Minorca, as yet imperfectly garrisoned,[1] was an isolated body of four ships under
Commodore Duckworth. Lord Nelson's command in the
central Mediterranean was disseminated, and the detachments, though not far out of supporting distance, were
liable to be separately surprised. Troubridge with four
vessels was blockading Naples, now in possession of the
French, and at the same time co-operating with the resistance made to the foreign intruders by the peasantry under
Cardinal Ruffo. Nelson himself, with one ship, was at Palermo, and the faint-hearted court and people were crying
that if he left them the island was lost. Captain Ball,
with three of the line, blockaded Malta, the only hope of
subduing which seemed to be by rigorous isolation. Far to
the eastward, up the Mediterranean, without a friendly port
in which to shelter, Sidney Smith with two ships, unsus-

---

[1] Two months later Lord Keith, having succeeded St. Vincent in the command, wrote to Nelson: "If Minorca is left without ships it will fall." (Nelson's Dispatches, vol. iii. p. 415, note.)

picious of danger from the sea, was then drawing to an end the defence of Acre.

Each of these British divisions lay open to the immensely superior force which Bruix brought. Not only so, but the duties of an important nature to which each of them was assigned were threatened with frustration. So large a fleet as that of Bruix might, and according to the usual French practice probably would, have numerous troops embarked.[1] No amount of skill could rescue Troubridge's division from such a disproportion of force, and with it would fall the resistance of Naples. Only flight could save the ships off Malta, and St. Vincent saw the blockade raised, the garrison re-enforced and re-victualled; as within his own memory had so often been done for Gibraltar, in its famous siege not twenty years before. Duckworth's little squadron could not prevent the landing of an army which would sweep Minorca again into the hands of Spain, and the British commodore might consider himself fortunate if, in so difficult a dilemma, he extricated his ships from a harbor always hard to leave.[2] Spain also had in Cartagena and Majorca a number of soldiers that could be rapidly thrown into Minorca under cover of such a fleet.

The British admiral instantly decided to sacrifice all other objects to the concentration of his fleet in such a position as should prevent the junction of the French and Spaniards; against which the presence off Cadiz of Keith's squadron, though inferior in numbers to either, had so far effectually interposed. He at once sent off dispatches to

---

[1] Bruix did not have over a thousand troops with him, the pressure on the land frontiers by the Second Coalition demanding all the force that could be raised to resist it; but the fleet carried twenty-four thousand seamen or artillerists, a force capable by itself of accomplishing much. The reputation of the admiral caused both officers and men to flock to his flag.

[2] "Port Mahon is a very narrow harbor, from which you cannot get out without great difficulty." (Collingwood's letters, August 18, 1799.) "Ships had better be under sail off Port Mahon than in the harbor." (Nelson's Dispatches, May 12, 1799.)

all his lieutenants; but the westerly gales that were driving Bruix to his goal made it impossible to get ship or boat to Keith. This admiral was only reached by an indulgence from the Spanish officials, between whom and the British an intercourse of courtesy was steadily maintained. These granted to Admiral Coffin, who had been appointed to a post in Halifax, passports to proceed to Lisbon through Spain; and Coffin on the way contrived to get a boat sent off to Keith, with orders which brought him to Gibraltar on the 10th. To Nelson the earl wrote that he believed the enemy were bound to Malta and Alexandria; and that the Spaniards, whom he was forced to release from Cadiz, would descend upon Minorca. Nelson received this message on the 13th of May. The day before, a brig coming direct from the Atlantic without stopping at Gibraltar had notified him of the escape from Brest, and that the French had been seen steering south. On the strength of this he drew from Naples and Malta all the ships-of-the-line except one before each, directing a rendezvous off Port Mahon, where he would join Duckworth; but when St. Vincent's letter came, he called them all in, leaving only frigates on each station, and ordered the heavy vessels to meet him off the island of Maritimo, to intercept the French between Sicily and Africa. He also sent to Duckworth to ask his help; but the commodore declined until he could communicate with the commander-in-chief, from whom he had received orders to keep his division in readiness to join the main fleet when it appeared.

St. Vincent's position, in truth, was one of utter and dire perplexity. If the French and Spaniards got together, he would have forty-four enemy's vessels on his hands: against which, by sacrificing every other object, he could only gather thirty until re-enforced by the Channel fleet, upon whose remissness he could hardly fail to charge his false position. To lose Minorca and Sicily, to see Malta snatched from his fingers when ready to close upon it, the French position in Naples established, and that in Egypt so strengthened as to become impregnable to either attack or reduction by want, such were the obvious probable consequences of Bruix's coming. Besides these evident dangers, he very well knew from secret official information that the Spanish court were in constant dread of a popular insurrection, which would give the French a pretext for entering the peninsula,—not, as in 1808, to impose a foreign king upon an unwilling nation, but to promote a change in the government which the distress of the people, though usually loyal, would probably welcome. In March he had received a communication from the Spanish prime minister, asking that a British frigate might be detailed to bring remittances from the Spanish colonies to Gibraltar, to be afterwards conveyed into Spain. The reason given for making this request of an enemy was that the want of specie, and consequent delay in public payments, especially to the soldiery, made revolution imminent. St. Vincent recommended his government to comply, because of the danger, in case of disturbances, that both Spain and Portugal might fall under subjection to France.[1]

Fortunately, amid the conflicting claims of diverse interests, the path of military wisdom was perfectly clear to one understanding its principles. St. Vincent might be agitated by apprehensions; but he knew what he must do, and did it. To get his own fleet together and at the same time prevent the allies from uniting theirs, was the first thing; and the point of concentration indicated for this purpose should be one that would cover Minorca, if he arrived before it was reduced. For Sicily, Malta, and all to the eastward, he must trust to the transcendent abilities of Nelson and his "band of brothers."[2] On the 12th, after two days of

---

[1] Brenton's St. Vincent, vol. i. p. 493.
[2] "I had the happiness to command a band of brothers." (Nelson's Dispatches, vol. iii. p. 230.) The best of his Nile captains were, for the most part, still with him.

hurried preparations, the British fleet sailed from Gibraltar. On the 20th it reached Minorca, found it still safe, and was joined by Duckworth's division, raising the force to twenty ships-of-the-line. St. Vincent here received information that the French had on the 12th been seen north of Minorca, heading for Toulon.[1] Sending this news to Nelson he sailed on the 22d in pursuit; but learning that the Spaniards after Keith's departure had left Cadiz, as he had expected, he decided to cruise off Cape San Sebastian on the Spanish coast. Seventeen sail of Spaniards had indeed reached Cartagena on the 20th; but in the passage from Cadiz eleven had been partly or totally dismasted, and this circumstance was sufficient excuse for not proceeding to a junction, to which the policy of their court was but little inclined.

On the 30th of May St. Vincent heard that the French had sailed again from Toulon, but for what purpose was not known. As it might follow the course of Bonaparte's expedition, east of Corsica, and fall upon Sicily and Malta, he sent Duckworth with four ships to Nelson at Palermo, and four hours later was joined by the first detachment of five sail-of-the-line from the Channel,[2] of whose nearness he doubtless had some intimation before parting with Duckworth. With twenty-one sail he now stood south-west toward Barcelona, then north-east for Toulon. On the 2d of June, when seventy miles from this port, his health gave way altogether. He turned over the command to Keith and departed to Port Mahon.

Keith continued steering to the northward and eastward. On the 5th of June he was joined by a small cruiser, which had seen the French fleet in Vado Bay the day before. Bruix had reached Toulon May 14, and sailed again on the 26th, taking with him twenty-two ships; the others being left in port for repairs. He steered east, carrying

[1] Nelson's Dispatches, vol. iii. pp. 366, 374.
[2] See ante, p. 306.

supplies and a few recruits for the army of Italy. On the
4th of June he had anchored in Vado Bay. A detachment
from the fleet threw the supplies into Genoa, and it would
seem that Bruix there had an interview with General
Moreau, then commanding the army of Italy. On the 6th,[1]
turning short round, he doubled on his tracks, following
close along the coast of Piedmont and Provence to avoid
the British,[2] passed again in sight of Toulon to obtain information,[3] and from there pushed on to Cartagena, where he
anchored on the 22d; thus making with the Spanish fleet
the junction which had been frustrated before Cadiz.

On the same day that Bruix turned, Lord Keith, who
had also passed close along the French coast between
Cannes and Nice,[4] standing to the eastward, reached as far
as Monaco. Then the wind shifted to the eastward, and he
wrote as follows to Nelson: " Soon after I despatched the
' Telegraph ' " (the vessel which saw the French in Vado
Bay) " last night, *the wind came fresh from the east*, which
is of course a fair wind for the enemy, if bound towards
you " (by the east of Corsica) " and a foul wind for me to
follow them, which is unfortunate; for, if my information
was just, I had no doubt of overtaking them before they had
left the coast of Italy; . . . but *the defenceless state of
Minorca*, without a fleet, the great force prepared (at Car-

---

[1] Jurien de la Gravière, Guerres Maritimes, vol. i. p. 288 (4th edition);
also James, Naval History, vol. ii. p. 264 (edition 1847). Other authorities
say the 8th. The reconcilement seems to be that Bruix did not take his fleet
to Genoa, but only a detachment; the main body anchoring in Vado Bay.
He would thus leave Genoa the 6th, Vado the 8th.

[2] " We avoided the enemy by skirting very close, and under cover of
foggy weather, the coasts of Piedmont and Provence." (Journal of Captain
Moras, special aid to Bruix. La Gravière, Guerres Maritimes, vol. i. p. 376.
Appendix, 4th edition.)

[3] " In our passage before Toulon we learned the vexations accidents which
had happened to the Spanish fleet, and went to rejoin them at Cartagena."
(Ibid. Also James, Nav. Hist., vol. ii. p. 264.)

[4] The British fleet was sighted off St. Tropez (Troude, vol. iii. p. 158);
and fired upon by coast batteries near Antibes on June 6th. (James, Nav
Hist. vol. ii. p. 262).

tagena) to attack it, added to my having so far exceeded my orders already, will oblige me to relinquish the pursuit, and return to the protection of that island. But I have detached to your lordship the 'Bellerophon' and 'Powerful' (seventy-fours), which I hope will arrive in time, as I am confident *the French are not thirty leagues hence at this moment.*"[1]

Being close in with the shore with an east wind, Keith could only stand off on the port tack, and it would appear that he still clung to the hope of a shift favorable for reaching Bruix; for on the 8th he was sixty miles south of Monaco,[2] not on the route for Minorca. There he received from St. Vincent, who, though relinquishing the immediate command of the fleet, retained that of the station, pressing orders to take a position off the Bay of Rosas. This was evidently intended to block the junction of the two fleets, though St. Vincent could not have known Bruix's purpose to return. Keith did not obey the order; but seems under its influence to have abandoned definitively his hope of overtaking the French, for he made sail for Minorca, and arrived there on the 12th.[3] Had he obeyed St. Vincent he could scarcely have failed to meet Bruix, for at the moment of receiving his letter the two fleets were hardly sixty miles apart, and both would have passed within sight of Cape San Sebastian, the natural landfall of vessels going from Toulon to Cartagena.

[1] Nelson's Dispatches, vol. iii. p. 379, note. This east wind seems to have been overlooked in the criticisms of Keith's conduct.
[2] Cape delle Melle bore, on the 8th, N. N. E., distant ninety miles. James, Nav. Hist., vol. ii. p. 262.
[3] Lord Keith's biographer (Allardyce) says he determined "to take Minorca on his way to Rosas" (p. 165); which was certainly a liberal construction, though not beyond the discretion of an officer in Keith's position. To take Minorca on his way to Rosas, from his position on the 8th, was to go two hundred miles to the former and one hundred and fifty more to Rosas, when the latter at the moment was not two hundred distant. He was a few miles nearer Rosas than Minorca, when he took the decision which finally wrecked the cruise.

Keith remained at Minorca but a few days, during which St. Vincent turned over to him the command of the station as well as of the fleet.[1] He sailed again on the 15th for Toulon; but the British had completely lost trace of the French from the time that they surrendered the touch of them obtained on the 5th of the month. From the 15th of June to the 6th of July[2] was passed groping blindly in the seas between Minorca, Toulon, and Genoa. On the latter date Keith regained Minorca, and there found the twelve ships-of-the-line which Bridport had detached from Ireland on the 1st of June, and which seem to have reached Port Mahon about the 17th of that month.[3] Scarcely an hour after his arrival,[4] information was received of the French having entered Cartagena. The ships that had accompanied Keith on the recent three weeks' cruise had to fill with water; but on the 10th he started for the Straits of Gibraltar with thirty-one ships-of-the-line, on a stern chase — proverbially a long chase — after the allies, known to be bound to the westward.

The latter, however, had a long start. Bruix, aware of the reluctance of the Spaniards, and secretly informed that in case of attack they could not be depended upon, hurried them away after a week's waiting, in virtue of stringent orders wrung from Madrid by the persistence of the French ambassador. On the 29th of June he sailed, having sixteen Spanish ships-of-the-line in company. On the 7th of July, just as Keith reached Minorca from his profitless cruise off Toulon, the allies were passing the Straits; and it happened, somewhat singularly, that the old Earl of St. Vin-

[1] Brenton's Life of St. Vincent, vol. ii. p. 24.
[2] It was during this time that Perrée's squadron was captured. See ante, p. 301.
[3] Mutineers belonging to the "Impétueux," one of the division, were tried by court martial in Port Mahon, June 19 and 20. (Osler's Life of Lord Exmouth, p. 192. Nels. Disp., vol. iii. p. 415, note.)
[4] James, Nav. Hist., vol. ii. p. 265 (edition 1847). Nels. Disp., vol. iii p. 415 note.

cent, who had seen them pass Gibraltar, bound in, had arrived in a frigate twenty-four hours before,—just in time to hear their guns as they went out. They entered Cadiz on the 11th of July, the day after Keith sailed in pursuit from Minorca. On the 21st, still numbering forty sail, they sailed from Cadiz, and on the 30th Keith with his thirty-one passed the Straits, after a moment's delay at Gibraltar. The British pressed their chase, and, despite its long start, came off Brest barely twenty-four hours after the French and Spaniards, who entered the port on the 13th of August. Lord Keith then went on to Torbay. The news of the junction of the French and Spaniards, and of their entering the Atlantic, had preceded him, and caused a renewal of the excitement about intended invasion to which Great Britain at this epoch was always prone. The arrival of the large force under his command restored confidence; but although, in conjunction with the Channel fleet, there were now as many as fifty-six ships-of-the-line assembled in Torbay, some time elapsed before the country would part with any of them, while so many enemies lay in Brest. Keith did not return to the Mediterranean until December, the chief command there being exercised by Nelson during his absence.

The exact aims of the French in this cruise, which from the inefficiency of their officers and seamen was as hazardous in its undertaking as it proved barren of results, have never been precisely ascertained. This uncertainty is probably due to the fact that the Directory itself was not clear as to what could be accomplished, and that Bruix had somewhat unlimited powers, based upon his confidential knowledge of the views of the government. It would seem that the first object, both in importance and in order, was a junction with the Spaniards in Cadiz. This being frustrated by Keith's division and by Bruix's distrust of the efficiency of his captains, the opportunities for offensive action, offered by the scattered condition of the British ships, were neglected in favor of going to Toulon; for Bruix seems to have neither felt nor betrayed any doubt as to his course. "The Brest squadron had such a game to play at Malta and Sicily," wrote St. Vincent to the First Lord, "that I trembled for the fate of our ships employed there, and for the latter island. Your lordship made a better judgment by fixing their operations to the coast of Genoa."[1] As a matter of fact, this is true; but as a question of military forecast, St. Vincent was perfectly right, and the action of the French can only be explained on the ground of distrust of their navy, or by the old faulty policy — traditional in all French governments, republican, royal, or imperial — of preferring ulterior objects to the destruction of the enemy's ships.

That the relief or re-enforcement of Bonaparte was intended seems improbable; although both St. Vincent and Nelson entertained this suspicion, upon which the latter acted. M. Thiers, indeed, finds Bruix's cruise inexplicable on any other supposition, but he does not assert the fact.[2] The feelings of the Directory towards that general were not strictly benevolent, and the ships carried neither troops nor supplies of importance; but the destruction of Nelson's scattered detachments, coupled as that might have been with the victualling of Malta, would have been a most worthy object, and one of very probable fulfilment. It is noteworthy that Nelson received his first news of Bruix's approach on the 12th of May, at Palermo, and on the 14th the French admiral entered Toulon. Now the distance from Gibraltar to Toulon is only one hundred and fifty miles less than that from Gibraltar to Palermo. Nelson could not have collected his ships in time to present a united front; and even could he, his whole force did not exceed ten or twelve to the enemy's twenty-four. As it was, Bruix's adventure, though daring in conception and active

[1] Brenton's Life of St. Vincent, vol. ii. p. 25.
[2] Histoire de la Révolution, vol. x. p. 392, note.

in execution, resulted merely in bringing back to France sixteen Spanish ships-of-the-line to be hostages for the continuance of the Spanish alliance, tottering under the adverse events of 1799; and this possibly was the great purpose of the Directory. If so, the excursion was political rather than military; and hence an opportunity, of a kind which, when rightly improved, has always been most pregnant of military consequences — concentration opposed to dispersion — remains to us merely an impressive lesson of what might have been, but was not. "Your lordship," wrote Nelson four years later to St. Vincent, " knows what Admiral Bruix might have done had he done his duty."[1] "The cruise of Admiral Bruix," says Captain Chevalier,[2] "was well conceived, but failed through the weakness of our allies and the inexperience of our own officers and crews. . . . The Spanish squadron brought to Brest, the gage of an alliance then very tottering, was the only result of this campaign. It is impossible to have any illusion as to the extent of the services rendered by the fleet on the coast of Italy. A division of frigates would have done as much."

The conduct of the British admirals in the Mediterranean, caught at so serious a disadvantage through no fault of their own, deserves to be considered. Dispersed in a fashion that was perfectly proper and efficient under the previous conditions, the arrival of Bruix imposed concentration, with a consequent enforced abandonment of some positions. St. Vincent's first step was to order Nelson to concentrate in the neighborhood of Sicily, while he himself drew Keith and Duckworth together at Minorca. This effected, the British would present two squadrons; one of twenty ships-of-the-line in the west, centring about Minorca; the other, four hundred miles distant, of fifteen or

---

[1] Nels. Disp., July 4, 1803, vol. v. p. 116.
[2] Mar. Fran. sous la Rép. p. 415.

sixteen ships,[1] gathered off the west end of Sicily to dispute the passage to Malta and Alexandria. This smaller division thus seems to have been much exposed; but, independently of its greatly superior efficiency to the French, it must be remembered that St. Vincent, as soon as he reached Minorca, knew that Nelson was in no immediate danger, for the French had given him the go-by and gone to Toulon. Cruising therefore off Cape San Sebastian, to intercept the junction of the Spaniards to the French, he was in constant touch of Minorca, barely one hundred miles distant, and, at the same time, was as near to Nelson as were the French in Toulon, whether they went east or west of Corsica. Being only one hundred and twenty miles from Toulon, and in such a position that a wind fair for the French to sail was also fair to bring his lookouts down to him, he could hope to overtake them, — if not in time to save Nelson, yet with the certainty of finding the French so badly handled that they could scarcely escape him. He no doubt reasoned as did Nelson to the ministry just before Trafalgar: " I ventured without any fear [to predict] that if Calder [with eighteen ships] got fairly alongside their twenty-seven or twenty-eight sail, by the time the enemy had beat our fleet soundly, they would do us no harm this year."[2] Save Malta, which could not have maintained the twenty thousand men in their fleet for a month and was otherwise barren of resources, the French would have had no port to fall back on and would have been lost to the republic.[3] Had St. Vincent cruised off Cartagena, where the Spaniards were, he would have been

---

[1] Ten or twelve British, four or five Portuguese; the former exceptionally well-ordered ships. (Nels. Disp., vol. iii. p. 365.)

[2] Nels. Disp., vol. vii. p. 16.

[3] To this must be added that, from conditions of wind and weather, Malta was very far from Toulon, much farther than Toulon from Malta. Of this Nelson complained often and bitterly in the later war, when commander-in-chief off Toulon. Malta was valuable, he said (Disp., vol. v. p. 107), as a most important outwork to India and for influence in the Levant; valueless against Toulon.

in better position to check them, but he would have uncovered both Minorca and Nelson to the French; both being nearer to Toulon than to Cartagena. Not only so, but Cartagena being three hundred miles farther from Toulon than Cape San Sebastian is, the British lookout ships would have had all that greater distance to go to their admiral, who, when found, would then be further from his chief points of interest than when off the Cape. As soon, however, as St. Vincent learned that the French had gone east from Toulon, being relieved from any immediate apprehension concerning the Spaniards, he re-enforced Nelson with four ships, raising his squadron to sixteen British against a possible French twenty-four.

It was during the week following the detachment to Nelson that St. Vincent left the fleet, and that Keith made the false move which has been so severely blamed. It appears to the author, from all the information accessible to him, that Keith took this step wholly independent of St. Vincent's special orders, which are alleged as controlling him. He acted in deference, partly, to the general orders given before turning over the command, and partly to his own views of the situation.[1] These seem to have differed from those of St. Vincent, who laid most stress on disabling the enemy's fleets; whereas Keith was dominated by the fear of losing Minorca. This feeling led him to deviate from the order to cruise off the Gulf of Rosas, as it also led him soon after, on two occasions, to direct Nelson to detach ships for the defence of the island; which Nelson, with very doubtful propriety, refused to do.[2] Minorca, in this case, very appositely illustrates the embarrassment of a fleet upon which an important seaport wholly

---

[1] This is plain from his letter of June 6 to Nelson. (Ante, p. 313.) Keith's failure is usually attributed to St Vincent's dispatches, received June 8; whereas the letter shows that he had decided to return to Minorca two days before receiving them.

[2] Nels. Disp., vol iii. pp. 408 and 414, with notes.

depends for security. In the present instance the beating of the French fleet and the protection of Minorca introduced two apparently divergent motives, which became personified in St. Vincent and his lieutenant. The former saw the best protection to the island to be in beating the fleet: Keith subordinated the latter to the former. With St. Vincent agreed Nelson's simple but accurate view of naval strategy: "I consider the best defence for his Sicilian Majesty's dominions is to place myself alongside the French."[1] Keith, on the other hand, in a somewhat later letter, expresses almost pathetically the embarrassment caused by his inferior strategic insight. "It is very hard I cannot find these vagabonds in some spot or other, and that I am so *shackled* with this defenceless island."[2] Properly every seaport should be able to hold out for a length of time, longer or shorter, according to its importance, entirely independent of the fleet. The latter will then be able to exert its great faculty, its mobility, unfettered by considerations of what is happening at the port. For so long the latter is safe; meanwhile the fleet may be absent. The best coast-defence is a navy; not because fortifications are not absolutely necessary, but because beating the enemy's fleet is the best of all defences.

After the vain pursuit of Admiral Bruix, Lord Keith brought his fleet into Torbay on the 17th of August. On the 18th Earl St. Vincent landed at Portsmouth, thus formally quitting the Mediterranean command, which he had held for three years and nine months. Four days afterwards, on the 22d of August, 1799, Bonaparte secretly embarked at Alexandria to return into France.

After the Syrian campaign the French army had re-entered Cairo on the 14th of June. On the 11th of July Sir Sidney Smith, with his two ships, anchored in Aboukir Bay, accompanying, or being accompanied by, a Turkish

---

[1] Nels. Disp., vol. iii. p. 380.
[2] Keith to Nelson, July 12, 1799; Nels. Disp., vol. iii. p. 419, note.

fleet of thirteen ships-of-the-line with a hundred other sail of frigates and transports. Embarked on board the latter were troops variously estimated at from ten to thirty thousand men.[1] On the 15th Bonaparte, at Cairo, learned that his anticipations of an attack by sea, during the fine season, had been realized. He promptly ordered Desaix to evacuate upper Egypt for the security of Cairo, and rapidly drew together in the neighborhood of Alexandria the detachments in lower Egypt. This concentration was effected on the 19th, but by that time the Turks had landed and stormed the Castle of Aboukir, which fell on the 16th. On the 25th the French attacked the enemy on the peninsula of Aboukir, and the same scene that had witnessed the destruction of Brueys's squadron a year before now saw the entire overthrow of the Mahometan army. All who had landed were either killed, driven into the sea and drowned, or taken prisoners. Among the latter was the Turkish commander-in-chief.

After the defeat flags of truce passed between Bonaparte and the British commodore, through which the former received English newspapers up to the 10th of June.[2] By them he learned the victorious advance of the second coalition, and the defeats of the French in Germany and Italy. His resolution was speedily taken to return to France. It has been disputed whether this was a sudden determination not before entertained, as asserted by his secretary Bourrienne; or whether it represents a purpose gradually and naturally formed. Napoleon himself in later years attributed his decision to information obtained from Phélippeaux in the trenches before Acre; when the combatants, separated by but a few yards, often exchanged words.[3] It is, however, certain that the thought had long been familiar to

---

[1] The larger number is the estimate in Napoleon's Commentaries, which ordinarily exaggerate the enemy's forces. (Vol. iii. p. 107.)

[2] Corr. de Nap., vol. v. p. 710.

[3] Commentaires de Napoléon, vol. iii. p. 89.

him; for, in a letter to the Directory as early as October 7, 1798, he had announced his intention of returning to Europe in certain very probable contingencies.[1] The same message was repeated a few months later.[2] In truth his keen military sagacity, resembling the most delicate yet most highly cultivated intuitions, had divined the misfortunes awaiting France at the time he learned by the Ragusan ship that Naples had declared war and that all[3] the powers were arming. During his own Italian campaign, even after the British had left the Mediterranean, his mind had been preoccupied with the danger from Naples; and he foresaw in Egypt the disasters that must result from an ex-centric movement of the French army in that quarter, if followed by any reverses in upper Italy. Bourrienne tells a story which illustrates vividly the superstitious vein in his character, as well as the foreboding of evil that he had carried with him into Syria. While before Acre, news was received that a Nile boat named the "Italy," in the employ of the French army, had after a gallant defence been blown up by her crew to avoid capture by the Arabs. The incident and the name made a strong impression upon Bonaparte. "My friend," said he to Bourrienne, "Italy is lost to France. All is over; my presentiments never deceive me;" nor could any argument rid his mind of this conviction, dependent rather upon his instinctive perceptions than upon a slight and fortuitous coincidence.[4] So, when he read Sidney Smith's gazettes, he cried again: "My presentiment did not deceive me! Italy is lost!"[5]

Admiral Ganteaume was directed to prepare rapidly two of the frigates which had fallen to France in her share of the spoil of Venice; and the persons intended to accompany the general were quietly notified. After the defeat of the Turks at Aboukir, Sidney Smith had resumed the blockade

---

[1] Corr. de Nap., vol. v. p. 56. [2] Ibid., p. 403 (Feb. 10, 1799).
[3] See ante, p. 291.
[4] Mém. de Bourrienne, vol. ii. p. 238. [5] Ibid., p. 305.

of Alexandria; but on the 9th of August he withdrew to
Cyprus, probably for water. Taking advantage of the opportunity, Bonaparte sailed, and after a tedious passage
landed at Fréjus on the 9th of October. One month later
the Directory was overthrown and the supreme power in
France passed into Bonaparte's hands.

Thus ended, so far at least as the great designer was concerned, Bonaparte's Oriental Expedition; an undertaking
which has been freely stigmatized as a dream, marked by
the eccentricities of its author's genius, not by his usual
keen intelligence. A dream it was, it is true; but not for
its Eastern impossibilities, nor for its wide flights of imagination, the faculty which Bonaparte possessed in so eminent
a degree, without which he never could have conceived his
extraordinary policy, and to which he usually joined a
width and depth of practical wisdom which balanced his
imagination and made possible the realizing of his visions.
That it was no dream to rouse and combine the nations of
the East under the headship of one man, witness the careers of the adventurers who there, from age to age, have
risen to empire; and who certainly were not superior in
genius, nor as leaders of men, to the great Corsican. Witness, too, the motley host which he gathered under one
standard, from all the highly organized nations of continental Europe, for that other great Eastern expedition in
which he wrecked his fortunes. The Egyptian enterprise
and all its brilliant hopes definitively failed at Acre, in
the march against Turkey through Syria; and it failed,
— why? Because a British seaman, by his command of the
sea and his support to the garrison, maintained the possession of a place, to advance beyond which, unsubdued, would
entail ruin. Forty years later an army, not of the superb
soldiers of the French revolution, but of native Egyptians,
led by Ibrahim Pasha, whom none will equal to Napoleon,
undertook the same march, captured Acre, and had progressed victoriously into the heart of Asia Minor when the

British navy again interfered and called a halt. How came it that a naval captain, with two ships-of-the-line and a few small vessels, controlled absolutely the far east of the Mediterranean? Because in Aboukir Bay, nine months before, Nelson had destroyed the French fleet. That magnificent battle not only signalized the genius for war of the British admiral, but proclaimed aloud the existence of a power destined ever, and in all parts, to clip the wings of the coming emperor. The Eastern enterprise of Bonaparte failed, not because of miscalculations as to what was possible in that far East, which Western people so ill can understand; but because he, to the end of his career, was never able rightly to appreciate the conditions of naval warfare. His perfect military insight was not mistaken in affirming that the principles of war upon the sea must be the same as upon land; it was by the failure to comprehend the circumstances to which the principles must be applied — the failure to realize the possibilities and the limitations of the naval warfare of his day — that the general and the emperor were alike led into fatal miscalculations. The Nile and Trafalgar, each the grave of a great conception, proclaimed the same cause and the same effect; underlying each was the inability of Napoleon to understand what ships could do and what they could not, according to the conditions of the sea and the capacity of the seamen.

There was, however, one radical fallacy underlying Bonaparte's Egyptian, or rather Oriental, expedition, — for in his mind it far outleaped the narrow limits of the Nile valley, — and that lay in the effect he expected to produce upon Great Britain. It is all very well to stigmatize, after Lanfrey's fashion, as the vagaries of a distempered fancy, the vast projects of Eastern conquest and dominion, which unquestionably filled his mind with dreams of a sweep to his arms rivalling that of Alexander and of the Roman legions. An extraordinary, perhaps even an extravagant, imagination was one of the necessary conditions of Napoleon's wonderful career. That it should from time to time lead him into great mistakes, and ultimately to his ruin, was perhaps inevitable. Without it, or with it in a markedly less degree, he might have died in his palace an old man and left his throne to a son, if not to a dynasty; but also without it he would not have produced upon his own age and upon all subsequent history the effects which he has left. To it were due the Oriental visions, to which, regarded as a military enterprise, the present writer is certainly not ready to apply the word "fantastic." But, as a blow directed against Great Britain, there was in them a fatal defect of conception, due more to a miscalculation of the intellect, a prejudice of his day, than to a wild flight of fancy.

In the relations of India to Great Britain, Bonaparte, in common with all Frenchmen of his age, mistook effect for cause. The possession of India and of other colonies was to them the cause of British prosperity; just as at a later time, and now, the wide extent of British commerce has seemed to many the cause of Great Britain's wealth and eminence among the nations. That there is truth in this view is not to be denied; but it is the kind of truth compatible with putting the cart before the horse, mistaking the fruit for the tree, the flower for the plant. There was less excuse for a blunder of this kind in a quick-witted nation like the French, for they had before their eyes the fact that they had long owned some of the richest colonies in the world; and yet the British had, upon their own ground, amid all disadvantages of position, absorbed the commerce of the West Indies, French as well as Spanish. In local advantages, Great Britain in the West Indies had not the tenth of what France and Spain had; yet she so drank the wealth of the region that one fourth of her envied commerce then depended upon it. So in India; Great Britain sucked the wealth of India, because of the energy and commercial genius of her people. Had Bonaparte's visions been realized and India dominated, Great Britain would not have been overcome. A splendid bough would have been torn from a tree, and, in falling, would have carried to the ground the fruit depending from it; but not only was the amount of the fruit exaggerated, but the recuperative power of the root, the aptitude of the great trunk to throw out new branches, was not understood. Had Bonaparte converted the rule of India from England to France, he would have embarrassed, not destroyed, British traffic therein. Like the banyan tree, a new sucker would have been thrown out and reached the soil in some new spot, defying efforts at repression; as British commerce later refused to die under the far more searching efforts of the Continental System.

The strength of Great Britain could be said to lie in her commerce only as, and because, it was the external manifestation of the wisdom and strength of the British people, unhampered by any control beyond that of a government and institutions in essential sympathy with them. In the enjoyment of these blessings, — in their independence and untrammelled pursuit of wealth, — they were secured by their powerful navy; and so long as this breastplate was borne, unpierced, over the heart of the great organism, over the British islands themselves, Great Britain was — not invulnerable — but invincible. She could be hurt indeed, but she could not be slain. Herein was Bonaparte's error. His attempt upon India was strategically a fine conception; it was an attack upon the flank of an enemy whose centre was then too strong for him; but as a broad effort of military policy, — of statesmanship directing arms, — it was simply delivering blows upon an extremity, leaving the heart untouched. The same error pervaded his whole career; for, with all his genius, he still was, as Thiers has well said, the child of his century. So, in his later years, he was beguiled into the strife wherein he bruised Great Britain's heel, and she bruised his head.

Yet his mistake, supreme genius that he was, is scarce to be wondered at; for after all the story of his career, of his huge power, of his unrelenting hostility, of his indomitable energy, unremittingly directed to the destruction of his chief enemy, — after all this and its failure, — we still find men harping on the weakness of Great Britain through her exposed commerce. Her dependence upon trade, and the apparent slackening of the colonial ties, foretell her fatal weakness in the hour of trial. So thought Napoleon; so think we. Yet the commercial genius of her people is not abated; and the most fruitful parts of that colonial system existed scarcely, if at all, in those old days, when her commerce was as great in proportion to her numbers as it is now. To paralyze this, it must be taken by the throat; no snapping at the heels will do it. To command the sea approaches to the British islands will be to destroy the power of the State; as a preliminary thereto the British navy must be neutralized by superior numbers, or by superior skill.

Like the furtive intrusion and hasty retreat of Bruix's fleet, the stealthy manner of Bonaparte's return to Europe proclaimed the control of the Mediterranean by the British navy, and foretold the certain fall of his two great conquests, Egypt and Malta. His own personal credit was too deeply staked upon their deliverance, both by his original responsibility for the expedition and by the promises of succor made to the soldiers abandoned in Egypt, to admit a doubt of his wish to save them, if it could be done. His correspondence is full of the subject, and numerous efforts were made; as great, probably, as were permitted by the desperate struggle with external enemies and internal disorder in which he found France plunged. All, however, proved fruitless. The detailed stories of the loss of Egypt and of Malta by France have much interest, both for the military and unprofessional reader; but they are summed up in the one fact which prophesied their fall: France had lost all power to dispute the control of the sea. From February, 1799, when a small frigate entered La Valetta, to January, 1800, not a vessel reached the port. In the latter month a dispatch-boat got in, bringing news of Bonaparte's accession to power as First Consul; which event, though two months old, was still unknown to the garrison. On the 6th of February Admiral Perrée, who had served on the Nile and in Syria to Bonaparte's great satisfaction, sailed from Toulon with the " Généreux," seventy-four, one of the ships that had escaped from Aboukir Bay, three smaller vessels, and one large transport. A quantity of supplies and between three and four thousand troops for the relief of Malta were embarked in the squadron. On the 18th they fell in with several British ships, under Nelson's immediate command; and after the exchange of a few shots, one of which killed Perrée, the " Généreux " and the transport struck to a force too superior to be resisted. The other ships returned to Toulon.

All further attempts to introduce relief likewise failed. During the two years' blockade, from September, 1798, to September, 1800, only five vessels succeeded in entering the port.[1] The " Guillaume Tell," which had lain in Valetta harbor since the battle of the Nile, attempted to escape on the night of the 31st of March, being charged with letters to Bonaparte saying that the place could not hold out longer than June. The ship was intercepted by the British, and surrendered after a brilliant fight, in which all her masts were shot away[2] and over a fifth of her crew killed and wounded. One of the vessels sharing in this capture was Lord Nelson's flag-ship, the " Foudroyant," but the admiral himself was not on board. Swayed by a variety of feelings, to analyze which is unnecessary and not altogether pleasant to those who admire his fame, he had asked, after the return of Lord Keith, to be relieved and granted a

---

[1] Chevalier. Mar. Fran. sous le Consulat, etc., p. 16.
[2] Nels. Disp. vol iv. p. 219, note.

repose to which his long and brilliant services assuredly entitled him. He thus failed to receive the surrender of the last of the ships which escaped from the Nile, and to accomplish the reduction of Malta, whose ultimate fate had been determined by his previous career of victory. The island held out until the 5th of September, 1800. Nelson on the 11th of July struck his flag in Leghorn, and in company with the Hamiltons went home overland, by way of Trieste and Vienna, reaching England in November.

The story of Egypt is longer and its surrender was later, — due also to force, not to starvation. An army powerful enough to hold in submission and reap the use of the fertile valley of the Nile, could never be reduced like the port of a rocky island, blocked by sea and surrounded by a people in successful insurrection. Nevertheless, the same cause that determined the loss of Malta operated effectually to make Egypt a worse than barren possession.

Bonaparte, though wielding uncontrolled sway over all the resources of France, found as great difficulty in getting news from his conquest or substantial succor to it as he had had, when in Egypt, to obtain intelligence from home. Unwearying official effort and lavish inducements to private enterprise alike proved vain. In the first week of September, 1800, the return of the "Osiris," a dispatch-boat that had successfully made the round voyage between France and Egypt, was rewarded by a gift of three thousand dollars to the captain and two months' pay to the crew. This extravagant recompense sufficiently testifies the difficulty of the feat; and over seven weeks later, on October 29, Bonaparte writes to Menou, "We have no direct news of you since the arrival of the 'Osiris.'" This letter was to be entrusted to Admiral Ganteaume; but three months elapsed before that officer was enabled by a violent gale to evade the British blockade of Brest. Appeals were made to Spain, and government agents sent throughout the south of France, as well as to Corsica, to Genoa, to Leghorn, to the

Adriatic, to Taranto, when Italy after Marengo again fell under Bonaparte's control. Numerous small vessels, both neutral and friendly, were from every quarter to start for Egypt, if by chance some of them might reach their destination; but no substantial result followed. For the most part they only swelled the list of captures, and attested the absolute control of the sea by Great Britain.

Kleber, the illustrious general to whom Bonaparte left the burden he himself dropped, in a letter which fell into the hands of the British, addressed to the Directory the following words:[1] "I know all the importance of the possession of Egypt. I used to say in Europe that this country was for France the fulcrum, by means of which she might move at will the commercial system of every quarter of the globe; but to do this effectually, a powerful lever is required, and that lever is a Navy. Ours has ceased to exist. Since that period everything has changed; and peace with the Porte is, in my opinion, the only expedient that holds out to us a method of fairly getting rid of an enterprise no longer capable of attaining the object for which it was undertaken."[2] In other words, the French force of admirable and veteran soldiers in Egypt was uselessly locked up there; being unable either to escape or to receive re-enforcement, they were lost to their country. So thought Nelson, who frequently declared in his own vehement fashion that not one should with his consent return to Europe, and who gave to Sir Sidney Smith most positive orders on no account to allow a single Frenchman to leave Egypt under passports.[3] So thought Bonaparte, despite the censure which he and his undiscriminating supporters have seen fit to pass upon Kleber. Six weeks before he sailed for Europe[4] he wrote to the

[1] Naval Chronicle, vol. iii. p. 149.
[2] Napoleon's Commentaries give Sept. 26, 1799, as the date of this letter, —only a month after Bonaparte sailed. (Vol. iii. p. 183.)
[3] Nels. Disp. vol. iii. p. 296.
[4] June 28, 1799. Corr. de Nap. vol. v. p. 622.

Directory: "We need at least six thousand men to replace our losses since landing in Egypt.... With fifteen thousand re-enforcements we could go to Constantinople. We should need, then, two thousand cavalry, six thousand recruits for the regiments now here; five hundred artillerists; five hundred mechanics (carpenters, masons, etc.); five demi-brigades of two thousand men each; twenty thousand muskets, forty thousand bayonets, etc. etc. *If you cannot send us all this assistance it will be necessary to make peace;* for, between this and next June, we may expect to lose another six thousand men."[1] But how was this help to be sent when the sea was securely closed?

Bonaparte and Kleber held essentially the same view of the situation; but the one was interested, like a bankrupt, in concealing the state of affairs, the other was not. Kleber therefore gladly closed with a proposition, made by the Turks under the countenance of Sir Sidney Smith, who still remained in the Levant, by which the French were to be permitted to evacuate Egypt and to be carried to France; Turkey furnishing such transports as were needed beyond those already in Alexandria. A convention to this effect was signed at El Arish on the 24th of January, 1800, by commissioners representing Kleber on the one hand and the commander-in-chief of the Turks on the other. The French army would thus be restored to France, under no obligations that would prevent its at once entering the field against the allies of Great Britain and Turkey. Sir Sidney Smith did not sign; but it appears from his letter of March 8, 1800,[2] to M. Poussielgue, one of Kleber's commissioners, that he was perfectly cognizant of and approv-

---

[1] At the same time he made requisitions for clothing for double the number of men actually in Egypt, notifying the officers concerned that he did so to deceive Europe as to the strength of the army. Corr. de Nap. vol. v. p. 721. This has a significant bearing on the charges, made by him against Kleber, of exaggerating his weakness.

[2] Annual Register, 1800; State Papers, p. 225. It may be added the commissioners first met on board Smith's ship.

ing the terms of an agreement in direct contravention of the treaty of alliance between Turkey and Great Britain, and containing an article (the eleventh) engaging his government to issue the passports and safe conducts for the return of the French,[1] which depended absolutely upon its control of the sea, and which his own orders from his superiors explicitly forbade.

The British government had meantime instructed Lord Keith that the French should not be allowed to leave Egypt, except as prisoners of war. On the 8th of January, over a fortnight before the convention of El Arish was signed, the admiral wrote from Port Mahon to notify Smith of these directions, which were identical in spirit with those he already had from Nelson. With this letter he enclosed one to Kleber, " to be made use of if circumstances should so require." This letter, cast in the peremptory tone probably needed to repress Smith, informed Kleber curtly that he had " received positive orders not to consent to any capitulation of the French troops, unless they should lay down their arms, surrender themselves prisoners of war, and deliver up the ships and stores in Alexandria." Even in this event they were not to be permitted to return to France until exchanged. The admiral added that any vessel with French troops on board, having passports " from others than those authorized to grant them," would be forced by British cruisers to return to Alexandria.[2] Smith, knowing that he had exceeded his authority, had nothing to do in face of this communication but to transmit the letters apologetically to Kleber, expressing the hope that the engagement allowed by him would ultimately be sustained. In this he was not deceived. The British cabinet, learning that Kleber had executed an essential part of his own agreements, under the impression that Smith had authority

---

[1] For the convention of El Arish, see Annual Register, 1800, State Papers, p. 217.

[2] Allardyce's Life of Lord Keith, pp. 226, 227.

to pledge his government, sent other instructions to Keith, authorizing the carrying out of the convention while expressly denying Smith's right to accede to it. Owing to the length of time required in that age for these communications to pass back and forth, such action had been taken by Kleber, before these new instructions were received, that the convention never became operative. The French occupation lingered on. Kleber, being assassinated on the 14th of June, 1800, was succeeded by Menou, an incapable man; and in March, 1801, a British army under General Abercromby landed in Aboukir Bay. Abercromby was mortally wounded on the 21st, at the battle of Alexandria; but his successor was equal to the task before him, and in September, 1801, shortly before the preliminaries of peace with Great Britain were signed, the last of the French quitted Egypt.

The terms under which the evacuation was made were much the same as those granted at El Arish; but circumstances had very greatly changed. The battle of Marengo, June 14, 1800, and the treaty of Lunéville, February 9, 1801, had restored peace to the Continent; the French troops would not now re-enforce an enemy to the allies of Great Britain. Not only so, but since the power of Austria had been broken, Great Britain herself was intending a peace, to which the policy of Bonaparte at that time pointed. It was therefore important to her that in the negotiations the possession of Egypt, however barren, should not be one of the cards in the adversary's hand. No terms were then too easy, provided they insured the immediate departure of the French army.

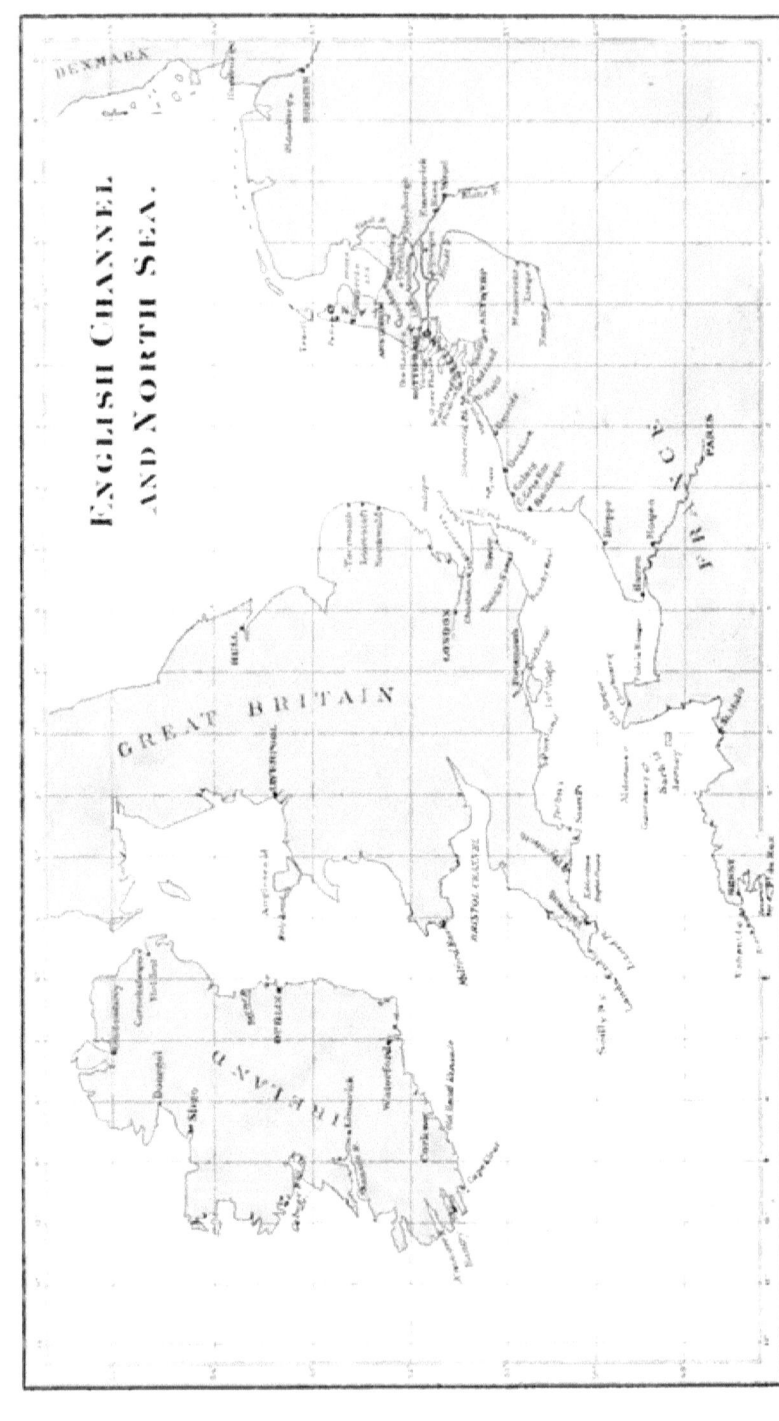

CHAPTER XI.

THE ATLANTIC, 1796–1801.—THE BREST BLOCKADES.—THE FRENCH EXPEDITIONS AGAINST IRELAND.

THE decision taken by the French executive in the latter part of 1795,—after the disastrous partial encounters of Martin with Hotham in the Mediterranean and of Villaret Joyeuse with Bridport in the Bay of Biscay,— to discontinue sending large fleets to sea, and to rely upon commerce-destroying, by single cruisers or small squadrons, to reduce the strength of Great Britain, remained unchanged during the following years, and was adopted by Bonaparte when the Consular government, in 1799, succeeded that of the Directory. This policy was in strict accord with the general feeling of the French nation, as well naval officers as unprofessional men, by which the action of the navy was ever subordinated to other military considerations, to "ulterior objects," as the phrase commonly ran,—a feeling that could not fail to find favor and expression in the views of the great director of armies who ruled France during the first fourteen years of this century. It amounted, however, simply to abandoning all attempt to control the sea. Consequently, whenever any enterprise was undertaken which required this to be crossed, resort was necessarily had to evasion, more or less skilfully contrived; and success depended, not upon the reasonable certainty conferred by command of the water, by the skilful massing of forces, but upon a balance of chances, which might be more or less favorable in the particular instance, but could never be regarded as reaching the degree of security which is essential, even in the hazardous combinations of the game of war. This formal relegation of the navy to a wholly inferior place in the contest then raging, was followed, under the embarrassments of the treasury, by a neglect of the material of war, of the ships and their equipments, which left France still at Great Britain's mercy, even when in 1797 and 1798 her Continental enemies had been shaken off by the audacity and address of Bonaparte.

Thrice only, therefore, during the six years in question, ending with the Peace of Amiens in 1802, did large French fleets put to sea ; and on each occasion their success was made to depend upon the absence of the British fleets, or upon baffling their vigilance. As in commerce-destroying, stealth and craft, not force, were the potent factors. Of the three efforts, two, Bonaparte's Egyptian expedition and Bruix's escape from Brest in 1799, have been already narrated under the head of the Mediterranean, to which they chiefly — the former wholly — belong. The third was the expedition against Ireland, under the command of Hoche, to convoy which seventeen ships-of-the-line and twenty smaller vessels sailed from Brest in the last days of 1796.

The operations in the Atlantic during this period were accordingly, with few exceptions, reduced to the destruction of commerce, to the harassment of the enemy's communications on the sea, and, on the part of the British, to an observation, more or less vigilant, of the proceedings in the enemy's naval ports, of which Brest was the most important. From the maritime conditions of the two chief belligerents, the character of their undertakings differed. British commerce covered every sea and drew upon all quarters of the world ; consequently French cruisers could go in many directions upon the well known commercial routes, with good hope of taking prizes, if not themselves captured. British cruisers, on the other hand, could find

French merchant vessels only on their own coast, for the
foreign traffic of France in ships of her own was destroyed;
but the coasting trade, carried on in vessels generally of
from thirty to a hundred tons, was large, and in the maritime provinces took in great measure the place of land carriage. The neutrals who maintained such foreign trade as
was left to the enemies of Great Britain, and who were
often liable to detention from some infraction, conscious or
unconscious, of the rules of international law, were naturally to be found in greatest numbers in the neighborhood
of the coasts to which they were bound. Finally, the larger
proportion of French privateers were small vessels, intended to remain but a short time at sea and to cruise in the
Channel or among its approaches, where British shipping
most abounded. For all these reasons the British provided
for the safety of their distant commerce by concentrating
it in large bodies called convoys, each under the protection
of several ships of war; while their scattered cruisers were
distributed most thickly near home, — in the English Channel, between the south coast of Ireland and Ushant, in the
waters of the bay of Biscay, and along the coasts of Spain
and Portugal. There they were constantly at hand to repress commerce-destroying, to protect or recapture their
own merchantmen, and to reduce the coasting trade of the
enemy, as well as the ability of his merchants to carry on,
under a neutral flag, the operations no longer open to their
own. The annals of the time are consequently filled, not
with naval battles, but with notes of vessels taken and
retaken; of convoys, stealing along the coast of France,
chased, harassed and driven ashore, by the omnipresent
cruisers of the enemy. Nor was it commerce alone that
was thus injured. The supplying of the naval ports, even
with French products, chiefly depended upon the coasting
vessels; and embarrassment, amounting often to disability,
was constantly entailed by the unflagging industry of the
hostile ships, whose action resembled that which is told of

the Spanish guerillas, upon the convoys and communications of the French armies in the Peninsular War.[1]

The watch over the enemy's ports, and particularly over the great and difficult port of Brest, was not, during the earlier and longer part of this period, maintained with the diligence nor with the force becoming a great military undertaking, by which means alone such an effort can be made effective in checking the combinations of an active opponent. Some palliation for this slack service may perhaps be found in the knowledge possessed by the admiralty of the condition of the French fleet and of the purposes of the French government, some also in the well-known opinions of that once active officer, Lord Howe; but even these circumstances can hardly be considered more than a palliation for a system essentially bad. The difficulties were certainly great, the service unusually arduous, and it was doubtless true that the closest watch could not claim a perfect immunity from evasion; but from what human efforts can absolute certainty of results be predicted? and above all, in war? The essential feature of the military problem, by which Great Britain was confronted, was that the hos-

---

[1] "At the theatre last night I had a conversation with General Kilmaine [commanding the division intended to send into Ireland]. He told me . . . the arsenals at Brest are empty; and what stores they have in other ports they cannot convey thither, from the superiority of the naval force of the enemy, which kept everything blocked up." (Wolf Tone's Journal, June 16, 1798.) In 1801 "the port of Brest lacked provisions. The difficulty of getting the convoys into it decided the First Consul to break up the fleet there and send part to Rochefort . . . The Spanish admiral (who had come there with Bruix in 1799) was invited to escort the division. To equip the necessary ships, this officer had to give them equipments taken from the others of his squadron, and could obtain provisions only for seventeen days. Baffled by the winds and by the constant presence of the enemy, the ships did not sail." A combined expedition against the Cape of Good Hope failed for the same reason. "The blockade of the Dutch ports was no less rigorous than that of the coast of France." "At Brest, they lived from day to day. Villaret Joyeuse was ordered to go out with ten French and ten Spanish ships to support the entry of convoys. He did not go, and received another mission." (Troude, Batailles Navales, vol. iii. p. 222.)

tile fleets were divided, by the necessities of their administration, among several ports. To use these scattered divisions successfully against her mighty sea power, it was needed to combine two or more of them in one large body. To prevent such a combination was therefore the momentous duty of the British fleet; and in no manner could this be so thoroughly carried out as by a close and diligent watch before the hostile arsenals, — not in the vain hope that no squadron could ever, by any means, slip out, but with the reasonable probability that at no one period could so many escape as to form a combination threatening the Empire with a crushing disaster. Of these arsenals Brest, by its situation and development, was the most important, and contained usually the largest and most efficient of the masses into which the enemies' fleets were divided. The watch over it, therefore, was of supreme consequence; and in the most serious naval crisis of the Napoleonic wars the Brest " blockading " fleet, as it was loosely but inaccurately styled, by the firmness of its grip broke up completely one of the greatest of Napoleon's combinations. To it, and to its admiral, Cornwallis, was in large measure due that the vast schemes which should have culminated in the invasion of England, by one hundred and fifty thousand of the soldiers who fought at Austerlitz and Jena, terminated instead in the disaster of Trafalgar. Yet it may be said that had there prevailed in 1805 the system with which the names of Howe and Bridport are identified, and which was countenanced by the Admiralty until the stern Earl St. Vincent took command, the chances are the French Brest fleet would have taken its place in the great strategic plan of the Emperor.

This far-reaching combination, so tremendous in its risks and in its issues that men have doubted, and always will doubt, whether Napoleon seriously meant to carry it through, was but the supreme example of the dangers to which Great Britain was exposed, and from which her fleets had to shield her. It was aimed, with the true insight of genius, directly at her heart ; and except from occasional assertions of the emperor, whose words can never be implicitly believed, there is really little cause for doubt that he was prepared to take many chances of ruin in order to execute an enterprise which, both in conception and details, was so clearly stamped with the characteristics of his intellect and temperament. But the widely scattered dominions of Great Britain offered many points, besides the British islands themselves, to the blows of an enemy ; and her navy had to protect not merely the heart but the extremities, each and all of which were threatened, in proportion to their value and their means of resistance, when a hostile squadron was loose upon the sea. How, then, should this service be performed ? By dividing the fleet among the points threatened, and establishing the line of defence close before the region to be defended ? Not so should the true maxim, that the British navy was the first line of defence, have been interpreted. As in all military campaigns, the front of operations of a powerful fleet should be pushed as far towards the enemy as is consistent with the mutual support of the various detachments, and with secure communication with their base. By so doing, not only are the great national interests placed more remote from the alarms of war, but the use of the region behind the front of operations, in this case the sea, is secured to the power that can afford to maintain its fighting line close to the enemy's positions.

Not merely to check great combinations threatening great disasters, but to protect as far as possible minor but important interests, and for the security of commerce itself, the true station for the British fleets, superior in temper if not in numbers to the enemy, was before the hostile ports and as close to them as might be. There, though their function was defensive, as in the last analysis that of the British Empire also was, they were ever ready, did opportunity offer, to assume the offensive. "Every opportunity will be given to the Toulon squadron to put to sea," wrote Nelson, "for it is on the sea that we hope to realize the expectations of our country," — a hope which it was given him to fulfil at Trafalgar, where the greater designs of Napoleon were forever crushed. This hope of Nelson's was, however, based upon a close watch of his port, to establish which by constant cruising before it he avowed his purpose;[1] and the enforced abandonment of this plan, from the crazy condition of several of his ships, was the first cause of the perplexities which pursued him through the campaign. Did an enemy's division escape, as from Toulon and at other times, the general policy was not invalidated by such occasional failure. The first line of defence had been pierced at a single point; there still remained the other lines, the fortified ports and the soldiers behind them, or, in a maritime region like the West Indies, a detachment of ships more or less adequate to contest the ground until re-enforced.

A wisely co-ordinated system of defence does not contemplate that every point is to hold out indefinitely, but only for such time as may be necessary for it to receive the support which the other parts of the whole are intended to supply. That the navy is the first line of defence, both in order and in importance, by no means implies that there is or should be no other. This forced and extravagant interpretation, for which naval officers have been largely responsible, of the true opinion that a navy is the best protection for a sea frontier, has very much to do with that faulty strategy which would tie the fleet, whatever its power, to the home ports, and disseminate it among them. Navies do not dispense with fortifications nor with armies; but when wisely handled, they may save their country the strain which comes when these have to be called into play, — when war, once remote, now thunders at the gates, and

[1] Nelson's Disp., vol. v pp 300, 306, 411, 498.

the sea, the mother of prosperity, is shut off. This kindly office did British seamen for Great Britain in the days of Napoleon, and mainly through those close blockades of which St. Vincent set the pattern before Toulon in the Mediterranean,[1] and afterwards before Brest, when he took command of the Channel fleet.

The port of Brest, regarded as the principal hostile arsenal round which must centre the operations of a great part of the British navy, has to be considered under two sets of conditions: 1st, as to its position, relatively to the British bases of operations and to points of British territory open to attack; 2d, as to its own immediate surroundings, how far they facilitated the action of the French navy, and what dispositions of the British fleet were necessary in order best to impede that action. The former question is strategic in its character, the latter tactical.

At the end of the peninsula which forms the northwestern extremity of France, there is a deep recess in the land, between two capes which lie nearly in the same north and south line, and are called Pointe St. Mathieu and Pointe du Raz. The former is the more northerly, and the distance separating the two is seventeen miles. A promontory making out from the bottom of the recess divides it into two bays of unequal dimensions, of which the southern is known as the Bay of Douarnenez and the northern as that of Brest. The entrance to the former is five miles wide and unobstructed, so that only partial shelter is obtained; it gives, however, a safe though rough anchorage, even in westerly gales. The Bay of Brest, of smaller surface, is entered by a passage three miles long and only one wide, called the Goulet. With such an approach, and further favored by the configuration of the surrounding land, perfect security is found there, as well as facility for carrying on the work of a fleet, when it would be impossible at the more exposed anchorage of Douarnenez.

[1] See ante, p. 212.

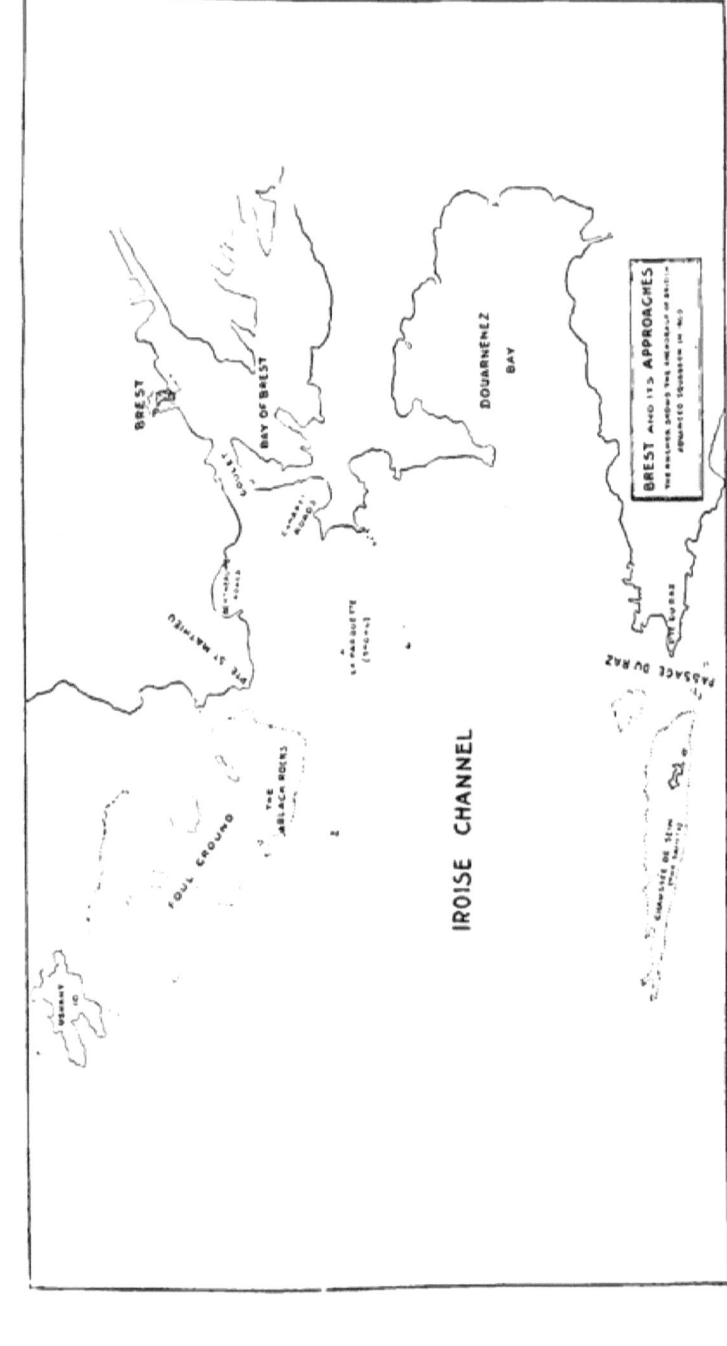

From the Goulet to Pointe St. Mathieu the distance is seven miles; and immediately outside the former are two open roadsteads, Bertheaume to the north and Camaret to the south, frequently occupied by French ships prior to a final start on an expedition, or when waiting for a wind.

Had these features constituted the whole of the hydrographic surroundings of Brest Harbor, the task of a British admiral would have been simpler. A singular combination of dangers conspired to force him, even in favorable weather, to a station much further from the coast, and at the same time tended to facilitate the exit of the French. From both Pointe St. Mathieu and Pointe du Raz a strip of foul ground, comparatively narrow, extends for fifteen miles directly out to sea. That from St. Mathieu trends west-northwest and terminates in the island of Ushant;[1] while from Pointe du Raz a succession of reefs, shoals, and low islands, the whole known as the Chaussée de Sein, stretches nearly due west to a point due south of Ushant and distant from it twenty-two miles. Between these two long, low barriers lay the principal approach to Brest, the Iroise Channel, — fifteen miles long and of a width varying from seventeen to twenty-two, nearly double that of the Straits of Gibraltar, — in which it was not possible to maintain a body of heavy vessels, particularly the three-decked ships, of ninety guns and over, which formed a large fraction of the Channel fleet and were singularly wanting in weatherly qualities. Their short, high hulls and heavy top-hamper caused them to drift rapidly in bad weather; and they needed plenty of open sea to leeward for this reason, and also that they might run before the wind, if too violent. To try to keep these formidable but unhandy vessels in the Iroise during the heavy westerly gales which prevail in the

---

[1] There is between Ushant and the reefs a narrow passage, practicable for ships-of-the-line, which was surveyed under Lord St. Vincent; but it could only be used with pilots, and was rather a convenience than an important feature.

Bay of Biscay,[1] with no refuge from the sea save the enemy's port under their lee, was to court destruction.

To keep the English Channel open in case of very heavy weather was therefore essential to the British fleet. The Island of Ushant, as favoring this object and also as a conspicuous, easily recognized off-shore position, became the strategic centre around which the movements of the main body of the fleet revolved, and to which all dispositions made to ensure the watching of Brest must have regard, as to their natural point of reference.

Given the superiority of force which the British navy usually possessed, a superiority none too great to bear the tremendous strain imposed by the dangerous weather and coasts it had to encounter, the supreme strategic factor was the wind. Brest is farther west than any English Channel port except Falmouth, which is on the meridian of Ushant. Falmouth, however, did not stand well as a port in the general naval opinion of the day, though it had warm advocates;[2] and it was undoubtedly wanting in room for a number of heavy ships to anchor together. East of Falmouth there were available the anchorages of Plymouth, Torbay, and Spithead, distant from Ushant respectively 120, 135, and 210 miles, Falmouth being only 100; but with the exception of Spithead, they were not secure in all winds.

---

[1] In the English Channel and the neighboring western coasts of Europe, winds from S.W. to N.W. prevail during three fourths of the days of the year, and are often exceedingly violent.

[2] See "Twelve letters to the Rt. Hon. Spencer Perceval," by Capt. James Manderson, 1812; in which it is also said that Mr. Pitt was towards the end of his life much impressed with the advantages of Falmouth's position. To this opinion is probably due the following statement in a magazine of the day, during Pitt's short second administration: "It is now (Feb. 1805) determined that the Channel fleet shall in future rendezvous at Falmouth, and moorings are immediately to be laid down for fifteen sail-of-the-line." (Nav. Chron., vol. xiii. p. 328.) Lord Exmouth seems to have shared this opinion. (Life, p. 140.) While Falmouth was by position admirably suited for a rendezvous, ships running for refuge to Torbay would have the wind three points more free, an advantage seamen will appreciate.

Plymouth Sound was exposed to the point of danger in south-west gales. Torbay, though safe in westerly weather, was at times dangerous, as well as difficult to leave, in the southeasterly storms, which were, however, exceptional.

Spithead was secure, and was moreover the roadstead of a great naval arsenal, as was also Plymouth Sound; but its distance, a hundred miles east of Torbay, with the wind prevailing three-fourths of the time from the westward, should have been considered an insuperable strategic objection to sailing ships destined to watch Brest, and especially to fleets. A sailing ship of fair qualities, proceeding against a dead head wind, makes good only one third of the distance she actually sails. With such a wind a port one hundred miles distant is actually three hundred, and with fleets progress is even slower. To this was added at Spithead a difficulty seemingly trivial, yet so insuperable as to be humiliating. With a south-east wind, favorable to go down Channel, three-decked ships could not get from the anchorage to St. Helen's (the outer roads only three miles distant), whence they could sail with a fair wind.

The whole theory of the blockade of Brest rested on the fact that the French fleet could not sail in such westerly weather as forced the British to take refuge in port,[1] and upon the expectation that the latter by diligence could regain their station with the first of the east wind, in time to prevent the enemy's escape. This expectation depended upon the greater rapidity of the British movements and consequently upon the distance of the point of refuge. For this reason Spithead was singularly unfit to be the rendezvous of the fleet; yet it was chosen and maintained by both Howe and Bridport during the seven years of their consecutive commands. To this they added the practice of keeping the main body of the fleet in port during the winter months.

---

[1] With the wind to the southward of south-east we know full well that no ship-of-the-line can get out of Brest. — *Letter of St. Vincent;* Tucker's Life, vol. ii. p. 119.

The Admiralty, doubtless, was ultimately responsible; but, even with the sharp lessons of the Irish expedition and Bruix's escape, it needed the advent of an admiral of St. Vincent's sagacity and temper to insure the adoption of a more rational and vigorous system. In his words to the second in command, — when the wild winter weather and his own declining years compelled him to withdraw from the flag-ship, — "You are on *no* account to authorize any ships to go to Spithead, unless you receive special orders from the Admiralty or from me,"[1] is summed up the simple, yet fundamental, difference between his policy and that of his predecessors. All his other careful arrangements to expedite the refitting of ships, and prolong their stay on the station, are but detailed instances of the same effort to save time, to keep his fleet concentrated at the decisive point, and in the largest mass possible.

After Howe finally retired from the command, Bridport established his headquarters at Spithead, where during the winter and early spring the main body of the fleet was commonly assembled. The commander-in-chief seems himself to have lived ashore, being in April, 1796, created general port-admiral with liberal appointments. Squadrons of seven or eight ships-of-the-line, about a fourth of the total force, cruised to the westward of Ushant, "in the soundings," during the winter, for periods of two or three months, returning to Spithead when relieved. Thus was practically realized Lord Howe's policy, to economize the ships and depend upon vessels kept in good order by staying in port to follow the French, when information of their sailing was received. This also was the general plan at the time of the French expedition against Ireland in the winter of 1796–1797.

The widespread discontent in Ireland, especially in the Protestant North, was well known to the Directory, with which, through the French minister at Hamburg, Irish

[1] Tucker's Life of Earl St. Vincent, vol. ii. p. 14.

agents had been in communication as early as April, 1796. Another, the somewhat celebrated Wolfe Tone, had in the first months of the year arrived in Paris from the United States with a similar mission. To their efforts was added the powerful influence of General Hoche, who had in other fields of action shown military ability of the highest order; and who, having established his claims upon the gratitude of his country by the pacification of La Vendée and Brittany, was now in command of the army in that quarter. In all directions circumstances seemed favorable. Bonaparte was in the midst of his great Italian successes; and the reverses inflicted upon Jourdan and Moreau in Germany by the Archduke Charles were neutralized, for the winter at least, by the necessity of drawing upon his troops to renew the Austrian armies in Italy. Spain had declared war against Great Britain; and there were hopes, destined to be frustrated by the lethargy of her movements and by the battle of Cape St. Vincent, that the Spanish fleet could be made to combine with the French for the purposed invasion. The mission of Lord Malmesbury, although the British government held its head high, seemed to indicate failing confidence; and the British navy, however successful in seizing the colonial possessions of its enemies in all parts of the world, had been unable, through the retirement of the French fleets from the sea, to win any of those brilliant victories which restore the courage of nations. St. Vincent, Camperdown, and the Nile were still in the future.

The proposed invasion was consequently resolved. It depended avowedly upon the co-operation of the disaffected inhabitants; but Hoche did not make the mistake of trusting to them for the most serious part of the work. No less than twenty thousand troops were to be embarked; and as the general recognized that the difficulties would by no means be over when Ireland was reached, — that the British navy, if successfully eluded by the expedition, would nevertheless seriously interfere with subsequent supplies, — he insisted upon carrying with him as much of these, and consequently as many ships, as could be had in Brest. Efforts were made to increase the force in that port. Five ships under Admiral Villeneuve were ordered round from Toulon;[1] Richery's squadron was expected from North America,[2] and the Spaniards were also called upon. These efforts, however, only caused delay, and contributed but two of Richery's ships to swell the expedition, the others being found too shaken to be sent at once to sea. Villeneuve did not arrive in time, and the Spaniards remained in the Mediterranean.

The number of seamen at the disposal of the government was limited, owing to many causes; among which the principal were discontent with the navy, and the superior attractions of privateering, which had led not merely to their choosing that service, but also to many being captured at sea and so lost to their country. This deficiency imposed a proportionate limit to the number of ships that could be fitted. There was a dearth likewise of good watch officers. Besides these controlling circumstances, there were also some manifest advantages in reducing to the smallest numbers the vessels composing an expedition, which was to avoid action, to make a short passage at the stormiest season of the year, and which it was all important should keep united and arrive together. For these reasons it was decided that the troops should be embarked on the ships-of-war to their fullest capacity. Each ship-of-the-line carried six hundred soldiers, making with her crew a ship's company of thirteen hundred souls. The frigates received about two hundred and fifty each. Although in this particular instance the arguments in favor of transporting the army in the ships-of-war outweighed those against, there is always a grave disadvantage to the handling and fighting of vessels encumbered by so many useless and generally sea-sick men.

[1] See ante, p. 220.   [2] See ante, pp. 202, 214.

Never, however, was a great expedition, destined to encounter extraordinary risks and to brave one of the stormiest of seas, more favored than this at the first was by the elements and by the mismanagement of its enemies. For nearly six weeks before it sailed the winds prevailed from the east; and during the passage, in midwinter, fine weather with favorable winds lasted until the bulk of the fleet reached the Irish coast. Nor was an enemy's vessel met, to take advantage of the crowded and inefficient condition of the French ships. Like Bonaparte's expedition to Egypt, though from other causes, Hoche's ships passed to their destination unseen by any foe powerful enough to molest. To the enfeebled state of the French navy, to the decay of its material, to the want of seamen, to the disappearance of the trained officers, and to the consequent disinclination of the superiors to undertake the expedition, is to be attributed the failure of an attempt in which their sympathies had never been enlisted. Hoche, who had supreme command of both army and navy,[1] found by bitter experience the delays which incompetent or ill-affected subordinates can impose, especially in a branch of service of which the commander-in-chief has not particular knowledge. Villaret Joyeuse, first appointed to command the fleet, being keenly aware of its defects, was averse from an enterprise which, in all reasonable probability, would lead to a meeting at once with the British and with excessively bad weather. He wished, as did also Truguet, the Minister of Marine, to take a heavy squadron of eight ships to India; whereby, if the first encounter with the enemy were evaded, a long passage with much good weather would permit the crews to be trained, while in the Indian seas they would be superior in force to their opponents. Truguet, however, harmonized this object with the proposed expedition by purposing to send the ships to India after their return from Ireland; while Villaret, who had spent in the ports the

---

[1] Chevalier, Mar. Fran. sous la Rép., p. 265.

years which the minister had passed in Paris, and knew intimately the deplorable state of both men and ships, had little hope of the latter coming back in any state to undertake his favorite project.

The hardly concealed bias of the admiral, and the apathy of the naval officers generally, inspired Hoche with doubts of Villaret's faithfulness to his task; and upon his urgent remonstrance Morard de Galles, who fifteen years before had been like Villaret among the bravest captains of the great Suffren, succeeded to the command. The new admiral brought to his duty the submissive devotion of a military man, and had not, as Villaret had, any counter-project of his own; but the radical defects of an organization, vitiated by years of neglect and false standards, could not be overcome by a man already advanced in years in the few short days of hurried preparation. Such as the French navy had become, through the loss of its heads and the vagaries of the legislature, such it sailed on the expedition to Ireland. "God keep me from having anything to do with the navy!" wrote Hoche. "What an extravagant compound! A great body whose parts are disunited and incoherent: contradictions of all kinds, indiscipline organized in a military body. Add to that, haughty ignorance and foolish vanity, and you have the picture filled out. Poor Morard de Galles! he has already aged twenty years; how I pity him!"[1]

The administrative difficulties, caused by poverty of resources, conspired with the non-arrival of Richery and Villeneuve to delay the expedition. Fixed first for the early autumn and then for the first of November, it was not able to sail till the middle of December. Richery had reached the anchorage of Île d'Aix[2] on the 5th of November with five ships-of-the-line; but not till the 8th of the following month could his vessels, racked by their long cruise, sail for Brest. On the 11th they entered the port,

---

[1] Rousselin's "Vie de Hoche," quoted by Troude, Bat. Nav., vol. iii. p. 6.
[2] Before Rochefort.

where upon examination two only of them were found fit for the Irish voyage; and the wait for these entailed a delay which had a singular effect upon the fortunes of the undertaking.

On the 15th of December the whole body of ships, except Richery's two, got under way, stood through the Goulet, and anchored that evening in Bertheaume and Camaret roads, ready for a start, — the wind still fair as fair could be, at east. The British, under the lax and cautious system pursued by Bridport and his lieutenants, had then no ships-of-the-line close up to the port, but only two or three frigates, and these Morard de Galles drove off with a small detached squadron, hoping thus to deprive the enemy of precise knowledge of his movements. Sir Edward Pellew, the senior officer of the frigates, sent one of them, the "Phœbe," to Admiral Colpoys, commanding the division of Bridport's fleet then cruising; which, in consequence of the preparations known to be going on in Brest, had been increased to fifteen sail-of-the-line, double the usual winter squadron. Contrary to Lord St. Vincent's sound maxim, "Well up with Ushant in an easterly wind," Colpoys's rendezvous was about eight leagues to the west of the island, and thither the frigate went to seek him; but his force, composed largely of three-deckers, having let go the shelter of the land, had been driven farther still to leeward, and being nearly fifty miles from Ushant was not found by the "Phœbe" till the 19th, three days after the French finally sailed.

Pellew, one of the most active frigate captains of the time, retired but a short distance from his pursuers, and next day, the 16th, again stood in for the French anchorage with his own ship, — well named the "Indefatigable," — and the "Révolutionnaire." At noon the enemy were again sighted, and not long after, Pellew's vigilance was rewarded by seeing them get under way. Richery's two ships, "Pégase" and "Révolution," came through the Goulet towards noon, and all the expedition began at once to lift their anchors between two and three P. M. of the short winter day. Dispatching the "Révolutionnaire" to the admiral, Pellew himself remained to watch the course taken by the enemy.

The imperative need of the French being to escape meeting the British, and to reach Ireland with force undiminished either by capture or straggling, Morard de Galles' first object was to avoid Colpoys's fleet. This was known to be in the direction of Ushant, having been seen on more than one occasion from the island, and by Richery when entering Brest. If the departure were unperceived, the uncertainty of the enemy as to the destination might be counted on to favor the further movements of the expedition. The French admiral therefore determined to use the advantage, inestimable to a naval port, which Brest possesses in a double entrance. Between the Pointe du Raz and the Chaussée de Sein [1] there is a channel known as the Passage du Raz. It is narrow, being less than three miles wide in one part, and is sown with dangers, formidable above all in the night season, during which it must be passed if the enemy were to be kept in ignorance; but with a fair wind and good pilots the thing could be done. Morard de Galles therefore gave the order to the fleet to head, upon getting under way, for the Passage du Raz, and informed the captains that, after clearing it, he intended to steer west for one hundred miles. Having provided for keeping the fleet together so far, each commanding officer was also given a sealed packet, directing him what to do in case of separation. It may be said here that these packets, — which were not to be opened unless in case of parting company, — directed to make Cape Mizen Head on the south coast of Ireland, near the entrance of Bantry Bay, the anchorage whence the landing was to be made. There the separated vessels were to cruise five days, waiting for orders.

[1] See map of Brest, p. 343.

At three o'clock the whole fleet was under sail, the sun was sinking fast, the weather gloomy and squally; and the vessels, unable to form from the inexperience of their officers, were running disorderly for the dangerous pass, the entrance to which, being fifteen miles from the anchorage they were leaving, could not be reached before dark. The flag-officers, except Richery, had quitted their own ships-of-the-line and gone aboard frigates, the two commanders, Hoche and Morard de Galles, being together on board the "Fraternité." As night fell, the wind hauled to the southward, threatening to become foul, under which conditions the passage of the Raz would be impossible. Moved by the danger, and considering that Colpoys was not within sight, the admiral by signal countermanded his order, and directed the fleet to put before the wind and run out by the Iroise channel. In the confusion and growing darkness this order was not understood. Morard's own ship and half a dozen more, one only of which was of the line, obeyed; but all the others continued for the Passage du Raz. Thus, at the very moment of starting, the two principal officers were separated from their command. In vain did Morard send a corvette to enforce his order by voice or by signal, — she was not understood; and the confusion was increased by Pellew, who, attaching himself to the leading ships, kept on with them through the Iroise, and by burning rockets and blue lights, and firing guns, rendered utterly incoherent the attempts of the French admiral to convey by similar means his meaning to his fleet.[1] In the midst of the turmoil the "Séduisant," of seventy-four guns, ran on a rock which lies across the entrance to the passage, and was totally wrecked, her guns and signals of distress adding to the uproar.[2] At half-past

---

[1] In performing this audacious service Pellew was somewhat favored by the fact that his ship was a French prize, easily mistaken for one of the expedition. He kept close, often within half gun-shot of the leading ship.

[2] The greater part of the "Séduisant's" crew was saved.

eight, the "Indefatigable" saw the ships with which she had kept company pass round the outer end of the Chaussée de Sein and steer to the southward, with the hope, doubtless, of rejoining their consorts. Pellew then made sail for Falmouth, where he arrived on the 20th of December. Had this port then been the rendezvous of the Channel fleet, or even of a strong detachment, there would still have been time, for the French did not reach Bantry Bay till the 22d; the wind was east, and the distance but two hundred and fifty miles.

On the morning of the 17th of December, the French were divided into three bodies out of sight of each other. With the two commanders-in-chief were one ship-of-the-line and three frigates. Rear-Admiral Bouvet, the second in command, had with him eight ships-of-the-line and nine other vessels. In accordance with his orders he continued to steer west during the 17th and 18th. On the 19th, having opened his sealed instructions and reached the longitude of Mizen Head, he changed the course to north, and the same day was joined by the third section of the expedition, thus concentrating under his command fifteen ships-of-the-line, and, with three unimportant exceptions, all the other vessels except those with Hoche and Morard. Grouchy, second to Hoche, was with Bouvet; so that the admiral now had with him practically the whole body of the expedition. Unfortunately the soul, the young, gallant, and skilful Hoche, the emulous rival of Bonaparte's growing glory, who saw in the Irish expedition the great hope of restoring the brilliancy of his own star, paling before that of his competitor,— Hoche was absent.

With a brief exception of southwesterly weather, the wind continued from the eastward during the whole of Bouvet's passage; and notwithstanding a good deal of fog, at times very dense,[1] all those who were with him on

[1] "Fog so thick we cannot see a ship's length. Has been foggy all day." (Wolfe Tone's Journal, Dec. 18.) "The state of the weather was such that it

the 19th — thirty-five out of the forty-three which composed the expedition — found themselves on the early morning of December 21st together, and in full sight of the Irish coast. "It is most delicious weather," wrote the eager, restless Irishman, Wolfe Tone, who was on board one of the ships, "with a favorable wind and everything we can desire, except our missing comrades. At the moment I am writing we are under easy sail, within three leagues at most of the coast, so that I can discern patches of snow upon the mountains. What if the general do not join? If we cruise here five days according to our instructions, the English will be upon us and all will be over. *Nine o'clock* (P. M.). We are now at the rendezvous appointed; stood in for the coast till twelve (noon), when we were near enough to toss a biscuit ashore. At twelve tacked and stood out again, so we have now begun our cruise of five days in all its forms. . . . We opened Bantry Bay; and in all my life rage never entered so deep into my heart as when we turned our backs. Continue making short tacks; the wind foul."[1]

The wind was now foul, not because of its own change, but because from the entrance of Bantry Bay to its head the direction is east-north-east. The wind that had been favorable for leaving Brest and for the passage was for the short remaining distance, not over thirty miles at the most, nearly dead ahead. Unfortunately, also, in sailing north along the meridian of Bantry Bay, the east wind had set the fleet imperceptibly to the westward, so that the land first seen was not Mizen Head, at the eastern side of the entrance, but Dursey Island, at the western.[2] Had the intended landfall been made, the ships might, by hauling close round Mizen Head, have fetched a point at least twelve miles inside of Dursey Island and there an-

was impossible for Admiral Colpoys to keep his own fleet under observation, and the air so hazy that fog guns had continually to be fired." (Parliamentary Hist. xxxiii. p. 12. March 3, 1797.)

[1] Wolfe Tone's Journal, Dec. 21, 1796.
[2] James Nav. Hist. vol. ii. p. 7. Chevalier, Mar. Fran. sous la Rép. p. 281.

chored. Now that fortune ceased to waft them with favoring gales, the weaknesses of the expedition became painfully apparent. Crews composed mainly of landsmen, with a very small sprinkling of able seamen, crowded and impeded at every turn by the swarming mass of soldiery, were ill able to do the rapid handling of ropes and canvas necessitated by a dead beat of thirty miles, against a strong head wind in a narrow bay, where every rod lost tells, and requires three or four rods of sailing to be regained; where sails must be reefed or hoisted, set or furled, at a moment's notice, and the canvas spread varies from half-hour to half-hour. Such a tug tasks the skill, as it proclaims the excellence, of the smartest single ship, though she find the channel clear of other vessels; but to a fleet of thirty-five, manned and equipped as those of Bouvet, and compelled to give way continually as they crossed each other's paths, it proved impossible to reach the head of Bantry Bay, where shelter would have been found from the east winds, which for the following week blew with relentless fury.

Through the night of the 21st and all day of the 22d, the fleet continued turning to windward; and toward nightfall the admiral anchored with eight of-the-line and seven other vessels off Bear Island, still twelve miles from the head of the bay. The other twenty ships remained outside under way. All the 23d it blew hard from the eastward, and nothing was done. On the 24th the weather moderated, and it was decided to attempt a landing, although no more ships had come in, — the twenty outside having been blown to sea. Those at the anchorage got under way, but made no progress. "I believe," wrote the exasperated Wolfe Tone, "that we have made three hundred tacks, and have not gained a hundred yards in a straight line." At sunset the division again anchored; and during the night the wind rose to a gale, which continued all the 25th and prevented any boat work. Several ships dragged, and some cables parted. Soon after nightfall the cable of Bouvet's flag-ship gave way, and the "Immortalité" began to drive upon Bear Island. A second anchor failing to hold her, the admiral cut both cables and put to sea, signalling the other vessels to do likewise and hailing to the same effect those near whom he passed, among others the ship on board which Wolfe Tone was. This, however, held on — her captain becoming the senior naval officer present — till the 27th. The wind then falling, a council of war was held, and decided that as there were but four thousand soldiers in the bay, and as neither cannon, ammunition nor provisions necessary for the landing remained at the anchorage, the attempt must be abandoned. The wind now changing to south-west and threatening a storm, this little division, reduced to six ships-of-the-line and four smaller vessels, sailed for Brest, where they arrived on the 12th of January. Rear-Admiral Bouvet had long preceded them, having reached Brest on the 1st of the month.[1] By the 14th, four weeks and a day after sailing from Brest, thirty-five of the expedition had returned safe, though greatly battered, to French ports, after various adventures not necessary to relate. Five, including the "Séduisant," wrecked on the night of sailing, had been lost or destroyed by their officers, and six captured[2] by the British.

The one still to be accounted for closed dramatically the adventure, which, having begun by the wreck of one ship-of-the-line, ended with the yet more deplorable destruction of another. This, called by the good revolutionary name "Droits de l'Homme," had clung tenaciously to the Irish coast till January 5th; but, finding herself alone and no hope remaining, started then to return to Brest. On the

---

[1] Bouvet was broken without trial by the Directory on the 15th of February, 1797, and was not restored to the navy until 1801, under the Consulate. Captain Chevalier's judgment is that "he despaired too soon of the success of the expedition, . . . and forgot that he should have been inspired only by the great interests entrusted by accident to his hands." (Mar Fran. sous la Rép., pp. 309, 311.)

[2] Chevalier. James makes the number captured to be seven.

13th she fell in with two British frigates, one the "Indefatigable," Pellew's ship. The two closed with her, and just before nightfall the French vessel carried away her fore and main topmasts. The wind was blowing hard from the westward, and her captain, fearing momentarily to meet enemy's ships of greater force and numbers, decided to run steadily for his own coast. At half-past five the "Indefatigable," whose sail power was untouched, drew up, and the battle began. An hour later her consort, the "Amazon," came within range. Through the long night, with a few intermissions at the choice of the uncrippled British frigates, the strife went on, — the embarrassed condition of the "Droits de l' Homme" being increased by the fall of her mizzen mast at half-past ten. The sea was running so high that the crews of the frigates fought up to their middles in water, while the ship-of-the-line could not use her lower tier of guns; and at the end the "Indefatigable," the sole survivor of the conflict, had four feet of water in her hold. At half-past four on the morning of the 14th, land, for which a lookout had been anxiously kept, was suddenly seen. The two British ships were then holding positions a little ahead, and on either bow, of the "Droits de l'Homme." Each hauled to the wind on its own side of the enemy; the "Indefatigable" to the south, the "Amazon" to the north. All three were embayed in Audierne Bay, an unsheltered beach thirty-five miles south of Brest, between Pointe du Raz and the Penmarck rocks. By strenuous efforts the "Indefatigable," after wearing twice, cleared the latter by three quarters of a mile. As she passed them in broad daylight, the "Droits de l'Homme" lay on her side at the bottom of the bay, the surf beating over her. The "Amazon," whose situation had allowed too little time for skill to play, was also aground two miles to the northward. Here, however, the resemblance ceased. The trained and disciplined British crew got safe to land. The unfortunate French ship, crowded to repletion with men for the most part wholly

unaccustomed to the sea, had had the further misfortune
to take the bottom on a bank at a great distance from the
beach. Three days of awful exposure, without food or
water, followed. Not till the 17th did the subsidence of
the gale allow relief from shore, and only on the 18th did
the last survivor quit the wreck. Out of thirteen hundred
men on board her when the battle began, two hundred and
sixty were killed and wounded, and two hundred and seventeen lost their lives through the wreck.

The singular circumstance that, despite the first separation of the fleet on the night of sailing, the disconnected
units were yet for the most part brought together and
together reached the coast of Ireland, and yet that from
this happy meeting the most important vessel of all, carrying the two commanders-in-chief, was excepted, creates a
legitimate curiosity as to the movements of the "Fraternité" during these critical days. On the 17th, this ship had
with her two frigates and one ship-of-the-line, — the "Nestor." On the 20th the other frigates had disappeared, the
"Nestor" alone remaining; but it was found, from subsequent examination of the logs, that had the fog which then
covered the ocean lifted, the "Fraternité" would have
been in sight of the main body, which then, under Bouvet,
was steering north to make Mizen Head. That night the
"Nestor" parted company. On the 24th of December the
"Fraternité" was pursuing her course for Bantry Bay,
where the main body had already arrived, when a ship resembling a ship-of-the-line was seen. As the stranger did
not reply to the signals made, the "Fraternité" took flight
to the westward, and, finding herself outsailed, threw overboard some of her guns. During the night the pursuer was
thrown off, and the frigate again shaped her course for
Bantry Bay; but the same easterly gale which drove Bouvet
from the anchorage was now blowing in her teeth. On the
29th Hoche and Morard fell in with the first of the expedition they had seen since the "Nestor" left them, and a sad

meeting it was. One, the "Scevola," was sinking; the
other, the "Révolution," which had been badly injured by
a collision in Bantry Bay, was saving the "Scevola's"
crew. In the dangerous condition of the "Révolution,"
now having twenty-two hundred souls on board, with provisions for but eight days, and having learned the dispersal
of the vessels in Bantry Bay, Hoche and Morard determined
to return. The two ships reached Rochefort on the 13th of
January. Whether Hoche, with his military ardor, the
high prestige of his fame, and the intense personal interest
felt by him in the success of the expedition, could have
triumphed over the material obstacles which defeated the
lukewarm energies of Bouvet, may be questioned; but it
was certainly an extraordinary circumstance that, of the
whole large body of ships, the one containing the two commanders was almost alone in her failure to reach the Irish
coast.

From the preceding account, it is evident that the success or failure of the French landing depended entirely
upon their ability to make the thirty miles intervening between the entrance and the head of Bantry Bay. Whatever may be thought of their prospects of ultimate success
in the conquest or deliverance of Ireland, — a matter of
pure speculation, dependent upon many conditions rather
political and economical than military, — it cannot be
questioned that they had succeeded in crossing the sea
and reaching almost their point of destination, not only despite the British navy but without even seeing it. On
December 21st the bulk of the expedition was at the mouth
of Bantry Bay. Not till the 22d did Colpoys, commanding
the fleet watching, or rather detailed to watch, off Brest,
know they had actually sailed; and then he did not know
in what direction. Bridport at Portsmouth received the
news on the same, or possibly on the previous day, through
Pellew's diligence and forethought. Not till the 31st of
December was it known in London that the enemy had

actually appeared off the Irish coast, and at that time Bridport's fleet had not even sailed. Only continued bad weather, and that ahead, prevented the landing which even Bouvet would not have hesitated to make under better conditions. Had no other harm resulted, the capture of Cork, only forty-five miles distant, was certain. "We propose to make a race for Cork as though the devil were in us," wrote Wolfe Tone in his journal; and how severe the blow would have been may be imagined, for in that place were collected stores and supplies to the value of a million and a half sterling, including the provisions for feeding the navy during the next year. Ireland was then the great source from which naval provisions were drawn.

Such a failure on the part of the British navy, with its largely superior forces, can scarcely be called less than ignominious, and invites now, as it did then, an examination into the causes. The outcry raised at the time by panic and disappointment has long ceased; but the incident affords a fruitful field for study, as to how far the disposition of the Channel fleet conformed to a reasonable interpretation of the principles of war, as applied to the sea.

It must be obvious to any one stopping to think, that, for a fleet charged with thwarting the combinations of an enemy's navy, there can be no point so well adapted as one immediately before the port from which the greatest fraction must sail. Once away, to an unknown destination, the position to be taken becomes a matter of surmise, of guess, which may be dignified by the name of sagacity if the guess prove right, but which should not be allowed to cover the original fault of disposition, if it could have been avoided. To multiply instances would be tedious; but reference may be made to two detailed elsewhere in this work, viz: Bridport, upon the escape of Bruix in 1799,[1] and Nelson after the escape of Villeneuve in 1805,[2] though in the latter case

---

[1] See ante, p. 306.   [2] See post, Chap. XVI.

the admiral's reasons for not cruising before Toulon were
not only adequate, but imperative.

A similar perplexity existed in the closing months of
1796. The government and the admiral of the Channel
fleet knew that a large expedition was preparing in Brest,
and they had reason to fear the co-operation with it of the
Spaniards. Opinion was somewhat divided as to the objective; according to reports industriously circulated by the
French government, it might be Portugal the ally, Gibraltar the outpost, or Ireland the dependency, of Great Britain.
One thing only was certain, that the surest and largest
component of the undertaking was in Brest. There soldiers were gathering, and there also arms were being shipped
largely in excess of the troops,[1] pointing to a hope of co-
operation by inhabitants at the point of landing. Such
conditions dictated certainly three things : 1, a force before
Brest superior to that of the enemy inside ; 2, inasmuch
as the heavier ships must keep the channel open, against
the danger of violent westerly gales, there should be an advance squadron of handier vessels close in with the port,
powerful enough to hold its ground if the enemy came out
and to keep touch with him if he sailed ; 3, since Ireland
was by far the most important of the interests threatened,
the government should have indicated it to the admiral as
the point to be covered, in case he did lose knowledge of
the hostile fleet. The first of these provisions sums up the
main strategic requirement, to effect which all other strategic dispositions should conduce. The second is tactical
in character, relating to the disposition of the force upon
the ground to which strategic considerations assign it. The
third presents the alternative, the second line of defence,
upon which, in case the first is forced, the defending fleet
falls back.

[1] Parliamentary History, vol. xxxiii. pp. 113, 116. Wolfe Tone states that
there were on board the ships of the expedition 41,160 muskets. (Journal, Dec.
22, 1796.)

Colpoys's fleet of fifteen sail was certainly not superior to the French. It might be considered adequate to frustrate the expedition, if met, but not sufficient to inflict the crushing blow that the policy and needs of Great Britain imperatively demanded. Moreover, a military body is not an inanimate object, like a rock, which once placed abides unchanged for years. It is rather a living organism, depending on daily nourishment, subject to constant waste, and needing constant renewal. If to station a competent force before Brest met the chief strategic requirement, its maintenance there embraced a number of subordinate strategic provisions, which in terms of land warfare are called communications. Ships meet with accidents; they degenerate by wear and tear; they consume water and provisions, their crews diminish by illness and need rest by occasional returns to port. These communications were not threatened by the French; but they were open to injury by insufficient forethought and by excessive distance, and from both they suffered. A division like Colpoys's may be renewed in two ways. Either it may be relieved by a body of similar number and go home; or it may be continually receiving fresh ships and continually sending old ones to the rear for rest. It need scarcely be said that the latter is by far the better, preserving a continuity of life and administration which the former breaks. Not only so; but the other system presupposes a squadron in port equal to that cruising, a reserve equal to the body in the field, — a fantastic proportion, which sacrifices every principle of warfare, and divides the available force into two masses, which do not even pretend to support but merely to replace each other.

A fleet charged with duty like that before Brest needs to be fixed at the highest number the resources of the nation can supply and supported by a reserve so proportioned that, by a constant coming and going, no ship at the front should ever be suffering from an exhaustion, either of condition or of supplies, against which diligent human forethought could

have provided. The station of this reserve is obviously a
matter of the utmost importance. It should, of course, be
as near as possible to the main body, and, for sailing ships,
favorably situated with reference to prevailing winds; for
a head wind meant not merely the loss of time caused by
itself, but often the loss of an opportunity which passes
with the time. Thus, on this very occasion, when the wind
blew fresh from the eastward, fair to go from Portsmouth
to Ireland, Bridport's ships were unable to use it, because
they could not make the stretch of three miles from Spithead to St. Helen's. Nor is the nearness of a dockyard
a controlling condition for the reserve, though it may be
admitted that dockyards should be placed with reference to probable theatres of war. On the contrary, a
yard is the last place to which to send an active ship.
Naval officers knew then, as they know now, that vessels at dockyards become valetudinarians, whose doctors,
like some others, flatter the ailments of their patients
to increase their practice. An available reserve is one
thing, a ship needing dockyard repairs quite another;
and no countenance should be given to any confusion
of the two by keeping the reserve at, or close by, a
yard. Properly, the reserve should be simply that
portion of the active force which, for the benefit of the
whole, is for a moment resting, but is ready at once to
proceed.

How very little the government of the day and the then
admiral of the Channel fleet realized these principles, is
evident by a few facts. The reserve was at Spithead, a
roadstead over two hundred miles distant. It was equal in
force to the division before Brest. "The government
thought it the wisest plan," said its authorized defender in
the Commons, "to separate the fleet into different divisions. One fleet was off Brest to watch the enemy and intercept the sailing of the expedition; and another at home
to relieve the fleet off Brest, if necessary, or to pursue the

enemy, if he should sail."[1] When the French had escaped, Colpoys received the news December 22d. His orders did not cover the contingency, and in his uncertainty he first decided to keep his station,[2] than which nothing could be more satisfactory to the French, who had made a long circuit to avoid that particular spot. Like all men in the dark, however, the admiral soon changed his mind and concluded to go off the Lizard, a cape near Falmouth, where he might receive information.[3] Here, in the entrance to the Channel, he found several ships in want of necessaries, and the weather such that he could not provide them from others.[4] This statement was disputed by the Admiralty, which, however, admitted that some of these ships had not water in abundance.[5] With a properly worked reserve, a few ships might have been short, — those, that is, whose turn was to go in next, — but it is evident that a very disproportionate number were here affected; for the explanation of these short ships being still out was, that Curtis's squadron of *seven* ships was to have relieved them, but had been delayed for certain causes.[6] Whatever the reason, the impotent conclusion was that Colpoys, a good officer under a bad system, put his helm up and ran into Spithead, where he arrived December 31st, more than a week after the French reached Bantry Bay.

While the subordinate was thus badgered by the inadequate measures of his government and his chief, the latter was leisurely preparing to relieve him off Brest. On the 21st or 22d, he was spurred up by news of the French sailing, and replied that in *four* days he would be ready, — a truly handy reserve with the British Islands about to be invaded. On the 25th he got under way, and demonstrated at once the fitness of Spithead as a station for the reserve.

---

[1] Dundas's Speech, Mar. 3, 1797, Parl. Hist. vol. xxxiii. p. 12.
[2] Ibid., vol. xxxiii. 13. [3] Ibid., vol. xxxiii. pp. 109, 111.
[4] Speech of Lord Albemarle, ibid., p. 109.
[5] Speech of Earl Spencer, First Lord of Admiralty, ibid., p. 111.
[6] Dundas, Parl. Hist. vol. xxxiii. p. 13.

Eight ships only succeeded in getting to St. Helen's that day, a sudden change of wind to south-east supervening: "which, although favorable for his getting to sea, was directly on the bows of the ships coming to join him from Spithead."[1] It was not thought prudent to sail with only eight ships, and through the delay of waiting for the others Bridport did not get away from St. Helen's (Portsmouth) until January 3, 1797, — the day before the last of the French abandoned Bantry Bay, — when he sailed with fourteen of-the-line, a mass equal to Colpoys's division which had just returned. An inadequate force at the decisive point, inadequately maintained, and dependent upon a reserve as large as itself, but unready and improperly stationed, — such were the glaring faults of the strategic disposition.

The tactical mistakes are equally apparent. The main fleet was stationed so far at sea as to derive no shelter from easterly storms. It contained several three-decked ships,[2] whose poor sailing qualities exaggerated to the last degree the drift consequent upon bad weather. As a result, at the critical moment, Colpoys, instead of being, according to St. Vincent's maxim, "close in with Ushant in an easterly wind," was over forty miles west of it, "working up against a fresh east-south-east wind,"[3] and the next day was driven to the northward by southerly weather. Under such conditions any look-outs in the "Iroise" were almost a vain show. It is of the essence of such a look-out, however, that it should not be driven from its post by a detachment so small that the enemy does not weaken himself by making it. Of what consequence in this way were three or four frigates, which the French could and should have driven off by a half dozen, backed by two sail-of-the-line? Properly to watch Brest required a strong de-

[1] James's Nav. Hist., vol. ii. p. 21.
[2] Of fifteen ships four were of ninety-eight guns or over. (Schomberg's Nav. Chronology, vol. iv. p. 525.)
[3] James, vol. ii. p. 20.

tachment of line-of-battle-ships of the medium class, which were handy and weatherly, and whose grip could only be loosened by fighting. The correlative, however, of such a big detachment is the main body close up, ready to support it. The whole theory hangs together. The advanced detachment close up, else it cannot watch; big enough, else it cannot stay; the main body also close up, else the advance guard is hazarded.

Under all these circumstances it is not strange that the careful British chronicler, James, has to record that "during the three or four weeks the French ships were traversing in every direction the Irish and English Channels, neither of the two British fleets (Bridport's nor Colpoys's), appointed to look after them, succeeded in capturing a single ship;" and "the principal losses by capture sustained by the enemy arose from the diligence and activity of a sixty-four-gun ship and four or five frigates, which, on the 29th of December, were lying in the harbor of Cork."[1] Yet, after satisfying himself that the French had gone back to Brest, Bridport returned to Spithead, and the old system was resumed. In Parliament the ministry strongly maintained that they had done all that could be expected; and the First Lord went so far as to say that even an inquiry would be considered an unmerited censure.[2]

It is no more than just to note, in this slack and shiftless conduct of the war, the same sluggish spirit that, after making all allowances for the undeniable grievances of the seamen, was also responsible for the demoralization of discipline in the Channel fleet, which soon after showed itself openly, — among the crews in the mutinies of 1797, and among the officers, at a later day, in the flagrant insubordination with which St. Vincent's appointment was greeted. Both show a lax hand in the chief naval commander; for, while a government is responsible for its choice of the

[1] James's Nav. Hist., vol. ii. pp. 20, 22.
[2] Earl Spencer's Speech, Parl. Hist., vol. xxxiii. p. 115.

latter, it must, especially in so technical a profession as the navy then was, depend upon him for the enforcement of discipline and for the choice of measures, at once practicable and adequate, to compass the ends of the war. Upon him, more than upon any other, must fall the responsibility of failure; for he knows, or should know, better than the government, what the fleet can be made to do, what the state of discipline really is, and what his own capacity to carry out the one and support the other. Only through him can the government act. When it disregards or overrides, without displacing him, mischief ensues; but the correlative of the generous confidence and hearty support it owes to him is, on his part, unceasing intense effort, or resignation.

It is a relief, and instructive, to turn to the methods of Earl St. Vincent. Having returned from the Mediterranean in August, 1799, he was chosen to succeed Bridport upon the latter's resignation in the following April. It is told that, when his appointment became known, one of the naval captains, at the table of the former commander-in-chief, gave the toast, " May the discipline of the Mediterranean never be introduced into the Channel fleet." If, as is said, the admiral (presumably Lord Bridport) suffered this to pass unrebuked, no words could depict more forcibly than the simple incident the depths to which his own dignity and control had sunk.[1] It is, perhaps, needless to say that St. Vincent met this temper with the same unbending firmness that he had shown in his former command.

It is not, however, in his discipline, but in his management of the Brest blockade, and the Channel fleet for the support of that blockade, that we are here interested. The force before Brest was largely increased, consisting at this time of never less than twenty-four sail-of-the-line, and, un-

[1] Tucker's Life of Earl St. Vincent, vol. ii. pp. 10 and 70; the latter reference being to a letter from St. Vincent to the First Lord of the Admiralty. The incident occurred on board Bridport's flag-ship, the " Royal George."

til ordered by the Admiralty to be reduced, was maintained by St. Vincent at thirty.[1] The rendezvous, or central station round which the main body was to revolve, and where, if possible, it was always to be found, was changed from eight leagues west of Ushant to "well in with Ushant in an easterly wind." How the commander-in-chief understood this order is shown by his instructions to his second in command, when the fleet was for a time turned over to him. "I recommend you in the strongest manner *never* to be farther than six or eight leagues from Ushant with the wind easterly; and if westerly to make the Saintes (Chaussée de Sein) as often as the weather will permit; and when the wind is such as to permit the French to slip out of Brest, to stand in on the first of the flood so far as to see the in-shore squadron."[2] In another letter to the same he says: "The principle on which the squadron acts, with the wind easterly, is to wear . . . during the night, so as to be within a couple of leagues of Ushant at daylight."[3] So constant was this practice during the summer and early autumn months, while he himself remained on board, that in one hundred and twenty-one days there was but one, and then owing to fog, in which the main body did not communicate by signal with the in-shore squadron stationed between Ushant and Brest.[4]

To sustain the ships in the greatest and most constant efficiency, in other words to maintain the communications, his care and watchfulness are incessant; and, though not expressly so stated, it is evident from the general tenor of his correspondence that the ships went in to refit and rest not in large numbers, but singly, or in small groups. "I am at my wits' end," he writes, "to compose orders to meet every shift, evasion, and neglect of duty. Seven-eighths of the captains who compose this fleet are practising every

---

[1] Tucker's Life of Earl St. Vincent, vol. ii. p. 58.
[2] Ibid., vol. ii. p. 13.
[3] Ibid., p. 114. [4] Ibid., p. 24.

subterfuge to get into harbor for the winter." [1] A constant pressure is kept upon all officers of the fleet, and especially upon those stationed to supervise at the anchorages for refittal and taking in stores, that vessels should lose no time and should come back as full as possible. The time for remaining "in Plymouth Sound or Cawsand Bay *never* ought to exceed six days, unless a mast is to be shifted, and in that event not more than ten days." [2] "A thousand thanks are due you," he writes to Rear-Admiral Whitshed, "for the pains you have taken to dispatch the ships which were necessarily sent into Cawsand Bay. Without such powerful aid, all my endeavors to fulfil the wishes of the Cabinet would be vain." [3] It was for this purpose he gave the order, so bitterly resented, that no officer, from the captain down, should sleep out of his ship, or go more than three miles from the beach.

Throughout he strove, according to his own practice and that of Suffren and Nelson,[4] to make the ships self-dependent, and to keep them out of the dockyards and on the station to the last moment. "Under the present impending storm from the North of Europe," wrote he in January, 1801, "and the necessity there is of equipping every ship in the royal ports that can swim, no ship under my command must have anything done to her at Plymouth or Portsmouth that can be done at this anchorage." [5] The question of wind and distance weighed heavily with him. Torbay and Cawsand Bay, an anchorage in Plymouth Sound, were made the ordinary resorts of ships going in to refit; and

---

[1] Tucker's St. Vincent, vol. ii. p. 114.
[2] Ibid., p. 80.   [3] Ibid., p. 78.
[4] See Nelson's letter to Earl St. Vincent, Feb. 1, 1800. (Nelson's Dispatches.)
[5] Tucker, vol. ii. p. 121. Modern ships, so much more complex, are much more liable to derangement than those of St. Vincent; and, unless such pains as his are taken to make them self-sufficing, their officers and the dockyards will make a heavier drain on the force of the fleet than in his day. Perhaps in no point will provident administration more affect the efficiency of the fleet than in this.

his orders to the second in command, when left in charge off Brest, were "on no occasion to authorize any ships to go to Spithead, unless by special orders from the Admiralty or from me." Finally, when his health compelled him to abandon the immediate command afloat, he again, as at Gibraltar during his Mediterranean career, took up his station at the point of next importance to the efficiency of the Brest fleet, settling himself in a house near Torbay, overlooking the anchorage, whence he directly supervised the refitting and speedy dispatch of the ships sent in for repair and refreshment. In short, when unable to be with the main body, he made a point of seeing personally to the reserve and to the supplies.

To mass the fleet before Brest,—to maintain it in a high state of efficiency, by the constant flow of supplies in transports and the constant exchange between worn and fresh ships,—and to fix a rendezvous which assured its hold upon the enemy,—such were the strategic measures adopted and enforced by St. Vincent. The disposition of the ships when before the port, with a view to prevent the evasion which was the height of French naval ambition, and to compel the enemy to battle if he came out, may be more properly called tactical. It may be given nearly in his own words. "A squadron of five ships-of-the-line is *always anchored* during an easterly wind between the Black Rocks and Porquette Shoal" (about ten miles from the entrance). "Inside, between them and the Goulet, cruise a squadron of frigates and cutters plying day and night in the opening of the Goulet; and outside, between the Black Rocks and Ushant, three sail-of-the-line cruise to support the five anchored."[1] A group of eight line-of-battle ships was thus always on the lookout,—a force too strong to be driven off without bringing on the general engagement which was the great object of the British, and so disposed that, if not the inner, at least the outer members could be

[1] Tucker's St. Vincent, vol. ii. pp. 13, 88.

signalled every day by the main body. The mutual support of all parts of the fleet was thus assured. "Unless this is done," wrote St. Vincent, "the ships appointed to that important service may not feel the confidence necessary to keep them in their post,— a failure in which has frequently happened before I was invested with this command."[1]

The seamanlike care with which, as a general officer, he studied his ground, is also evidenced by his remarks, some of which have already been quoted. "I never was on a station so readily, and with so little risk maintained as that off Ushant with an easterly wind" (with which alone the enemy could get out), "owing to the length and strength of flood-tide;"[2] and he adds, in another place, "If the flood flows strong, you will find *much shelter* between Ushant and the Black Rocks during the day."[3] The investment of Brest was completed by stationing detachments, amounting in all to from two to four ships-of-the-line with numerous frigates, to the southward of the Passage du Raz and thence to Quiberon Bay, forming a chain of lookouts to intercept vessels of all kinds, but especially the coasters upon which the port depended for supplies; while other cruisers were stationed all along the shores of the Bay of Biscay, from the mouth of the Loire to Cape Finisterre, and their captains specially incited and encouraged to approach and scour the coast. In the various "cutting out" expeditions engaged in by these, the numerous small vessels captured are usually stated to have been loaded with stores for the Brest fleet. By this means, if the enemy did not come out and fight to break up the blockade, he must soon be reduced to impotence by exhaustion of the commonest supplies. As there were in Brest, in 1800, forty-eight ships-of-the-line, French and Spanish, a combination resulting from Bruix's cruise of the year before, this end was soon obtained, as French accounts abundantly testify.[4]

[1] Tucker's St. Vincent, vol. ii. p. 14.   [2] Ibid., p. 14.   [3] Ibid., p. 115.
[4] See Troude, Batailles Navales, 1800, 1801, vol. iii. pp. 190, 222, 223.

The immediate adoption and enforcement of these measures, after St. Vincent succeeded to the command, illustrate clearly the inevitable dependence of the government upon the admiral of the Channel fleet, and its inability to conceive or enforce the system by which alone so necessary yet hazardous a service could be effectually performed. Only a thorough seaman, and of exceptional force of character, could both devise and execute a scheme demanding so much energy and involving so heavy a responsibility. It was hard to find a man of St. Vincent's temper to carry out his methods; and the government was further handicapped by a tradition requiring a certain rank for certain commands. So strong was the hold of this usage that even St. Vincent, in 1801, yielded to it, lamenting that Nelson, " of whom he felt quite sure, had not rank enough to take the chief command " of the vitally important expedition to Copenhagen; which was entrusted to Sir Hyde Parker, " of whom he could not feel so sure, because he had never been tried."[1] Later, when First Lord of the Admiralty, Earl St. Vincent was fortunate enough to find in Admiral Cornwallis a man who, whatever his intellectual grasp, possessed all the nerve and tenacity of his predecessor; but the necessary rank was too apt to bring with it a burden of years, accompanied by the physical weakness which, in lesser men, led to failing energy and shrinking from responsibility, and by actual prostration drove even St. Vincent ashore in the winter weather. His predecessor, Lord Bridport, had been well on in the seventies, and his first successor, Sir Hyde Parker, announced his intention " not to risk staying with the whole fleet off Brest at this season [winter], when it blows hard from west or west-south-west," [2] — a decision which may have been no more than prudent, but the open avowal of

---

" We had at Brest (in 1800) neither provisions nor material. The Franco-Spanish fleet there was of consideration only from its numbers." (Chevalier, Mar. Fran. sous le Consulat, p. 10.)

[1] Tucker's St. Vincent, vol. ii. p. 136.

[2] Naval Chronicle, vol. iv. p. 520.

which, taken with Nelson's opinion of him,[1] seems to show that, though a brave and good officer, he was not equal to the stern work demanded.

Lord St. Vincent, though perfectly satisfied with his own arrangements, doubtless never cherished the vain hope that no evasion of them could ever be practised. On the contrary, he had at the very outset of his command, and in the comparatively genial month of May, the experience of a terrific hurricane, which drove his fleet headlong to Torbay, and rejoiced the hearts of the cavilling adherents of the old system. That the fleet must at times be blown off, he knew full well; and also that the escape of the enemy, in whole or in part, before its return, was possible, though it ought not to be probable. To provide against this contingency, he recommended the government to give to the officer commanding the in-shore squadron, who would remain, special orders in a sealed packet to be opened only in case the enemy got out.[2] The failure to provide Colpoys with such specific directions had been charged by the Opposition, and most justly, as a grave fault of the government in 1796.[3] It is right and wise to leave great discretion to the officer in command on the spot, — minute instructions fetter rather than guide him; but a man in Colpoys's situation, bewildered as to the enemy's objects, aware only that the first line of defence is forced, but ignorant where the second will be assailed, is entitled to know precisely what the government considers the most important among the interests threatened. This decision is one for the statesman rather than the seaman. Not only, in 1796, was Ireland distinctly the most vulnerable point, but the ministers had information, almost to certainty, that there was the enemy's aim.

In 1800, as when Bruix escaped in 1799, circumstances

[1] See *post*, Chap. XIII.
[2] Tucker's St. Vincent, vol. ii. p. 105.
[3] Parliamentary History, vol. xxxiii. pp. 111–116.

were somewhat different. The disaffection, or at least the disloyalty, of the Irish had been shown to be a broken reed for the enemy to lean on; while in the Mediterranean the French had acquired, in Egypt and Malta, interests peculiarly dear to the First Consul. Those valuable possessions were in deadly straits, and the attempt to relieve them was more probable than another attack on Ireland. St. Vincent, therefore, wrote to the then head of the Admiralty, saying with perfect propriety that it became him, " in the situation I stand at this critical period, to suggest to your lordship any ideas for the good of the public service," and suggesting that Sir James Saumarez, commanding the inshore squadron, should have specific orders that, " if the combined fleets get out before I can return to the rendezvous, he should in that case push for Cadiz with the eight ships-of-the-line stationed between me and the Goulet; for I," he added, " shall have sufficient force to protect England and Ireland, without counting upon his eight sail." Such instructions completed the scheme; precise, but not detailed, they provided for the second line, in case the careful precautions for guarding the first were foiled.

The dispositions adopted by St. Vincent remained the standard to which subsequent arrangements for watching Brest were conformed. From Commander-in-Chief of the Channel fleet he became, in February, 1801, First Lord of the Admiralty. In this position he naturally maintained his own ideas; and, as has before been said, found in Cornwallis a man admirably adapted to carry them out. In May, 1804, the ministry with which he was connected resigned; but, although as an administrator he provoked grave criticism in many quarters, and probably lost reputation, his distinguished military capacity remained unquestioned, and the methods of the Brest blockade were too sound in principle and too firmly established to be largely modified. During the strenuous months from 1803 to 1805, when Great Britain and France stood alone, face to face, in a state more of watchful tension than of activity, the Channel fleet kept its grip firm on the great French arsenal. Nelson's justly lauded pursuit of Villeneuve would have been in vain, but for the less known tenacity of Cornwallis; which, by preventing the escape of Ganteaume, was one of the most potent factors in thwarting Napoleon's combinations. Wherever else the great naval battle which has immortalized the name of Trafalgar might have been fought, the campaign would have taken a different form but for the watch over Brest conducted on St. Vincent's lines.

The result of this strict blockade and of the constant harrying of the French coasts from Dunkirk on the North Sea to the Spanish border, was to paralyze Brest as a port of naval equipment and construction, as well as to render very doubtful the success of any combination in which the Brest fleet was a factor. This result has been, historically, somewhat obscured; for abortive attempts to get out obtained no notoriety, while an occasional success, being blazoned far and wide, made an impression disproportioned to its real importance. When Ganteaume, for instance, in January, 1801, ran out with seven ships-of-the-line, — the blockading fleet having lost its grip in a furious north-east gale, — more was thought of the escape than of the fact that, to make it, advantage had to be taken of weather such that six of the seven were so damaged they could not carry out their mission. Instead of going to Egypt, they went to Toulon. The journals of the day make passing mention of occasional sorties of divisions, which quickly returned to the anchorage; and Troude, in a few condensed sentences, under the years 1800 and 1801,[1] vividly shows the closeness of the watch and the penury of the port. Remote from the sources of naval supplies in the Baltic and the Mediterranean, with the sea approaches to both swarming with enemy's cruisers, and in a day when water carriage, always

[1] Batailles Navales, vol. iii. pp. 187-190, 222, 223.

easier and ampler than that by land, was alone adequate to the transport in sufficient quantity of the bulky articles required for ship building and equipment, it became impossible to fill the storehouses of Brest.

Partly for this reason, yet more because his keen military perceptions—at fault only when confronted with the technical difficulties of the sea—discerned the danger to Great Britain from a hostile navy in the Scheldt, Napoleon decided to neglect Brest, and to concentrate upon Antwerp mainly his energies in creating a navy. In later years this prepossession may have partaken somewhat of the partiality of a parent for a child; and he himself has said that there was a moment, during his receding fortunes in 1814, when he could have accepted the terms of the allies had he been able to bring himself to give up Antwerp. In close proximity to the forests of Alsace, Lorraine, and Burgundy; able to draw from the countries bordering on the Rhine and its tributaries flax and hemp, and from the mines of Luxemburg, Namur and Liège iron, copper and coal,—the naval resources of Antwerp could be brought to her on the numerous streams intersecting those countries, and were wholly out of reach of the British. Many were the difficulties to be overcome,—docks to be excavated, ships to be built, seamen gathered and trained, a whole navy to be created from nothing; but the truth remained that the strategic position of Antwerp, over against the mouth of the Thames and flanking the communications of Great Britain with the Baltic, was unequalled by any other single port under the emperor's control.

The expedition against Ireland, thwarted by the elements in 1796, was never seriously renewed. It remained, to the end of his short life, the dream of Hoche. Transferred from the army of the Ocean to that of the Sambre and Meuse, his career there was cut short by the preliminaries of Leoben, by which Bonaparte extricated himself from the dangers of his advance into Carinthia. Sacrificed thus, as

he felt, to the schemes of a rival, Hoche supported with all
the weight of his interest an expedition of fifteen thousand men, who, under the pressure of the Directory, were
gathered in the Texel in the summer of 1797 for an invasion of Ireland under convoy of the Dutch navy. Here
again Wolfe Tone for two months fretted his heart out,
waiting for the fleet to sail ; but, though the period seemed
most propitious, through the mutinies in the British fleet
and the cessation of hostilities on the continent, a peculiar
combination of wind and tide were wanting to cross the bar,
and that combination did not come. In October the Dutch
ships-of-war, numbering sixteen small ships-of-the-line, put
to sea by themselves, and on the 11th met the fleet of Admiral
Duncan, of equal numbers but distinctly superior in broadside force. The British, having the wind, bore down and
attacked—passing when possible through the enemy's line,
so as to cut off his retreat to the Dutch coast, then less than
ten miles distant. The battle, known by the name of
Camperdown, from a village on the adjoining shore, was
fought with all the desperation that in every age has marked
the meetings of the British and the Dutch. It closed with
the defeat of the latter, who left nine ships-of-the-line and
some frigates in their enemy's hands. This put an end
to the Texel expedition. Hoche had died a few weeks before, on the 18th of September; and with him passed away
the strongest personal interest in the invasion of Ireland,
as well as the man most able to conduct it.

The following year, 1798, open rebellion existed in Ireland, and the Directory undertook to support it with troops
and arms ; but the equipment of Bonaparte's Egyptian expedition absorbed the energies of the Ministry of Marine,
and there was no Hoche to give the enterprise the development and concert essential to a great success. A small
division of four frigates sailed from Rochefort on the 6th
of August, carrying twelve hundred troops under General
Humbert, who had served in the expedition of 1796 and

shared the shipwreck of the Droits de l'Homme. This squadron escaped observation, landed its detachment on the 21st of the month, and returned safely to France; but the small corps, unsupported by regular troops, again demonstrated the imprudence of trusting to the co-operation of insurgents. On the 8th of September Humbert was obliged to surrender with the bulk of his force.

A week later, before the news reached France, a ship-of-the-line, appropriately called the "Hoche," and eight frigates, under the command of Commodore Bompart, sailed from Brest, carrying a second division of three thousand troops. Though they escaped the eyes of Bridport's vessels, if there were any in the neighborhood, by running through the Passage du Raz, they were seen on September 17, the day after sailing, by three British frigates; one of which, after ascertaining that the French were really going to sea, went to England with the news, while the others continued to dog the enemy, sending word to Ireland of the approaching danger as opportunity offered. On the 4th of October, in a gale of wind, the enemies separated, and the French commodore then made the best of his way towards his destination, in Lough Swilly, at the north end of Ireland; but the news had reached Plymouth on the 23d of September, and when he drew near his port he found the way blocked by three British ships-of-the-line and five frigates, which had sailed at once for the insurgent district. An engagement followed, fought on the 12th of October, under circumstances even more disadvantageous than that of mere numbers, for the "Hoche" shortly before the action had lost some of her most important spars. Of the little squadron, she and three frigates were compelled to surrender that day, and three more were intercepted later by British vessels, so that only two of the expedition regained a French port. The enthusiastic and unfortunate Irishman, Wolfe Tone, was on board the "Hoche" and wounded in the action. He shortly afterwards committed suicide in prison. A third French division had sailed from Rochefort on the very day the "Hoche" was captured. It succeeded in reaching Ireland; but learning the fate of Bompart's squadron, returned without landing the troops. This was the last of the expeditions against Ireland that sailed from French ports. Other interests and other rulers combined with the pronounced naval ascendency of Great Britain to give a different direction to the efforts of the republic.

END OF VOL. I.

www.ingramcontent.com/pod-product-compliance
Lightning Source LLC
Chambersburg PA
CBHW030549300426
44111CB00009B/915